CONTENTS

INTRODUCTION

Menopause is not a disease of the hormonal system that requires years of drug treatment. Rather, it involves many dimensions: mental, emotional, physical and spiritual. Many of the symptoms during the menopausal years, such as hot flashes, night sweats, memory problems, fatigue, weight gain, loss of libido or headaches are blamed on the decreased production of hormones, estrogen and progesterone. However, it is a natural process for the ovaries to take a well-deserved holiday during these years. The main reason so many women today have symptoms during the hormonal transition is due to imbalances in the adrenal glands, liver, thyroid and intestines.

The stressors we are faced with on a daily basis such as increased work load, lack of physical and spiritual exercise, insufficient rest, poor diet, environmental toxins including the increase in xenoestrogens (estrogen mimickers), all contribute to these organ imbalances. For example, symptoms of adrenal stress may include fatigue, anxiety, headaches, insomnia, alcohol intolerance, decreased libido, or memory problems. Sounds familiar to common menopause symptoms?

The adrenal glands also produce hormones and these glands are asked to pick up the slack while the ovaries go on holiday. Most women that have problems during menopause, have functional adrenal problems due to the added stressors mentioned above.

Supporting the body with a healthy diet and lifestyle, starting at an early age, is the first step to hormonal health. If the menopausal years are symptomatic, then we must treat the cause of the symptoms.

If the red oil light comes on in your car and you choose to ignore it and instead put a band-aid over it (treat the symptom) you will have major car problems a few miles down the road. It is the same with your body. Find out what it is your body is trying to tell you and what you need to do to support it.

This new book on hormonal health explains in detail the effects of stress on the various organs responsible for hormonal balance, the variety of symptoms involved, what can be done to prevent and treat these organ imbalances as well as natural nutritional or botanical options for women who do require additional support during the menopausal years. In addition the authors provide detailed information on safe and effective treatments for osteoporosis, new information on breast cancer, premenstrual syndrome, cardio-vascular disease and other conditions related to women's health.

Rather than continually waiting for "new and improved" drugs that offer better health through chemistry, let's get back to basics and start taking more responsibility for our own health and our environment.

Life is a continuous adventure that requires mental, emotional, physical and spiritual stamina during the hormonal transitional years and always. This book offers many tips and insights that can help women accomplish this through Healthy, Hormone Balancing.

NO MORE HRT:
Menopause
Treat the Cause

———

DR. KAREN JENSEN, ND
LORNA R. VANDERHAEGHE, BSc

QUARRY
HEALTH
BOOKS

Health Venture Publications, Ontario
www.Hormonehelp.com

Jensen, Karen,
Vanderhaeghe, Lorna R.

No More HRT: Menopause Treat the Cause

Includes references and index.
ISBN 1-55082-325-6

1. Menopause—Popular works. 2. Women's Health—Nutritional aspects. 3. Hormone aspects. I. Title

The publishers acknowledge the support of the Government of Canada, Department of Canadian Heritage, Book Publishing Industry Development Program.

Health Venture Publications

Act Natural Corporation
Health Venture Publications
5948 3rd Line RR #1
Hillsburg, ON
N0B 1Z0

ISBN 1-55082-325-6

Cover Design: Richard Bakker
Cover Photograph: Donna Newman

Printed and bound in Canada

This publication contains the opinions and ideas of its authors and is designed to provide useful advice in regard to the subject matter covered. The authors and publisher are not engaged in rendering medical, therapeutic, or other professional services in this publication. This publication is not intended to provide a basis for action in particular circumstances without consideration by a competent professional. The authors and publisher expressly disclaim any responsibility for any liability, loss, or risk, personal or otherwise, which is incurred as a consequence, directly or indirectly, of the use and application of any of the contents of this book.

Visit our website www.hormonehelp.com

ACKNOWLEDGMENTS

We would like to thank Deane Parkes for just being 'Deane' and for his commitment to the broader vision for our health industry in Canada. His vision encompasses all people in the industry working together towards a common goal: to educate the public about gaining and maintaining optimal health. It is an honor and a pleasure for us to be a part of the team. Our heartfelt thanks go to John Barson for responding to our many cries for computer help during this book's production.

Thank you to Lorna Vanderhaeghe for her commitment to this book and for her sense of humor, insights, knowledge and work ethic. Lorna and I share a common vision with our interest, enthusiasm and dedication to women's health. Our primary purpose is to educate women of all ages on the importance of gaining and maintaining optimal health on all levels, the physical, mental, emotional and spiritual.

The greatest gift in my life has been my three children. They have, without a doubt, been my greatest teacher and have taught me about unconditional love. I have absolutely no words to express the gratitude for such blessings in my life. When I was presented an award at graduation from naturopathic college, it really should have been my children on stage, not me, because without them I could not have accomplished what I did.

My patients over the years have been the fuel for the fire that has kept my passion alive in this field of medicine. The honour of being part of their healing journey and to see them embrace their lives and turn things around for themselves brings me great joy and continued inspiration. It is the empathetic listening to my patients' concerns and experiences that keeps me in touch with the reality of medical practice and stops me from blindly accepting the mountains of statistics and rigidity of the often questionable results of scientific studies and treatments.

Writing this book has only reminded me that I cannot accomplish my life's goals without the support of others and the gift of the grace of Divine Spirit in my life.

Karen Jensen

To my children, Crystal, Kevin, Kyle and Caitlyn, you have given me so much love and joy. I am very grateful for your patience and understanding while I went back to University to complete my degree and through the years of writing books and lecturing all over the world. To my grandsons Matthew and Hayden, you are two very special gifts in my life. You are all my heart and soul and the reason I continue to research and spread the word about nutritional medicine and the health of our planet. To my husband John thank you for everything. Mom, thank you for providing me with the genetic constitution and the drive to succeed. Thank you to Tanja Hutter for burning the midnight oil to complete this book. You have been with me through all three of my books and I could not have done it without you.

My love and respect goes out to Karen for her camaraderie, laughter and for her trust. Timing is everything and we did it!

Many people have left a powerful impression on my life, their love, support and faith in my abilities have help mold the person I am today. My maternal grandmother's death from invasive breast cancer when I was ten years old planted the seed for my foray into disease prevention. My passion for sharing knowledge comes from my own life experiences, your shared stories and my desire to ensure that no woman or man has to endure so much physical suffering—when the answers are so easily found in nature.

Lorna Vanderhaeghe

This book is for all women and we trust that it will empower you to seek safe and effective medical care. Thousands of women have written us to tell their nightmares experiences of unnecessary hysterectomy, years of suffering with endometriosis, fibroids, ovarian cysts and misdiagnosis. No More HRT: Menopause Treat the Cause is written with love and understanding and provides the information for you to take charge of your health!

1

OPTIMAL HEALTH: BUILDING THE FOUNDATION

"The significant problems we have cannot be solved at the same level of thinking with which we created them."
—Albert Einstein

The natural cycles of life bring change and growth to all living things—change and growth that we must learn to embrace if we are to enjoy life's full potential. The hormonally driven transition to menopause is one of the significant times of change and growth in every woman's life.

Today, many menopausal women are seeking safer alternatives to the standard "treatment" for menopausal symptoms, hormone replacement therapy (HRT). While this search for alternatives is certainly a positive beginning, it needs to be taken a little further. The foundation underlying this book is the truth that *hormonal health depends completely on the overall health of the individual, on all levels—physical, emotional, mental, and spiritual.* The purpose of this book is to offer safe and effective ways to support the transition into menopause by creating health with appropriate diet and lifestyle choices, natural remedies, exercise, rest and relaxation, and spiritual practices such as prayer and contemplation. *Optimal health throughout life, and thus during the transitional years as well, is the goal.*

Clearly, the natural approach encompasses much more than hormonal suppression with hormonal drugs, the standard—and unnecessarily risky—treatment currently offered for everything from premenstrual syndrome (PMS), perimenopause to menopause. But once a woman begins to work towards achieving optimal health and becomes healthier, she will likely find that any unwanted symptoms of hormonal imbalance can be handled safely and effectively with nutrition, exercise, and botanical and homeopathic remedies.

CREATING OPTIMAL HEALTH

What are the basic steps required if we are to create optimal health? The first step is knowing what optimal health is. Health is much more than the absence of disease.

"Health is the normal and harmonious vibration of the elements and forces composing the human entity on the physical, mental and moral (emotional) planes of being, in conformity with the constructive principle (great law of life) in nature."—Henry Lindlahr

Daily Lorna and I encounter many people who claim they are in good health and say that they are mainly concerned with wanting to prevent disease and maintain health. In further discussions, however, it is not uncommon for us to discover that they have had cancer or another chronic disease, or are taking prescription medications for various conditions. Because the symptoms, or visible manifestations of disease, are no longer present, these people think that they are healthy. Their limited conception of what constitutes health is supported by conventional medical models that see health as simply the absence of disease.

But optimal health is definitely more than the absence of disease. When we are experiencing optimal health, we enjoy a vibrant sense of well-being on all levels: physical, emotional, mental, and spiritual. We are in a state that promotes optimal function, regeneration, and repair of the body's cells, tissues, and organ systems at all times. *We are in harmony with ourselves and our environment.*

In the field of health, as in any area of life, it is crucial to understand what it is we are trying to achieve. Then we will be in a position to more readily assess the ability of different medical approaches, based as they are on distinct philosophies, to meet our needs. We will also be able to make more informed choices regarding health promotion and disease prevention and management.

The next step in achieving optimal health is assuming responsibility for our health. Too often we turn that responsibility over to someone else, frequently our medical doctor.

When people are asked why they are taking a certain prescription medication, most do not know. They are simply following their doctor's orders. Frequently, though, doing what one is told to do without understanding why one is doing it does little to change a situation. Instead, ask questions, demand answers, get second and third opinions. Take responsibility for what you put into your body.

It is easy to feel intimidated when it comes to asking questions and requesting answers from your medical doctor. Allopathic medicine appears to be very complicated, untouchable, and unknowable except by those trained in the coveted profession. It presents you, the patient, with big medical words and illegible handwriting so you can't understand your prescription. Medical doctors, not used to having their authority questioned, may become annoyed or indignant at your questioning. Yet the word "doctor" does not mean medical deity. It comes from the Latin *docere*, which means to teach.

Of course, the medical establishment could not present itself as the all-knowing authority, privy to the mysteries of life and death, without the cooperation of patients. Many patients are reluctant to tell their medical doctor that rather than fill their prescription, they took a naturopathic treatment that resulted in the improvement of their condition. Where does their fear come from? We believe it is rooted in an attitude many of us were raised with: *the doctor's word is gospel.*

Karen's father was 52 when he started coughing up blood. He went to his doctor, whom he had known all his life, was examined, and was told that there was nothing to worry about—he was the healthiest man in the valley. My father was indeed a rugged, strapping man who really did look healthy. No x-rays were taken, so I suggested to my father that he get another opinion to determine the cause of the blood. But my father wouldn't call his doctor's authority into question, even though there was obvious cause for doing so. Later, when he did seek another opinion, he was told he had lung cancer. He died one year later. No one person is the final authority over another. Yet so often, we surrender our personal responsibility and inner knowingness to someone or something external to ourselves.

We really need to understand the words "cause" and "effect." Our life can become a puppet show of sorts, demonstrating the effects of another person's attitudes or opinions. Unquestioning compliance will let us fool ourselves into thinking that we don't have to carry the onerous burden of responsibility for ourselves. If something doesn't turn out the way we expect, we can always blame the situation on the person pulling the strings. For example, let's say a woman takes the birth control pill for years, or hormone replacement therapy (HRT) at menopause, and ends up with breast cancer. People who have accepted the role of being an "effect" would feel it was the doctor's fault for prescribing the medicine and would not take any responsibility for their part.

The alternative to a life lived dancing to others' tunes is to become the *cause* of events in one's life—to make informed choices and to take responsibility for them no matter what the outcome. Once you choose to become the "cause" in your life and more specifically in your health care, you will see that you always have options and choices. We believe that there is always a greater plan at work encompassing everything in our lives, including our health experiences. When we listen to our inner knowing and wisdom, we will be directed to make the choices that are right for us. *What is right for one is not necessarily the answer for another.* Embrace your life, be grateful for every experience, and make your decisions based on as much knowledge as you can. Then follow the highest knowledge: your inner connection with Spirit.

If you haven't already done so in your life, we hope you are now inspired to begin taking your health care into your own hands. You won't be alone. Today, more and more people are becoming increasingly aware of the various health care choices available to them and they want more information on how to achieve and maintain optimal health through safe, effective medicines.

"Individuals must take greater responsibility for their health at the earliest opportunity. This means adopting habits such as a healthy diet, adequate exercise and the avoidance of tobacco early in life and maintaining them for the rest of their years."—*The World Health Report 1998: Life in the 21st Century: A Vision for All*

Now that you're ready to ask some questions and dig a little deeper, let's look at some basic information you will need to make well-informed choices on the road to optimal health.

Medicine is both a science and an art. It is a science as it presents facts and evolves principles; an art as it applies these principles to individual patients. For its present accomplishments, it is indebted to both scientific research and to empirical discovery. For a patient, dealing with the medical world, despite all its mystique, it need not be complicated. As a patient you have two basic choices:

- You can take the *proactive* approach, by making health care choices that promote ever greater vitality, or that are specifically intended to prevent disease from occurring.

- You can take the *reactive* approach, not doing much about your health until symptoms or disease strike, at which point you begin the search for an effective treatment.

Know Your Options

There are two main philosophies of medicine, and each takes differing approaches to health promotion, disease prevention, and disease treatment.

The *mechanistic* school of thought sees the body as a machine made up of various interlocking parts. Mechanists take the approach that each body part and function can be understood and treated in isolation from all other parts and functions. Life and death are explained as being simply products of complex chemical and physical reactions. Mechanistic thinking is the foundation for allopathic medicine (discussed below).

> "The mechanistic view of the human organism has encouraged an engineering approach to health in which illness is reduced to mechanical trouble and medical therapy to technical manipulation."—Fritjof Capra

The *vitalistic* school of thought holds that life is much more complex than a series of chemical reactions, and that a living system is more than just the sum of its parts. Each body, says vitalism, is animated by an organizing force, a vital force that directs the body and its healing processes. Vitalism is the philosophy underlying naturopathic, homeopathic, Ayurvedic, shamanistic, traditional Chinese, osteopathic, chiropractic, and other forms of medicine. The vitalistic world view was known to the ancient Greeks and is found in the writings of Hippocrates (460–377 BC), "the Father of Medicine."

> "The natural healing force within each one of us is the greatest force in getting well."—Hippocrates

The vital force was also described by the alchemist Paracelsus, in the sixteenth century: "The vital force is not enclosed in man, but radiates round him like a luminous sphere, and it may be made to act at a distance. In these semi-natural rays the imagination of man may produce healthy or morbid effects. It may poison the essence of life and cause diseases, or it may purify it after it has been made impure, and restore the health."

Let's take a closer look at the mechanist and vitalist schools of thought as they are found in allopathic and naturopathic medicine, respectively.

ALLOPATHIC MEDICINE

Allopathic medicine, or allopathy, is in western, industrialized countries the commonly accepted form of health care. Allopathy is based on the mechanistic model. Disease and its accompanying signs and symptoms are seen as the result of a disruption of chemical reactions. Treatment of disease addresses the symptoms through the use of drugs, surgery, or both, without addressing the underlying cause of the illness. Allopathic health promotion and disease prevention focuses mainly on early detection of disease or of pathological changes, detectable in laboratory tests, likely to lead to disease.

Allopathic treatment models generally do not recognize that the body's chemical reactions take place within a larger context and are disturbed and varied by many internal and external factors, just as the magnetic needle will vary in its movement because of interfering forces.

NATUROPATHIC MEDICINE

Naturopathic medical care, or naturopathy, is a form of primary health care that draws on both science and tradition, and is based on the philosophy of vitalism. Put together, the root words "naturo" and "patho" (from the Greek) mean a natural way to relieve suffering.

The naturopathic approach sees symptoms as being a result of a person's response to disease-causing factors—as the body's attempt to maintain balance and defend itself. Natural methods and substances are used to support and stimulate the body's inherent self-healing ability and thereby restore the overall health of the individual. Above all, naturopathic doctors seek to remove the roots of the illness by identifying and treating the cause or causes. Treatments are carefully chosen to bring about healing of the whole person, without harming the patient or suppressing the symptoms.

Naturopathy prefers to prevent disease rather than to treat it. This is done through natural methods that strengthen the vital force within the person, giving the vitality needed to fend off potential sources of illness. Naturopaths are able to effectively prevent disease because they recognize that diseases rarely develop overnight. Disruptions in the optimal function of the organ systems usually occur years before a disease is diagnosable by standard laboratory procedures. Sensitivity to the subtle signs and signals of such disruptions can guide early intervention.

In addition, naturopaths, remembering the Latin root of the word "doctor," believe that the most important role of the physician is to educate patients on how to be healthy.

Today, people are seeking the benefits of naturopathic medicine in increasing numbers because they have experienced the restrictions of allopathic medicine.

"It is more important to know what sort of person has a disease than to know what sort of disease a person has."—Hippocrates

The following lists summarize the major differences between allopathy and naturopathy:

Allopathic Disease Care

- Treats or suppresses symptoms, rather than treating the whole person and the underlying causes.
- Often interferes with the body's self-healing ability.
- Has many side effects.
- Relies largely on costly technology.
- Requires a pathological (disease) diagnosis before treatment can begin.
- Is very important in emergency and disease care.

Naturopathic Health Care

- Focuses on the person, rather than on the disease.
- Looks for the underlying causes of disease.
- Supports the body's inborn ability to heal itself.
- Uses therapies that can prevent illness and promote healing.
- Believes the doctor should be a teacher.
- Holds to the credo "Do no harm."
- Believes that health promotion is the best disease prevention.

Adapted from the American Association of Naturopathic Physicians

The Integrated Approach to Health Care

As you can see from the summaries above, **no one system of medicine has all the answers!** And naturopathy and allopathy are but two of the world's major medical systems. There are many ways of understanding the language of the body, and each approach has its strengths and limitations. I would encourage people first of all to prevent problems by working for optimal health, and next, to seek to understand the underlying cause of any health conditions and to treat them with appropriate non-invasive, non-toxic therapies whenever possible, provided by naturopathy or one of the other vitalistic schools of therapy, such as homeopathy, traditional Chinese medicine, Ayurveda, osteopathy, chiropractic, and others. (Some of these medical traditions will be discussed in more detail later in this book.) However, if symptoms are so debilitating or life threatening that more immediate treatment is called for, allopathic medicine can usually provide excellent crisis intervention.

But don't stop with only the symptomatic treatment—*address the cause.* If the underlying cause is not addressed, then the body will react in a similar way again or manifest deeper symptoms. For example, if your red oil light comes on in your car and you simply tape a piece of paper over the light and continue to drive, what happens? You end up with much bigger problems down the road. The same is true of our physical vehicle, the body. If you ignore your symptoms, by covering them up with symptomatic treatment, there will be much bigger problems later on.

Let us give you an example to illustrate the point. One of the most common ways in which suppressing symptoms results in greater problems is the treatment of eczema with corticosteroids. The skin is the largest elimination organ in the body. When eczema is suppressed, the expression of the imbalance goes deeper. Most people taking the corticosteroid treatment for eczema end up with asthma. When asthma is treated with non-suppressive remedies, the eczema comes back; it, in turn, is treated with non-suppressive remedies. Only then is the person healed of eczema.

Another powerful example of the difference between the allopathic and naturopathic approaches to illness is found in the attitude of the two schools to the use of antibiotics. Naturopathic physicians have always argued that the "terrain" in which illness occurs—that is, the susceptible host—must be addressed, not only the apparent disease-causing agent. However, when antibiotics emerged after World War II, the naturopathic approach faded into the background.

The reciprocal relationship between the host and microbe was forgotten with the advent of antibiotics because the initial positive results produced by the wonder drugs were obtained quickly and easily. But now, as we begin to encounter "superbugs" resistant to almost all antibiotics, we find ourselves paying a huge price for the "quick fix" and can no longer rely on symptomatic treatment alone. The causes of our susceptibility to infection in the first place have to be addressed.

> "The doctor of the future will give no medicine, but will interest his patients in the care of the human frame, in diet, and in the cause and prevention of disease."—Thomas Edison

The allopathic model, while responsible for corticosteroids, antibiotics, and the like, has nevertheless achieved remarkable results in prolonging life and relieving pain through the relief of symptoms and the removal of organs. However, it has fallen short in preventing chronic disease and promoting optimal health. In fact, treatment of chronic disease currently accounts for 85 percent of the national health care bill in the United States. This situation is due to the focus of allopathic medicine on disease, not on the prevention or recognition of earlier manifestations of disease.

AT THE CROSSROADS

More and more people are sick and tired of being sick and tired. They are also frustrated with and fearful of the current options, drugs and surgery. Recently, a research team at the University of Toronto medical faculty analyzed several studies on adverse drug reactions in the United States. According to the researchers' estimates, published in the *Journal of the American Medical Association* (April 14, 1998), the annual number of deaths related to drug reactions in the United States is between 76,000 and 137,000. Only heart disease, cancer, and stroke kill more Americans.

As patients become increasingly aware of statistics like these, they are challenging their medical doctors more and more about what caused their illness, why it persists despite pharmaceutical treatment, and what alternatives to standard invasive and toxic therapies are available. Often physicians are questioned about diets and nutritional or botanical supplements as patients look for instruction and guidance in this area. Limited by time constraints, medical politics, and a lack of education in naturopathic therapies, physicians become frustrated and patients become disillusioned.

Some patients simply turn to other practitioners. According to Statistics Canada, in 1996 at least 3.3 million Canadians paid more than $1 billion for health care services provided by naturopaths, chiropractors, homeopaths, massage therapists, and Chinese doctors. These are services not covered by

Canada's state-run health insurance plans. General use of alternative medicines and treatments has nearly doubled in five years.

A recent study published by the *New England Journal of Medicine* described
survey results that found that more than one-third of those questioned chose
complementary medicine over allopathic methods because of standard medicine's emphasis on drugs and diagnostic testing while ignoring the whole
person. Clearly we are at a crossroads in health care.

> "People are beginning to realize that it is cheaper and more
> advantageous to prevent disease rather than to cure it."—Henry
> Lindlahr (writing in 1913)

To think we knew this as early as 1913. There are times when treating
symptoms with drugs or surgery is absolutely necessary. At the same time, it is
always critically important to address the underlying causes of any condition.

To make health care choices within an either/or framework is too limiting. And, indeed, it is becoming increasingly common for patients to be
under the care of an allopathic doctor and a naturopathic doctor at the same
time. *Integrated* or *complementary* health care bridges the gap between mechanism and vitalism, allopathy and naturopathy.

The success of a complementary approach is highly dependent on good
communication between the practitioners involved. It is unfortunate that
most allopathic doctors are still under the illusion that allopathic treatment
is the only way and are not interested in understanding the approach taken
by naturopathic physicians. Perhaps one of the reasons for this resistance is
the allopathic profession's common charge that naturopathic treatments are
"not scientific" and are unproven. Ironically, the majority of allopathic
procedures—more than 80 percent!—are unproven.

According to Dr. David Eddy, a consultant to the United States
Committee for Quality Assurance, many current allopathic treatment protocols do not rest on a solid foundation of scientific or clinical evidence. To
investigate further, Eddy asked physicians to look at 21 practice guidelines
to see if they were supported by good scientific studies. The physicians rated
the scientific evidence supporting 17 of the 21 guidelines "poor" or "none."
Many treatments that have not been subjected to controlled trials can be
effective; however, when they carry risks, the supportive scientific evidence
needs to be there. Many of the therapies and treatments in complementary
medicine have not been adequately studied either, but they carry extremely
low risks, making them very safe.

There is also the question of how well those scientific studies that support allopathic treatments have been done. David Moher, a Canadian epidemiologist, has found so many errors in medical drug trials that are so broad and deep that the British science journal *Lancet* fears his research could "cast serious doubts on the validity of current clinical research." Moher and a team of Canadian researchers found that in most drug trials the treatment results were exaggerated from 30 to 50 percent, and they found startling errors in the way 85 percent of the studies chose their control groups. "There is a right way and a wrong way to do clinical trials," says Moher, and "what we have discovered is that the majority of clinical trials are not being done correctly." He says that this "bad bookkeeping" is not a localized but a common phenomenon.

"Science is not about truth: it is about the reliability of knowledge."
—Professor Paul Davis, University of Adelaide

Fortunately for patients, the lines of communication are slowly beginning to open. Is it possible for the "twain" to meet despite such differences in medical philosophies? Maybe not, but more important is that the medical professions stay open and strive for a common goal: the prevention and treatment of disease with the safest, most non-invasive therapies possible, so that patients receive the most optimal health benefits possible.

If your medical doctor does not support the choices you make regarding your health, find another who is respectful of your decisions and open to discussing the options—after all, it is your health!

Some medical doctors are going the "alternative medical" route because they see the increased interest among patients in less toxic and invasive treatments. However, many of these doctors are still very mechanistic in their approach, because they have not been through the years of training required to understand the philosophy and principles underlying naturopathic therapies. Their use of these remedies is still based on treating symptoms without addressing the underlying cause. For example, they might prescribe less harmful, more natural hormonal therapy. A naturopathic physician may suggest the same substances, but at the same time will be focusing on treating the weakness in the body so that the ongoing use of hormones will not be necessary.

Further, no standards are in place to evaluate the knowledge and skills of medical doctors venturing into the field of natural medicine. Currently, their broad scope of practice allows any medical doctor to practice acupuncture, homeopathy, botanical medicine, or nutrition without adequate knowledge or guidelines. By comparison, naturopathic doctors study the principles and philosophy of natural healing and natural modalities for four years after completing three years of premedical sciences at university. Standards of practice and regulation are required for *all* medical doctors who are treating patients with natural substances.

IN CONCLUSION

Naturopathy has been considered by some the "medicine of the past." Yet, despite all the technological advances made by allopathic medicine, we still have epidemic Type II diabetes, heart disease, obesity, and cancer as well as new, and increasingly lethal, viral strains and antibiotic-resistant bacteria.

As we move into the twenty-first century, the need for a safe, economical, and integrated approach to health care becomes more and more necessary. The naturopathic approach to healing offers the foundational philosophy that is so necessary if we are to achieve and maintain optimal health in our ever-changing environment.

Let us continue our exploration of the road to optimal health, then, by exploring, from a naturopathic perspective, the factors that influence our health, for better or worse, every day.

2

―――――――――

MINIMIZING STRESS

"It is highly dishonorable for a Reasonable Soul to live in so
Divinely built a Mansion as the Body she resides in, altogether
unacquainted with the exquisite structure of it."
—Robert Boyle, 1627–1691

One of the characteristic features of all living beings is their ability to
maintain the constancy of their internal milieu despite changes in
their surroundings. Whenever this self-regulating power fails, disease or even
death occurs. Truly, life is largely a process of adaptation to the circumstances in which we live, and the secret of health and happiness lies in our
successful adjustment to the ever-changing conditions created by the world
around us and by our inner search for truth. The greater our self-knowledge
on all levels, and the greater our willingness to take responsibility for express-
ing our truth, the greater will be our ability to adapt to and embrace life.

"States of health or disease are, at the heart, the organism's success
or failure at adapting to environmental challenges."—René Dubos

The great majority of illnesses have a number of causes. To better understand hormonal health, we must look at some of the factors that influence it.

The hormones that regulate the reproductive cycles and transitions, such
as menopause, as well as a myriad of other body functions, are produced by
the organs of the endocrine system. The endocrine system consists of a
number of glands that secrete hormones directly into the bloodstream. All
the hormones produced by the endocrine system influence one another,
creating a balance. One of the main causes of ill health, and in particular of
hormonal problems, is the effect of stressors on those self-regulating balances.

Stressors are events or situations, internal or external, pleasant or
unpleasant, that require our body systems to adapt and respond in order to
maintain balance, or homeostasis. Stress can result in compromised func-

tion of the adrenal glands, the body's first line of defense against stressors (for more information, see Chapter 3). Most of us know what this feels like, know when whatever we are doing or is being done to us is strenuous and tiring. Often stress is non-specific, simply caused by everyday life. The body adjusts its adaptive reactions accordingly.

Exposure to stressors results in a cascade of stimuli throughout the nervous system that then stimulates the endocrine system, particularly the adrenal glands, and affects the whole body. It is the nervous and endocrine systems that first receive the information regarding the stress because both play important roles in maintaining balance during exposure to stressors. As a result, the health of the endocrine system is greatly affected by stressors.

When the stressor (regardless of its origin) is unrelenting, the body may lose its ability to adapt to it—the defence mechanisms become exhausted. Exhausted defence mechanisms are incapable of protecting the body. Not only that, such exhaustion burdens the body in other ways because in its presence the load of internally produced toxins is increased and the elimination of toxins of both internal and external origin is decreased. Internal toxins naturally occur as a result of metabolism or body functions, and with the added burden of the environmental toxins the toxic load can become too great and decrease the body's ability to cope, or adapt. The symptoms of disease are signs of the fight to maintain the balance of our tissues, despite the damage.

The stages of stress-induced damage were first studied by a Canadian doctor, Hans Selye. He gave us a greater understanding of how stress affects the entire body.

> "To understand the mechanism of stress gives physicians a new approach to treatment of illness, but it can also give us all a new way of life, a new philosophy to guide our actions in conformity with natural laws."—Hans Selye, M.D.

Dr. Selye calls the body's mechanism for dealing with stress the general adaptation syndrome (G.A.S.). The G.A.S. has three stages: (1) the alarm reaction, (2) resistance, and (3) exhaustion.

Stage 1: Alarm Reaction. There is an initial reaction by the body to a stressor, followed by recovery time. For instance, someone who works long hours on a project may come down with a cold or flu, and recover in a few days because the balancing mechanisms (stress adaptation abilities) are strong.

Stage 2: Resistance. Ongoing stress requires the body to continuously respond and adapt; the person must push harder to keep going. The result is depletion of the reserves. The person gets a cold or flu, but instead of recovering after a few days' rest, they find the illness lingering for a much longer time. Even when better the person never feels as well as before. The body's ability to cope with stress has been lowered.

Stage 3: Exhaustion. There are no reserves left for adapting to stressors, resulting in fatigue, malaise, and lack of will. The person who started in Stage 1 and pushed through Stage 2 is now completely exhausted mentally, emotionally, and physically. The reserves are so depleted that the person easily becomes sick and the symptoms of disease become chronic and more degenerative. If the person continues to push forward or to suppress the symptoms, the disease process goes even deeper into the body and may finally result in failure of the whole system.

It is the relationship between the stressors and the body's stress resistance that decides when, and to what extent, ill health will result:

- The greater our stress resistance is in relationship to the stressor, the less likely we are to become ill.

- Conversely, if a stress is so great that it overwhelms our stress resistance capability, illness is far more likely to occur.

By simultaneously decreasing the number and intensity of stressors in our lives and increasing our ability to handle them, we can restore our self-regulating mechanisms and maintain balance.

Just as one part of the body is directly connected to the whole, we as a whole are directly connected to our outer environment and thereby influenced by it. Jokingly we say that it must be a full moon when people around us are acting unusually strange. But even closer than the moon are other external factors such as chemical, thermal, climactic, and electromagnetic stressors, all of which have direct effects on our health.

Rather than focusing on the specific ways in which we manifest our symptoms as a result of stress, we can learn that it is in our power to determine how to effectively diminish our overall stress burden.

Each of us will benefit from reducing stressors, but the obvious benefits will vary depending on our overall stress resistance capabilities, which are determined by our individual strengths and weaknesses.

We can begin by reducing the many stresses in our lives that are chronic for almost all of us—our lifestyles are in many ways far more stressful than a few decades ago. These stresses fall into two main categories: external and internal.

EXTERNAL STRESSORS

External stressors originate in our environment and include chemicals and other air, food, and water pollutants, including radiation, as well as noise, weather changes, and electromagnetic fields. We can diminish these external stressors once we have a better understanding of their sources and of how they are transmitted to us.

Electromagnetic Stress

Currently spreading all over the world is a new form of environmental pollution: electromagnetic fields (EMFs), emitted by thousands of sources. The typical person today regularly receives electromagnetic radiation at concentrations up to 200 times more intense than those experienced by our ancestors; most of this synthetic energy field has been created in the last half-century. Some common sources of electromagnetic radiation are televisions, computers, laser printers, electric blankets, hair-dryers, curling irons, refrigerators, fluorescent lights, high-tension wires, underground cables, cash registers, video games, x-ray machines, and microwave ovens, to name a few. We have evolved in the absence of artificial energy fields such as are emitted by these devices; for millions of years our development has taken place within the influence of the earth's natural electromagnetic fields. The machines that surround us are literally conductors that drain away life energy—and we wonder why, after being surrounded by these electrical "zappers" all day, we feel drained.

The human body consists of billions of subatomic particles twirling and spinning in a self-organizing manner. The subatomic particles form atoms; many of these form molecules, which then group into more complex molecules. Atoms and molecules are held together in large part by electromagnetic bonds. Electromagnetic pollutants continuously assault these bonds; many physical symptoms can result. Because the allopathic approach to medicine does not recognize the body as being an electromagnetic system, these symptoms are categorized as "etiology unknown" (cause not known).

Yet EMFs can cause psychological symptoms such as tension, frustration, and apprehension, and physical symptoms such as lowered immune function, eye damage, infertility and other hormonal problems, digestive disturbances, headaches, fatigue, and chronic disease such as cancer.

It is interesting to note that crowding animals, in conjunction with exposing them to other environmental stressors such as fluorescent lighting, caused changes in the animals' endocrine systems, resulting in emotional instability (increased aggression or lethargy), uncontrolled blood sugar, delayed sexual maturity, lower birth rates in offspring, and lower estrogen levels.

It is not conceivable to think that we can go back to the days of candles and washboards, but we do need to understand how to minimize the negative influences of synthetic electromagnetic fields.

EMFs: Stress Reduction Tips

- Using a Trifield Meter, measure the EMFs emitted in your home and office by the various sources mentioned, and make adjustments as needed (see the tips below) to ensure that the overall field level remains within the safety range. The overall magnetic field in your environment should be lower than four or five milligauss, and the overall electric field lower than four or five kilovolts per meter.

- Use safe-screen computers and protective plates that decrease the electromagnetic radiation emitted by a computer. And turn the computer off when not using it.

- Do not use electric blankets, and keep your sleep space free of EMF-radiating devices.

- Get out to the country, away from concentrated EMF fields, regularly. (Go hug a tree!)

- Avoid living close to high-voltage power lines.

- Do not use a microwave oven, or, if you must, have it checked for leaks.

- Use full-spectrum light bulbs. They emit lower levels of electromagnetic radiation than do fluorescent lights.

Stress Related to Weather and Seasonal Changes

Changes in weather force the body to constantly adapt. The effects of weather on health have been recognized for millennia, and were mentioned by Paracelsus (1493–1541). Dressing inappropriately for the weather, or being caught in unexpected circumstances, can lead to stress because we become too hot or cold. Along similar lines, heat waves or cold snaps can tax our endurance and lower our immunity. In places where the barometric pressure changes frequently, the incidences of migraine headaches and asthma also increase.

> "He who knows the origins of winds, of thunder, and of the weather, also knows where diseases come from."—Paracelsus

In temperate and northern areas, seasonal changes also affect the amount of available natural light. In winter, when natural light is decreased because days are short and often cloudy, many people suffer from Seasonal Affective Disorder (SAD). They become depressed, sleep more, eat more, feel tired, are easily overwhelmed, and have difficulty concentrating.

As well, aggravation of premenstrual syndrome may arise as a consequence of increased exposure to fluorescent lighting and decreased exposure to full-spectrum, natural lighting. In the absence of natural light, the pineal gland secretes less of the hormone melatonin. Women who suffer from PMS appear to have an abnormal pattern of melatonin secretion in the days before menstruation. This is treatable with exposure to full-spectrum lights in the evening; these act on the pineal to lengthen the period of melatonin release and thereby reduce PMS.

Weather and Seasonal Changes: Stress Reduction Tips

- Go outside, without glasses on, for a minimum of one hour each day. You will get out of the toxic indoor office environment and increase your exposure to natural light.
- Use full-spectrum lighting wherever possible.
- If you are weather sensitive, giving your adrenal glands additional support, especially when weather changes are anticipated, can help prevent unwanted symptoms. Adrenal support is discussed in detail in Chapter 3.
- Homeopathic medicines can help your body adjust to changes in weather. The homeopathic medical system was developed by a German

physician, Samuel Hahnemann (1755–1843). Dr. Hahnemann found that disease symptoms represent the body's efforts to heal itself and felt that treatment should help stimulate this process. The word "homeopathy" is derived from the Greek "homoios," meaning similar, and "pathos," meaning suffering. The first law of homeopathy states that a substance that *causes* symptoms in a healthy person can help *cure* a sick person with similar symptoms: "like cures like." In essence, the homeopathic remedy mirrors to the body the nature of the illness it is experiencing; as the body's awareness of its situation is increased, so is its ability to overcome the illness.

Homeopathic remedies come in gradated potencies. The potency of a remedy in this case is indicated by a number and the letter C. Following are some useful homeopathic remedies for weather-sensitive persons, as well as the potency range in which they should be taken. Use any homeopathic remedy at least 20 minutes before or after eating. Pure water, however, does not interfere with a remedy's action.

— Bach Flower Rescue Remedy, a preparation made of flowers, can help with physical and emotional stress. Take two to three drops as needed until symptoms have improved.

— Phosphorus (9C to 30C) can help those who are worse during electrical and thunder storms; take three pellets or 10 to 15 drops every hour until symptoms improve.

— Rhododendron (9C to 30C) helps those who are sensitive to barometric changes (symptoms include headaches, asthma, or neuralgias); take three pellets or 10 to 15 drops every two to three hours until symptoms improve.

Chemical Stress

Over the past few decades it has become evident that chemicals introduced into the environment through human activity are having a profound influence on our health—there is a direct relationship between environmental toxicity and disease. Indeed, the contamination of both our indoor and outdoor environments with substances of potential harm—toxic chemicals that accumulate in the tissues of all plants and animals—has become a central problem of our technological times. Chemical toxins in our foods and environment cause an acceleration in the production of free radicals inside the body, molecules that are extremely reactive and can cause cell injury and dysfunction, inflammation, and degenerative diseases. Chemicals also increase the need for nutrients, as the body must have certain vitamins and minerals to neutralize free radicals and to transform chemical substances into excretable compounds.

Unfortunately, the average person would be hard pressed to avoid exposure to chemical toxins, and usually encounters several each day.

For example, according to extensive research done by Dr. Russell Jaffee, a scientist at Serammune Physicians Lab in Reston, Virginia, in 1988 the use of pesticides in the United States exceeded 1.1 billion pounds, an increase of 109 percent from 1964. Another finding from Jaffee's study was that more than 16 million people showed impaired immune function due to the effects of these pesticides, resulting in susceptibility to chronic viral and bacterial infections and a general decreased ability of the body to repair itself. The World Health Organization (WHO) estimates that every year 5 000 people die from the effects of pesticides. Potentially harmful amounts of pesticides can be found in our water supply, the air, and our food supply.

OH, CANADA!

A class of chemicals called persistent organic pollutants (POPs) are found in industrial chemicals and pesticides and are also byproducts of the pulp and paper industry. The breast milk of women from the province of Québec's Gaspé and Hudson Bay regions is among the most toxic in the world, containing 25 times more POPs than the WHO considers acceptable. The average Canadian breast-fed baby consumes almost 15 times more of certain POPs per day than is considered acceptable by the WHO. A study conducted by Greenpeace analyzed the levels of POPs in human tissue and noted that Canadians have the highest levels in the world of three types of POPs: dioxin, PCBs, and chlordane. These chemicals have been linked to rising breast and testicular cancer rates and falling sperm counts.

Canada's federal government issued its Toxic Substances Management Policy in 1995, a document that called for virtual elimination of POPs by 1997. Yet, as we enter the new millennium, Canadians still have the highest levels in the world of some of the most toxic POPs!

Other sources of chemicals in our environment include air pollutants from industrialization and temperature inversions (a temperature inversion occurs when a layer of cold air traps a layer of warm air below it, and toxic emissions from industry and cars build up in the warm layer), indoor contaminants from secondhand cigarette smoke and emissions from carpets, paints, and furniture. We increase our chemical stressor load every time we use alcohol, caffeine, tobacco or prescription drugs, drycleaning fluid, nail polish and plastic wrap. Food and drink regularly carry toxins into our bodies. Additives in colouring and packaging are common in processed and junk foods. According to the Canadian Environmental Law Association (CELA), there are traces of toxic chemicals in drinking water and just about every type of food common in the Canadian diet: butter, milk, and cheese; pork, beef, chicken, and eggs; and cereals, honey, fruits, and vegetables. The report goes on to say that the variety of toxic chemicals in food is astounding, and ranges from paint strippers and pesticides to urinal deodorizers and wood preservatives. Another serious food contamination problem is the use of growth hormones (especially BGH, or bovine growth hormone) and antibiotics in modern animal husbandry.

We can't escape our past. It was recently reported that toxins accumulated in glaciers are melting into rivers: PCBs, DDT, and other banned substances are making their way back into our lives. A renowned Columbia icefield scientist, the University of Alberta's D. Schindler, says, "Every day I see new environmental mistakes being made in a very cavalier fashion."

In 1998, scientists working for Health Canada questioned the safety of BGH for human consumption. However, the scientists were heavily pressured into changing their initial reports. Many parties had vested interests at stake: as BGH increases the yield of individual cows, it results in increased profits for the dairy and beef industry. Of course, BGH also turns a profit for the pharmaceutical companies who produce it. At the time of this writing, drug companies provided 70 percent of the funding for the Health Protection Branch. It is imperative that everyone write the government and Health Canada to voice concerns about foods such as milk produced with BGH from the U.S. being allowed into the Canadian market. If such foods are released in Canada, it is vital that labelling be mandatory so that the public is aware of what drugs are in the foods. For more information see the "Further Reading" section at the back of this book.

While the debate over further contamination of the food supply continues, a recent study reported that Canadian rates for several cancers are among the highest in the world:

- The breast cancer rate per 100 000 women is 76.8 in Canada, compared with 24.3 in Japan, 26.5 in China, and 20.4 in Zimbabwe. Only American women get breast cancer more often.

- Colorectal cancer rates in Canadian men are second only to those found in the Czech Republic.

- Prostate cancer occurs 10 times more frequently in Canadian men than Japanese men.

- Stomach cancer rates in Japanese women are four times higher than in Canadian women. This difference is thought to be due to the high consumption of smoked and cured foods by the Japanese.

The researchers presenting these alarming statistics suggest that possible causes for the high Canadian cancer rates include diet and lifestyle, including smoking, and exposure to environmental pollution, especially chlorinated compounds.

Clearly, the chemicals that we continue to add to our foods and water supply do affect our endocrine systems and overall health.

Years before a cancer takes hold, however, we may not even realize that environmental toxins are having an impact on us. Because most chemical pollutants cause not a specific disease but rather a range of symptoms, allopathic doctors are unable to offer a diagnosis and therefore are generally unable to offer any treatment. For example, how do medical doctors deal with the millions of people whose lab tests are all normal but who just don't feel well, who complain of being tired all the time? These people are generally told they are fine and just need a rest, or that they are depressed and need to take a holiday or some antidepressants.

Women diagnosed with depression are suffering from endocrine or liver imbalances resulting from the effects of prolonged exposure to environmental chemicals. Once this situation is addressed, the depression disappears. The experience of these women bears out the hypothesis that our health may be threatened not so much by one individual chemical as by the total chemical load we are burdened with over time. Remember that it is increasing load and decreasing resistance that together cause a breakdown in adaptation mechanisms.

As noted above, today's increased burden of chemicals and other environmental stressors increases the demand for nutrients that the body uses to detoxify and excrete chemicals, as well as to rebuild tissues damaged by toxins. But our soils are depleted in nutrients because the basic principles of crop rotation are not followed and liberal use of artificial fertilizers and chemicals has upset the soil's natural life-giving balance. The result is nutritionally inferior food. Twenty years ago our chemical exposure wasn't as great and our foods were higher in nutrients, but in today's world many people consume more toxins than nutrients, and the effects of chemicals on their biological processes are exacerbated.

The litany of chemical terrors could go on and on—the study of chemical pollutants and their influence on health is a vast topic. We have touched only on the basics here to give you an introductory understanding of why it is vital to your optimal health that you know how to effectively reduce your chemical stress load.

CHEMICAL TOXINS: STRESS REDUCTION TIPS

- Eat natural unprocessed, chemical-free foods, organically grown whenever possible.

- Antioxidants are substances that neutralize free radical molecules. Increase your intake of antioxidants, including vitamins A, C, and E; the minerals zinc and selenium; carotenoids, such as beta carotene; and plant compounds called proanthrocyanidins, found in grape seed and pine bark extracts. For more information on antioxidants, see Chapter 3.

- Store foods in glass rather than plastic containers. Do not microwave foods in plastic.

- Minimize pollutants in your home and work environment by using air cleaners and water purifiers. Avoid chlorinated water not only for drinking but for bathing and showers as well. Buy a shower water filter.

- Carefully select your building materials, paints and finishes, and furniture. Low- and no-chemical alternatives are possible.

- Don't use pesticides or herbicide on your lawn or garden.

- Use only biodegradable cleaning supplies and detergents.

- Wear clothing made of natural fabrics. Avoid dry-cleaning.

- Speak out to the policy makers regarding the use of chemicals in foods and the larger environment.

- Detoxify and cleanse your body regularly (see Chapter 3)

Nutritional Stress

We are eating more and more of less and less. And according to a Statistics Canada report released in 1994, Canadians are now spending more time in hospitals than they were in the 1970s.

Many of our health problems can be directly linked to a lack of basic nutrition and increased chemicals in our foods. As we have seen, the body requires higher levels of nutrients to counter the added environmental challenges of today's world. However, the nutritional content of the food we eat is often lacking, or destroyed by the time it gets to our tables, for a number of reasons.

- **Soil conditions.** The condition of the soil a food is grown in is the most important factor determining its nutrient content. Many soils today are depleted because of poor farming practices, which are "remedied" with chemical fertilizers. These increase crop yield but do nothing to improve the soil's or food's nutrient content. In fact, fertilizers deplete such nutrients as iron, vitamin C, zinc, and trace minerals.

- **Food transport.** Today, fruits and vegetables are often picked before they are ripe, shipped long distances and stored before sale for long periods, sometimes under fluorescent lighting. At every step along the way, nutrients are depleted.

- **Chemical animal husbandry.** Antibiotics and growth hormones given to animals and pesticides and herbicides used in growing animal feed accumulate in the fat cells of animals. When we consume animal products we ingest a high concentration of these chemicals, which in turn are stored in our fat tissue. These toxins carry serious long-term health risks and also undermine our health in the short term.

- **Food additives.** Additives are another serious source of nutritional stress. Did you know that there are 1,200 legal additives for ice cream and more than 3,000 used in commercially processed foods?

- **Food processing.** We pay a high price in stores and food outlets for our convenient lifestyles, but the price we pay in our health is even greater! While a moderate amount of food processing is necessary in today's world, it must also be recognized as the single greatest destroyer of nutrients. In some cases nutrients may be added back, but certainly not in the way nature intended. Unfortunately, our North American concept of the food basics seems to be focused on highly processed foods—fast food pizza, sugar-laden baked goods and doughnuts, and other refined-flour products such as sugar cereals, burgers and fries, coffee, potato chips, soda pop and other snacks—all of which are non-foods. Non-foods contain little, if any, nutritional value except unwanted fats and calories; they deplete the body of nutrient stores and cause nutrient malabsorption, block essential metabolic pathways, increase the load of toxins and cancer-causing substances in the body, and stress and irritate all organ systems.

• **Irradiation.** As though our food wasn't depleted enough, now threatens another nutritional nightmare—food irradiation. This technology bombards food with radioactive isotopes, and the processing plants produce radioactive wastes that need to be disposed of. Currently being promoted for its ability to kill bacteria and molds, irradiation also damages the molecular structure of food, making it less absorbable by the body. A study performed in 1984 by Ralston Scientific Services for the United States Army found that mice fed diets rich in irradiated chicken died earlier and had a higher incidence of cancerous tumours.

Other major sources of nutritional stress are found in the quality of the fats and oils we consume, and in the extent of contamination of the water supply.

FATS AND OILS

Contrary to popular belief, optimal health depends largely on having appropriate amounts of fat in our diet—but it must be the right fats. Most people today have become "fat-phobic"; they have come to believe that all fats are the same and cause disease, especially cardiovascular conditions.

Fats and oils come in many forms—there are short-chain, long-chain, saturated, unsaturated, monounsaturated, polyunsaturated, and essential and non-essential fatty acids. Rather than go into great detail about the various compositions of these fats, I will simply highlight their key characteristics so you can have a better understanding of why some fats are better for health than others.

Essential Fatty Acids: The "Good" Fats

Essential fatty acids (EFAs) are important to health and have many roles in the body. They are the only fatty acids not manufactured by our bodies;

consequently, they must be supplied by the diet. There are two categories of EFAs: omega-3 and omega-6 fatty acids, also called alpha-linolenic and linoleic acid, respectively.

Alpha-linolenic acid is primarily found in fish oils such as herring, salmon, mackerel, sardines, and halibut and in flaxseed oil, soybeans, walnuts, and green leafy vegetables. Deficiency symptoms include inflammatory conditions, water retention, dry skin, high blood pressure, platelet aggregation or stickiness associated with heart disease (platelets are blood cells involved in blood clotting), low metabolism, growth retardation and poor brain development, learning disability and behavioural changes, and vision impairment.

Linoleic acid is found primarily in vegetable and seed oils such as evening primrose oil and safflower, sunflower, grape seed, and almond oils. Signs of deficiency include eczema-like eruptions, slow wound healing, sterility in males, miscarriage, hair loss, weak immunity, and arthritis.

The EFAs are ideally ingested in a particular ratio. Western diets are typically overabundant in omega-6 fatty acids. It is estimated that the average diet in the west contains more than 10 times the amount of omega-6 fatty acids that are required for health. It has been proposed that in adults the ideal intake of EFAs is four parts omega-6 fatty acids for every one part omega-3 fatty acids.

Saturated Fatty Acids

There are short- and long-chain saturated fatty acids (SFAs). Short-chain SFAs are usually liquid at room temperature, partly soluble in water and easy to digest, making them readily available for energy production in the body. Sources of short-chain SFAs include butter, coconut oil, and palm kernel fats. Refined sugars and starches are converted to short-chain SFAs in the body.

Long-chain SFAs are solid at room temperature and insoluble in water. Sources include pork, beef, and mutton.

Unsaturated Fatty Acids

Included in this group are monounsaturated fatty acids (MUFAS) and polyunsaturated fatty acids (PUFAS). These substances are liquid at room temperature. The most commonly ingested MUFA is the oleic acid found in olive oil, almonds, and other seed oils and in the fat of most land animals. It stimulates the flow of bile; people with a diet high in olive oil have lower levels of cholesterol and lower blood pressure than those eating margarine and

SOURCES OF ESSENTIAL FATTY ACIDS

Omega-3 Fatty Acids (Alpha-Linolenic Acid)

- Fish oils (herring, salmon, mackerel, sardines, halibut)
- Flaxseed oil

Omega-6 Fatty Acids (Linoleic Acid)

- Almond oil
- Brazil nut oil
- Canola oil
- Evening primrose oil
- Flaxseed oil
- Grape seed oil
- Hazelnut oil
- Peanut oil
- Pecan oil
- Pumpkin seed oil
- Safflower oil
- Sesame seed oil
- Sunflower seed oil
- Walnut oil

large quantities of butter. Olive oil fits into the "no harm" category but does not provide many of the essential fatty acids.

Toss the Tuna — According to an advisory panel to the U.S. Food and Drug Administration (FDA), pregnant women and those in their childbearing years should limit their tuna consumption and in 2001 the FDA had also put out the same warning for shark, king mackerel, swordfish, and tilefish. About 8 percent of U.S. women of childbearing age have enough mercury in their blood to be at risk and The National Academy of Sciences estimates that 60,000 newborns a year could be at risk of learning disabilities because of mercury their mothers absorbed during pregnancy.

The Processing of Oils

Most commercially available oils are highly processed. The most harmful stage of oil processing is hydrogenation, a means of making oils into solids.

Oil is saturated with hydrogen atoms by mixing it with a metal catalyst and subjecting it to extremely high temperatures, as high as 196° Celsius. The molecular structure of the hydrogenated oil changes into substances the body finds unrecognizable and unuseable—trans-fatty acids, potentially carcinogenic and disruptive of the normal metabolism of essential fatty acids. In North America, some "food" goods are estimated to have a trans-fatty acid content as high as 60 percent. Hydrogenated oils are commonly used in margarines, shortenings, ice cream, candy, and snack foods. In Holland foods containing trans-fatty acids have been banned.

The production of other oils uses temperatures ranging from 95 to 260° Celsius, temperatures that destroy nutrients and create trans-fatty acids. Don't be fooled by the commercially produced oils that are labelled "cold pressed"; even these oils are subjected to high heat from friction generated by giant oil presses. Because no external heat has been applied, however, these products can legally be called cold pressed. Buyer beware.

For your optimal health, choose expeller-pressed, unprocessed oils. Extra virgin olive oil is also safe, since it can be extracted from olives without high heat being generated in the process.

One way to offset the damaging effects of trans-fatty acids is to consume high levels of the beneficial fatty acids found in flaxseed, sesame, soy, evening primrose, olive, and fish oils. Vitamin E also helps prevent negative effects from heated oils.

If oils are dangerous when heated, how can we safely cook with them? Some oils offer more heat stability than others. Use sesame oil, olive oil, cocoa butter, palm oil, or butter when cooking at *low heats*. If the oil becomes black or brown during cooking, discard it.

Butter versus Margarine

It is not logical to presume that butter, a saturated fat that humans have been consuming for hundreds of years, has caused the abrupt rise in the incidence of heart disease since the 1900s. There is, however, a correlation between the rise of heart disease and the replacement of the butter churn, olive press, and expeller-pressed oils with the industrial oil refineries.

Margarine is a hydrogenated oil and contains many toxic chemicals; no "health" margarine is available and it doesn't matter whether the label says it is polyunsaturated or not. A natural, polyunsaturated fat that is solid at room temperature does not exist—any margarine has to have been chemically altered by hydrogenation and totally denatured to get that way. Butter, on the other hand, is a saturated fat in its natural state. Butter contains healthy fatty acids, vitamins, and minerals; choose butter over margarine.

Avoid refined heated oils, fried and deep-fried oils, margarines, shortenings, and partially hydrogenated oils. Moderate your intake of saturated fats from pork, beef, mutton, and dairy products.

Guilt-Free Butter
Mix together:
- 250 mL of butter (at room temperature)
- 250 mL of flaxseed or olive oil
  Store in the refrigerator.

This recipe helps you get more of the essential fatty acids and at the same time reduces your intake of saturated fats. Use this combination on popcorn, baked potatoes, toast, cooked corn ... it tastes great.

Cholesterol: The Good, the Bad, the Misunderstood

Cholesterol has received such bad publicity that most people think that any cholesterol is bad and are unnecessarily preoccupied with their cholesterol intake. But as I discuss in detail later, cholesterol is the raw material from which all hormones are made. Some hormone synthesis uses low-density lipoprotein (LDL) cholesterol while other uses high-density lipoprotein (HDL) as the raw material. HDLs remove excess cholesterol from the body. LDLs carry cholesterol from the liver to the bloodstream and the cells. Contrary to popular belief, HDL cholesterol is not "good," nor is LDL cholesterol "bad." Rather, both, in proper balance, are required for specific body functions.

There is a difference between dietary cholesterol and blood cholesterol. Dietary cholesterol comes from food, whereas blood cholesterol is made by the body and found in the bloodstream. Eating foods containing dietary cholesterol will not necessarily put cholesterol into the bloodstream. Cholesterol is made by the body from fats, sugars, and proteins, and the more heated oils and refined sugars you consume, the more cholesterol your body will make. Free radical damage also causes the body to produce more cholesterol (see Chapter 3).

Eggs have gotten a "bad rap" as a contributor to high cholesterol levels, but this theory is unfounded. Yet doctors and dietitians continue the bad press. When I was residing in California in the early 1990s, a commercial put out by the egg industry pictured eggs dressed in convict uniforms being released from prison cells. Rap music played in the background, while the eggs sang, "Eggs got a bad rap." This advertising was based on studies that showed eggs do not have a negative influence on cholesterol. Nature knows best: eggs contain lecithin, which emulsifies the cholesterol in them. Homogenized milk does more damage to arteries than eggs or meat ever will because the fat globules in it have been mechanically altered to such a small size that they can be absorbed directly into the bloodstream. (For more information on fats and heart disease, see Chapter 9.)

WATER

Nearly 70 percent of the human body is made of water—and nearly every bodily function, from the transportation of nutrients to the elimination of toxins, is done through this medium. Ingesting adequate amounts of water (2.5 L) is critical for optimal health. Conditions linked to inadequate water intake include allergies, arthritis, angina, asthma, cardiovascular problems (high blood pressure, high cholesterol, edema), chronic pain (back pain, headaches), dyspeptic conditions (gastritis, heartburn, ulcers), gastrointestinal conditions (appendicitis, colitis, hiatus hernia), and obesity.

Over the years our natural water supplies have become contaminated by acid rain, chemical leaching, and industrial waste, as well as two very toxic chemicals added to municipal water supplies, chlorine and fluoride. Chlorine is an inorganic mineral that reacts with naturally occurring organic compounds to form organochlorines, which are extremely mutagenic and carcinogenic substances. Fluoride is certified rat poison and is toxic at any level. Yet many people ingest large amounts from water, foods and beverages made with fluoridated water, toothpaste, and mouth wash. More and more children have fluorosis, a condition in which the teeth become mottled, discoloured with opaque white patches, and malformed. Teeth are an excellent indication of what is happening to the bone as well. The effects of fluoride on bone health are discussed in Chapter 8.

The literature on "good" water suggests that most experts agree that the purest water you can drink is distilled or "purified" water. Reverse-osmosis filtered water is another wise choice as long as you change the filters regularly and you have a good-quality system.

Nowadays we wonder why we are having hormonal problems, why we feel chronically fatigued, and why our children and grandchildren have allergies, learning disorders, and chronic colds and ear infections. The fact is that these conditions will only get worse and develop into even more serious chronic diseases unless we start eating real, unprocessed foods and drinking pure water.

Nutritional Stress Reduction Tips

- Avoid all non-foods.
- Replace non-foods with organically grown, fibre-rich whole grains and fresh fruits and vegetables, and hormone- and chemical-free animal products.
- Limit consumption of refined carbohydrates (i.e., sugar, white breads, pasta) and increase consumption of complex carbohydrates such as whole grains and legumes. Use concentrated carbohydrates such as honey, dried fruits, and fruit juices in moderation.
- Avoid saturated fats, heated oils and margarines, fried foods, and processed cooking oils. Increase your consumption of the essential fatty acids.
- Increase your protein intake from vegetarian sources such as legumes and fermented soy products.
- Increase your intake of green leafy vegetables.
- Decrease your intake of milk and dairy products, chocolate, and chocolate-containing foods.
- Decrease your salt intake.
- Drink only unfluoridated, unchlorinated water, and drink a minimum of 2.5 litres of water daily!
- Minimize or eliminate the consumption of soft drinks; drink beer and wine in moderation and spirits sparingly, if at all. Coffee and tea can be taken in moderation, one to two cups daily at the most—they are diuretics and flush much-needed fluids from your body.
- Take antioxidant supplements to provide additional support for the body. (See Chapter 3)
- Take a good multivitamin and mineral supplement such as Femmessentials for added nutritional insurance.

"If we do not change the way we are going, we are going to end up where we are headed."—Red Skelton

Structural Stress

You need a healthy physical structure to support the rest of your life—musculoskeletal structure and function have a profound influence on the rest of the body's state of health. Don't wait for joint pain or osteoporosis to start taking care of the framework. The first rule of structural health? Exercise is not an option!

Life once demanded that we be active, but today we spend much of our day in sedentary jobs that require extensive periods of sitting, either at a computer or in meetings, usually in chairs that do not support the body properly. The number of hours spent doing sedentary work limits recreational and exercise time. Because of these time pressures, many people do not even try to exercise, since they believe that to benefit from exercise they must complete strenuous workouts every day. Yet a study published in the *Journal of the American Medical Association* found that people who walk vigorously for 30 minutes at a time, at least six times a month, reduce their risk of premature death by up to 44 percent; even those who exercised less frequently had a 34 percent lower mortality rate than completely sedentary people. However, exercising on only six days a month will not keep you fit.

Regular exercise benefits psychological health, improves sleep, balances hormones, slows aging, strengthens connective tissue and bones, supports the immune system, decreases blood pressure, increases energy levels, increases metabolism, enables better weight management, and reduces other stress-

STRUCTURAL STRESS REDUCTION TIPS

- Exercise and stretch regularly. Aim for a minimum activity level of three 30-minute exercise sessions per week.

- Take the steps needed to improve your posture so as to decrease structural trauma in daily activities.

- Schedule regular massages and chiropractic care. Most people require a minimum of two such appointments per month. More may be necessary, especially at first.

related conditions. In light of facts like these, how can we not find time for exercise? Some people are concerned about the amount of money they have to spend on their health and yet somehow still do not find time for exercise, which costs nothing but time. What good is all the money in the world if you do not have your health?

If you are not sure how to start integrating exercise into your schedule, please refer to *The Complete Athlete: Integrating Fitness, Nutrition and Natural Health*, by John Winterdyk and Karen Jensen. (See the "Further Reading" section at the back of this book.) This book offers simple guidelines and tips for the beginner athlete as well as specific recommendations for elite athletes. We use the term "athlete" to describe everyone because we are all athletes competing in the exercise of life—some of us just go at it with more vigour.

In addition to our activity level, nutritional habits and genetics influence the health of the bones, joints, and muscles (see Chapters 7 and 8), as do rest and postural habits. Posture demonstrates the nature of our relationship to gravity. Gravity is the most constant influence on the physical structure, requiring

THE EXTERNAL STRESSORS: A SUMMARY

- **Electromagnetic fields.** Sources include computers, fluorescent lights, hair dryers, microwave ovens, power lines, televisions, waterbeds, and anything else that is plugged in.

- **Weather and seasonal stressors.** These include overheating and overcooling, seasonal changes in weather and natural light patterns, and barometric shifts.

- **Chemical stressors.** The various forms of chemical stressors include toxic metals, cosmetics, plastics, persistent organic pollutants, junk food diets, alcohol, caffeine, tobacco, and both legal and illicit drugs.

- **Nutritional stress.** Modern agricultural and food processing practices have seriously depleted the nutritional content of most foods; pollutants contaminate the water supply.

- **Structural stressors.** Sedentary lifestyles and poor posture stress the musculoskeletal system and the internal organs and functions.

ongoing adaptation. A number of natural therapies, such as yoga, the Feldenkrais method, Pilates, and postural integration (Rolfing), are available for those who would like to reduce trauma and stress on the musculoskeletal system by learning to work with gravity's influence with more grace and ease.

Now that we have reviewed some of the external stressors that may affect our health, we will look at some of the internal stressors.

INTERNAL STRESSORS

In our interactions with the environment, the inner and outer worlds continuously and reciprocally influence one another. Internal stress is frequently a direct result of modern life. Environmental toxins, improper diet, inappropriate use of drugs, and hectic, sleep-deprived lifestyles all affect our nutritional status, intestinal health, and mental, emotional, and spiritual health. However, we can address our internal stressors, and in the process will often find that we are making changes to our external world as well.

Mental, Emotional, and Spiritual Stress

> "Visualization takes advantage of what might almost be called a 'weakness' of the body: it cannot distinguish between a vivid mental experience and an actual physical experience."— Bernie S. Siegel, M.D.

Once we fully understand that we do have choices in our lives, we come to realize that the majority of limitations we have are those we create with our own beliefs.

What we constantly image will become our individual reality. What we constantly image as a society will become our collective reality, and each one of us has an important say in this process. The more feeling there is behind the images, the more potently they are likely to manifest in the physical world. The most powerful images are those fuelled by love (see Chapter 10 for more on love).

These concepts have a critical role to play in our journey to health. If our thought forms help to create our reality, we can use them to contribute to the creation of health—or of disease.

A continual focus on limiting beliefs, worries, or unpleasant situations harms the physical body. I can't tell you how many times I hear people say such things as "I get allergies every year at this time," or "I worry myself sick about my children," or "I dread getting up in the morning because I hate my job." Thoughts like these do not just float around in the ethers; they create powerful effects on you and those around you. If you have enough destructive thoughts, they will result in physical, mental, or emotional problems. Every thought, if strong enough, solidifies into a future condition.

Test yourself to see how many disruptive thoughts you regularly entertain. For one day, write down each limiting, unpleasant, or negative thought you have—thoughts that begin with the words "I can't," "I should," "If only," "I don't like," "You made me," "I didn't want to," "I'm sick," "I have no money," "I had no choice," and so on. Don't forget the uncompassionate, belittling, or blaming thoughts you might have about other people. And putting someone on a pedestal in comparison to you isn't very healthy either. You will be amazed how much time you spend in unproductive, harmful thought patterns—and every time we allow our thoughts to run along such tracks we dissipate our vital energy. One of my patients recorded more than 300 destructive thoughts in one afternoon. And we wonder why we end up sick and tired at the end of the day!

"The greatest thing in this world is not so much where you are but in what direction we are moving."—Oliver Wendell Holmes

Our destructive thought patterns often occur even when there is no particular external stimulus to initiate them. Once we start to gain control over these thought patterns, we can begin to look at how we respond to the actual circumstances of our lives.

Life is an impeccable teacher and continually offers opportunities for growth. When everything is smooth and going well, how many people take the time for inner reflection and communication with their higher power, however they might define or name this being or force? Not many. How many people daily give thanks for all the small blessings in their life? Not many.

However, when presented with a chronic illness or pain, most people are faced with themselves and start doing much more soul searching.

When something "good" happens in our lives, we rarely ask God, "Why me?" When something unpleasant or painful happens, we almost inevitably ask God, "Why me?"

The most successful soul searchers are those who learn that rather than be upset or disappointed when faced with unpleasant or painful situations, it's best to change one's attitude—to gracefully and gratefully accept that a difficult situation is a chance to learn and grow. When we take this approach, all conditions and experiences will work to our benefit.

Even at those times when the situations in our lives or in our health seem permanent, it is the attitude we hold towards the experience that contributes to our growth—or hampers it. Christopher Reeve, the movie actor and "superman," became a quadriplegic. His body may be paralyzed for the rest of his life, but his incredible strength of spirit and heart in response to his circumstance has provided inspiration for millions of people. His attitude to his situation has turned what could have been a long descent into bitterness and hopelessness into an opportunity for growth, learning, and joy. He and so many others continuously make us marvel at the courage of the human spirit.

Life often gives us what we want, with a twist. The twist is what we can use for our growth.

Karen's Personal Journey

When I was in my twenties, I was essentially disabled because of unrelenting and excruciating back pain. Specialists determined that I had a degenerative spinal condition and that I would be in a wheelchair by the time I was 35. Drugs and bed rest were presented as my only treatment options. Another specialist said that my condition was all in my head and that I needed psychiatric counselling and medication. In the face of these opinions, I at first felt helpless, and that I had no choice; the authorities had spoken—I could do little about my health situation.

However, it didn't take me long to become extremely frustrated by my lack of action on my own behalf, and I decided that the dire prognoses I had received did not have to become my reality. My search for a way to change the situation began.

I came into this life with a very strong will. At times this quality makes life difficult for those around me, but in this case it was my greatest gift. It gave me the persistence and determination I needed to act against the opinions of my family and the status quo, which was very difficult over thirty years ago, when allopathic doctors were still unquestioned authorities. It was only through determination and searching that I came to discover other options available to me. The path was long and painful, but for 12 years now I have suffered no back pain and I am *not* in a wheelchair. The journey I embarked on also contributed significantly to my decision to change careers and begin practising naturopathic medicine. More important, in my estimation, is that

MENTAL, EMOTIONAL AND SPIRITUAL STRESS REDUCTION TIPS

- Love is the essential healing force in the universe and brings us everything we need. Focus on how to express love in every act and word, and love will return to you in abundance.

- Cultivate an attitude of gratitude for everything in your life. Look for the opportunity to learn and grow in every situation.

- Remember that thoughts, especially when accompanied by strong emotion, eventually manifest in physical reality. If you want to change your physical reality, change the focus of your thoughts. Especially replace disruptive, unpleasant, worrying, and limiting thoughts with loving and liberating thoughts.

- As soon as you have decided to change your reality, give thanks that it has happened and act as if the change has already taken place. What do you learn from doing so? How do you feel? What else can you do to fully bring the new reality into physical manifestation?

through my experience I gained compassion, patience, and understanding for others who are less fortunate, who are handicapped in some way, or who are faced with situations that are painful or devastating and appear hopeless. For that I am forever grateful; the years of pain seem a small price to pay for wisdom of the heart. I only ask that I will continue to see "gifts of opportunity" in all that life presents to me so that I may continue to grow and learn.

Thoughts significantly affect everything in our lives, including our physiology and therefore our health. Listen carefully to your spoken and unspoken thoughts and observe where they are leading you.

"In mechanical terms, the motor is the mind, but the fuel is the heart. Thus every thought combined with feeling brings into action certain physical tissue, parts of the brain, nerves or muscles. This produces an actual change in the conditions of the tissue, regardless of whatever body it be."—Paul Twitchell

Sleep Deprivation Stress

We will not be able to direct our thoughts properly if we are fatigued from lack of sleep. Many people do not get enough rest because the invention of electricity allows us to stay up till all hours, disrupting the natural cycles of darkness and daylight, sleeping and waking. The age of modern technology promised to offer more time for rest and relaxation but has only increased the demands on us. Too often, we steal from our sleep time to meet those increasing demands. Yet adequate sleep is essential for good health. Special immune functions take place during sleep, body tissues are repaired and regenerated, and dreams arise to help us deal with the stresses of the past day. In fact, dreaming has been shown to be essential for maintaining our physical, emotional, and mental balance. The world's religions also comment on the importance of dreams for our spiritual life.

STRUCTURAL STRESS REDUCTION TIPS

- It's simple, get adequate rest. Sleep in a room that is as dark and quiet as possible. Some people may require only six hours' sleep, while other feel better with eight or nine. Listen to your body; it knows best. (For more information on support for insomnia, see Chapter 6.)

Digestive Stress

From the moment of conception to the last breath of life, our bodies are constantly changing. Cells and molecules, when they are worn out or no longer needed, are expelled from our bodies and are replaced by new substances and biological structures. If constant self-renewal did not take place, we would soon waste away, and that would be the end of us.

It is food that provides the raw material for new body structures and components. In order for this basic building material to be absorbed by the body it must first be digested. If digestion is not efficient, absorption of nutrients into the bloodstream is inefficient, or doesn't occur at all. Furthermore, without a healthy digestive process we will not only develop increasing deficiencies of key nutrients needed to maintain biochemical processes, we will also increase our load of undigested food particles. These are toxic to us.

DIGESTIVE STRESS REDUCTION TIPS

- *Go to your table with a light heart and a relaxed mind.* Eating too rapidly causes less saliva to be secreted and food is dumped into the stomach in much the same condition it entered the mouth. This causes extra work for the stomach enzymes. Eating hurriedly, or while angry or worried, also inhibits the release of gastric enzymes. *Do not eat if you feel stressed or extremely rushed*—you won't digest properly and will create yet more stress for your body.

- Avoid drinking fluids with meals, as this dilutes the digestive enzymes, making them less efficient. If you feel the need to drink fluids in order to swallow your food, you are not chewing long enough.

- Avoid cold fluids, especially with meals. According to traditional Chinese medicine, drinking cold fluids injures the stomach's energy.

- Practice temperance. Eating too much food at one sitting overtaxes digestion, causing more harm than good. Ancient philosophy has passed down a credo that is as relevant today as ever: *"I do not live to eat and drink; I eat and drink to live."*

Obviously, good digestion starts with choosing good food, discussed in the section "Nutritional Stress" above. Another major contributor to poor digestion is the manner in which we eat.

STRESS DUE TO BOWEL IMBALANCES

Another major possible source of ongoing digestive stress can be microbial imbalances in the digestive tract, especially in the large intestine or bowel. Naturopathic doctors and related health care professionals have for decades considered microflora imbalances due to an overgrowth of yeast a trigger for many diseases. There are approximately 250 species of yeast; the major species that grows in humans is *Candida albicans*. Allopathic medicine treats a yeast overgrowth symptomatically when there are overt manifes-

POSSIBLE CONDITIONS DIRECTLY AND INDIRECTLY RELATED TO CANDIDA (IMBALANCE IN THE GUT)

Candida and friends rob the body of nutrition and cause increased toxicity that can contribute directly or indirectly to the following conditions:

- Adrenal/thyroid problems
- Allergies
- Arthritis/Ankylosing spondylitis
- Asthma
- Blood sugar problems (diabetes, hypoglycemia)
- Celiac disease
- Chronic fatigue syndrome/Fibromyalgia
- Cognitive difficulties
- Colitis/irritable bowel syndrome
- Crohn's disease
- Depression
- Diarrhea/constipation
- Endometriosis
- Fatigue
- Food cravings
- Gas/bloating
- Hormonal imbalance
- Hyperactivity
- Insomnia
- Liver spots
- Liver stress
- Malabsorption
- Menstrual problems
- Over/under weight
- Premenstrual syndrome
- Premature aging
- Skin rashes and hives
- Vaginal yeast/bladder infections
- Water retention

tations such as vaginal yeast, or thrush or fungal problems (athlete's foot, fungal toenails).

It is normal for everyone to have small amounts of yeast and other potentially harmful microorganisms in the intestines. As long as the "friendly bacteria" continue to outnumber the potentially "bad microbes," all will be well. Friendly bacteria form vitamins B12, K, and folic acid, and prevent the overgrowth of yeast and harmful bacteria. However, if the friendly bacteria in our colons are killed by antibiotics, or if the immune system becomes weakened, perhaps because of one of the stressors we have already discussed, or because of other influences we will consider further on, various microorganisms and "yeasty beasties" will multiply readily. The latter can also mutate into an aggressive fungus. The result of overproliferation of yeast and other harmful fungi and bacteria in a susceptible host is intestinal imbalance and toxicity.

Darkfield microscopy can detect indicators of immune dysfunction in the blood when high levels of microbial imbalance are present. The relationship between the immune system and microbial imbalance, or dysbiosis, has not been thoroughly studied to date, but one recent study, completed in 1996, confirms these clinical observations. The researchers found that 60 percent of patients with autoimmune disease were positive for Candida antibodies, while only 7.5 percent of the control group were positive. The connection between the presence of Candida and autoimmune disease, as well as a direct association between Candida and diseases involving a severely compromised immune system, such as cancer, are now widely accepted.

Why is candida so damaging? Yeast's metabolic wastes, including gas, alcohol, and acetylaldehyde, enter the bloodstream; the liver has to detoxify these substances, and becomes stressed. The toxic waste products of yeast metabolism also spread to other areas of the body, causing a multitude of symptoms and conditions. Candida is also accompanied by the proliferation of bacteria that ferment foods, creating gas and toxic compounds, and which can indirectly increase the body's total estrogen levels.

Poor digestion contributes directly to Candida overgrowth. As discussed above, without a healthy digestive process we suffer from increasing nutrient deficiencies as well as from an increased toxic load due to undigested food particles. The immune system is forced to react to partially digested foods, as it recognizes them as foreign substances. When the immune system is occu-

CANDIDA QUESTIONNAIRE

General History

_____ Have you taken tetracyclines (e.g., Minocin) for acne for one month or longer?

_____ Have you taken, or do you take, antibiotics for infections more than four times per year?

_____ Have you taken birth control pills for more than two years?

_____ Have you taken birth control pills for six months to two years?

_____ Have you taken prednisone or other cortisone-like drugs (e.g., asthma medication)?

_____ Does the smell of perfume, tobacco, or other odours or chemicals make you sick?

_____ Do you crave sugars and breads?

_____ **Total Score**

Symptoms

Enter (1) if symptom is mild; (2) if moderate or frequent; (3) if severe or constant.

_____ Experience vaginal discharge or irritation

_____ Experience frequent bladder infections or incontinence

_____ Experience premenstrual syndrome or fluid retention

_____ Have difficulty getting pregnant

_____ Have frequent infections (sinus, lung, colds, etc.)

_____ Have allergies to foods or environmental substances

pied with protecting us from these foreign particles, its ability to fight disease-causing yeasts and microbes becomes impaired.

Furthermore, when the immune system is overworked, one result is an increase in the production of abnormal fatty acids called leucotrienes, the

_____ Feel worse on rainy and snowy days, around molds or musty basements

_____ Experience feelings of anxiety and/or irritability

_____ Have insomnia

_____ Experience gas and bloating

_____ Experience constipation or diarrhea

_____ Have bad breath

_____ Have a difficult time concentrating; feel "spacey"

_____ Experience muscle weakness or painful joints

_____ Have nasal congestion

_____ Feel pressure behind or irritation of the eyes

_____ Have frequent headaches

_____ Generally "not feeling well" without an explanation or diagnosis

_____ Have thyroid problems

_____ Have muscle aches or weakness

_____ **Total Score from all sections**

Scoring:

50 or less indicates mild _Candida_

50 to 90 indicates moderate _Candida_

90 to 120 indicates severe _Candida_

result of an immune system response called the fatty-acid mediated response system. Leucotrienes bind with the chloride molecules found in the body's salt. The stomach needs chlorides to make stomach acids, so the leucotriene activity results in decreased stomach acid and even weaker digestion. The lack of acids in the stomach also leads to an excess in the gastrointestinal tract of alkaline substances called bicarbonates. As the digestion is further weakened, of course, the immune system receives even less support for its activities and more undigested particles to deal with. A vicious circle now needs to be broken.

As we mentioned earlier, when it comes to preparing for a healthy hormonal transition, many women are interested only in what remedies they need to take, or which prescription hormones are safer. Granted, many women can benefit from some extra support from botanical and homeopathic medicines, nutritional supplements, lifestyle changes, and in some cases hormone replacement during the perimenopausal and menopausal years. However, creating hormonal health goes much deeper than that! One of the main underlying causes of most hormonal problems is poor digestion and dysbiosis.

Vaginal yeast infections and bladder infections are the more commonly recognized manifestations of increased yeast levels, but several other conditions that may be blamed on menopause are instead actually a direct result of dysbiosis interfering with the healthy functioning of the bowel, liver, adrenal glands, and thyroid gland (all discussed later).

Imbalances in the gut can manifest in many ways, and may have a number of causes. The questionnaire on the previous page will help you determine what degree of dysbiosis you have. It is adapted from one developed by William Crook, M.D. Over the years we have read many books and studies and observed the many symptoms and possible causes of candida.

Candida-related stress reduction is a little too complex to fit into a list of short tips. If, after reviewing the possible conditions related to dysbiosis and answering the questionnaire, you feel you have symptoms related to dysbiosis/Candida overgrowth, we recommend that you review the recommendations for treatment given in Chapter 3. There are also many books on Candida available at your library or local bookstore that can offer additional information. Please refer to the "Further Reading" section at the back of this book for a list of titles.

Bowel health is central to a healthy body and particularly to a healthy hormonal system (a more detailed discussion is in Chapter 3). However, our bowels are often contaminated with toxins that can leach into the bloodstream. Toxins form in the bowel for a number of reasons; among the most detrimental are poor-quality foods and an imbalance of the microintestinal flora. Another cause of bowel toxicity is scanty evacuation.

BOWEL TOXICITY STRESS REDUCTION TIPS

- If you suspect Candida, take immediate steps to bring your intestinal flora back into balance. See Chapter 3.

- Eat unprocessed foods - whole grains, beans, vegetables, fruits, nuts - high in natural fibre. Plant fibres found in natural foods absorb harmful compounds and encourage regular evacuation.

- Avoid antibiotics whenever possible; instead seek safer, natural immune-enhancing treatments for infections. Antibiotics kill beneficial bacteria in the colon, allowing yeast and other harmful organisms to flourish.

- Simple sugars and other refined foods stress the digestive and immune systems and encourage Candida proliferation.

- Avoid hormone replacement therapy, birth control pills and steroid medications such as cortisone whenever possible - investigate the natural alternatives. These drugs encourage yeast overgrowth since they increase blood sugar levels.

- Take steps to reduce the various stressors in your life. Unrelieved stress lowers immunity, enhancing the possibility of bowel toxicity.

Many people do not understand how they could have a toxic colon when they have "regular" bowel movements—we have been continuously surprised that people believe that "regular" could range from once a day to once every two weeks, depending on who we were talking with. Hippocrates knew of the importance of colon health and suggested that we need to evacuate the bowels after each meal. And what is a normal bowel movement? At least 30 to 45 cm of fecal matter should be excreted per bowel evacuation. If we worked towards this goal, most disease could be eliminated, along with our waste matter. People often tell us that they have one bowel movement weekly and their medical doctor has told them that this is normal for them.

It is not normal for anyone to have fewer than two to three good bowel movements daily.

IN CONCLUSION

The nervous system and the adrenal glands are the primary organs that initially respond to stressors. When they are unable to adapt, all other organ systems are affected.

The general weakening of our ability to maintain hormonal balance and the increase in chronic disease occurring today are the results of accumulated stresses borne by almost everyone in our society over many years: inadequate nutrition, exposure to environmental toxins, sedentary jobs and lifestyles, and familial, social, and spiritual meltdown.

We can change these disheartening trends by taking responsibility for our health on all levels. In so doing, we will become more motivated to extend our movement towards health to include our environment.

In the next chapter, we will begin to consider in more depth how to build optimal health, from the inside out.

THE INTERNAL STRESSORS: A SUMMARY

- **Mental and emotional stress.** We stress ourselves mentally and emotionally when we habitually entertain unwholesome thoughts that elicit anger, fear, worry, and anxiety.

- **Spiritual stress.** It is stressful to have a lack of trust in the Holy Spirit/God/the Universal Wisdom, and not take time for prayer and contemplation (for details, see Chapter 10).

- **Inadequate sleep.** Not getting enough sleep disrupts our physical, emotional, mental, and spiritual health.

- **Poor eating habits.** Eating in a rush or when angry or upset interferes with digestion.

- **Dysbiosis.** The overgrowth of harmful organisms in the intestinal tract compromises immunity, affects hormone levels, stresses the liver, and interferes with digestion and nutrient absorption.

- **Colon toxicity.** Antibiotics, hormonal drugs, poor food choices, stressful lifestyle, and poor evacuation can lead to a build-up of toxic substances in the colon.

CLEANSING, DETOXIFICATION, AND STRENGTHENING

"The human body is the universe in miniature. That which cannot be found in the body is not to be found in the universe. Hence the philosopher's formula, that the universe within reflects the universe without. It follows, therefore, that if our knowledge of our own body could be perfect, we would know the universe."—Mahatma Gandhi

In the past 150 years there has been incredible progress in medicine, science, and industry. However, as we have discussed, these developments have come with a tremendously high price; the side effects of our chemical-dependent technology are the contamination of our atmosphere and water and the pollution and depletion of our soil and foods. Although the human body has an incredible ability to adapt, these contaminants are accumulating faster than our bodies are able to handle them. In many people, the toxic burden is resulting in altered metabolism, enzyme dysfunction, nutritional deficiencies, and hormonal imbalances.

WHY IS DETOXIFICATION IMPORTANT?

We know that drugs, preservatives, pesticides, and other pollutants can remain stored in the body long after the initial exposure. For example, the residues of DDT (DDE and DDD) have a half-life of between 20 and 50 years in the fat tissues of humans. Indeed, the predominant storage site for most chemicals is in fatty tissues. From these tissues, toxins re-enter the bloodstream during illness, exercise, and periods of fasting, emotional stress, or excessive heat. When these chemicals enter the bloodstream, every organ in the body is continually exposed at low levels. Remember, it is not a single agent that causes serious problems—it is the total load. Remember, too, that while the effects of many individual chemicals have been studied, little is known about how the many chemicals potentially in circulation in our bodies interact with one another to affect us.

The Kellogg Report — a 1989 comprehensive research report that sheds new light on the effects of diet, environment, and lifestyle on the diseases so prevalent in today's world—states that 1 000 new compounds are introduced each year. The number of foreign chemicals in our surroundings (drugs, pesticides, food additives, environmental and industrial pollutants) now totals roughly 100 000. The magnitude of the situation becomes more visible when we consider the following statistics, from the 1989 Toxic Release Inventory Report, published by the Office of Toxic Substances of the U.S. Environmental Protection Agency:

- Four hundred chemicals have been found in human tissue: 48 in fat tissue; 40 in breast milk; 73 in the liver; 250 in the blood.
- In the United States in 1989, more than 550 million pounds of industrial chemicals were dumped into public sewage.
- More than 1 billion pounds of chemicals were released into groundwater.
- More than 180 million pounds of chemicals were discharged into surface water.
- Almost 2.5 billion pounds of toxic emissions were pumped into the atmosphere.

"The reasonable man adapts himself to the world; the unreasonable one persists in trying to adapt the world to himself. Therefore all progress depends on the unreasonable man."—George Bernard Shaw

Note that the above statistics refer to only one country's—the United States'—emissions! Water and air do not stop their movements at political boundaries. These toxic chemicals find their way into our bodies through the air we breathe, the food we eat, and the water we drink. Although the body has systems in place to eliminate toxins, it cannot always handle the overload that is present in today's environment. The result is a variety of diseases.

How do environmental toxins do their damage? The major mechanism is via their contribution to producing free radicals. Free radicals are highly reactive molecules generated by body cells through normal metabolism and exposure to radiation, heated oils, environmental pollutants, and microbes. Because of their atomic structure, these molecules compulsively react with other molecules in cells and cell membranes, thereby damaging these structures. Many free radicals are highly toxic, mutagenic, and carcinogenic. The major sources and generators of free radicals include:

- fried foods and heated oils
- nitrates and nitrites in meats
- toxic chemicals in the air
- cigarette smoke, or smoke from forest fires
- exposure to medical or electromagnetic radiation (e.g., computer terminals)
- strenuous exercise
- chlorinated water
- a high-fat diet
- prolonged physical and/or emotional stress

One of the best ways to maintain our health is through exercise, which supplies oxygen to our cells. Exercise can, however, also increase free radical levels as a consequence of aerobic respiration in the cells. Oxygen in the body is therefore a paradox: we can't live without it, but its presence generates free radicals. Don't let this lead you to believe that the extra oxygen used during sensible exercise is bad for you: *hypoxia, or lack of oxygen, in the tissues is the fundamental cause of all degenerative diseases.*

Antioxidants are free radical "scavengers." These substances readily react with free radical molecules, sparing other molecules from being mutated or damaged. When the body is deficient in antioxidants, the risk of disease due to chemical exposure increases. Antioxidant supplements for optimal health in a polluted world will be discussed in detail later in this chapter.

Many studies document illness in humans resulting from chemical exposure. Cancers of virtually every organ system, liver disease, immune system damage, pulmonary damage, nervous system disease, psychological changes, kidney damage, and hormonal, reproductive, and fertility impairment have all been observed. Before the outbreak of serious disease, the body will often warn of a toxic overload with a number of possible symptoms: allergies, back pain, bowel problems, headaches, insomnia, joint pain, mood changes, respiratory problems, sinus congestion, or skin eruptions, psoriasis and acne. These conditions indicate a need for cleansing.

In response to such symptoms, many naturopathic doctors and related health care practitioners recommend a variety of "detoxification" programs. These programs aim to improve bowel and liver health so that toxins circulating in the bloodstream because of poor functioning of these two organs can be eliminated from the body. These programs also move toxins out of their storage sites in the fatty tissue, support the liver's ability to break them down, and support the functioning of the other major organs of elimination: the skin, the lungs, the kidneys, and the gastrointestinal tract. In this chapter we will describe a step-by-step program for detoxifying the body and strengthening the organs of elimination.

INTESTINAL CLEANSING

Good intestinal function is extremely important to our ability to detoxify our body. As discussed in the last chapter, diets high in refined foods and excess sugar, medications, exposure to toxins, and high stress make the gastrointestinal tract susceptible to microbial imbalances that undermine health.

The following treatment for *Candida*/intestinal problems is very effective and easier to follow than some of the more restrictive programs.

Candida/Intestine Treatment Recommendations

There are four components to the treatment that are used for cleansing the bowel and decreasing the toxic overload:

a. Making dietary changes to starve out *Candida* and harmful bacteria.
b. Cleansing the bowel of harmful microflora and accumulated toxins.
c. Restoring beneficial microflora.
d. Building the immune system.

FOLLOWING THE MODERATE *CANDIDA*/INTESTINE DIET

The objective of the dysbiosis diet is to reduce the intake of foods that encourage the growth of harmful yeast and bacteria. This diet needs to be carefully followed during the entire 10-week period that the "colonic cocktail," which cleanses the bowel of harmful microflora, is in use.

Foods to Avoid

- Sugars of all types, and foods that contain refined or simple sugars
- Dried fruits (e.g., raisins, prunes, dates)
- Fruit juices, both fresh and frozen
- Yeasted breads, pastries, and other baked goods (Alternatives to yeasted baked goods include corn tortillas and burritos, unyeasted crackers or rice cakes, sprouted breads, and yeast-free and sugar-free breads)
- Alcoholic beverages and malt products
- Processed and smoked meats
- Peanuts, cashews—these commonly contain the mold aflatoxin, which can aggravate intestinal problems.
- Cow's milk (can be used in moderation on cereal or in coffee) and ice cream (alternatives include soy milk and goat's milk)
- Antibiotics

Foods That Can Be Eaten Freely

- Fresh, hormone-free meats, poultry, and fish
- Eggs
- Raw nuts (except peanuts and cashews; see above) and seeds
- Cold-pressed, unrefined flaxseed and olive oil
- Low-carbohydrate vegetables such as all green leafy vegetables (chard, kale, celery, lettuce, spinach), broccoli, cabbage, and Brussels sprouts
- Organic butter and yogurt (in the absence of allergies to dairy products)

Foods That Can Be Eaten Cautiously

- Organic fruits—eat no more than three per day.
- Cereals and other whole grain products. These should always be yeast-free and sugar-free.

- High-carbohydrate vegetables (e.g., squash, potatoes, carrots, beets)
- Cheese may be eaten in small amounts, two to three times per week

Intake of foods in the "eat with caution" category needs to be monitored day by day. For example, if you have a high-carbohydrate vegetable for lunch (such as sweet potatoes), then have only a small serving of grain or pasta for dinner. Various products decrease the load of toxic microbes.

- Caprylic acid is a natural compound with antifungal properties that is effective in treating intestinal imbalances.
- Chlorophyll, the substance that makes plant cells look green, binds with toxic chemicals and heavy metals and has antibacterial and antiviral properties.
- Grapefruit seed extracts, taheebo tea, and garlic all kill off unfriendly microbes.
- Psyllium seed is a bulking agent that helps to eliminate toxins by encouraging regular bowel movements and by binding with stored waste products that normally are not eliminated.

The Colonic Cocktail

This cleansing mixture, which combines several of the antimicrobial and antitoxic substances listed above, is jokingly referred to by Karen's patients as "sludge." Use it in combination with the candida/intestine diet.

- Mix 2 teaspoons of psyllium with water and a little grapefruit juice, and stir to a drinkable consistency. Then add 1 tablespoon of caprylic acid.
- Drink this mixture once or twice daily, morning or evening, followed by 250 mL of water. Add liquid chlorophyll to the water if you wish.
- Take this mixture for at least six weeks, then take it twice weekly for another four weeks.

Efficient bowel elimination is important for microbial balance. It can be encouraged with the herbs buckthorn (*Rhamnus cathartica, Rhamnus frangula*) and cascara sagrada (*Rhamnus purshiana*). These herbs increase peristalsis, or the muscular contractions, of the bowel, thereby assisting with the removal of toxins.

RESTORING BENEFICIAL MICROFLORA

The two most important friendly bacteria in our bodies are *Lactobacillus acidophilus* and *Bifidobacterium bifidum*. *Lactobacilli* and *Bifidobacteria* in the intestines inhibit the growth of unfriendly organisms by producing antimicrobial factors. *Lactobacillus* also inhibits a bacterial enzyme that reduces estrogen reabsorption and may therefore reduce the risk of estrogen-dependent diseases.

Lactobacillus and *Bifidobacteria* are found in the fermented foods that most cultures use, such as yogurt, miso, tempeh, keifer, sauerkraut, and fermented juices. These foods, as well as supplements (called probiotics) containing the beneficial bacteria, benefit human health. North Americans do not regularly use fermented foods, with the exception of yogurt. Unfortunately, the friendly bacteria in yogurt usually include little, if any, *Lactobacilli*. Using a high-quality *Lactobacillus acidophilus* and *Bifidobacterium bifidum* supplement will therefore provide greater colonization of the friendly bacteria than simply eating yogurt. Look for products that include fructo-oligosaccharides (FOS), such as asparagus, garlic, onions, and artichokes. FOS feeds the friendly bacteria, particularly *Bifidobacteria*, once they are in the gastrointestinal tract, and is not absorbed from the intestines.

Lactobacillus casei is another probiotic agent that can reduce diarrhea and enhance immune function.

How much of a particular probiotic supplement you take will depend on how many live organisms are present per capsule or teaspoon. Most people need to take enough of a supplement to supply 5 to 10 billion live *Lactobacillus acidophilus* and *Bifidobacterium bifidum* cells daily. We recommend daily use of probiotics while following the dysbiosis diet and cleansing protocols, and regular use thereafter. If you eat foods that are high in friendly bacteria (see above), then you do not need to take a daily supplement, though we suggest using one at least two days a week to maintain adequate levels of the friendly microbes.

OPTIMIZE YOUR IMMUNE SYSTEM

What causes one person to catch a cold or flu and another to avoid it? Why do serious outbreaks of infectious disease leave some individuals untouched? What allows someone to be incapacitated by allergies? Why does one person with HIV never contract full-blown AIDS and another succumb and die? The answers lie within the most powerful curing machine hardwired into our body—the immune system.

The body's ability to protect itself from the onslaught of offending viruses, bacteria, fungi and cancer can be enhanced or weakened by a number of factors. We have each experienced a cold that sets in after an extraordinarily stressful event: too many days of celebration and/or unrelenting stress. More serious events such as the death of a loved one, a divorce or the loss of a job can weaken our immune system and make us susceptible to heart attack, a debilitating autoimmune disorder such as rheumatoid arthritis or even cancer. Years of a poor diet, inadequate nutrients, continual stress, negative emotions, a lack of exercise and environmental poisons have all contribute to the inability of our immune system to properly defend us. Fortunately, the body is wonderfully regenerative and our internal army of immune cells can be enhanced in a matter of weeks by simply improving our nutrition, reducing stress, adding immune-specific nutrients, exercising and seeking emotional well-being.

Defenders of our Immune System

Our immune army is a highly specialized front-line defense that identifies, remembers, attacks and destroys disease-causing invaders and abnormal or infected cells. When this internal army is functioning optimally few viruses, cancer cells, bacteria, fungi or parasites are allowed to set up house and wreak havoc. The immune system is so determined to annihilate invaders that it can often go awry and begin to damage the body itself, as happens in autoimmune diseases including lupus, rheumatoid arthritis or multiple sclerosis.

Our immune system is made up of cells, each with a specific duty. Natural killer cells (NK) are often the first cell a virus or bacteria encounters and if the NK cell is effective these invaders will never be able to infect cells. NK cells are also our cancer-fighting cells. Macrophages are like pac-man cells digesting and destroying offending agents. T-cells are the generals of our immune arsenal they include helper T-cells and cytotoxic T-cells. Cytotoxic T-cells fight viruses and bacteria that managed to get past the NK cell and are now inside cells. Helper T-cells are especially important because these cells control the secretion of important immune factors called cytokines that modulate or keep the immune system in balance and functioning at peak performance.

There are two types of helper T-cells, T-helper-1 and T-helper-2 cells. When these two types of helper T-cells are in balance we are healthy. When we are sick with cancer, infectious diseases such as herpes, hepatitis C, colds and flu, pneumonia or HIV our T-helper-1 cells are suppressed and are not able to release enough of the 'good guy' immune factors. When we have allergies, fibromyalgia, osteoarthritis, autoimmune diseases such as Type-1 diabetes or Crohn's or Celiac's disease our T-helper-2 cells are overactive and secreting too many of the inflammatory immune factors. The key to maintaining health is to keep these two types of helper T-cells in balance. The six steps to optimizing immune function focus on enhancing T-helper-1 cells and controlling the T-helper-2 cells.

Food that Harms and Food that Heals

Sugar is one food that should come with a warning label stronger than that found on cigarette packages. Sugar causes our Natural Killer cells to become inactive. As little as one teaspoon of sugar shuts off NK cells for up to six hours leaving us vulnerable to cancer invasion and growth and infectious disease. While sugar is toxic to the immune system fruits and vegetables, nuts and seeds optimize immunity. Organic foods should be chosen over pesticide-laden foods, fresh wild fish and lean free-range chicken and turkey over red meat and purified water should make up the bulk of our diet.

Nutrients to Enhance Immune Function

Vitamin A, C, E and B complex, reduced L-glutathione, selenium, zinc, magnesium, coenzyme Q10 and sterols and sterolins have important immune enhancing properties.

Vitamin A is a clear immune vitamin. If you are deficient in this vitamin you will be prone to infections, especially colds and flu. Wounds and stomach ulcers will not heal quickly. Important for immune cells vitamin A helps mucous membranes maintain their structure and keep invaders out. It also helps with cell division and enhances T-cell counts. Vitamin A has also been shown to halt hair loss in those undergoing chemotherapy. Recommended dosage: at least 1,500 IU should be taken daily.

Vitamin C increases IgA which is integral to stopping invaders from entering our digestive tract. Vitamin C also has antiviral, antibacterial and anticancer properties. Recommended dosage: 1,000 mg per day.

Vitamin E along with vitamin C and selenium increase our resistance to infection and protects us against the damaging effects of stress. It also enhances our T-cell function and the release of the good guy immune factors interleukin 2 and gamma interferon. Vitamin E has been found to improve B cell activity and antibody production. Recommended dosage: 100 IU - 400 IU per day gets your immune system going.

Vitamin B6 with a B complex is essential for maintaining optimal hormone levels and a healthy immune and nervous system. B6 is required for good thymus gland and T-cell activity and it enhances Natural Killer cell function. Without vitamin B6 the immune system is like an army without weapons waiting for attackers to descend. B6 should always be taken with a complex of B vitamins. Recommended dosage: 25 -50 mg of each B vitamin.

Magnesium is required for over 300 enzymatic reactions in the body and that alone makes it important to the immune system. Magnesium keeps pro-inflammatory immune factors in check effectively reducing pain and swelling for those with fibromyalgia and osteoarthritis. Recommended dosage: a minimum of 100 mg per day is needed.

Zinc truly is the most important immune mineral. Zinc increases the size of the thymus gland, the conductor of the immune orchestra. Without a healthy thymus the immune system is powerless. Zinc has been studied for its antibacterial and antiviral properties.. Zinc is one of those nutrients where more is not better. Too much zinc can cause immune suppression so don't take doses higher than 300 mg per day. Recommended dosage: 15mg per day.

Selenium deficiency may be the cause of cancer. It was found that women who live in areas where the soil selenium levels were poor had higher rates of cancer per capita. As well in Africa the worst rates of HIV are in areas where soil selenium levels are very low. Selenium is needed to fight off bacteria and viruses and ensure our T-cells and NK cells work hard. Recommended dosage: 100 - 200 mcg per day.

Coenzyme Q10 has been found to halt tumors, have antibacterial and antiviral properties. By the time we are 50 years of age our coenzyme Q10 levels are half the levels of our twenties. Thirty milligrams per day is a maintenance dose, but over 320 mg have been used to treat breast cancer with excellent tumor inhibiting action. Recommended dosage: 30 mg daily.

Reduced L-Glutathione is my favorite nutrient. No other antioxidant is as important to overall health as glutathione. It is the regenerator of immune cells and the most valuable detoxifying agent. Low levels are associated with early death and viral infections. Optimal levels control insulin, halts inflammatory processes, detoxifies alcohol, eliminates carcinogens, keeps cholesterol from oxidizing. Recommended dosage: 45 mg per day.

Or simply take Multimune, a combination of the ten nutrients mentioned above.

• Moducare, sterols and sterolins, plant nutrients, have been researched extensively worldwide for their anticancer, antiviral and antibacterial properties. Professor Patrick Bouic, head of immunology at the University of Stellenbosch, Cape Town has found that sterols and sterolins balance the action of the T-helper-1 and T-helper-2 cells. Within 4-6 weeks immune function is normalized and symptoms of disease disappear. Allergic reactions cease, autoimmune disease goes into remission, cancerous tumors shrink and general well-being is observed. Double-blind, placebo controlled trials have shown that sterols and sterolins increase our DHEA, control the negative immune factors Interleukin-6 and Tumor Necrosis Factor both implicated in autoimmune disease and increase the good guy immune factors gamma interferon and Interleukin-2. The adrenals will also make DHEA from plant sterols and sterols ensuring we always have adequate DHEA hormone levels. Prof. Bouic has performed human trials using sterols and sterolins on the following diseases HIV, rheumatoid arthritis, HPV induced cervical cancer, tuberculosis, stress induced immune suppression, prostate, and rhinitis with excellent results. For adrenal support remedies, see page 76.

> *Recommended dosage:* For the first week take 2 capsules, 3 times daily then 1 capsule, 3 times daily thereafter. Do not take with meals.

• **Echinacea (*Echinacea augustifolia, Echinacea purpurea*)** has historically been used to boost the immune system and purify the blood. It is antiviral and antibacterial and is an excellent remedy for colds, flus, *Candida* overgrowth and intestinal problems, upper respiratory tract infections, and other common infections. We recommend Echinamide Echinacea. Echinacea should be taken at the onset of a cold or flu to shorten the duration of the infection. Echinacea is not recommended for those with autoimmune disorders, asthma, fibromyalgia or HIV.

> — *Recommended dosage:* 1 to 2 mL fluid extract (1:1) three times daily; 200 to 500 mg solid extract (4:1) three times daily; 2 to 4 mL root tincture three times daily; 325 to 650 mg dried root three times daily.

Immune-supportive herbs should not be taken continuously. When rebuilding a weak immune system, take an immune-supportive herb for a week, then take a week off. Do this for three months; thereafter use the herb as needed for acute conditions.

Immune Protection Comes from Stress Reduction

Poor nutrition combined with excess stress causes most disease. When we are exposed to stress, be it emotional, physical, environmental or nutritional stress our body sends out the stress hormone cortisol. This hormone then causes two things to happen our DHEA levels to drop and our Interleukin-6 levels to rise. DHEA is the most important immune hormone and it is also called the anti-aging hormone. DHEA is negatively affected by cortisol. Interleukin-6, is an inflammatory immune factor that causes inflammation, pain, swelling and it is known to exacerbate autoimmune and fibromyalgia symptoms. IL-6 also removes calcium from bone into blood causing osteoporosis and osteoarthritis.

Stress reduction is extremely important. Take the stress and your immune system test and find out where you are on the stress scale. If you scored 12 or over, you are putting yourself at risk for immune system overload. Immediately adopt the recommendations above and focus on stress reduction. Between 6-12, you are still coping with the stressors in your life but you need to slow down, say no once in a while and register for a yoga class. Between 1-5, you are in the peak range for stress management and if you keep this pace you will reach the finish line healthy.

Spiritual Well-being Needed

All body systems are intricately connected to the immune system. Research performed at the University of Rochester, New York has shown that our nervous system is in direct communication with our immune system and therefor thoughts and emotions effect our immunity. Happiness and feelings of self-worth are paramount to good immune health. The power of prayer and spiritual well-being have been proven to enhance T-cells making our internal army more effective.

Exercise: Too Much Can Be Bad

Low to moderate exercise is beneficial to health and enhances immunity. Walking is the most effective immune-maximizing activity providing movement for the body while clearing the mind. Boost the intensity and duration of an exercise routine however, and too much of a good thing can be bad. The moral is 'everything in moderation.' If you are exercising more than 4 times a week you may be putting your immune system into suppression. Exercise

STRESS TEST TO DETERMINE IMMUNE STATUS

Unusual tiredness and/or dizziness..3
Unexplained irregular heartbeat and/or shortness of breath...........3
Smoke, drink alcohol or caffeine or take prescription drugs............3
Sugar or aspartame consumption...3
Headaches and/or muscle tension or joint pain...............................3
Lack of sexual desire..3
Nausea or irritable bowel/digestive problems..................................3
Overexercising (more than 4/week) or no exercise at all.................3
You don't take vitamin or mineral supplements...............................2
Poor nutrition...2
Feelings of anxiety or depression...2
Feelings of guilt..2
Feelings that you can't cope or you feel trapped............................2
Being self-critical or lacking confidence...2
Feelings of inadequacy..2
Fear of getting a disease such as cancer...2
You use antibacterial soaps...1
Not wanting to socialize with friends..1
Suppressed anger..1
Inability to relax...1
Fidgeting or restlessness..1
Excessive appetite/loss of appetite...1
Loneliness..1
Insomnia or difficulty falling asleep...1

Total Score _____

How did you score?

If you scored 12 or over, you are putting yourself at risk for immune system overload.

Between 6 and 12 you are still coping with the stress in your life, but you need to slow down.

Between 1 and 5 you are in the peak range for stress management and if you keep this pace you will reach the finish line healthy.

moderately 3 times a week for no longer than one hour and ensure you add the nutritional supplements recommended above to protect your immune system. Walk, walk, walk!

The body has remarkable regenerative abilities we only have to give it the tools to repair itself. Stress reduction, nutrients and good nutrition and regular exercise will help your immune system do its job of fighting off bacteria, viruses, parasites and more.

Antioxidant Supplementation

If you feel you need more antioxidant support than can be supplied by your diet, a basic antioxidant supplementation program includes the following vitamins and minerals. I have placed a (w) beside those antioxidants that are water soluble and an (l) beside those that are fat (lipid) soluble.

- Beta carotene, 25 000 to 50 000 IU daily (w)
- Selenium, 200 to 400 mcg daily (w)
- Vitamin A, 10 000 to 50 000 IU daily (l)
- Vitamin C, 1 000 to 3 000 mg daily (w)
- Vitamin E, 400 to 1 200 IU daily, or vitamin E with tocotrienols, 400 to 1 200 IU daily (l)
- Zinc, 30 to 60 mg daily (w)

- Keep life simple: take a good multivitamin like FemmEssentials

You can add to this basic program with the following antioxidant supplements. All act to protect water-based substances; lipoic acid has the unique ability to protect lipid-based substances as well. Extra nutritional support is very useful for enhancing the immune system. One of the most important influences weakening the immune system and ultimately causing disease is free radical damage, discussed above. Antioxidants neutralize free radicals and strengthen immunity. They are found abundantly in many common foods.

Green tea is rich in antioxidants and may prevent cancer of the stomach, esophagus, and lungs as well as offering protection against cardiovascular problems, according to recent studies. Green tea does contain caffeine, so sensitive sleepers need to drink it in the morning. It is an excellent alternative for coffee drinkers, in that it provides a bit of a boost as well as offering health benefits.

- **Amino acids**. Methionine and cysteine, sulphur-containing amino acids, are needed to keep an adequate concentration of glutathione within the cells. Glutathione, in the form of glutathione peroxidase, a free radical scavenging enzyme, plays a critical role in the defence against harmful compounds. Foods that contain high levels include beans, fish, liver, eggs, brewer's yeast, protein powders and nuts.

- **Bioflavonoids,** in concentrated supplemental form, exert antiallergic, anti-inflammatory, antiviral, anticarcinogenic, and cardio-protective effects. Flavonoids are unique in the antioxidant activity in that they are active against a very wide range of free radicals.

  — *Recommended dosage:* 250 to 400 mg mixed bioflavonoids (most commonly including quercetin, rutin, and hesperidin) twice daily.

- **Lipoic acid** is one of the most versatile and powerful bioflavonoid antioxidants. It seems to have the ability to protect both water- and lipid-based substances from free radical damage. Lipoic acid enhances the actions of vitamins C and E and the coenzyme glutathione (an antioxidant made by the body); it is also useful in treating diabetes for its ability to normalize blood sugar and prevent cataracts.

  — *Recommended dosage:* 200 to 400 mg daily.

- **Lycopene** is one of more than 600 known naturally occurring carotenoids. Lycopene is extremely high in tomatoes; it is what gives them their red colour. Current research indicates that lycopene has anti-cancer effects.

  — *Recommended dosage:* 10 mg twice daily.

- **Proanthocyanidins (PCOs)** are the most popular bioflavonoids and very powerful antioxidants—50 times more powerful than vitamin E and 20 times more powerful than vitamin C in their ability to offset oxidative damage. They are found in foods such as blueberries, grapes, fruits, and some nuts and vegetables. The supplemental forms (which are highly concentrated) come from Maritime pine tree bark or grape seed extracts. An excellent product that contains grape seed extract is grapes+, available in most health food stores. Studies indicate that coronary heart disease mortality rates decrease when high levels of flavonoids are taken.

  — *Recommended dosage:* 100 to 200 mg daily.

ONGOING BOWEL MAINTENANCE

We recommend that a complete gastrointestinal balancing—using the *Candida*/intestine diet, the 10-week colonic cocktail program, and daily doses of probiotics and immune strengthening herbs as described above during the 10-week period—be done once or twice yearly. The rest of the year, use a good probiotic and psyllium or other supplemental fibre on a regular basis. Such a program is especially valuable for any woman who is experiencing hormonal imbalances related to menstruation, the perimenopause, or menopause.

Once you have completed the *Candida*/intestine program, you can go another step and embark on a 10-to-14-day detoxification and elimination program, described later in this chapter.

Now that your gastrointestinal tract is well on its way to optimal functioning, it is time to consider your liver. It is probably feeling better already, since, as we shall discover, the health of the bowel has an enormous influence on the health of the liver.

THE LIVER, THE GREAT DETOXIFIER

> "If we look at the liver as being a powerhouse we will realize we can only throw sand in it so long before the energy output decreases."—John Matsen, N.D.

Historically, naturopathic doctors have centred much of their approach to health and healing on cleansing and detoxifying the liver. The liver is a remarkable organ and is the central chemical laboratory in the body. It is a critical organ in three areas of physical functioning.

- The liver plays an important role in metabolism. Metabolism is the process whereby nutritive material is built up into living matter or broken down into simpler substances to be used in special functions of the body. Perhaps the most important metabolic function of the liver is the detoxification or inactivation and excretion of toxic chemicals, drugs, and hormones, both those made by the body and those that come from outside sources. The liver inactivates these substances and eventually they are excreted by the bowels, lungs, kidneys, or skin. The liver is also involved in fat, carbohydrate, and protein metabolism and vitamin and mineral storage.

- The liver is a major blood reservoir, filtering more than 1.4 L of blood per minute. It removes bacteria, toxins, and various other unwanted substances from blood circulation.

- Every day the liver manufactures and secretes approximately 1 L of bile. Bile is necessary for the absorption of fat-soluble material from the intestines, including many vitamins, and its secretion helps eliminate many toxic substances.

In Chinese medicine, bodily organs are viewed as being a focal point of a particular kind of energetic expression. The liver, then, is a focal point of liver (or wood) energy, which exists throughout the body and expresses itself in a number of functions. In Chinese medicine the liver energy system governs the peripheral and central nervous system and the eyes and tendons. It is responsible for muscle tone and peripheral motor activity. The liver is also seen to provide energy and vitality to the sexual organs.

The Chinese consider the liver the organ most strongly affected by our emotions. Conversely, the Chinese and many other cultures have long recognized that when the liver is stressed, anger, depression, and irritability are more likely to arise. When a person's liver is functioning harmoniously, there is never stress or tension; the person stays calm and relaxed.

Many factors determine whether the liver performs its critical functions well. Too much pressure on the liver from overeating, too much rich or poor-quality food, environmental stresses, overwork or emotional stress can cause liver overload, leading to a decreased ability to clear toxins and hormones and manufacture bile. An overloaded liver allows toxic and waste material to pass into the blood, and it accumulates in the body instead of being eliminated.

The Liver and the Excretion of Hormones

Let's now consider in more detail the pathway the liver uses to clear away estrogens and other hormones, as well as many other compounds.

This pathway is called the enterohepatic circulation and refers to the circulation of substances from the liver to the small intestines and bowel and back again. How well this pathway functions determines whether our estrogen and other hormone levels stay balanced. The pathway proceeds as follows:

- Substances, such as hormones, are altered or broken down in the liver and excreted into the bile.

- The liver secretes the bile into the small intestines. Much of this bile and its load of excreted substances will be eliminated in the feces.

- Some of the hormones excreted by the liver into the bile may be reabsorbed through the walls of the small and large intestines if there is microflora imbalance (the mechanism is discussed below), and will then return to the liver via a group of veins called the portal blood system. The portal blood system is also responsible for bringing nutrients from food in the digestive tract to the liver for processing.

Any disruption of the liver circulation contributes to increased levels of both hormones and chemicals in the body.

You may have heard the term "conjugated estrogen." The liver is responsible for conjugating (or coupling) estrogens and other steroid hormones, certain drugs and many chemical compounds. Successful conjugation of hormones requires that they be bound to another substance, usually glucuronic acid, sulphate, glycine, or glutathione, before secretion into the bile. The conjugated estrogen is then secreted into the bile. A decreased rate of estrogen excretion through this process, as well as of the other substances mentioned, may result from liver overload and bowel toxicity. The liver's ability to form conjugates may also be decreased if such nutrients as niacin, vitamin B6, magnesium, or methionine and cysteine, important sources of organic sulphates, are deficient.

Even mild liver dysfunction may lead to enough decrease in estrogen excretion rates that hormonal balance is disrupted.

Not only liver dysfunction prevents successful estrogen clearance. Bowel health is another key to this process. As noted above, after the liver forms estrogen conjugates, it excretes them through the bile into the small intestine. The conjugates must stay in their original form throughout the entire length of the intestinal tract in order to be eliminated in the feces. If elimination time is too long or if *Candida* is present, there will be an increase in gastrointestinal bacteria that produce an enzyme called beta-glucuronidase. This enzyme cleaves estrogen from its glucuronic acid carrier. Once separated from the glucuronic acid, the estrogen is once again biologically active and is reabsorbed into the bloodstream, and has to be processed by the liver all over again.

However, there are ways to control the estrogen reabsorption. One way is to dramatically cut back on your meat intake because eating meat raises the level of the enzyme beta-glucuronidase in the gut. The phytochemical indole-3-carbinol assists in the conjugation of estrogen, so eat at least two vegetables daily from the indole-rich family such as broccoli, cauliflower, cabbage, kale and collards. Calcium-D-glucarate prevents break-up of the estrogen conjugate. It can be taken in a supplemental form, such as EstroSense which also contain indole-3-carbinol and other liver-supporting herbs.

Now that we have a sense of how important the liver is, we need to look more closely at how to create healthy liver function.

"Sluggish" or "Congested" Liver

The following naturopathic principles recognize a condition we call "sluggish" or "congested" liver. A person with a congested liver has liver dysfunction, but the dysfunction is not yet at a level that is detectable through standard laboratory tests. However, the effects of suboptimal liver functioning on health, and in particular on hormonal health, are profound because of the liver's important role in so many metabolic processes. Possible causes of liver congestion include:

- Dietary stresses: saturated fats, refined sugars and grains, a preponderance of low-fibre foods, alcohol, tobacco
- External toxins from the environment: chemicals in food, water, and air
- Internally generated toxins, including bacterial toxins originating in the intestines
- Drugs: antibiotics, diuretics, synthetic hormones, steroids, and many others
- Obesity
- Type II diabetes
- Viral hepatitis, mononucleosis
- Hereditary disorders

"As about nine-tenths of the diseases flesh is heir to are caused by ignorant or willful abuse of the stomach and liver, every person should make it their business to study themselves, their habits and appetites; and if wrong, correct them as far as possible, for good health is far better than riches."—H.C. Wood, M.D., 1905

Although "congestion" is a functional condition as opposed to a pathological condition, it can create a variety of physical, emotional, and mental symptoms, ranging from headaches and indigestion to anger, depression, and mental rigidity. We have summarized the common signs and symptoms of liver congestion in the table below.

A Little Help for Our Friend the "Live-er"

The steps you need to take to detoxify a congested liver depend on how severe the problem is. Start with the simple dietary and lifestyle measures outlined below and see how they make you feel. If you feel your liver needs further support, begin using herbs that support liver functions (discussed below), and possibly lipotropic factors as well.

Food and Lifestyle Choices that Support the Liver

- Start your morning with fresh lemon juice in water; this helps flush and decongest the liver.

- Eat beets or drink beet and vegetable juice regularly. Beets are an excellent liver cleanser.

- Chlorophyll drinks and other green drinks such as greens+ can be used regularly to aid in liver cleansing.

- High-quality protein foods are necessary to restore and sustain the liver. Free-range eggs, fish, raw nuts and seeds, and whole grains are beneficial. Eating calves' liver or chicken livers is also beneficial, but make sure the animal was organically raised. Remember what the liver does—cleanses and detoxifies.

- Nutritional antioxidants such as vitamin E, zinc, and selenium (discussed earlier in this chapter) are essential for protecting the liver from free radical damage.

- Liver restoration also requires lots of fresh air, exercise, adequate rest, natural foods, and good water.

COMMON SIGNS AND SYMPTOMS OF LIVER CONGESTION

PHYSICAL

- Allergies; chemical/environmental sensitivities
- Chronic indigestion or distended abdomen
- Constipation
- Difficulty rising in the morning
- Eye problems (red, itchy, watery, spots in vision)
- Fatigue
- Headaches and migraines
- Hot feet at night
- Insomnia or inability to sleep deeply
- Menopausal problems, PMS
- Muscular pain and tendon problems
- Rigid, inflexible body
- Tension in neck and back

EMOTIONAL

- Aggression
- Anger
- Depression
- Irritability
- Mental rigidity
- Moodiness
- Negativity
- Resentment

LIVER SUPPORT REMEDIES

Civilizations throughout history have been aware of the healing action that specific herbs have on the liver. Known as cholagogues (the Greek word "khole" means bile), these plants trigger the liver's production of bile. As bile production is increased, the liver is gently cleansed. As toxins are cleared, the liver cells can more easily access nutrients and the liver becomes toned.

During a cleansing or detoxification program, such as the *Candida*/intestinal program, we suggest that a liver-supportive herb such as dandelion or burdock be taken two to three times daily for the length of the program. Formulas such as live-tone and EstroSense are good remedies to support and cleanse the liver. EstroSense is specifically formulated to balance estrogen levels. To keep the liver healthy in our toxic and stressful world, we suggest that a liver-supportive herb be taken initially for a period of six weeks then decrease it to ten days every month. The most effective commonly used liver-supportive remedies are discussed below:

• **Burdock root (*Arctium lappa*)** has traditionally been used as a blood cleanser to support the liver and hormonal health, making it very effective in the treatment of eczema and other skin conditions. Studies show that it is also effective as an immune system enhancer, in the stabilization of blood sugar, and as an antibiotic, antifungal, and antitumour agent

   — *Recommended dosage:* 500 to 750 mg dried powdered root per day; 2 to 4 mL tincture per day.

• **Dandelion root (*Taraxacum officinale*)** is considered the ideal liver remedy because it is completely non-toxic and gently restores liver function. It is rich in vitamins, minerals, and protein, and is higher in beta carotene and other carotenoids than carrots—dandelion has 14 000 IU of beta carotene per 100 g compared with 11 000 IU for carrots. Dandelion enhances the flow of bile, improving such conditions as liver congestion, hepatitis, gallstones, and jaundice. Dandelion also supports the kidneys during cleansing and detoxification of the liver and bowels. Dandelion can be taken by itself or in combination with other liver support herbs.

   — *Recommended dosage:* 125 mg solid extract (4:1) two to three times daily; 30 to 50 mL root tincture two to three times daily; 2 to 4 g powdered dried root two to three times daily.

• **Globe artichoke (*Cynara scolymus*)** has a long history of use in the treatment of many liver conditions and has demonstrated significant liver protecting and regenerating effects.

   — *Recommended dosage:* 500 mg powdered herb three times daily.

• **Milk thistle (*Silybum marianum*)** contains some of the most potent liver-protective substances known, including silymarin, which is a mixture of flavonoids, with silybin being the most active. Silymarin inhibits the action of free radicals that damage liver cells. It also stimulates protein synthesis, which results in the production of new liver cells to replace the damaged ones.

   — *Recommended dosage:* Take enough milk thistle in tincture or dried form to obtain between 70 and 210 mg silymarin three times daily.

The dosage for solid extracts of milk thistle standardized to contain 70 percent silymarin is 100 to 300 mg three times daily.

• **Tumeric (*Curcuma Longa*)** has been used traditionally as a seasoning in the cuisine of many cultures while in more recent time, researchers are finding that it has some very important healing benefits. Tumeric lowers the activity of cancer-causing agents (carcinogens) such as xenoestrogens, while increasing their detoxification from the body. It is a potent antioxidant and a powerful liver detoxifier as well as offering anti-inflammatory action.

— *Recommended dosage:* 100 mg daily.

• **Indole-3-carbinol (I3C)** is a phytochemical that improves detoxification of excess estrogen or xenoestrogens, as well as other toxic substances, from the body. I3C also inhibits the growth of prostate cancer, and reduces tumor development of the cervix and endometrium. Please note that for women with breast cancer who are taking tamoxifin, I3C is complementary and works with tamoxifin to inhibit the growth of estrogen-dominant cancers.

— *Recommended dosage:* 300 mg daily

• **Calcium-D-glucarate** is found in fruits and vegetables such as apples, grapefruit, oranges, broccoli and Brussels sprouts. It is a powerful antioxidant that increases the activity of other antioxidants such as vitamin C and carotenoids. Calcium-D-glucarate helps to rid the body of toxic substances through the conjugation system in the liver (see page 64) and prevents the estrogen conjugates from breaking up as they travel through the intestines enroute out of the body. Human studies are beginning to determine that it lowers the risk of breast cancer, bladder cancer, colon cancer, prostate cancer, lung cancer and liver cancer.

— *Recommended dosage:* 200-300 mg daily.

An excellent formula to prevent estrogen-dominant conditions is EstroSense or for general liver support, liv-tone.

ADRENAL STRESS SYMPTOMS

____ Symptoms present since stressful event (e.g., divorce)
____ Blurred vision
____ History of asthma/bronchitis
____ Headaches
____ Environmental sensitivities
____ Hypoglycemia
____ Food allergies
____ Poor concentration
____ Low energy, excessive fatigue
____ Post-exertional fatigue
____ Dizziness upon rising
____ Arthritis, bursitis
____ Irritability
____ Increase/loss of skin pigment
____ Nervousness/anxiety
____ Aching muscles
____ Shortness of breath
____ Tired feet
____ Cold extremities
____ Low back pain
____ Insomnia
____ Knee problems
____ Depression
____ Ulcers
____ Excessive urination
____ Excessive perspiration
____ Muscle twitches
____ Heart palpitations
____ Edema of extremities
____ Eyes light-sensitive
____ Crave salt
____ Crave sugar/junk food
____ Crave coffee
____ Alcohol intolerance
____ Recurrent infections
____ Digestive problems

THE ADRENAL GLANDS

The adrenal glands are among the most important organs in the body and yet receive little attention in allopathic medicine unless something goes extremely wrong, such as Addison's disease. Naturopaths, however, consider it very important to help their patients establish good adrenal health by accessing the earlier signs of low adrenal function. (For more information see the Adrenal Stress Symptom list.) These small glands release sex hormones and stress response hormones that guide our whole body's reaction to a stressor. They are thus the organs responsible for the "front-line" work of adaptation to stress. The accumulated effects of internal and external stressors have a profound impact on the adrenal glands, an impact that then ripples out into the area of hormonal health.

"Adaptability is probably the most distinctive characteristic of life."—Hans Selye, M.D.

The two adrenal glands sit on top of each kidney and contains two major components: the cortex and the medulla. In response to triggers from the brain, the medulla secretes hormones called catecholamines (epinephrine and norepinephrine), chemicals that stimulate an area of the brain called the hypothalamus and so permit the body to respond to stress by increasing blood sugar levels, the breathing rate, cardiac output, blood flow to the muscles, lungs, and brain, and cellular metabolism—the famous "fight-or-flight" response. The cortex is responsible for the production of a wide range of hormones called glucocorticoids (i.e. cortisol) and mineralocorticoids (i.e. aldosterone and testosterone). These hormones are essential to regulating metabolic, excretory, reproductive, mineral balancing, and immune defence functions.

The secretion of corticosteroids by the cortex in response to stress is one of the most important functions of the adrenals, as these hormones help us adapt over the longer term to the stresses of life. Various corticosteroids stimulate the conversion of protein to energy, so that energy levels remain high even after the glucose used in the fight-or-flight reaction has been used up. Others of these hormones help maintain elevated blood pressure and create changes needed for dealing with such stresses as emotional shocks, infection, high work load, weather changes, environmental chemicals, physical or emotional trauma, and the like.

CORTISOL, THE HALLMARK OF STRESS

The hormone cortisol is secreted by the adrenal glands in response to stress, whether physical, psychological, chemical or environmental and cortisol is gaining attention as the hallmark of stress. However, cortisol is more than a simple marker of stress levels; it is necessary for the functioning of almost every function of the body. Excess or deficiencies of this crucial hormone can cause a variety of physical symptoms, which if not treated, will lead to more serious chronic disease states and even death. Some of the important functions of cortisol include: the regulation of hormones, glucose metabolism, immune system, hormones and cardiovascular functions; glucose metabolism; as well as regulating the body's use of proteins, carbohydrates, and fats. Our ability to adapt to stress depends upon optimal function of the adrenal glands and regulation of cortisol secretion.

If a person has chronic stress, cortisol levels will remain elevated and research now correlates chronically elevated cortisol levels with blood sugar problems, fat accumulation, compromised immune function, infertility, exhaustion, chronic fatigue, bone loss, high triglycerides levels and heart disease. Memory loss has also been associated with high cortisol levels. As you can see, continual stress can indeed have a negative impact on many areas of your health. The extreme end of hypersecretion of cortisol results in a Cushing's syndrome.

An additional problem of long-term elevations of cortisol is that the adrenal glands may wear out and no longer be able to produce even normal levels of cortisol. This is called "adrenal exhaustion" resulting in conditions such as chronic fatigue syndrome or in extreme cases, Addison's disease.

The adrenal cortices secrete both male and female sex hormones, the estrogens and androgens, and become the prime producers of estrogen and progesterone during the transitional years, when the ovaries "go on vacation." In today's world, most women (and people in general) have some degree of adrenal compromise. Women are generally working a full time job and raising children and juggling hundreds of other of demands of daily life. Poor adrenal health directly affects a woman's ability to smoothly make the transitions inherent in female life.

Cortisol has a natural rhythm. Your body produces more cortisol in the morning than in the evening, giving you the energy you need to begin your day. The cortisol levels should drop by 90% in the evening as you leave the stresses of the day behind and you start to unwind and relax. A recent study found that women who work outside the home and have family responsibilities tend to have elevated evening cortisol levels. Men, on the other hand, have lower cortisol levels in the evenings. The difference may reflect the additional responsibilities women have after they get home from their day jobs. It may also answer why more women have difficult sleeping, particularly during the perimenopausal and menopausal years. Elevated cortisol levels at night will prevent sleep or cause very light sleep with frequent waking.

SPOTLIGHT ON: SLEEP, MEMORY, DEPRESSION AND BREAST CANCER

Sleep: A study published in the *Journal of the American Medical Association* (*JAMA*) in August 2000, found that increasing age was associated with an elevation of evening cortisol levels that became significant only after age 50 years. Sleep became more fragmented and REM sleep declined.

Changes in sleep quality are linked to specific changes in several hormone levels as well. There is a vicious cycle with sleep and impaired adrenals. If the adrenals are weak, the sleep will be poor; if sleep quality is poor the adrenal glands become exhausted. Support your adrenal glands if you have sleep problems.

Depression: Recent research has found that approximately half of patients with major depression have high levels of cortisol and that high cortisol levels might be a cause rather than a symptom of depression, as previously thought. "The idea that stress hormones may actually affect the brain's biochemistry and cause depression is an evolving concept," said Owen Wolkowitz, M.D., co-author of the study published in the September 1999 issue of *Psychosomatic Medicine*. "Recent studies have amassed enough evidence to suggest that at least some cases of depression may be a disease or disorder of the endocrine system which manifests itself in the brain rather than in the body."

Scientists will now be looking for drugs that lower cortisol levels. However, rather than taking drugs to simply mask the symptoms of the condition, you should treat the cause by supporting your adrenal health.

Memory Problems: If it's been a really rough day at work all week and you can't remember where you put your keys or your own phone number, it may be that high levels of the stress hormone cortisol are interfering with your memory. High cortisol levels are relevant to the kind of memory that helps us function moment-to-moment but other areas of memory suffer. The good news is that once the stress and cortisol levels decreases, memory performance returns to normal. Some people however, are constantly on a cortisol inducing treadmill, not knowing how to get off.

Breast Cancer: A study published in the Journal of the National Cancer Institute, June 2000, found that women with advanced breast cancer who have abnormal daytime levels of cortisol are significantly more likely to die sooner than patients with normal levels of this stress hormone. The researchers also found that women with increase cortisol levels had fewer immune system cells known as natural killer cells, and this reduced immunity was associated with the higher mortality rate. The study also reported that women with abnormal cortisol patterns during the day were more likely to have sleep disruptions at night.

Guess What?
Early Morning Exercise May Be Bad For You!

A recent study involving competitive swimmers, published in the *British Journal of Sports Medicine*, July 2002, found that levels of the stress hormone cortisol were higher in the morning compared to the evening before exercise and in general cortisol was significantly higher after exercise. The researches from the Brunel University's Department of Sport Sciences concluded that the body clock and early morning exercise suppresses the immune system. The study concluded that the best time to train is in the evening when cortisol levels are lower.

Based on Karen's clinical experience, she sees many patients with low adrenal function who cannot exercise in the evening because their cortisol levels are higher in the evening due to the effects of chronic stress. Evening exercise stimulates the adrenal glands to excrete more cortisol that can cause insomnia in many people. An Adrenal Stress Index test (ASI) explained later in this section can help to determine your own cortisol rhythm.

In traditional Chinese medicine specific emotions are associated with a particular organ/energy system. (In allopathy, the head is separated from the rest of the body and sent off to a psychiatrist or psychologist to fix!) The Chinese tradition says that the adrenals are the "site of the will." When the adrenal chi is weak, anxiety and fear will increase, and a person will be weak-willed; conversely, excessive fear and anxiety will weaken the adrenal chi. Many people with strong wills, who push beyond what the body is telling them, end up with lowered adrenal energy.

"On a personal note, I (Karen) can trace low adrenal function symptoms back to my early teens and then in my twenties they became worn out due to too much physical and emotional stress. This low adrenal condition resulted in many years of severe back pain as a result of spinal degeneration. However, it did cause me to search into the alternative areas of medicine and eventually led me to where I am today."

Do you need adrenal support? We encourage you review the 'Adrenal Stress Symptoms' list overleaf. Most people are surprised to find that many of their symptoms are related poor adrenal function. How did you do?

The dexamethasone suppression test, also referred to as ACTH suppression test or Cortisol suppression test, is the lab test commonly used to measure cortisol blood levels. However, rarely will this test show alterations in cortisol levels that are considered extreme enough to be considered a health problem.

Most adrenal conditions are due to sub-optimal function of the adrenal glands and it is therefore difficult to diagnose mild to moderate adrenal compromise by using a cortisol suppression test only as the results will probably fall within the normal range.

Naturopathic Adrenal Tests

Adrenal Stress Index (ASI): an excellent method for assessing adrenal maladaptation to stress.

The ASI is an accurate and convenient method for assessing adrenal function for assessing adrenal function by testing cortisol levels in the saliva. Saliva cortisol results have been used in stress research for over 10 years. The body's level of cortisol displays what is known as a diurnal variation, meaning normal levels of cortisol vary throughout a 24-hour period. With a home kit the patient can collect samples of saliva throughout the day making it possible to the diurnal rhythms.

Glucose Tolerance Test: There is a frequent relationship between hyperinsulinism (low blood sugar) and functional hypoadrenalism. A five to six hour glucose tolerance test can rule out blood sugar irregularities such as dysglycemia, discussed in Chapter 9.

Postural (Orthostatic) Blood Pressure: is an easy in-clinic assessment of adrenal function. The blood pressure is taken while the patient is in the reclining position and twice when the patient is brought to a standing position. In a normal response the blood pressure will be approximately 10 mg/hg higher in the standing position than in the lying position. With adrenal insufficiency the blood pressure will drop 5 mg/hg or more when the patient moves from the lying to standing position. Generally, the orthostatic blood pressure is a reliable indication of the adrenal state, with a few exceptions: athletes and people taking cortisone. Competitive athletes are constantly pushing their adrenal glands to the point the adrenals are constantly on overdrive making it difficult to assess adrenal function based on this measurement only. prednisone or other forms of cortisone mask the normal adrenal function.

You can support the the adrenal glands with vitamin and mineral supplements, botanical medicines and by balancing workloads, rest, family time, physical and spiritual exercise, and personal play time.

UNDRESS YOUR STRESS: SUPPORT YOUR ADRENAL GLANDS

ADAPTOGENS

Herbs that assist us in adapting to stress by supporting the adrenal glands are aptly called adaptogens.

ability to cope with stress—whether it be physical, environmental, or mental and emotional. Adaptogens have many important properties, but the most important is their *normalizing effect*, regardless of the condition—they help the body maintain homeostasis, the constant internal state necessary for health and life itself. For example, if blood pressure is high, an adaptogen will help lower it; if it is low, the same adaptogen will help normalize it.

During menopause the work load of the adrenal glands is increased. At this time, the adrenals must not only help us cope with life's ordinary strains but also with all the emotional and physical stresses that attend the menopausal transition. And as mentioned above, they must begin replacing the sex hormones once produced by our ovaries. Because adaptogens support adrenal function, they can be very important to well-being during menopause.

Some of the common health-enhancing and adrenal-supporting functions of adaptogens include:

- improving blood sugar metabolism;
- supporting the endocrine (hormonal) system;
- protecting and supporting the immune system;
- providing liver protection and support;
- increasing stamina and endurance;
- strengthening the cardiovascular and respiratory systems;
- strengthening the brain and central nervous system; and
- protecting cells from antioxidant damage.

ADAPTOGENIC HERBS

All herbs discussed below can be used by both women and men.

"It seems to me that man's ultimate aim in life is to express himself as fully as possible, according to his own lights. and to achieve a sense of security. To accomplish this you must find your own optimal stress level, then use your own adaptation energy at a rate and in a direction adjusted to your *own* innate qualifications and preferences."—Hans Selye, M.D.

- **American ginseng (*Panax quinquefolius*); Asian ginseng (*Panax ginseng*).** The word "ginseng" is said to mean the wonder of the world. The properties of American and Asian ginseng are similar to those of Siberian ginseng (below), but these herbs tend to be more yang. They have therefore been traditionally used more for men. American ginseng contains the same active ingredients as *Panax ginseng* but in different proportions. As a result American ginseng tends to depress the central nervous system, increase the synthesis of cholesterol, and lower blood pressure. *Panax ginseng*, on the other hand, slightly stimulates the central nervous system and increases blood pressure.

  Both herbs provide support for the adrenal glands and increased ability to withstand stress, counter fatigue, enhance mental performance, and support the immune system.

  — *Recommended dosage:* If using a standardized supplement (4 to 7 percent ginsenosides) take 100 mg root powder two to three times daily. If using non-standardized ginseng, take 1 to 2 g once or twice daily.

- **Siberian ginseng (*Eleutherococcus senticosus*)** is known as the "King of Adaptogens." It is respected for its ability to support adrenal function and enhance immune function. Toxicity studies have demonstrated that it is virtually non-toxic. Research on Siberian ginseng began in the 1940s when I. I. Brekhman and colleagues were searching for an economical replacement for Asian ginseng. In Russia, Siberian ginseng is well known for its ability to increase stamina and endurance in athletes.

Siberian ginseng can be used to counter fatigue, give immune support, improve decreased mental abilities, and support the body during periods of high physical exertion.

— *Recommended dosage:* 100 to 200 mg solid extract standardized to contain 1 percent eleutherosides three times daily; 2 to 4 mL fluid extract (1:1) one to three times daily; 2 to 4 mL tincture three times daily; 200 to 400 mg powdered root three times daily.

- **Russian Rhodiola (*Rhodiola rosea*)** is one of the newer adaptogens to North America but it has been intensively studied for over 35 years in Russia. Russian researchers have observed that rhodiola increases resistance to a variety of chemical, biological and physical stressors as well offering anti-fatigue, anti-depressant, immune-enhancing, anti-cancer and cardioprotective effects. It also improves the nervous system and mental function by increasing blood supply and protein synthesis. Rhodiola has found to be beneficial in the treatment of insomnia, work performance, fatigue, hypertension, memory problems and depression.

— *Recommended dosage:* 80 mg two to three times daily.

- ***AdrenaSense*** is a new adaptogenic product containing many of the valuable adrenal support herbs. It was formulated as a coping remedy for the times when life is too stressful (available in spring 2003).

— *Recommended dosage:* 2 to 4 capsules daily.

- **Ashwagandha (*Withania sominifera*)** is referred to as "Indian ginseng" and it has been used in Ayurvedic medicine, the traditional medical system of India, for more than 2,500 years. While numerous studies have explored this herb's ability to improve stress tolerance, combat fatigue, improve memory problems, enhance immune modulation and benefit inflammatory conditions such as arthritis, recent research has examined its positive effect on those suffering from hormone imbalances and low thyroid function. Ashwagandha is an excellent remedy for nervous system complaints such as anxiety and insomnia.

— *Recommended dosage:* 300 mg solid extract standardized to contain 5 percent withanolides, two to four times daily.

• **Brazilian ginseng/suma (*Pfaffia paniculata*).** Suma is both the common name and the trade name for this plant. In Brazil, it is also called *para todo*, a Portuguese phrase meaning "for everything"—traditionally it is used as an energy and rejuvenating tonic as well as a general cure-all for many types of disorders. Suma is an excellent herb for the cardiovascular system, central nervous system, reproductive system, digestive system and the immune system. In Europe Suma is commonly used to treat fatigue, menopausal symptoms, impotence and other sexual difficulties, respiratory problems, blood sugar imbalances and diabetes, and cancer and other diseases related to chronic immune deficiencies. Suma is a source of beta-ecdysterone that are used widely to help athletes increase muscle mass and endurance.

— *Recommended dosage:* 300 mg powdered root three times daily.

• **Schizandra (*Schizandra chinensis*).** In traditional Chinese medicine Schizandra is commonly used as a general tonic herb to purify the blood and restore the liver that is associated with aging. It is also used as an adaptogenic herb to counter the effects of stress and fatigue. Scientific studies show it has normalizing effects in cases of insomnia, gastrointestinal problems, and immune system disorders. Schizandra improves mental function and enhances physical and intellectual endurance.

— *Recommended dosage:* 60-80 mg two to three times daily.

• **Jiaogulan (*Gynostemma pentaphyllum*)** has been studied extensively in China. It is a very powerful adaptogenic herb. Preliminary studies suggest that its regulatory effects are even more powerful than those of other Asian ginsengs. Jiaogulan has demonstrated antibacterial, antiviral, and anti-inflammatory activity as well as the ability to regulate blood pressure, balance reproductive, mental, and digestive function, enhance immune response, and increase athletic endurance. It is also very beneficial for hormonal balance. It has also been shown to be effective in increasing fat metabolism and establishing favourable HDL to LDL ratios in the blood. Finally, it is rich in amino acids and antioxidants.

— *Recommended dosage:* 80-100 mg capsule standardized to 20% gypenosides, two to three times daily.

THE OVERALL CLEANSE

We now know how to cleanse our colon and support the adrenal glands and liver through the use of botanical medicines and nutrition. Given the current state of our environment it is usually important to take another step in the detoxification of our bodies. Short overall internal cleanses give our digestive system and stress-response organs a much needed rest and the opportunity to do some "house cleaning" and rebuilding. After a cleanse, nutrient assimilation also usually improves.

Traditionally, fasting has been used to rid the body of toxins and facilitate healing. There are typically two types of fasts: those that allow water only, and those that include freshly made juices. The cleansing program outlined here is less severe, as it starts with a cleansing diet for the first seven days and then moves into a three- to seven-day juice fast. I find that most people today carry such a heavy load of toxins that as the body begins to cleanse, it requires more supportive nutrients than are supplied by traditional fasts to aid the organs of elimination in their work—otherwise they may become overwhelmed.

As the body eliminates toxins some people may experience uncomfortable side effects. These effects are temporary and may include constipation due to loss of fluids and no fibre, headaches, inability to concentrate, nausea, or rashes or skin outbreaks. These symptoms usually occur within the first 48 hours of the cleanse. They should not last longer than three to four days, although in some people they may continue for up to seven days. If you are concerned, or symptoms persist, consult your naturopathic doctor or natural health practitioner.

You may also find yourself revisiting past traumatic events, in memory or in dreams, or experience tears or anger for no apparent reason. To keep toxins moving outwards at all levels, it is very important to ensure that your bowels continue eliminating regularly, and to remember to drink the required amount of water during a cleanse—a minimum of 2.5 L per day. You can add lemon juice to give your liver extra help.

Following are the complete instructions for a 10- to 14-day detoxification and cleansing program.

TEN- TO FOURTEEN-DAY
DETOXIFICATION AND CLEANSING PROGRAM:
GENERAL GUIDELINES

Do each one of the things on this list *daily* throughout your cleanse:

- Drink at least 2.5 to 3 L of purified water.
- Make sure you have two to three substantial bowel movements. If you have difficulty achieving this, use buckthorn or cascara sagrada, discussed earlier in this chapter.
- Exercise moderately on at least five of the seven initial days of the cleanse.
- Reduce personal obligations and rest more.
- Sleep for at least eight hours each night.
- Have regular detoxification baths (described below) and, if available, sauna sessions.
- Spend at least 20 minutes in meditation, contemplation, or prayer to relax your body and mind.
- Throughout the day, take a moment here or there to visualize your body, mind, and spirit as healthy. Know that you *are* healthy! See Chapter 10 for more information on mental, emotional, and spiritual exercises.

DETOXIFICATION AND CLEANSING PROGRAM:
THE FIRST SEVEN DAYS

Your diet during the first seven days will be restricted to whole grains and vegetables and small amounts of fruit, condiments, and oil.

- Choose two to three grains for the week from the following list: brown rice, brown basmati rice, quinoa, millet, hulled barley, and buckwheat. You may have two to three moderate servings daily.

- Eat as much as you like of the following: steamed vegetables, raw vegetables, and vegetable juices. Have a minimum of three servings of vegetables and two 250 mL glasses of fresh vegetable juice daily. Vegetable juice recipes are given below.

- In addition, drink 50 to 75 mL of red potato juice daily. This juice is made by mixing the juice of red potatoes with the juice of celery stalks; use two to three stalks per serving.

THE DOS AND DON'TS OF CLEANSING

AVOID COMPLETELY	PERMITTED SUBSTITUTES
• Alcohol	• Herbal teas
• Tobacco	• Fresh herbs for flavor
• Coffee and caffeinated tea	• Sea salt used sparingly, herbal salt substitutes (ground herbs) and sea vegetables (wakame, hijiki, dulse)
• Sugar of any kind, including honey, molasses, corn syrup, maple syrup, barley or rice malt and table syrup	
• Table salt	• Soy milk (250 mL) or tofu (175g) once daily
• Dairy products	• Ground flaxseed and flaxseed oil
• Eggs, chicken, beef, pork, lamb, fish and any other sources of animal protein	
• Butter and margarine	
• Heated oils	

- Eat fruit sparingly, no more than three pieces daily, and eat any fruit at least one-half hour before or two hours after your other meals.

Cleansing Juices

Drink these juices right after they're made so that nutrients aren't lost. If you do not have a juicer and cannot buy one, most health food stores or restaurants will sell you freshly made vegetable juices.

Carrot, Beet, and Garlic or Ginger Juice

Juice 4 to 5 carrots, 1 small beet, and 1 to 2 fresh cloves garlic or a small piece of ginger.

Carrot-Apple Delight

Juice 1/2 apple, 4 to 5 carrots, and a small piece of ginger (optional).

Green Vitality

Juice 3 to 4 kale leaves, 1 bunch parsley, 1 cucumber, 2 to 3 celery stalks, and 3 to 4 carrots.

"Yard by yard, life is hard; inch by inch, life's a cinch." If you feel ready to take the next step—or the next yard—I recommend embarking on a juice-only cleanse for three to seven days after the initial seven-day detoxification. Trust your intuition. You may need to wait to take this step until you have done more to build up your overall health. Wait four to six months, then start again with the seven-day restricted diet. This time, you'll likely feel ready to move on to the juice cleanse.

DETOXIFICATION AND CLEANSING PROGRAM: DAYS 8 TO 10 OR 14

During this period, drink only fresh vegetable juices of your choice. Have at least six to eight glasses of juice daily and drink 2.5 to 3 L of water daily as well, with the juice of one or two lemons. Make sure you have regular bowel elimination and continue to follow the general guidelines outlined at the outset of this cleansing protocol.

After the juice cleanse, slowly begin to eat again. For the first three days, follow the dietary suggestions outlined for Days 1 to 7, then slowly introduce legumes, beans, tofu, and raw nuts and seeds over the next few days. By the end of five days you can reintroduce hormone-free animal proteins such as fish, chicken, eggs, veal, and the like.

During your cleanse, give your eliminative organs as much support as possible by using various detoxification aids often. For instance, during a cleanse, I suggest three detoxification baths (described below) each week. Experiment with the other aids and use your intuition to guide you in determining how frequently you use each one. These techniques are valuable between cleanses as well to lower the accumulated internal toxins.

Detoxification Baths

Detoxification baths use hot water to increase blood flow to the skin's surface and open the pores, thereby encouraging perspiration and toxin elimination. Start the baths slowly, as some people experience symptoms, especially if the toxic load is great. If you experience dizziness, headaches, fatigue, nausea, or weakness during a bath, stop, and next time, bathe for a shorter period. A detoxification bath involves the following steps: Wash thoroughly with a gentle natural soap and a skin brush or coarse wash cloth and rinse thoroughly; fill the tub with water as hot as is tolerable (filtered if possible) and begin with a five-minute soak. Gradually increase your time in the detoxification bath to 30 minutes if you are not experiencing any symptoms. After soaking, shower and scrub thoroughly with soap to rinse off toxins that have accumulated on the skin. Drink at least two to three glasses of water before, during, and after your bath. Shower filters are inexpensive and can be purchased at health food stores and Home Depot.

EPSOM SALT BATHS

Epsom salt baths help eliminate toxins by increasing the blood supply to the skin and by drawing from the body water and, with it, toxins. Epsom salts also contain sulphur, which is well known for its medicinal and detoxification properties. Add 250 mL Epsom salts to a regular bath and gradually increase the amount to 1 L per tub. Stay in an Epsom salts bath no longer than one-half hour.

Other substances you can add to the bath to help detoxification include:

- **Apple cider vinegar,** which works similarly to Epsom salts. Add 250 mL to your bath, gradually increasing to 500 mL per tub.

- **Baking soda.** Soda baths used to be a common household remedy for colds, flus, and skin irritations. Baking soda (sodium bicarbonate) balances the pH and is good for cleansing. Use 250 mL baking soda per tub.

- **Clay,** which draws out toxins. Use 125 to 250 mL clay per tub. Green clay is most commonly used for this purpose.

Sauna: The Age-Old Cure-All

"Give me a chance to create fever, and I will cure all disease."
—Paemendides (writing 2 000 years ago)

Sweating is good for you! The primary storage site for toxins is the fatty tissue. The heat generated in exercise removes toxins from the fat, and the increase in blood flow moves them into general circulation. Perspiration from exercise and saunas then eliminates the toxins from the body. Many studies that have measured chemical and heavy metal levels in the sweat and blood during and after exercise and sauna use confirm the effectiveness of these methods for removing toxic chemicals from our bodies. The research indicates that sweating confers the following benefits:

- High body temperatures during infection combat the growth of viruses or bacteria and strengthen the immune system. A fever or sauna will have similar effects in this regard.

- Sweating burns calories and speeds up the metabolic processes of the endocrine system and other organs.

- Sweating excretes toxins and metabolic wastes from the body, including cadmium, lead, nickel, sodium, sulphuric acid, and excess cholesterol.

- Sweating in a hot environment such as the sauna is the only detoxification program that has proven successful in removing chemical pollutants that accumulate in fat cells, such as PCBs, dioxin, and breakdown products of DDT.

- Sweating stimulates dilation of the peripheral blood vessels (blood vessels that lie close to the skin). This relieves pain and speeds the healing of sprains, strains, bursitis, diseases of the peripheral blood vessels, and arthritis.

- Sweating promotes relaxation.

- Finally, sweating improves recovery time in athletes after intense training sessions.

A detoxification sauna should be preceded by 20 minutes of exercise and followed by a cleansing shower. People can lose up to a litre of water during a 20-minute sauna, so be sure to replace lost fluids. Do not spend more than 30 minutes in a sauna.

There are two basic types of saunas, dry and wet. Dry saunas are preferred for detoxification because they increase natural sweating, speeding up the detoxification process more than the water-saturated air of a wet sauna can do.

Dry Brushing

Dry brushing the skin prior to a sauna, detoxification bath, or shower removes dead skin and improves circulation to the skin, helping open the pores for elimination of toxins. Use a special brush made for the purpose, available from many health food stores. Do up to five minutes of long strokes over every area of the body, always moving towards the heart.

Lymphatic Drainage

The lymphatic system circulates lymph fluid throughout the body. In lymph fluid, toxic wastes and bacteria are carried to lymph nodes, where these materials are engulfed and destroyed by large cells called macrophages. Clearly, it is always important, and especially so during cleansing, that the lymphatic system remain uncongested. Lymphatic massage can be done daily to help facilitate detoxification.

Castor Oil Packs

Castor oil from the castor bean plant (*Ricinus communis*) has been used therapeutically since ancient times in Egypt, India, China, Persia, Africa, Greece, Rome, Southern Europe, and the Americas. Pharmaceutical and medical references to castor oil date back to the seventeenth century. Recent studies confirm the therapeutic effects of castor oil.

Castor oil is used topically, in a castor oil pack, to enhance the functioning of the lymphatic system and the immune system. It is also a powerful detoxifier, able to draw toxins out of the body from as far as 10 cm down.

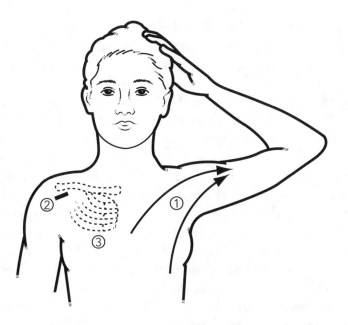

Most of the lymph vessels are located alongside veins and flow towards the heart. The main lymphatic duct empties into a vein near the top of the chest. Tightness or imbalance in the action of the upper chest muscles causes decreased chest expansion, thus putting pressure on this duct and decreasing the lymph flow.

By massaging the areas indicated, you will stimulate and stretch these muscles, increasing rib cage expansion and allowing freer flow of lymph. You may find your chest is sore at first, but this soreness will diminish with consistent treatment, indicating that lymph is flowing better.

1. Lift one arm over the head as shown. With the opposite hand, massage upwards from mid-chest to shoulder and along the side of the chest in the direction of the arrows, using the heel of your hand. Alternate strokes on both sides of the breast for 20 strokes. Then repeat the massage on the other side of the body. Note: Some people find this easier to do while the back is supported. If that is the case, stand against a wall, sit in a chair with good back support, or lie on a bed while doing the massage.

2. Use the thumb or fingers to rub back and forth deeply and briskly under the tip of the shoulder.

3. Find the tops of the first three ribs, just below the collar bone. Rub along the tops of these ribs from the centre of the chest to the outer edge of the chest for at least one minute on each side.

Massage all areas twice daily for one week, then once per day for a second week. After that treat yourself to a massage every time you shower.

Adapted from Patricia Wales, N.D., and Verna Hunt, N.D.

To use a castor oil pack you will need to collect the following supplies: large wool or flannel cloth, a plastic sheet (a green garbage bag will do), a bath towel, pure, cold-pressed, hexane-free castor oil, a heating pad or hot water bottle, and old clothes.

To make and use the pack: Fold the wool or cotton flannel so that it is three or four layers thick and measures 15 to 20 cm on each side. Pour enough castor oil onto the cloth so that the cloth is wet but not dripping. Lie on an old sheet or towel and apply the cloth to the area you wish to detoxify, then cover the pack with the plastic. Apply gentle heat for at least one hour. An alternative method is to apply the pack, cover with plastic, wrap a towel around the entire area, secure it with ties or pins and wear overnight or for a minimum of one hour. For general detoxification, apply the pack over the liver area, from below the right nipple straight down to the waist. Cleanse the skin after treatment with soda water made with 10 mL of baking soda per litre of water. Treatment can be applied daily.

You may keep the flannel or wool pack in a plastic container for future use, adding more castor oil as the cloth dries out.

IN SUMMARY

Undertaking a one- or two-week detoxifying program at least once a year and making regular use of the detoxification aids while taking action to support and strengthen the intestines, liver, and adrenal glands are key steps in recovering from many symptoms and conditions, and starting down the road to optimal health.

Now that we have laid the foundation for overall optimal health, we will go on in the next chapter to begin looking in more detail at the organs and processes most specifically involved in maintaining hormonal health during the transitional years.

4
———

HORMONAL BALANCE AND
THE ENDOCRINE SYSTEM

"Feminine wisdom is the intelligence at the heart of creation. It
is holistic, intuitive, contextual, and functions as a field of infinite
correlation."—Deepak Chopra, M.D.

As we discussed in Chapter 2, our bodies seek to maintain balance, a set
of constant internal conditions, regardless of the various internal and
external influences and pressures that affect us constantly. A number of
"control systems" regulate and adjust internal conditions in response to
stressors. One of these is the nervous system, which catalyzes adaptive
responses through electrical impulses delivered through neurons. Another
control system is the endocrine system, which affects bodily activities by
releasing chemical messengers called hormones into the bloodstream.
The nervous and the endocrine systems coordinate their activities—the
nervous system routinely sends messages to the endocrine system to stimulate or inhibit the release of hormones. (When we consider this relationship between the endocrine and nervous systems, it becomes even
more apparent how brain activities involving thoughts and emotions
could affect hormones.)

THE ENDOCRINE GLANDS

The endocrine system includes a number of organs—the hypothalamus,
pituitary, thyroid, parathyroids, adrenals, pancreas, ovaries, testes, pineal,
and thymus. All of them, not just the ovaries, powerfully influence the
health of our hormonal system during our reproductive years and throughout the menopausal and postmenopausal years.

Each endocrine gland secretes hormones that help maintain balance by changing the physiological activities of the cells of an organ or of cells in groups of organs; or the hormone may directly affect the activities of all the cells in the body. The amount of hormone released by an endocrine gland is determined by the body's need for the hormone at any given time. Through complex feedback mechanisms involving many body systems, hormone production is regulated so that there is no over- or underproduction of particular hormones. However, there are times when the regulating mechanisms do not function properly and hormonal imbalances occur. The stress factors discussed previously and transitional hormonal times such as puberty and menopause have a tremendous effect on the endocrine system's ability to maintain balance.

The "Hormonic" Symphony

In women the endocrine organs that most influence hormonal balance during the transitional years are the adrenal glands, pituitary, hypothalamus, thyroid, and ovaries. And although they are not endocrine organs, remember the role of the liver and the large intestine in hormonal health. Together, these many organs can be thought of as an orchestra playing a complex, beautiful, and ever-changing musical work, a "hormonic" symphony.

The pituitary regulates so many hormones that it can be considered the "concert master" of the hormonal orchestra, taking its orders in the form of releasing hormones from the conductor, the hypothalamus. The pituitary sends out its instructions to the other endocrine organs via various stimulating hormones. It is through the leadership of the hypothalamus and pituitary that the hormonal symphony orchestra is able to continue playing tuneful music.

However, during times when the hormonal levels must fluctuate more dramatically, such as after ovulation and through the transitional years, the orchestra may go out of tune. Players such as the thyroid or adrenal glands may not be able to adjust to the new notes the body wants to play. The adrenals may be exhausted from prolonged stress before menopause, and are unable to meet the demand for more hormones. Sometimes the concert master, the pituitary, cannot stimulate the glandular orchestra to play loud enough or in proper harmony. In naturopathic practice we recognize an important interaction between the thyroid and the adrenals. When this partnership becomes stressed during such times as the transitional years, pregnancy, or other physiological or emotionally stressful times, many women become symptomatic.

Karen's Personal Lesson

"When it came to thinking about or preparing for menopause, I would always jokingly say, "I'm not going to go there—maybe if I ignore the whole issue I won't even notice menopause!" I was wrong! About four years ago, almost overnight I stopped sleeping and as a result, became completely exhausted and barely able to function. I didn't sleep for three months. I would just sit on the floor and cry most of the night while my husband slept soundly, until about five o'clock in the morning, when I would finally be able to go to sleep—only to have to get up for work at seven. Naturopathic remedies were unable to help me sleep, and the side effects I experienced from trying prescription drugs were worse for me than not sleeping at all. I became extremely frustrated that I was able to help most of my patients with similar problems but seemed unable to heal myself.

As it turned out, I needed a deeper understanding of my situation. At first I had put my symptoms down to adrenal stress. I had just come through a year of extreme negative stress in my life, and what little adrenal reserve I did have was most certainly depleted after the event. I did all that I could to support myself. Things started improving, but slowly. I continually reviewed my symptoms to try to find an answer. I began to suspect that my thyroid had succumbed to the overtaxing of my adrenals during the previous year, and now, faced with the added stress of continual insomnia, had decided to slow down—which was good for my thyroid, but not good for me.

To check my thyroid, I monitored my basal temperature (see page 100 for information on home thyroid tests) and found all the readings to be below normal. I visited my M.D., who is very open to my approach to medicine, and we put our heads together. Lab tests indicated that testosterone levels were low. My thyroid stimulating hormone (TSH) level fell between 0.2 to 6.0 microinternational units per millilitre of blood, the standard unit of measurement for thyroid hormone. TSH is produced by the pituitary to stimulate thyroid function. The lower the thyroid function, the higher the TSH levels go as the pituitary tries to stimulate the thyroid into greater activity. (Conversely, TSH levels that are lower than 0.2 indicate clinical hyperthyroidism, or thyroid overactivity.) My TSH level was not high enough to indicate clinical hypothyroidism, that is, disease as defined by allopathic parameters. The thyroid hormones triiodothyronine (T3) and thyroxin (T4) were low, but still within normal limits.

Over the years in my practice, however, I have determined a more sensitive range for TSH (1.0 to 3.0) to indicate functional/subclinical hypothyroidism. Many people's TSH falls within the conventional parameters for normal (0.2 to 6.0), but most people with levels greater than 3.0 have symptoms of low thyroid function. Naturopathic doctors refer to such people as having subclinical, or functional, low thyroid. So although I was within the clinical normal range, I was not within the functional normal range, and I had many of the symptoms related to low thyroid function.

According to my observations, if diagnosis of thyroid imbalance is based solely on a TSH reading, without taking other symptoms into account, it will be another 10 to 12 years before thyroid hormone levels drop low enough to call forth an allopathic diagnosis of low thyroid function. In the meantime, the person with low thyroid symptoms will go through much unnecessary suffering.

I immediately adjusted my naturopathic program to include natural thyroid and a short-term prescription for testosterone. Within a very short time my sleep patterns and energy level started to return to normal.

I really had not thought of my symptoms as related to menopause, since I didn't have any of the other common symptoms such as hot flashes or night sweats. Yet, sure enough, my menstrual periods ended during this time. *I did go there!* In fact, I went quickly and suddenly.

During the perimenopausal years, as estrogen and progesterone production by the ovaries begins to decrease, the adrenals are meant to increase their manufacture of these hormones to make up for the deficiency. In my case—and I have seen this happen in many of my patients too—menopause occurred rapidly, not allowing the adrenals adequate time to adjust. From a naturopathic perspective, women who experience sudden changes related to menopause usually have low adrenal function, which can become even more compromised under the pressures associated with hormonal changes.

As a consequence of my experience I have read just about everything there is to read on the topic of menopause-related symptoms and signs to better help myself and my patients before, during, and after this transitional stage of life.

This story also demonstrates the important part the thyroid plays in the hormonal orchestra. Let's now consider the thyroid in more detail."

THE THYROID GLAND

The thyroid, located at the front of the throat, sets the rate of body metabolism, thereby regulating nearly every cell in the body. Therefore, any change in thyroid functioning will have far-reaching effects. The following hormones and substances directly affect the thyroid or are released by it:

- **Thyrotropin releasing hormone (TRH)** is secreted by the hypothalamus, a brain centre that coordinates the actions of the nervous and endocrine systems. TRH triggers the pituitary to secrete TSH.

- **Thyroid stimulating hormone (TSH)** is secreted by the pituitary in response to TRH. TSH stimulates the production of thyroid hormones and the growth of thyroid cells (excess TSH causes thyroid enlargement, or goitre).

- **Calcitonin** is a thyroid hormone involved in the homeostasis of blood calcium levels. It lowers the amount of calcium and phosphate in the blood as needed by inhibiting bone breakdown and accelerating the assimilation of calcium. Thus, the thyroid is involved in bone health and diseases such as osteoporosis.

- **Thyroxin (T4)** is the most abundant thyroid hormone. It is synthesized from tyrosine and includes four molecules of iodine per molecule of hormone.

- **Triiodothyronine (T3)** is the most active thyroid hormone, with four to ten times the activity of T4. It includes three molecules of iodine per molecule of hormone.

At any given time, most T3 and T4 molecules in the body are bound tightly to blood proteins. Only a small amount of each circulates as "free" hormone, which is physiologically active. For example, unbound T4 accounts for approximately 0.05 percent of total T4. Unbound hormone levels are seldom measured by medical doctors, yet these levels are most accurate for determining thyroid function.

Because the thyroid hormones have such broad effects, keeping the thyroid healthy is another key to optimal health. An important influence on thyroid health is adrenal health.

The Thyroid-Adrenal Relationship

If there is inadequate thyroid hormone, the adrenal glands are affected, and if there are inadequate levels of some of the adrenal hormones the thyroid does not function properly. The adrenal-thyroid feedback interaction is orchestrated by the nervous system.

Adrenal stress also affects the thyroid's "job description." We mentioned previously that the adrenals are the main stress adaptation organ. When the adrenal glands are overworked the body converts progesterone (a precursor hormone) into adrenal hormones, which depletes needed progesterone. Some of the many reasons this is undesirable will become clearer in Chapter 7, which discusses progesterone in relation to bone health. Both the thyroid and progesterone have a normalizing antistress action on the pituitary and thereby help the adrenals—which, like the thyroid, are stimulated by the pituitary—with stress adaptation. When progesterone levels are low because of its conversion into stress-fighting hormones, the thyroid suddenly has to take on the task of destressing the pituitary with little outside help.

Furthermore, the thyroid, as we have seen, governs the metabolic rate. If the adrenals are depleted, the thyroid will "whip" them, hormonally speaking, into order to maintain the proper rate. However, the endocrine system does not continue this strategy forever. Instead, over time the thyroid decreases hormone production in order to conserve adrenal energy (and its own). When this first happens the patient may have symptoms of both adrenal and thyroid imbalance. If the symptoms are not addressed, over time they will come to be predominantly related to one gland or the other.

Allopathic medicine does not recognize the symptoms of poor adrenal function until the glands become so compromised that disorders such as Addison's disease or Cushing's syndrome become diagnosable. Until this diagnosis the patient will most likely have suffered for years from symptoms of hypo- and/or hyperadrenal function. Years of chronic stress eventually cause low adrenal function, but prior to the organ becoming compromised, there are usually periods of overactivity that, if untreated, usually result in low adrenal function. Some people, however, stay in the overactive state for a prolonged period. In the mid-1970s, Raymond Peat, PhD, pointed out that menopausal symptoms resemble those of Cushing's syndrome, a disease related to overactivity of the adrenal cortex. For example, hot flushes, night sweats and insomnia, common menopausal symptoms, are also symptoms of Cushing's syndrome. More evidence that, as will be emphasized again and again in this chapter, a lack of diagnosable disease is not the same thing as hale and hearty organ function.

We discussed in detail the symptoms of poor adrenal function, and what can be done about it, in Chapter 3. Now let's look at some of the symptoms and signs of poor thyroid function. Two terms that will repeatedly be used in reference to the thyroid are "clinical" and "functional":

- **Clinical.** When the results of a medical test are of clinical significance, they lie outside normal parameters as defined by allopathy. For example, a diagnosis of clinical hypothyroidism (underactive thyroid) is made by allopaths only when TSH levels are higher than 6.0. This allows for a very broad definition of what is normal. (High TSH levels indicate hypothyroidism because the pituitary is trying to stimulate the thyroid into action.)

- **Functional/suboptimal.** When laboratory tests show results that fall in the normal range, yet the patient has the classic symptoms of the condition being tested for, naturopaths consider the patient to have a functional disease, or suboptimal function of the organ in question. For example, in functional hypothyroidism (suboptimal thyroid function) lab results will fall into what is considered the normal range, yet the patient will have many of the classic symptoms of clinical hypothyroidism, and more sensitive tests of thyroid function, such as basal temperature, will show abnormal results.

Functional Thyroid Problems

It is common for the thyroid to be functionally, or even clinically, out of balance in women who experience hormone-related problems such as premenstrual syndrome (PMS), infertility, ovarian cysts, fibroids, endometriosis, fibrocystic breasts, dysmenorrhea (menstrual pain), metrorrhagia (heavy bleeding), or menopausal symptoms.

Yet patients who come to Karen with functional low thyroid will usually have had an incredibly frustrating time searching for a diagnosis that explains their symptoms. These people may have all the classic symptoms of underactive thyroid (see below) and yet the standard laboratory tests fail to show any problem. As stated previously, we simply cannot rely on lab tests alone and ignore symptoms. This holds true in any health situation and is particularly the case when it comes to diagnosing thyroid imbalances. The normal levels for thyroid tests are so broad that most patients with functional problems are not clinically diagnosable. Yet it takes very little change in the pituitary stimulating hormone, TSH, to cause dramatic changes in thyroid function. It is a mystery to us why the allopathic definition of the normal range for TSH is so wide, given the extreme sensitivity of the thyroid to even minute variations in TSH levels.

It is common for women to have symptoms of thyroid over- or under-activity, particularly during the perimenopause and menopause. If the situation is addressed at this point, further depletion of both thyroid and adrenal function can be prevented. If not, most women are given estrogen for their complaints, which further shuts down the thyroid: high estrogen levels interfere with the thyroid hormones, particularly the utilization of T3, the most biologically active thyroid hormone.

How many women have experienced weight gain and increased blood pressure at menopause once they start taking synthetic estrogen? Because estrogen is an antagonist to thyroid hormone, the metabolic rate slows down. As this happens, many women develop difficulties with fat metabolism, because one of the functions of the thyroid hormones is to stimulate fat metabolism. Weight control problems result. In addition, serum cholesterol or triglyceride levels may increase. If this has been your experience, we suggest that you read Chapter 6 carefully, as it gives alternatives to synthetic hormone replacement therapy. Thyroid activity can also be inhibited by high levels of androgens (male sex hormones) circulating in the blood. For more information on the effects of androgens and the tests available to determine various hormone levels, see Chapter 6.

Depression and fatigue are the most common thyroid symptoms in menopausal women. Allopathic doctors frequently mishandle the conditions, with women being given antidepressants or hormone replacement therapy or both. In 1993, Dr. Frank Tallis reported in the *British Journal of Psychiatry* that up to 14 percent of the patients referred to him for depression or some other emotional disorder turn out to have clinical hypothyroidism (underactive thyroid). Once the hypothyroidism was treated, the emotional cloud lifted. What if Tallis included in his reckoning the many people with functional hypothyroidism? How high would the correlation between thyroid dysfunction and emotional symptoms rise?

According to both naturopathic and traditional Chinese medical philosophy, the thyroid is also influenced by the liver. The liver chi, or energy, governs the flow of fluids through the body. When it is congested or stagnant, swelling (edema) occurs. This congestion may occur in the thyroid area. It may be imperceptible, or a lump not large enough for us to feel may be felt by our internal sensing mechanisms. When a noticeable enlargement of the thyroid occurs—called goitre—this is also a sign of liver congestion.

The liver is indeed related to all hormonal imbalances.

Research indicates that thyroid problems are on the rise because of the widespread poor nutritional status of people today, as well as the high levels of environmental toxins to which we are exposed. As we mentioned in Chapter 3, the body's ability to eliminate toxic compounds and so support good thyroid functioning depends on the strength of its detoxification systems, which, in turn, are directly influenced by diet and lifestyle.

Allopathic medicine does not often consider the thyroid a major player in the hormonal orchestra, yet its functioning is central to endocrine balance. When we review the symptoms of low thyroid function below, you will see that they include insomnia, night sweats, mood swings, migraine headaches, memory problems, low energy, hormonal problems, palpitations, depression and irritability, and increased cholesterol levels—symptoms that are identical to common menopause-related difficulties.

The following lists give the most common symptoms and signs of under-active and overactive thyroid function. Very commonly encountered symptoms are set in bold text.

Common Signs and Symptoms of Hypothyroidism (Low Thyroid Function)

- **Cold hands and feet, cold intolerance, low body temperature**
- **Constipation**
- **Chronic fatigue,** weakness, lethargy
- **Edema** (swelling of eyelids or face)
- **Depression and irritability;** sudden change in personality; nervousness
- **Hair loss;** dry, coarse skin, hair, or both; cracking in the heels and skin
- **Hormonal imbalances** (fibroids, ovarian or breast cysts, infertility, miscarriage, painful periods, endometriosis, heavy periods, PMS, menopausal symptoms, frequent menstrual cycles)
- **Impaired memory; poor concentration**
- **Slower metabolism,** may show up as weight gain, either general or on the hips
- Shortness of breath; feeling unable to breathe deeply
- Goitre
- Headaches and dizziness that are worse in the morning, better in the afternoon

- Heart palpitations
- Insomnia; racing thoughts
- A metallic taste in the mouth; this symptom indicates a need for iodine.
- Poor vision

An underactive thyroid may result in the following findings at the doctor's office:

- **Slow Achilles reflex (see home thyroid tests)**
- **Low basal temperature** (see home thyroid tests)
- **High TSH; low T3, T4, or T7;** presence of thyroid antibodies
- Doughy abdomen
- Carpal tunnel syndrome
- Elevated cholesterol levels
- Low progesterone to estrogen ratio
- Slow pulse

Common Signs and Symptoms of Hyperthyroidism (Overactive Thyroid)

- **Increased appetite; weight loss, muscle wasting, and weakness**
- **Heart palpitations**
- **Nervousness and anxiety; mood changes; agitation; talkativeness**
- **Shakiness, trembling, or tremor**
- **Increased sweating, oversensitivity to heat; warm, moist palms**
- Bone aches
- Staring/bulging eyes; eye complaints
- Goitre
- Insomnia
- Dry, thin skin

An overactive thyroid may result in the following findings at the doctor's office:

- **Fast pulse; irregular heartbeat**
- **Tremor**

- **Low TSH; elevated T3 or T4**
- Brisk Achilles reflex
- High basal temperature
- Osteoporosis

Many people who have all the signs of thyroid difficulty may never receive appropriate treatment because the traditional lab tests are so insensitive to early changes in function. Abnormal TSH, T3, or T4 levels will be found in more advanced cases, but rarely in the multitude of subfunctional or subclinical low- or high-thyroid patients naturopathic doctors see. To confirm a diagnosis of functional thyroid imbalance, naturopathic doctors will also use the following evaluative tools.

LABORATORY TESTS: TSH, T3, AND T4

In Canada most doctors test only the TSH level. If it is within the normal limits, they do not do any further thyroid tests. Yet it is quite common for patients to have normal TSH and T4 levels but low T3 levels. T4 is the most abundant thyroid hormone (50 times more T4 is present in the body than T3), but T3 is far more active. Many people are unable to convert T4 into T3 at the rate needed, and will continue to experience low thyroid symptoms even if given medication that normalizes TSH levels, because the T3 level remains low. For additional information on T3, please refer to the work of Dr. E. D. Wilson, *Wilson's Syndrome: The Miracle of Feeling Well* (see the "Further Reading" section).

ACHILLES TENDON REFLEX

The response of the Achilles tendon to a light tap is a good general indicator of thyroid function. In patients with low thyroid the tendon reflex will be sluggish, whereas in hyperthyroid cases it will be brisk and rigid. Results, however, must be evaluated in combination with the additional information provided by symptoms and basal temperatures.

HOME THYROID TESTS

Basal Temperature

Monitoring the basal temperature is the most sensitive and accurate way to evaluate thyroid function and it is also the simplest and least expensive. The thyroid sets the thermostat for the body and regulates the rate of metabolism in nearly all of the cells. Therefore the most reliable window on thyroid function is the basic body temperature, or basal temperature. Some health care practitioners call basal temperature the axillary temperature. It is measured at the same time every day—as soon as you wake up in the morning, before arising.

The research on basal temperature as the most accurate measurement for thyroid function was done by Dr. Broda Barnes, who has more than forty years of clinical experience with thyroid patients. The "Further Reading" section of this book lists two of his titles, *Heart Attack Rareness in Thyroid-Treated Patients* and *Hypothyroidism: The Unsuspected Illness*.

Evaluating your basal temperature can easily be done at home; the information gained is very helpful to any holistically oriented medical practitioner.

- Shake down the basal thermometer the night before and leave it at the bedside

- Immediately on waking put it under your arm and leave it in your armpit for 10 minutes

- The temperature should be recorded for at least one week, but more accurate information will result from recording it for a full month, especially if you are menstruating

Normal basal temperature averages between 36.5 and 36.7° Celsius. Basal temperature will vary slightly in menstruating women, depending on the stage of the cycle. Having an average temperature below the normal range could indicate a hypothyroid state; a temperature above this range could indicate a hyperthyroid state.

You can expect your temperature to vary throughout the day, and to increase from the basal level as the day progresses. If you measure your temperature in the middle of the day and it is below normal, you can strongly suspect low thyroid function.

If your TSH level is above 3.0, your basal temperatures are low, and you experience some or many of the symptoms indicated for the condition, you most likely are suffering from functional low thyroid. If your TSH is under 1.0 and your basal temperatures are higher than normal, then your thyroid is working too hard and is overactive. This condition usually precedes hypothyroidism because when the thyroid has worked too hard for too long, it becomes tired and has to slow down.

If your basal temperatures are not normal and you are exhibiting symptoms of thyroid imbalance, you may want to consider providing your thyroid with some support.

Iodine Test

Purchase some iodine at the local pharmacy and apply to an area of the body (i.e. inner arm) and leave it on overnight. If the iodine is absorbed by morning, this could indicate that you have a functional thyroid function problem.

GENERAL TREATMENT FOR ALL THYROID IMBALANCES

Dietary and lifestyle changes can help normalize thyroid function.

- People with thyroid imbalances require more high-quality protein than others. Eat moderate amounts of whole grains and high-quality, hormone-free muscle and organ meats. Dr. Peter D'Adamo, author of *Eat Right for Your Type* (see "Further Reading" section), has found that those with type O blood have a tendency towards low thyroid function. Type Os, says D'Adamo, need large amounts of animal protein and do poorly eating a high-grain, high-carbohydrate diet.

- Eat your heaviest meal at breakfast. Breakfast should include lots of protein and minimal carbohydrates. Good breakfast choices include boiled or poached free-range eggs, a tofu–fermented soy milk shake (soy milk, 1/4 block tofu, and fruit) or Women's Whey with fermented soy, yogurt with nut granola, or chicken, fish, or meat if you have a good appetite. Foods to breakfast on cautiously include breads, especially those made with refined flours and refined breakfast cereals, and concentrated carbohydrates such as oatmeal and fruit juices.

- Eat foods rich in the mineral iodine (see Ocean Vegetables next). The thyroid needs iodine to make thyroid hormones. Iodine-rich foods include beef, lamb, and beef liver (hormone-free); eggs; raw nuts and seeds; seafoods such as clams, oysters, sardines, and other saltwater fish; sea vegetables such as wakame, hijiki, kelp, nori, arame, and dulse; and fresh fruits and vegetables, especially green peppers, lettuce, and pineapple. Raisins contain iodine as well.

- Be careful how much cabbage, Brussels sprouts, broccoli, kale, Chinese cabbage, and other *Brassica* family plants you eat. These contain goitrogens, which cause a decrease in the absorption of iodine. Other foods high in goitrogens include turnips, mustard greens, cassava roots, soybeans, peanuts, pine nuts, and millet. Cook these foods before eating them—cooking usually inactivates goitrogens.

- Use only pure, cold-pressed oils, and in moderation.

- Avoid coffee, tea, refined carbohydrates (white flour and pasta), sugar, fried foods, and fruit juices.

- Exercise daily for 20 minutes, if possible. Exercise is particularly important for hypothyroidism. It stimulates the thyroid gland and increases metabolism. For tips on how to start an exercise program or on how to fine tune the one you follow, please refer to *The Complete Athlete: Integrating Fitness, Nutrition and Natural Health*, by John Winterdyk and Karen Jensen. (See the "Further Reading" section.)

- Earlier in this chapter we touched on the importance of liver and adrenal health for thyroid health. If you haven't already begun implementing the suggestions for liver and adrenal support given in Chapter 3, do it now!

- *Candida*/intestinal problems cause constant stress to the adrenals, lowers nutritional status, and causes build-ups of toxins that can harm the thyroid. If you show any signs of gut problems, begin a treatment program, as outlined in Chapter 3, as soon as possible.

In addition to making diet and lifestyle changes, you can support your thyroid with nutritional supplements. Since the majority of North Americans are unfamiliar with sea vegetables, we will discuss them in more detail.

OCEAN VEGETABLES: THE ULTIMATE FOOD

In North America most people do not incorporate ocean plants into their regular diet. In many Asian countries, however, sea vegetables are staple foods. You may elect to make them a staple food as well once you have a fuller understanding of the benefits of eating these incredible foods.

Ocean plants are so valuable because they provide extremely concentrated nutrients. They are rich in minerals and trace minerals, containing 10 to 20 times the minerals of land plants; they are also high in protein.

Ocean plants protect and support the thyroid gland (its importance is discussed in Chapter 4), support the immune system, and remove radioactive elements, carcinogens, and environmental pollutants from the body. They are high in calcium. Hijiki, arame, and wakame each have 10 times more calcium per unit of weight than milk. In addition, sea vegetables build yin energy, detoxify the body, improve lymphatic drainage, activate liver chi, alkalize the blood, lower cholesterol, and improve metabolism.

An optimum intake is about 5 to 15 g daily, measuring the sea vegetables in the dried state, before soaking or cooking.

Several types of sea vegetables can be easily incorporated into the diet. Here they are, in order according to preparation time, from shortest to longest:

• **Dulse** and **nori** can be used as snacks without soaking or cooking. Dried sea vegetables make a quick and easy snack that provides good nutrition. You can add these two to salads, soups, rice, and other dishes. Or toast these sea vegetables briefly (nori requires a few seconds, dulse a minute or two) in an unoiled pan or over an open flame; then crumble over rice or vegetables as a condiment.

• **Wakame** and **arame** require soaking for approximately 15 minutes and can then be added to salads, soups, and other dishes.

• **Hijiki** is one of my favourite ocean plants. Hijiki requires soaking for at least a few hours, then simmering for 45 minutes to one hour in the soaking water, to conserve minerals. You can add onions, peppers, carrots or any of your favourite vegetables to the simmering hijiki. Traditional flavouring for hijiki in Japan includes soy sauce (tamari) and a dash of mirin (rice cooking wine). Serve the hijiki with rice or cold as a salad (tasty with a tahini/rice vinegar dressing).

• **Kombu** can be soaked overnight and used in soups. Or simmer the kombu for an hour or two in its soaking water and use the broth for cooking grains and making soups.

Specific Treatment Recommendations for Functional Hypothyroidism

Following are specific remedies for the improvement of functional hypothyroidism.

IODINE

Thyroid hormones are made from the amino acid tyrosine and iodine—therefore, iodine is essential for a healthy thyroid. Kelp (*Fucus vesiculosus*), Irish moss (*Chondrus crispus*), and other sea vegetables, such as dulse, nori, arame, hijiki, and wakame, are all very high in iodine. In fact, kelp not only supplies the thyroid with all the iodine it requires but also contains many other important nutrients, such as protein, essential fatty acids, sodium and potassium salts, and other minerals, including trace elements—minerals required in tiny amounts—essential for the thyroid and the rest of the body. Irish moss is closely related to kelp and supplies abundant quantities of iodine and trace elements.

In Japanese cultures, where diets are high in kelp and other sea vegetables, thyroid disease is virtually unknown, but is on the increase in Japanese whose diets are becoming more westernized.

— *Recommended dosage:* 125 mL sea vegetables daily, measure after soaking.

HOMEOPATHIC REMEDIES

A number of homeopathic remedies have a long history of use in thyroid problems. All homeopathic remedies need to be taken at least 20 minutes before or after eating. Pure water, however, does not interfere with their action.

• **Thyroidinum, 7C; Spongia tostada, 6 to 12C;** and **Natrum muriaticum, 6 to 12C,** all regulate the thyroid. Choose one of these remedies and take three pellets, or 10 to 15 drops, two to three times daily.

• **Sepia, 6C to 12C.** Homeopaths often prescribe sepia for menopausal or other hormone-related symptoms. Women who can benefit from sepia commonly have symptoms such as liver spots, dry eyes, cold hands and feet, dryness of the skin and mucous membranes (throat, lungs, vagina, intestines), irritability, and fatigue. These women are also apt to have low thyroid and low adrenal function. The usual dosage is three pellets, or 10 to 15 drops, two to three times daily.

• Consult the list of homeopathic remedies for menopausal support given in Chapter 6, as some of these may be useful for your particular symptoms.

Specific plants have been observed to affect the thyroid.

• **Siberian ginseng (*Eleutherococcus senticosus*)** is an excellent general tonic and adrenal support.

— *Recommended dosage:* 100 to 150 mg standardized solid extract (4:1) twice daily; 1 to 2 g of the dried herb daily.

• **Ashwagandha (*Withania Sominifera*)**, a great adaptogenic herb mentioned in the adrenal support section, has been proven helpful for people with low thyroid function. Adrenal support in general will help to stabilize the function of the thyroid.

— *Recommended dosage:* 2 to 4 capsules daily.

For more information on adrenal support, see Chapter 3.

GLANDULAR SUPPLEMENTS

Supplements containing carefully processed animal thyroid gland tissue are sold in health food stores. They are extremely low in thyroid hormones but do contain proteins that help the thyroid rebuild itself. When used in combination with the nutritional support required for the thyroid, they are suitable for people with mild hypothyroidism. Most glandular supplements are combined with kelp and the essential vitamins and minerals required for good thyroid nutrition.

— *Recommended dosage:* 50 to 150 mg daily, unless advised otherwise by your health care practitioner.

Treatment for Clinical Hypothyroidism

When thyroid hormone levels have decreased to the point that lab results are abnormal, most people require supplemental support from thyroid hormones for a time, until the other glandular imbalances are corrected.

Synthetic thyroxin (T4), under the names Levothyroxine or Synthroid, is the most commonly prescribed drug for hypothyroidism. These medications fool the pituitary into thinking the thyroid is functioning properly, so TSH levels usually normalize in cases of hypothyroidism. However this does *not* mean that the thyroid is getting stronger. On the contrary. For the thyroid, having this drug in the body is analogous to you having someone come in to do your housework. Why exert yourself to help out if someone else is doing the work for you? When T4 is given, the thyroid feels the same. It sits back and becomes even slower. That is why most allopathic doctors tell patients that once they are on thyroid medication, they will always be on thyroid medication.

Yet it is possible to wean yourself away from thyroid medications once the underlying imbalances—adrenal fatigue, dysbiosis, liver congestion, nutritional and dietary deficiencies, and bowel toxicity—are addressed. I do not recommend that someone who has been taking prescription thyroid hormones attempt this weaning on their own. Find a naturopathic doctor or holistically oriented medical doctor in your area to oversee the process.

While you are still on medication, you may also wish to consider switching to desiccated natural thyroid. It contains all the thyroid hormones, thereby providing hormonal support in the form most similar to that which the thyroid produces on its own. For this reason it is preferred by naturopathic physicians and complementary medical doctors. Most medical doctors are not familiar with desiccated thyroid because synthetic hormones have become more popular. However, my experience has been that when patients request a change in their medication to this preferred form, most doctors are willing to monitor the results to ensure effectiveness.

A final note: please have your thyroid levels checked regularly if you are taking Synthroid or Levothyroxine. It is very common for menopausal women to develop medication-induced hyperactive thyroid without exhibiting any of the symptoms of thyroid hyperactivity. This can have an extremely negative effect on the heart and bones.

Specific Treatment Recommendations for Functional Hyperthyroidism

The general guidelines given for thyroid support and for hypothyroidism, including daily intake of sea vegetables, all apply in hyperthyroidism as well.

The homeopathic remedy thyroidinum, taken at a higher potency than for hypothyroidism, and a number of botanical remedies are also appropriate.

• **Thyroidinum, 9C to 12C,** suppresses thyroid activity. Take three pellets two to three times daily.

• **Astragalus (*Astragalus membranaceus*)** is a Chinese herb that strengthens the natural defences of the body. Astragalus root tones the immune system, cardiovascular system, and the liver and adrenal glands. Research reported in Chinese journals demonstrates that it effectively inhibits chronic active hepatitis, hyperthyroidism, insomnia, and other conditions.[3]

    — *Recommended dosage:* 250 to 500 mg solid extract (4:1) two to three times daily.

• **Passion flower (*Passiflora incarnata*)** is a tonic herb with sedative action that helps decrease many of the symptoms of an overactive thyroid: anxiety, tension, irritability, insomnia, and nervousness. It also relaxes the muscles. Its sedative effects are not strong enough to interfere with the alertness of people who need to remain active and awake.

    — *Recommended dosage:* 150 to 200 mg solid extract (4:1) twice daily.

• **Siberian ginseng (*Eleutherococcus senticosus*).** The excellent toning effect of this herb on the adrenals has already been discussed several times. For more information on this plant, see Chapter 3.

    — *Recommended dosage:* as for functional hypothyroidism.

When hyperthyroidism is due to an autoimmune imbalance, immune system modulators such as Moducare can be beneficial. For more information on the immune system, see page 53.

Treatment for Clinical Hyperthyroidism

When a patient is medically diagnosed with hyperthyroidism, the symptoms are usually severe enough to warrant immediate attention. In these cases, it is necessary to use the commonly prescribed medications, methimazole or propylthiouracil.

However, it is usually possible to decrease and eventually stop the medications once the liver, immune system, and adrenal glands are supported and we suggest that three months before decreasing the use of medication, the patient begin taking astragalus, passion flower and Moducare, and begin implementing the recommendations given here and in Chapter 3 for bowel, liver, adrenal, and thyroid support. As in the case of clinical hypothyroidism, we strongly advise you to seek out the care of a naturopathic or holistically oriented medical doctor.

Now that we have considered the thyroid in some detail, let's look at another important player in the hormonal symphony orchestra, the ovaries. They too turn out to have a relationship with the thyroid.

THE OVARIES

Pity the ovaries! They are usually the organs that get the "bad rap" during menopause and in other hormone-related disorders. True, they definitely play an important role, but as you can see, they are only one player in the orchestra. The ovaries produce and discharge ova, the female reproductive cells, or eggs, at ovulation. They also secrete female and male sexual hormones. They are directly influenced by the hypothalamus and the pituitary. In naturopathic medicine we also observe an indirect relationship between the ovaries and the thyroid gland. One of the reasons may be that next to the thyroid, the ovaries contain the greatest concentration of iodine in the female body, so when iodine is deficient we see effects in both organs.

Ovaries start to join in with the hormonal orchestra at puberty; since they are still maturing at the time, they may be implicated in some wild

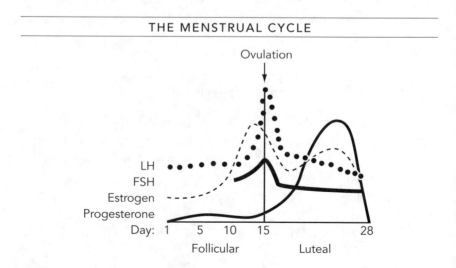

THE MENSTRUAL CYCLE

Ovulation

LH
FSH
Estrogen
Progesterone
Day: 1   5   10   15   28
       Follicular   Luteal

hormonal fluctuations and cause quite a few discordant notes. But things eventually settle down for most women, and the orchestra becomes more harmonious in its playing of the monthly cycle for the next three decades.

The Menstrual Cycle

In order to have a greater understanding of the hormonal fluctuations involved in the transitional years, it is important to know what happens during the menstrual cycle. The cycle is divided into the follicular phase and the luteal phase, and it is regulated by complex interactions between the hypothalamus, pituitary, and ovaries.

The hypothalamus directs the pituitary to secrete two hormones that are directly involved in the menstrual cycle: follicle stimulating hormone (FSH) and luteinizing hormone (LH). These in turn stimulate the ovaries to produce estrogens, progesterone, and androgens. The hypothalamus is in turn affected by these sex hormones and adjusts its instructions to the pituitary accordingly. When there is clear communication between the glands the hormones are in balance. Normally all hormones are released in short bursts every one to three hours so as to maintain constant levels in the blood.

DAYS 1 TO 5: MENSTRUATION

Normally, menstruation occurs the first five days of the cycle. This monthly bleeding takes place because of the sharp decline in estrogen and progesterone levels at the end of the luteal phase if pregnancy did not occur—these hormones maintain the womb's endometrial lining, the capillary-rich tissue in which a fertilized embryo implants itself. If no embryo implants, estrogen and progesterone levels fall, and the endometrium sloughs off, tearing capillaries and causing bleeding. Low estrogen levels promote FSH secretion, stimulating ovarian structures called follicles to begin secreting more estrogen. As well, LH stimulates the growth to maturity of new ova at this time.

DAYS 6 TO 14: FOLLICULAR STAGE

The ova continue to mature during the follicular stage. After the menstrual period and until ovulation, FSH (primarily) and LH stimulate the ovarian follicles to produce estrogen to support the growth of the endometrium. The rising estrogen levels trigger a mid-cycle LH surge, which causes ovulation some time between Days 12 and 14 of the cycle. In ovulation, the follicle that has been nurturing the growing egg ruptures, and the egg is released into the abdominal cavity, to be swept up by special structures at the ends of the fallopian tubes, canals which lead into the womb.

DAYS 14 TO 28: LUTEAL STAGE

The luteal stage occurs after ovulation and lasts approximately 12 days. Progesterone levels are higher relative to estrogen, as the ruptured ovarian follicle (corpus luteum) secretes large amounts of progesterone, needed to prepare the endometrial lining for implantation of a fertilized egg. If the egg is not fertilized, both estrogen and progesterone levels drop. When the uterus begins to shed the endometrial lining, menstruation begins. The menstrual cycle continues for roughly 30 years, from puberty to menopause, unless pregnancy or hormonal problems interrupt it. Any extreme ups and downs in the estrogen/progesterone ratio, when either hormone is excessive or deficient, results in symptoms.

The Liver, Bowel, and Thyroid: Their Influence on the Menstrual Cycle

Other organs that affect the menstrual cycle via their effects on female hormone levels are the liver, the large intestine, and the thyroid. Remember, sex hormones are broken down in the liver, a process that is necessary to help pull down the appropriate end of the hormonal teeter-totter on schedule. To review, the liver's main function is to detoxify the body, and the more toxic the large intestine and other organs, the larger the burden on the liver. An overburdened liver has a decreased ability to break down excess sex hormones, especially estrogen. This can cause a build-up of excess estrogen in the system and a variety of uncomfortable hormone-related symptoms.

Adequate thyroid gland function is necessary for the production of progesterone, according to researcher L. Rubel. In addition, both progesterone and thyroid hormone can be considered primary regulatory hormones. Both of them regulate metabolism, have a normalizing, antistress action on the pituitary gland, and are consumed by stress. In addition, each has a supportive and promoting action on the other.

As you can see, promoting the health of the thyroid is truly an important aspect of achieving optimal health and making the transitional years as smooth as possible. In the next chapter, we will begin a detailed examination of the transitional years themselves.

5

WOMEN IN TRANSITION: PERIMENOPAUSE AND MENOPAUSE

"As the art and science of medicine advances and becomes more eclectic in its approach, gathering from all systems the best and safest treatments, medical practitioners who want to meet the needs of the times must be individuals committed to progress and truth. The light of tomorrow within them must modify the light of today."—Karen Jensen, N.D.

In the last chapter, we introduced the idea of the hormonal symphony orchestra, made up of the various glands responsible for producing our hormones. As with any orchestra, when the musicians of the hormonal symphony are just learning a new tune, the music can be somewhat discordant for a time. As the orchestra learns to adjust to the new "hormonic melody" that comes with each stage of life—puberty, ovulation, menses, pregnancy, perimenopause, and menopause—many women experience various unwanted symptoms.

This chapter examines the nature of the perimenopausal and menopausal shifts and looks at possible accompanying symptoms.

WHAT IS PERIMENOPAUSE?

Many women are not aware that hormones can start to shift as early as 35 years of age. Usually, however, the hormonal shift starts three to six years before the last period, as the body approaches menopause. The relatively consistent up-and-down rhythm your hormones followed during your reproductive years is now shifting as wildly as it did during puberty. Sometimes estrogen will be high, progesterone low, other times progesterone will be high and estrogen low, and still other times, deficiencies or excesses of both will be present. "Oh fun!" you say—but enjoy the ride, and know that there are things you can do to make the transition smoother for yourself.

Some women will start to notice the hormonal changes through such symptoms as menstrual irregularities, breast tenderness, brain fog, insomnia, weight gain, hot flashes, or intermittent sweats, mood changes, fatigue, or changes in vaginal secretions. For some the changes may be subtle, while others may experience full blown perimenopausal symptoms by the time they are forty. If the process is this advanced at such a relatively young age, diet and lifestyle history, stress levels experienced to date, and the number of years hormones were manipulated with birth control pills will probably all have had a role to play.

Menstrual irregularity is one of the more common perimenopausal symptoms. The periods start to become erratic, some starting earlier, some later—the odd one may even be missed. Sounds like puberty, when things are just starting up, doesn't it? A study done in 1965 found that the symptoms of perimenopause are closer to those of pubescent girls than to those of postmenopausal women. Well, we survived puberty didn't we? So this too shall pass.

The ups and downs of the perimenopause are often mistakenly called menopausal symptoms, but let's not get hung up on semantics. The bottom line is that most women will probably experience symptoms to varying degrees for a few years before menstruation stops completely and for a few years after. For some postmenopausal women, the symptoms go on for many years.

MENOPAUSE

At the physical level, menopause is defined as total cessation of the menses for six months or more, generally accompanied by symptoms. The hormonal fluctuations now are not so dramatic as during the perimenopause; the orchestra has become more familiar with the new melody that it is expected to play. In most of us, however, it will still be experiencing some difficulty:

- Only ten to fifteen percent of women have no discernible symptoms at the menopause.
- Ten to fifteen percent of women have very severe symptoms at this time, sometimes severe enough that they require hospitalization.
- Seventy to eighty percent of women have mild to severe symptoms.

What Does Menopause Feel Like?

The major sign of the menopause, of course, is the cessation of the monthly menstrual period. In many traditional societies this was considered the time in which a woman came into her full power and wisdom. In the research for this book, we also learned of one tribe in which the women believed that if they stopped menstruating they would die. These women would menstruate well into their eighties. See Chapter 10 for more on the power of attitude.

Menopause can also bring the following symptoms in its wake:

- Acceleration of the aging process—overnight wrinkles appear (T, A)
- Anxiety or panic attacks (A, C)
- Bloating and indigestion, gas (T, C)
- Increase in blood pressure or cholesterol (A, T, L)
- Bone pain (often associated with osteoporosis/osteopenia) (A)
- Inability to breathe deeply (air hunger) (A)
- "Crawly" skin sensations, especially of the lower limbs (restless leg syndrome)
- Low energy (A, T, L, C)
- Increased facial hair, particularly around the chin and upper lip
- Heart palpitations (T, A)
- Hot feet, worse in bed (L)
- Hot flushes and/or night sweats (L, C)
- Insomnia, or interrupted sleep (A, T, C, L)
- Itching around the vaginal area, with or without discharge
- Joint and muscle aches and pains (L, T)
- Diminished libido, painful intercourse (A, T)
- Lightheadedness, dizzy spells, vertigo (A)
- Memory problems brain fog (A, C)
- Mood changes, depression, irritability, or anger (L, A)
- Migraine headaches (L, C)
- New food or environmental sensitivities or allergies (C, L, A)

- Urinary incontinence (worse with coughing or laughing)
- Vaginal or urinary tract infections (C)
- Weight gain, usually around or on the abdomen, hips, and breasts (T)

Some of you will probably recognized that many of these symptoms, while commonly attributed to perimenopause or menopause, are actually associated (from the naturopathic perspective) with adrenal dysfunction (A), thyroid dysfunction(T), liver congestion(L), and *Candida*/intestine problems (C). Please note that beside each symptom noted above, I have included the organs which, when are imbalanced, cause these symptoms.

We're outta here! We won't accept that these things have to happen in our lives. They don't have to happen in yours either. *There is life after and during the transitional years!*

We don't become "dried up"; we spend one-third of our lives in the postmenopausal years. Let's embrace the wisdom and power our transitions have given us and accept that *menopause is not a disease* that needs to be treated with drugs for years on end.

We commonly hear that there is so much more focus on the treatment of menopause today than in our parents' generation because women are living longer and thus the so-called menopause-related diseases are on the rise. Clearly this does not make sense. Karen's grandmother and a great-grandmother lived as long, if not longer, than most women do today; we are sure many of you could say the same.

It is difficult not to get caught up in the attitudes fostered by the medical profession and the media, that women in this stage of life are drying up, wrinkling and shrinking away. The menopausal transition is seen as a pathology, a disease of the endocrine system that needs to be treated. Certainly, symptoms are more common nowadays. The quality of our food is extremely compromised, being deficient in nutrients and containing added hormones and antibiotics. This, coupled with environmental toxins, has a profound effect on our hormonal system. The problem, however, is with the food supply and environment, not with menopause itself. Just as many women are now working to reclaim the transition of menarche (the onset of menstruation), and give it the honour and respect it is due, so we can change our attitudes to the menopausal transition. As we do so, others' attitudes will change as well.

MENOPAUSE AND AGING

Some of you may find this difficult to believe, but there are many women (I see some in my practice) who have such a difficult time with the decline of their youthfulness (their perky body, unwrinkled skin, youthful hair) that they will not even let the word "menopause" escape their lips—they associate aging with unbearable loss. These women have totally "bought into" the standards of appearance set by media images of glamorous models and actresses. When we accept the *false images* propagated by the media, changes in our physical appearance can spark severe emotional difficulties.

WE ARE WHO WE ARE

To any of you who may be in this predicament, we offer the following ideas.

We are who we are: *we are soul*, that beautiful, incredible, divine spark of the Creator in each and every one of us. The physical body is simply equivalent to a rental vehicle that carries us around throughout this lifetime. Like any vehicle, the better it is maintained, the better it will treat us. As our vehicle gets on in years it just means that the soul has been riding through life for a longer time and has had more opportunity to learn from the many experiences the years have provided.

What happens when a well-maintained car goes by? It's a head turner, right?

Granted, life can be hard, not only on our physical vehicle but also on our minds and emotions (some healers think of these as the mental and emotional bodies), and all our bodies deserve our gratitude and thanks for carrying us through our lives. When you see yourself in the mirror, imagine each wrinkle as a lesson learned and greater wisdom gained; give thanks for this gift of life. And for every one of those wrinkles, give yourself a hug—because you earned each and every one on this journey of life. Congratulations!

As we grow in wisdom and love, our inner beauty is reflected outwardly, ever more strongly. Don't let the packaging fool you; it will age, guaranteed, and some people will see only the ravages of age as you walk by—but some never see the true beauty of soul.

Those who know how to see know that true beauty is reflected in the eyes: the windows of the soul.

The picture below gives us a good opportunity to ponder our own perceptions. Do you see an old woman or a young woman? Can you see both at once?

OLD WOMAN/YOUNG WOMAN

"Reality is but an image of another picture not yet seen."—Plato

THE SEASONS OF SEXUALITY

On the long, often intense, days spent writing this book I (Karen) would almost daily take a couple of hours off to run and hike up a mountain, recharging my energy with the beauty and vitality of the Rockies. In the days before one of these outings I had been debating whether I should include in this book anything about the change in sexual desires I have observed in almost every woman close to menopause whom I see in my practice or know personally. Most books I have read support the perspective that decreased libido in relation to menopause isn't normal, and that this too can be fixed with hormone replacement therapy (HRT) and attitude. I have never felt comfortable with this perspective, but wondered if I was the only one out there who felt it was completely normal for the sexual desire to also go through transition during this stage of life, because sexual desire is, after all, hormonally driven.

On this hike, it seemed as though overnight autumn had come into the air; the hot days of summer were being replaced by the cooler days of fall, which would prepare us for the winter months. Suddenly I saw that the natural change of seasons could represent the different stages we go through in our sexuality:

- **Spring** is the season in which the Chinese perspective holds that yin, or watery, energy is decreasing and the yang, or fiery, energy is increasing. Spring represents the beginning of a new cycle; it corresponds to puberty and its hormonal fluctuations preparing us for the reproductive years and new birth.

- **Summer** is the season in which yang energy predominates, representing a highly energetic, vital time: the reproductive years.

- **Autumn.** In autumn, yang energy decreases and yin energy increases. Autumn is rich in colour and texture, and carries a hint of sadness as we leave the hot, vibrant days of summer. Autumn corresponds to the menopausal years. The autumn years then prepare us for the quieter, more introspective months of winter.

- **Winter** is the season in which yin energy almost completely predominates: these are the postmenopausal years. The kidney is the organ associated with the winter season in Chinese medicine; winter's snow and ice is white, which corresponds to our own experience of greying hair. It is a time to prepare for the start of another cycle: helping prepare our grandchildren for adult life.

All of us, men and women alike, go through these seasons of sexuality. The transitions need not be threatening to us if we remember that sexual expression is simply a way in which we share love and affection with our partner—and the ways we choose to express ourselves sexually can change. Lovemaking that includes intercourse is a means of reproduction and also involves a very high degree of intimacy, through which we express our love. However, intimacy does not have to mean intercourse. Sexual expression can be accomplished in so many ways, and the right way for each person will vary throughout life. When I see an older couple walking down the street holding hands, and observe the way they look at each other with love, complete acceptance, and respect, I see deep intimate expression. When the changes of the sexual seasons reverberate in our and our partners' lives, the most important thing we can do is to learn to accept them and then find new ways to express to one another the love that was once given voice in the heat of passion.

The menopausal years are a time of variability—one day is cold and crisp, the next day boasts such brilliant sunshine that it is enough to quicken your step and make you feel that you are experiencing summer again.

Physiologically speaking, once any unpleasant symptoms of the hormonal changes have improved, and natural hormonal support or HRT is in place, the libido will rise somewhat, *but it won't be those crazy days of summer again*.

Learn to embrace the seasons of sexuality, and as you find yourself in the autumn—or even the winter—seek out new and creative ways to express yourself sexually, ways that authentically reflect who you are at this time in your life.

Simply learning to flow with change, as we have been discussing here, and working towards overall optimal health, as discussed in previous chapters, will often alleviate symptoms. Symptoms that persist probably need to be addressed in a more focused way. In this chapter we will discuss natural support for the most common menopausal symptoms: hot flushes and night sweats, insomnia, and restless leg syndrome. If you are sad about the loss of your libido, please see "testosterone" in Chapter 6.

HOT FLUSHES AND NIGHT SWEATS

Hot flushes or flashes, sometimes accompanied by night sweats, are the most common complaint of women in the perimenopausal years. It is estimated that a third of women have hot flashes by three years before menopause; by one year before, almost half of women experience them. In 20 percent of women with hot flushes, they persist for up to four years after menopause.

The intensity of the flushes and the areas of the body most affected vary from woman to woman. For instance, I didn't experience hot flushes as typically described. Instead, frequently my feet would heat up the minute I went to bed. I always knew I was in for a rough night when this happened. I looked up the symptom in all of the menopause books I had, and asked my medical doctor and other women about it, but no one had heard of hot feet associated with menopause. A few years later, my mom and I were talking about her experience during menopause, and she mentioned that her sister didn't have any of the same symptoms as her but just kept complaining about "these darn hot feet!"

So remember that symptoms during this time can be very individual—some of you may experience unique manifestations of the changes in the hormonic symphony.

No one really knows what causes hot flushes. It is postulated that the main factor is elevated FSH and LH levels, caused by the pituitary's efforts to stimulate the ovaries to produce more estrogen. At menopause, the ovary does not respond to the expectations of the hypothalamus because it has too few follicle cells remaining—the cells that produce estrogen and progesterone. FSH can reach higher levels than are normally reached in the reproductive years; LH also increases above the previous norm. The increased heat and sweating occurs because of the body's effort to cool down.

Women have different attitudes about these heat spells; some welcome them and see the hot flashes as a useful way to get excess heat out of the body now that they are no longer menstruating. Traditional Chinese medical theory states that deficient yin leads to increased heat (yang) in the blood, and the hot flashes give these women a strong signal that their body needs rebalancing. Some women also use the heat surges to help them "flash" into menopause easier and faster. Others are simply annoyed at their hot flashes because of the social embarrassment they feel and the general inconvenience and discomfort involved.

Night sweats can be debilitating for some women during the menopausal transition. Night sweats typically involve waking up to find one's night clothes and bed linen soaked in sweat. Some women may get back to sleep, and other than feeling a little damp in the morning, they are not greatly inconvenienced by night sweats. Others are unable to get back to sleep and spend most of the night tossing and turning. In these cases, there are often factors other than hormonal imbalance at work, such as adrenal imbalance, deficient yin chi, intestinal microbial imbalances, and the like. These factors will be discussed in more detail in the section below on insomnia.

In any case, not sleeping leaves these women physically and emotionally drained.

Many women who take HRT find relief from the discomforts of hot flushes and night sweats. If you are reconsidering synthetic hormone use, cannot take HRT because of contraindications in your family history, or simply want to use natural therapies, here are some specific suggestions that can help with hot flushes and night sweats. In addition, please refer to Chapter 6 for information on natural hormonal support.

Hot Flushes and Night Sweats: General Tips

To treat your hot flushes and night sweats, start off with following simple changes and see whether they bring relief. If not, you'll want to try stronger remedies such as homeopathics and botanicals, discussed below.

- **Avoid alcohol.** Many women become very alcohol-sensitive during the transitional years. Alcohol increases heat in the body and for some, even very small amounts will cause night sweats. Alcohol is implicated in more serious difficulties as well. A recent study published in the *Journal of the American Medical Association* stated that women who have two to five alcoholic drinks per day have a 41 percent increase in their risk of developing breast cancer.

- **Avoid highly spiced foods.** Garlic, peppers, and the like, especially at the evening meal, may exacerbate symptoms.

- **Exercise regularly.** A study of 900 menopausal women showed that those who exercised regularly (a minimum of 3.5 hours per week) had milder and less frequent hot flashes.

- **Detoxify and support the liver.** See Chapter 3 for complete instructions.

- **Try nutritional supplementation.** Vitamin E (400 to 800 IU per day), vitamin C (500 to 1 000 mg per day) and beta carotene (25 000 to 50 000 mg per day) can help with hot flashes, or keep it simple with FemmEssentials and MenoSense.

- **Avoid polyester fabrics.** Polyester fabrics make you perspire more easily even if you are not going through hormonal changes. Use only natural fabrics for clothing, and cotton sheets, cotton or wool blankets, and cotton night clothes.

Homeopathic Remedies
for Hot Flushes and Night Sweats

Please note that the homeopathic remedies discussed below can help with hot flushes if they are matched as closely as possible to your individual symptoms. These remedies also offer support for other menopause-related symptoms. There are stars beside the most common remedies for hot flushes.

All remedies are taken within the potency range of 12C to 30C unless stated otherwise. They need to be taken at least 20 minutes before or after any food. Having pure water with a remedy is fine. If you prefer drops to pellets, one pellet is equivalent to five drops. For example, if the dosage given below is three pellets, take fifteen drops.

If you fit the symptoms of more than one remedy, you can alternate two to three remedies at the same time: take one remedy; two hours later another, and so on. We suggest that no more than three homeopathic remedies be taken at the same time.

• **Belladonna (deadly nightshade)** benefits those who experience sudden intense flushes of heat accompanied by a reddened face. Sometimes throbbing in the head or behind the eyes occurs with the flushes.

> — *Recommended dosage:* 3 pellets as needed, up to every hour if necessary, for symptoms.

• **Calcarea carbonica (carbonate of lime)** is a common remedy for women experiencing hormone-related conditions. Typical symptoms indicating a need for calcarea carbonica include sweats that come mostly on the head, fearfulness, and arthritic complaints.

> — *Recommended dosage:* 3 pellets three to five times daily, or take as needed, up to every two hours if necessary.

• **Cimicifuga (black cohosh).** The type of person who benefits from this remedy often experiences a restless and unhappy state of mind, may feel troubled or be irritable, cannot sleep, may have a sinking sensation in the stomach, may sometimes have pain in the left side or fullness and dull aching in the top of the head. Note: some of you may be familiar with the herb black cohosh (*Cimicifuga racemosa*), from which the homeopathic remedy is made. Do not, however, confuse the homeopathic application of cimicifuga with its botanical, or herbal, application. They are different and not interchangeable.

> — *Recommended dosage:* 3 to 5 pellets daily, more during the night if needed.

• **Gelsemium (yellow jasmine)** benefits those who often feel "dull, dumb, and droopy" as hormonal changes occur. Other symptoms that indicate a need for gelsemium include headaches with rushes of blood to the head creating a sensation of fullness or a "weird" head feeling, dizzi-

ness, a bruised feeling or throbbing in the head, dimness of sight, and
drowsiness. Nausea may be present as well.

— *Recommended dosage:* 3 pellets three to five times daily.

- **Lachesis* (venom of bushmaster snake).** Don't let the source of this
remedy scare you—this is not a promotion for "snake oil." Lachesis is one
of the most common remedies used by homeopaths, naturopathic doctors,
and complementary medical doctors in the treatment of menopausal
symptoms such as hot flushes, burning sensations on the top of the head,
profuse flow if still menstruating, lightheadedness, vertigo or fainting
spells, and increased flatulence. Some women who need lachesis experience headaches on waking because of congestion of blood flow. Emotional
symptoms include being bossy, overbearing, nervous or anxious, or jealous,
or having fits of rage.

This remedy may be needed intermittently or regularly during
menopause.

— *Recommended dosage:* 3 pellets every few hours if hot flushes are
extreme; lachesis can be taken for insomnia or hot flashes up to
every hour if necessary. Take as needed until things settle. Then
use 3 pellets three to five times daily if required.

- **Lycopodium (club moss)** is an excellent liver remedy. Women who
need this remedy suffer from a lack of confidence and tend to be very
indecisive. They might also carry a great deal of suppressed anger that
may come out in various ways. Physical symptoms include poor memory
and "fuzzy" brain, digestive difficulties such as gas and bloating, and a
pronounced energy dive in the late afternoon. Many of their ongoing
aches and pains, such as headaches, neck or shoulder pain, are worse on
the right side.

— *Recommended dosage:* 3 pellets three to five times daily.

- **Natrum muriaticum (sodium chloride).** This remedy helps those
who are emotionally sensitive and as a result become introverted. Many
people who benefit from this remedy carry deep emotional pain caused
by events in the past, may carry grudges, have difficulty crying except
at movies or when listening to sad music, and have difficulty with
being intimate. Physical symptoms indicating a need for this remedy
include feeling worse in warm air, hair loss, hair growth on the face,

vaginal dryness, frequent warm flushes, and headaches before, during, or after menstruation.

— *Recommended dosage:* 3 pellets three to five times daily.

• **Nux vomica/colubrina (poison nut).** Women who can benefit from this remedy have a tendency to overdo things and drive themselves too hard, especially at this time of life. They can get grumpy and irritable, sometimes harbouring a lot of anger. Physical symptoms include headaches, constipation with or without nausea, waking frequently at night, and backaches.

— *Recommended dosage:* 3 pellets three to five times daily.

• **Pulsatilla (wind flower)** is a common remedy for women who are very emotionally sensitive, especially during times of hormonal change such as puberty, the menopausal years, or menstruation. People who need pulsatilla are easily brought to tears, have very changeable moods, get upset at small things, lack energy, need lots of caring and support, and feel hot all the time. Their feelings of being hot worsen in bed; they tend to feel more comfortable outdoors in fresh air.

— *Recommended dosage:* 3 pellets three times daily; use again at night if needed, up to 1 pellet every two to three hours.

• **Sanguinaria (bloodroot)** is a remedy for women who flow profusely during the transitional years (or at other times) and who experience vertigo; rushes of blood to the head, sometimes with a buzzing in the ears and flushes of heat; headaches beginning in the back of the head and passing over the right eye; headaches with nausea and chilliness, sometimes accompanied by vomiting; and acrid vaginal discharge with offensive odor. People who need sanguinaria feel better in the open air or after lying down or sleeping.

— *Recommended dosage:* 3 pellets three to five times daily; the remedy can be used more often if necessary for headaches or heavy flow.

• **Sepia* (cuttlefish ink).** Along with lachesis, sepia is one of the most common menopausal remedies. Some of the symptoms that indicate a need for this remedy include liver spots and other liver congestive signs; dryness of the mouth, eyes, vagina, and skin; cold hands and feet; possible low thyroid and adrenal function with low blood pressure; palpitations of the heart that are worse in the evening or in bed; excessive talkativeness; congestion of blood (varicose veins, poor circulation); flushes of heat at night as well as in the daytime; darting pains in the head; exhaustion; and a feeling of not having enough energy to listen to anyone else's concerns or problems. People who need sepia often don't have anything left to give— they are "burned out" by life and very tired; they can be irritable or depressed because they feel so drained. Sepia brings their equilibrium back.

— *Recommended dosage:* 3 pellets three to five times per day. If hot flashes are persistent, the remedy can be taken every few hours. Women whose symptoms are mainly in the emotional area sometimes feel better taking sepia 200C. In this case, the dose should be 3 pellets once or twice weekly.

• **Thuja (arbor vitae).** Women who experience profuse night sweats and do not find relief from other remedies or the general supplement recommendations below will often benefit from thuja.

— *Recommended dosage:* 3 pellets three times daily; increase as needed for night sweats.

The following botanical remedies are very helpful if you suffer from hot flashes or night sweats. You will find these herbs discussed in detail in Chapter 6, which deals with both synthetic and hormone replacement therapy and natural hormonal support. MenoSense or meno are combined herbal formulas that can be used for support during the menopausal years.

• Black cohosh (*Cimicifuga racemosa*)
• Chaste tree (*Vitex agnus-castus*)
• Dong quai (*Angelica sinensis*)
• Licorice (*Glycyrrhiza glabra*)

INSOMNIA

During the perimenopausal years, many women become "light" sleepers, waking frequently for no apparent reason and finding themselves sometimes unable to get back to sleep. Often women who go to their medical doctor with this complaint are treated with antidepressants when the real cause of the difficulty is hormonal changes.

In traditional Chinese medicine, insomnia is caused by deficiencies of yin energy (deficient "blood of the heart"). The spirit (*shen*) that governs the mind needs the yin energy for stability, otherwise the mind becomes unstable and begins to wander. Insomnia, scattered thoughts, confusion, loss of memory, excess or no excitement, irrational behaviour, depression, poor circulation, aversion to heat, hot flashes, and in very severe cases, mental illness, can result from the instability created by deficient yin.

If you are consistently waking at the same time every night, this could indicate an imbalance in a specific organ system/energy complex. Traditional Chinese medicine has developed a "clock," shown on the next page, that charts the peak activity time for each organ/energy complex. This medical system also suggests that the organ's time of minimum activity occurs 12 hours after its peak interval.

To enhance yin energy, it is important to reduce liver congestion (see Chapter 3) and yang (heating) foods that deplete yin energy, such as coffee, alcohol, tobacco, animal products (use in moderation, as they stimulate liver heat), cloves, ginger, garlic, and other hot spices.

Recent research published in the Journal of the American Medical Association June 2002 found that even a week of mild sleep deprivation had a negative effect on hormone levels. In addition results showed that a lack of sleep can contribute to high blood pressure, heart disease, diabetes and inflammatory responses. For those of you who experience or have experienced insomnia, you know how debilitating lack of sleep can be and how it affects every area of your life.

You can also use the general tips and remedies given below to address sleep problems. As has already been emphasized with respect to hot flushes, remedies for insomnia work best when you are also addressing your individual areas of weakness, be they in the liver, bowel, adrenal, or thyroid, with the recommendations given in Chapters 2, 3, and 4.

Insomnia: General Tips

Start with these basic changes to restore restful sleep. If you need further support, see the homeopathic and botanical remedies described below.

• **Cut out stimulants.** Avoid caffeinated beverages (coffee, pop, tea), especially past noon.

CHINESE "ORGAN CLOCK"

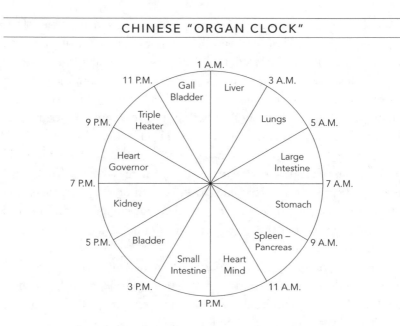

- **Do not eat a large meal late in the evening (after 7 p.m.).** In fact, try to avoid any snacking after your dinner. You may want to try a glass of fermented soy milk or Women's Whey with fermented soy before bed. Many women find that soy products encourage restful sleep.

- **Take your calcium supplement at bedtime.**

- **If you wake frequently to urinate, keep your fluid intake high during the day** and avoid drinking water or herbal teas in the evenings.

- **Exercise regularly.** You will see this suggestion in every self-help category. Exercise is not an option! Studies show that it helps induce restful sleep.

- **Take time one or two hours before bed to write down all the "to do's" for the next day.** Your mind will settle more easily.

- **Avoid using your television, radio, telephone, or computer** for at least one hour before bedtime. Instead, read a relaxing, "easy" book.

- **Take a hot bath before bed.** If a hot bath does not aggravate your hot flashes, it can be very relaxing, especially with added essential oils such as lavender or chamomile.

• **Apply a few drops of lavender and chamomile essential oil** on the temples and between the eyebrows. Karen has found that if she mixes blue chamomile essential oil in some lotion and applies it over her liver area, her sleep improves immensely. If you show the signs of liver congestion, this technique may also offer some benefit.

• **Take time for meditation, contemplation, or prayer before you retire.** As covered in Chapter 2, optimal health encompasses the physical, emotional, mental, and spiritual aspects of life. Symptoms always involve more than just physical and hormonal factors. Nightly meditation and prayer help you clear your mind and quiet your nervous system. Before your contemplation, ask your higher power for answers and understanding around the sleep disturbances.

Insomnia Remedies

Homeopathic remedies balance the entire system, so it's not uncommon that they help with more than one symptom. I reiterate, the best way to choose a homeopathic remedy is to pick the one that is most closely associated with your overall symptom picture. If you are in doubt, consult a homeopath or other qualified health care practitioner.

• **Chamomilla (German chamomile).** This remedy is for the insomniac who is drowsy but restless on attempting to sleep and lies awake filled with mental agitation, restlessness, and irritability. The person will be emotionally overreactive to life circumstances and other people's actions. This person will also tend to be impatient and somewhat intolerant of being spoken to.

— *Recommended dosage:* 3 pellets three to five times daily as symptoms dictate, and 3 pellets before bed and as required on waking during the night.

• **Coffea cruda (unroasted coffee)** benefits insomnia when the sleepless person is quiet, the senses are all acute, distant noises are heard with great distinctiveness, and the mind is active and busy with plans and ideas. The next day the person will experience brain fatigue and exhaustion. People who benefit from coffea also sometimes experience dull headaches, have a more difficult time getting to sleep after an animated conversation, cannot sleep after 3 a.m., and have great difficulty dealing with noises, odours, and light; they are also very sensitive to touch.

— *Recommended dosage:* 3 pellets before bed and as needed upon awakening.

• **Gelsemium (yellow jasmine).** People who can benefit from gelsemium cannot fully get to sleep even though exhausted. Their urge to continue thinking is uncontrollable and they will often exhibit all the symptoms of nervous as well as physical exhaustion.

— *Recommended dosage:* 3 pellets before bed and then as needed to quiet the mind.

• **Nux vomica/colubrina (poison nut).** People who require this remedy are able to sleep in the evening; they will fall asleep in their chair or upon going to bed but will wake very early (between three and five in the morning) and cannot get back to sleep. They are then very drowsy and tired during the day, feeling more tired than they did before going to bed; sometimes their daytime tiredness is accompanied with a dull headache and tiredness behind the eyes. They will also often have constipation or digestive problems.

— *Recommended dosage:* 3 pellets three to five times daily as symptoms indicate, and 3 pellets before bed and upon waking during the night.

Plants to the rescue! The following botanical remedies for aiding restful sleep are much lower in side effects than prescription tranquilizers and drugs. All are available at most health food stores in convenient capsule form.

• **St. John's wort (*Hypericum perforatum*).** Recent studies have demonstrated that St. John's wort is extremely effective in improving symptoms of anxiety, depression, and feelings of worthlessness. In addition to improving mood, it has also been shown to improve sleep quality. St. John's wort is known in Europe for the treatment of enuresis (bedwetting) and mental symptoms associated with menopause, or "menopausal neurosis," as it is described in the older herbal journals.

— *Recommended dosage:* Take up to 900 mg solid extract standardized to contain from 0.125 to 0.3 percent hypericin daily. I recommend starting with 300 mg one hour before bedtime. If that is not sufficient, take another 300 to 600 mg after dinner. Note: Regularly consuming more than 1 500 mg of standardized St. John's wort extract can increase photosensitivity (sensitivity to light), in which case prolonged exposure to sunlight needs to be avoided.

- **Valerian (*Valeriana officinalis*).** This plant has been shown to improve sleep quality and reduce the time required to get to sleep. It does not cause any "hangover" in the morning, as sleep medications such as benzodiazepines commonly do.
  - *Recommended dosage:* 400 to 700 mg solid root extract (4:1) 30 to 45 minutes before bed. I suggest using valerian capsules rather than tincture, as the taste of the latter is enough to put most people off, unless you like the flavour of dirty socks.

- **Passion flower (*Passiflora incarnata*).** Used alone or in combination with the other sedative herbs listed, passion flower is a mild sedative that reduces anxiety and nervous tension and encourages sleep. It induces normal, undisturbed sleep causing no "hangover." It also has antispasmodic and anti-inflammatory action and is used to treat premenstrual tension, muscle cramping, and inflammatory conditions.
  - *Recommended dosage:* 200 to 400 mg solid extract (4:1) one hour before bed or during the evening.

- **Chamomile (*Matricaria chamomilla*).** Chamomile flowers are a nervous system tonic that reduce anxiety and gently relax the nervous system. They are generally used in tea form; to assist with a restful sleep, take a cup of chamomile tea one to two hours before bed.

- **Skullcap (*Scutellaria lateriflora*); Chinese skullcap (*Scutellaria bicalensis*).** Skullcap is an excellent tonic herb and is commonly used for nervous system complaints. Its flavonoid content is responsible for its effectiveness as an anti-inflammatory, antiviral, antiretroviral, antitumour, and antibacterial agent. In China, skullcap has traditionally been used to "cleanse heat." According to Chinese medicine, insomnia is caused by heat (excess yang) in the heart organ system particularly, but it can be related to excess yang and deficient yin of other organ systems as well.
  - *Recommended dosage:* 5 to 8 g dried root daily.

- **Hops (*Humulus lupulus*).** Hops, in addition to their role in beer brewing, induce sleep and have been used for this purpose for many years. In the past the "hops pillow" was popular for promoting sleep. Hops are also used in the treatment of nervous tension and have been found to contain very high levels of phytoestrogens.

  Recommended dosage: 2 to 5 g solid extract (4:1) of the flowers (strobiles) daily.

- **Griffonia (*Griffonia simplicifolia*)** has, in recent years, attracted the attention of researchers interested in its effect on the nerve transmitter serotonin. Serotonin is the key to many brain functions such as weight problems, depression or insomnia. Griffonia acts by providing the body with an amino acid, 5-HTP that easily crosses the blood-brain barrier and is converted to serotonin in a natural process.

  — *Recommended dosage:* 100 to 200 mg daily to be taken one hour before bedtime.

When Prescription Drugs May Be Necessary

We realize that some of you with chronic sleep problems will have probably tried all of the above suggestions—been there, done that! And indeed, for some of you, menopause-related insomnia will be so debilitating that you may need to use prescription medications for a time until endocrine balance is re-established. We strongly suggest that you discontinue these medications as soon as possible or use them only intermittently when absolutely needed.

Many of the prescription insomnia medications, particularly the benzodiazepines (Diazepam, Halcion), are addictive, and if you take them too long, there is actually a strong withdrawal when you want to stop. Long-term use requires a continued increase in dose to maintain control of symptoms. The side effects of Halcion, such as daytime anxiety, can occur after as few as 10 days of continuous use. Benzodiazepines also interact with many other drugs such as analgesics, antihistamines, and tricyclic antidepressants;

most people are not aware of drug interactions. From a naturopathic perspective, taking a drug to be able to sleep does not address the many and varied underlying cause of the problem.

RESTLESS LEG SYNDROME

I (Karen) would like to end this chapter with a symptom that is very annoying and uncomfortable for women—"restless leg syndrome." The feeling is difficult to describe, but I will try, based on my own experience and the symptoms my patients have described. When restless leg syndrome is present, you want to rip your legs off because of a deep crawly feeling in the legs that forces you to get up and move around or have someone rub deeply. If you weren't able to move it could drive you crazy.

We have found that restless leg syndrome is related to blood sugar imbalances (dys-glycemia) and anemia and/or folic acid deficiency. We recommend a natural iron support such as Floradix Liquid Iron in an herbal base or Aqueous Liver Extract, taken along with 1 mg folic acid per day. Taking 200 to 400 mcg chromium and 400 mg magnesium per day, in combination with a good diet (no refined sugars or grains; lots of whole grains, vegetables, sea vegetables, protein, and fruits) helps balance blood sugar. Once these changes are implemented, the symptoms are generally relieved within a few days.

HORMONE REPLACEMENT THERAPY

"Although analytical approaches to the body and its intake and surroundings have provided for much useful information, such fragmented investigations have also obscured dynamic interrelationships which have an important bearing in medicine."
—Theron Randolph

This chapter deals with the big question in every perimenopausal and menopausal woman's mind: "Will I use hormone replacement therapy or not?" It is divided into two parts: in the first we look at the major hormones whose ups and downs will affect the quality of life of your transitional years; in the second we consider how to give yourself natural hormonal support, or synthetic hormonal support if needed, in the most effective and safest way possible.

By this point in the book, of course, you understand that there is much, much more to hormonal health during the menopausal transition than just deciding for or against hormone replacement therapy (HRT). Nevertheless, this decision is an important one, and it will have consequences in our lives and the lives of others.

We all come to menopause with different histories, different genetic strengths and weaknesses, different personal situations, and at different points on the journey to optimal health. No one can make the decision for us about whether to use HRT. This chapter aims to give you the information and resources you need to make an informed decision for yourself.

PART ONE: THE HORMONES
To begin, let's look at the hormones our body makes, day in and day out.

Steroid hormones are derived from cholesterol and include the sex hormones as well as the adrenal hormones cortisol and aldosterone. As you can see in the "Hormone Formation" diagram, cholesterol is the precursor substance needed for the synthesis, or creation, of all steroid hormones and in essence can be called the "mother" hormone. Both high-density lipoprotein (HDL) cholesterol ("good" cholesterol) and low-density lipoprotein (LDL) cholesterol (so-called bad cholesterol) are substrates (raw material) for hormones; LDL is used for hormone synthesis by steroid-producing cells in the ovaries, liver, fatty tissues, and brain; HDL is used in the adrenal glands.

The main female hormones are progesterone and estrogen; the main male hormones are testosterone and androstenedione. Women also require testosterone, in lower levels than men, however, and men also require progesterone and estrogen, but in lower levels than women. All steroid hormones are converted into more soluble excretion products in the liver. Normally, approximately 20 percent of these excretable hormones are secreted into the bile and then excreted in the feces; the remainder are released into the blood and are passed into the urine by the kidneys.

Some authors refer to progesterone as the "mother" hormone and pregnenolone as the "grandmother" hormone, but as you can see, without cholesterol none of the hormones can be made.

"We're going on a journey through a remarkable kingdom, a place in which miracles and magic are everyday occurrences. In no other place in this world are more wondrous things happening than inside each of us."—Tom Monte

Of the hormones in the diagram, three in particular are of great concern to women in transition: the estrogens—estradiol, estrone, and estriol. In this chapter we will also consider progesterone, an underappreciated contributor to the hormonal melody, and the androgens (male hormone).

THE ESTROGENS AND ESTROGEN REPLACEMENT

Most women do not realize that a single hormone called estrogen does not exist. This word is the name not of one substance but for a class of hormones, produced by the ovaries and adrenal glands. There are at least two dozen identified estrogens, and they have a multitude of functions. Every organ, including the brain, heart, ovaries, and liver, has receptor sites that receive their hormonal messages. The estrogens' functions include:

- stimulating breast tissue growth;
- stimulating the endometrium's growth during the follicular phase of the menstrual cycle (see Chapter 4);

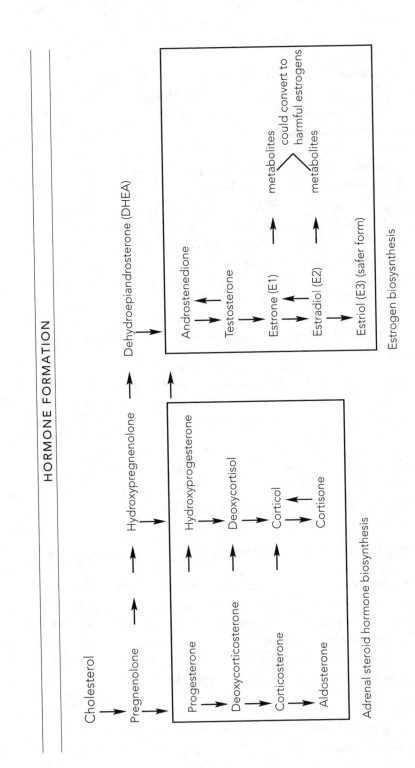

HORMONE FORMATION

Cholesterol → Pregnenolone → Hydroxypregnenolone → Dehydroepiandrosterone (DHEA)

Adrenal steroid hormone biosynthesis

Progesterone → Deoxycorticosterone → Corticosterone → Aldosterone

Hydroxyprogesterone → Deoxycortisol → Corticol → Cortisone

Estrogen biosynthesis

Androstenedione → Testosterone → Estrone (E1) → Estradiol (E2) → Estriol (E3) (safer form)

Estrone (E1) → metabolites
Estradiol (E2) → metabolites
} could convert to harmful estrogens

- helping maintain function of internal sexual organs;
- stimulating the menstrual cycle; and
- at puberty, stimulating growth of external genitalia and internal sexual organs, and establishing body fat deposition and body hair patterns.

Of the many types of estrogen, the most important are estrone (E1), estradiol (E2), and estriol (E3).

- **Estrone (E1)** is converted from estradiol in the liver and from the precursor hormones androstenedione, progesterone, and dehydroepiandrosterone (DHEA) in the fat cells and in some organs. Thus, women who have had their ovaries removed and those experiencing late menopause are still able to secrete high levels of estrone. Estrone has the potential to convert to toxic estrogens.
- **Estradiol (E2)** is produced directly by the ovary from cholesterol and is the principal estrogen secreted by the ovaries premenopausally. Most commercial estrogens are forms of estradiol, or combinations of estrone and estradiol. Estradiol is converted to estrone in the small intestine, and this conversion is reversible. Both estrone and estradiol can be converted to estriol. Estradiol also has the potential to convert to toxic estrogen.
- **Estriol (E3)** is a safer form of estrogen that is not further converted or changed, remaining estriol once it is formed. It has been commonly believed that most estriol results from the conversion of estradiol and estrone, primarily in the liver. Researchers have concluded that there may also be direct secretion of estriol by the adrenals and ovaries or that other precursors exist. It has also been reported that there is direct conversion of androstenedione to estriol.

At menopause, the ovaries greatly slow down their production of the estrogens, and, as touched on previously, the adrenals must help to compensate by producing the precursor hormones DHEA and androstenedione, which can be further converted to estrogen. If the adrenals are depleted, signs of estrogen deficiency will appear. As we have seen, the naturopathic approach to this problem is to support the adrenals. Allopaths take a different approach. They note that deficiency of estrogens is implicated in many menopausal symptoms, as the following list of supplemental estrogen's benefits makes clear:

- Promotes temporary increases in bone density by increasing calcium uptake and inhibiting cells that break down bone (osteoclasts).

- Decreases depressive feelings.

- Prevents hot flashes.

- Increases libido.

- Improves memory and symptoms of Alzheimer's disease.

- Improves skin tone, decreases wrinkling.

- Prevents vaginal dryness and thinning.

EE: Estrogen (Replacement) Enthusiasm

Given supplemental estrogen's list of benefits, why wouldn't every woman want to take estrogen replacement? Well, there are a few possible reasons ...

Estrogen enthusiasm (EE) around menopause dates back to the early 1960s. Before then, the aura around estrogen was one of *caution*. One estrogen enthusiast, A. Walsh, ignored the cautions and in 1965 she introduced the book *Now! The Pills to Keep Women Young! ERT: The First Complete Account of the Miracle Hormone Treatment That May Revolutionize the Lives of Millions of Women!* She was sure right about that last statement.

Hot on the heels of Walsh came Dr. Robert A. Wilson, who wrote an article for *Newsweek* magazine in January 1964 entitled "No More Menopause" and, with financial backing from Ayerst Laboratories, a book entitled *Feminine Forever* that did wonders for the sale of Premarin, an estrogen replacement drug derived from pregnant mares' urine and made by Wyeth-Ayerst. The basic attitude underpinning the promotion of estrogen in Walsh's writing is summed up in the following words from *Feminine Forever*: "The unpalatable truth must be faced that all postmenopausal women are castrates ... From a practical point of view, a man remains a man until the very end." Wilson's book and its effect on Premarin sales were the beginning of the *billion-dollar* relationship between estrogen and menopause. Premarin is now one of the most widely sold drugs in North America, with sales reaching $940 million a year. The drug is about to hit its demographic sweet spot—the huge wave of baby boomers coming into menopause, expected to exceed 50 million by the year 2000. Today estrogen is sold in a variety of forms: pills, patches, creams, and injections—choose your flavour of the month!

Advertising in the 1960s promoted estrogen as the woman's fountain of youth—no more wrinkles, no more menopause, and so on—and the advertising today (aimed mostly at allopathic doctors) promotes a similar picture. In my mind, the image created of the miracle youth pill is all too similar to the one found in the wide promotional campaigns mounted in the 1960s to prove the safety of DDT and cigarettes! The advertising for DDT included pictures of children playing in DDT spray and cartoons of smiling cows running around singing tunes like "DDT is good for me ... "

JUST AN ASIDE ...

DDT enthusiasm was once as rampant as estrogen enthusiasm. Paul Muller, a Swiss pharmacist, won a Nobel Prize in medicine and physiology in 1939 for discovering DDT. DDT use peaked during the early 1960s, with millions of kilograms in use around the world. But by 1973 the Environmental Protection Agency banned it in the United States because of its toxic effects on humans and animals—after more than a billion kilograms had been used in the United States alone. Now, more than thirty years after its "peak performance" in 1962, we are all still dealing with the *extremely* negative health impacts. One of DDT's breakdown products is DDE, a molecule similar to estrogen. Such synthetic estrogens in the environment are called xenoestrogens, and they are commonly found in pesticides and other substances. It is well documented that DDT and other pesticides are contributing to widespread endocrine problems, including the increased incidence of breast cancer.

The warning bells around supplemental estrogen really start ringing in my ears when I consider that most estrogen is synthetic or derived from horse urine. It *is alien* to our bodies. As the story of DDT and DDE demonstrates, synthetic chemicals can have unexpected effects.

"The whole imposing edifice of modern medicine, for all its breathtaking successes, is, like the celebrated Tower of Pisa, slightly off balance."
—Prince Charles

ANOTHER BIG "WHOOPS"?

Are the cumulative effects of HRT and xenoestrogens the sleeping DDT of the millenium? Newly published research is confirming that the widespread use of these substances is another big "whoops:!

A STROLL DOWN MEMORY LANE

Do you remember diethylstilbestrol (DES), a synthetic weak estrogen, FDA-approved and given to women between the early 1940s and early 1970s to treat breast cancer, prevent miscarriage, and reduce menopausal symptoms? Up to six million women in the United States and Europe took DES. Research has since revealed that DES causes birth defects, reproductive problems, infertility, and cervical cancer in women whose mother took the drug during pregnancy, and testicular cancer, undescended testicles, and increased risk of prostate cancer in men whose mothers took the drug. The "morning after" pill still in use is basically DES. DES was at one time also used in livestock husbandry (the same way estrogens and growth hormones are used today) until 1979, when it was banned because it was found at unsafe levels in supermarket beef.

We are seeing the negative effects of DES many years after the drug's introduction and removal. Are we perhaps doing things backwards? In the past, when indigenous groups of people who lived closer to the land were making a major decision, they carefully considered the possible impact it could have on them for up to seven generations into the future.

Today, tonnes of synthetic pharmaceutical estrogen, administered to menopausal women in larger quantities than their bodies absorb, estrogens given to animals to increase their weight and the farmer's yield, and xeno-estrogens from chemical breakdown products are flooding our rivers and ecosystems. We then ingest them again in our foods and water. What goes around, comes around… and around…

The risks involved in placing xenoestrogens in the body (and we will have more to say about them later in this chapter) become even less palatable when we realize that the pharmaceutical companies expose women to those risks because of their desire to make large profits.

Bioidentical Hormones vs. Patentable Hormones

It currently costs approximately $3 million to get a new drug approved for use—money that is spent mainly on researching the compound's efficacy and safety. Thus, if a company cannot expect to make a profit on a drug because it cannot patent it—that is, cannot claim it as its property alone and thereby shield itself from competition—then it makes little economic sense to do the necessary studies, especially given that most pharmaceutical companies expect extremely high profits. Bioidentical hormones—hormones that have the same molecular shape as hormones produced by the human body—cannot be patented. Hormones whose molecular shape has been altered from the human pattern by the pharmaceutical firm can be patented. As a result, any company that produces products containing bioidentical hormones could be in for a great deal of competition from other companies. Therefore, there are few studies on the effects of bioidentical hormones compared to studies on patentable hormones. What little we do know about bioidentical hormones indicates that they are much safer to use than synthetic ones. But because they cannot rake in the big bucks, they aren't manufactured or promoted en masse the way synthetic estrogens are. It is simply a matter of economics.

Estrogen and the Medicalization of Menopause

Estrogen hit the mass market in the 1960s without adequate testing, and once the marketing machine set sales in motion, it has continually been among the top 10 selling drugs in North America.

Now, most allopathic doctors believe that menopause is essentially a *disease* of the endocrine system that needs to be treated with drugs, and that all women need estrogen for optimal health during and after the menopausal transition.

There is something fundamentally disturbing about turning a natural event such as menopause into a disease that demands decades of drug treatment.

CALLING ALL WOMEN! WAKE UP, SPEAK UP!

Most of the menopausal and postmenopausal women reading this book were raised in an era in which it was generally considered wrong to question authority, particularly if you were a woman. Women were expected to just do what they were told, and not learn to think for themselves. It was somewhat acknowledged that teenagers were going to "act up," but that this would only be temporary, and soon they would "grow up" and learn to comply with the attitudes and options provided by the authorities in the churches, political system, schools, and medical establishment. The thought revolution began in the 1960s and the youth and women's movements started speaking up on various issues. I feel that somewhere along the line we went back to sleep—where are those "thought rebels" today? Are any of you out there? It is time to reawaken!

Question authority. *Let your inner knowing and common sense be your truth sensor, no matter what.* The greatest gift you can ever give to yourself is freedom of thought, especially the freedom to make your own decisions regardless of the opinions of others.

When it comes to making decisions on hormone replacement and other health concerns, you need to consider both the science of the matter and what those investigating the wisdom of nature have to say. The information you gain from these approaches to mapping reality, coupled with your own inner knowingness, will give you your truth.

THE MYTH OF THE MAGIC OF ESTROGEN REPLACEMENT

Just as a magician can create illusions by tricking the audience into thinking that something is happening when it isn't, the estrogen industry has managed to create the illusion that estrogen confers many benefits unavailable elsewhere. Meanwhile, behind the illusion, the real picture, which includes estrogen therapy's destructive side effects, is mostly ignored or downplayed.

Claims are made for HRT that do not always stand up to close scrutiny. HRT is prescribed for perimenopausal and menopausal women for a variety of symptoms such as hot flashes, night sweats, insomnia, and the like, but the two most commonly promoted reasons to take HRT are for the prevention and treatment of osteoporosis and protection from heart disease. Do the claims hold up under closer examination?

ESTROGEN AND OSTEOPOROSIS

Osteoporosis is a disease involving progressive loss of bone mass. This book covers osteoporosis in detail in Chapter 7 and offers prevention and treatment suggestions in Chapter 8.

The medical consensus is that estrogen can slow down the progression of osteoporosis but cannot cause new bone growth. This position is held because studies show that estrogen inhibits the cells that break down bone. When I review the mechanisms of bone remodelling, what I note is that the medical profession does not take into sufficient account that the cells that break down bone break down old and damaged bone. Estrogen thus inhibits this important process, preventing substandard bone from being removed by the body. As old bone accumulates, taking up space, the cells that build new bone cannot do their job efficiently, and therefore less new bone is formed. Over a prolonged period, the result of estrogen therapy is a build-up of old, brittle bone.

Estrogen—and levels rise when HRT is taken—causes excessive absorption of calcium. An excessive calcium uptake combined with decreased bone breakdown can result in a condition called osteoporosis, or hardening of the bones. In this condition, the bones may have more density, but their hardness means they lose flexibility, and they become very brittle. More is not necessarily better. Now I realize that some studies supporting the use of estrogen for bone health look impressive on first glance. But look a little deeper.

Some studies indicate that estrogen therapy does decrease bone breakdown (or resorption) and seemingly stabilizes bone mass, with a minimal increase in bone density at best, but it must be taken for a decade or more to reduce fracture incidence! In my practice, however, I commonly see women who are taking estrogen, some since an early age (because of hysterectomy), and yet have severe osteoporosis. I have never seen the "magic" effects of estrogen on bone health.

Indeed, one major finding of an eight-year study involving more than 9,500 American women, reported in 1995 in the *New England Journal of Medicine*, was that *current estrogen use by women over 65 had absolutely no benefit in preventing hip fracture*. The report also pointed out that other studies had mentioned that the only benefit estrogen has in possibly preventing bone loss is in the first few years of menopause.

In addition, the most authoritative medical textbooks do not support the conventional medical view that estrogen is a treatment of choice for osteoporosis. The prestigious *Harrison's Principles of Internal Medicine*, 12th edition, 1991, states that estrogens may decrease bone resorption but bone formation does not increase in estrogen's presence and, indeed, eventually decreases. *Scientific American Medicine*, 1991, agrees that estrogens decrease bone resorption, but associated with this is a decrease in bone formation. Also discussed are the very significant risks of estrogen use, one being a sixfold increase in the risk of developing endometrial cancer.

The other condition for which estrogen is highly touted is cardiovascular disease.

ESTROGEN AND CARDIOVASCULAR DISEASE

The relationship between heart disease prevention and estrogen is a massive topic, so here we will cover only general studies. Having done a great deal of reading on this subject, we can assure you that no matter the level of detail with which we covered all the studies and opinions, the result would still be the same: there have been no completed controlled studies that prove the touted benefits of HRT and cardiovascular health. In fact, the initial reports of controlled studies now show that estrogen is "biting the dust" when it comes to preventing cardiovascular disease (see page 279).

Most of us know that cardiovascular problems are the primary cause of death in men, but many people, including health care practitioners, are unaware that heart disease is the main cause of death in women 50 and older. Two out of three women in this age group are at risk for developing cardiovascular disease. Men are at greater risk for cardiovascular disease at any age; however, cardiovascular disease rates increase in both men and women as they age.

Perimenopausal, menopausal, and postmenopausal women—older women—are recipients of the most highly promoted drug in medical practice, conventional HRT.

Granted, HRT can provide relief from unpleasant symptoms experienced by some women during the transitional years, but we strongly advise short-term use only, and only if natural remedies do not give enough relief.

Until a few years ago, skepticism was the prevailing response to the use of HRT as a treatment for cardiovascular disease. Now most cardiologists, gynecologists, and family doctors seem to be blindly accepting pharmaceutical promotional information and would appear to be convinced that estrogen should be given to virtually every postmenopausal woman for prevention and treatment of cardiovascular disease. They are toeing the conventional party line that says use of HRT reduces the risk of myocardial infarction (heart attack) by about 50 percent.

No matter how hard we try we just can't figure out the logic behind such general acceptance of the estrogen-for-cardiovascular-health equation by such a large group of intelligent professionals. A quick look in any drug manual reveals that estrogen in any form is associated with risks for a multitude of cardiovascular diseases.

Several studies do show reduced risk of coronary disease in HRT users. These studies, however, are *epidemiological*—they compare the prevalence and spread of disease of different groups of people in various communities. In fact, *all* the studies that show benefits of estrogen for cardiovascular disease are epidemiological—*no large, randomized, controlled study on this topic has yet to be completed.* Recently one of the long-term controlled studies, initially to be completed in 2008, was stopped prematurely due to the increased risk for breast cancer, heart attack, stroke and blood clots.

The epidemiological studies have been highly criticized by many experts. The first major criticism levelled against these studies has been around the issue of selection bias: the study results do not take into account that the study is trying to compare apples and oranges. Clearly, say the critics, many more factors than estrogen use or non-use are involved in whether the women studied develop coronary disease.

California researchers reported in 1991 that the current use of estrogen or estrogen and progestagen does not significantly decrease the risk of myocardial infarction in postmenopausal women.

Despite the lack of corroboration in the research to date, claims that estrogen prevents osteoporosis and reduces heart disease by 50 percent have become the basis for recommending estrogen to virtually every post-menopausal woman in North America.

Clearly, though, the estrogen edifice is built on a very shaky foundation. Today, an increasing number of allopathic doctors and a dominant number of complementary practitioners see a much more limited role for estrogen replacement therapy, particularly in relation to cardiovascular diseases.

To better understand the naturopathic position on estrogen and cardio-vascular disease, let's look into some allopathic books—the *Compendium of Pharmaceuticals and Specialties* (CPS) of the Canadian Pharmacists Association and the American *Physician's Desk Reference* (PDR). Here are the warnings given in these texts regarding estrogen use and cardiovascular diseases (medical terms are explained in the glossary): increased blood pressure, altered coagulation tests, aggravation of migraine headaches, myocardial infarction or coronary thrombosis, neuro-ocular lesions (retinal thrombosis and optic neuritis), and thrombophlebitis, pulmonary embolism, or cerebral thrombosis.

As well, several studies show that estrogen increases blood coagulation and venous thromboembolism (blood clots in the legs) in women taking oral contraceptives or ERT.

In the past twenty years it has been well established that an increased risk of cardiovascular disease is the most important concern regarding oral contraceptive use and supersedes other side effects such as cancer, depression, and immune deficiency. *It is the estrogen in oral contraceptives that affects blood clotting systems.*

The first study on estrogen and heart disease took place in men and showed that giving them estrogen significantly increased their risk of heart attack: the study was discontinued. *Yet it's considered okay to give estrogen to women.* Confusing? You bet!

HDL:LDL RATIO—THE HALLMARK OF HEART DISEASE RISK?

How can estrogen possibly be promoted as protective for the heart given its recognized side effects? Well, you might say, it has been shown to increase high-density lipoprotein (HDL) levels ("good" cholesterol), and isn't that important? Indeed, the Post-Menopausal Estrogen/Progestin Intervention (PEPI) study results, reported in 1995, indicated improved HDL levels, increased fibrinogen (blood-clotting factor) levels, and decreased levels of low-density lipoprotein (LDL, the "bad" cholesterol) in women using estrogen.[11] The study lasted only three years, so estrogen's effect on heart attacks could not be studied. HDL levels were the study's primary focus. The general result in all groups was that HDL levels *initially* increased, but within six to twelve months they fell; LDL levels fell to their lowest point during the same period. *Triglyceride levels increased in every group except the one that received placebos.* The media began to report this study as proof that HRT/ERT prevents heart disease. Unfortunately, the media missed many details, including an important point ...

HIGH TRIGLYCERIDES MAY PREDICT HEART DISEASE RISK

Triglycerides are a very important risk factor for coronary disease—an increased incidence of cardiovascular disease occurs when increased triglyceride levels are present along with low HDL levels. In fact, the triglyceride to HDL ratio is the strongest predictor of heart attack; it is a much more accurate predictor than the ratio of HDL to LDL. Increased triglyceride levels alone are correlated with a threefold increase in rate of heart attacks; increased triglycerides combined with low HDL levels are correlated with a *sixteenfold* increase in the incidence of heart attacks.

In the PEPI study, HDL is the *one variable* considered, while fibrinogen, triglycerides, and the numerous other factors involved with heart disease are ignored. The association between estrogen use and embolism, stroke, thrombosis, obesity, edema, depression, myocardial infarction, eclampsia, epilepsy, and thyroid suppression are also ignored.

In a study done in 1995, E. Barrett-Connor looked at the effects a blood hormone levels in relation to heart disease. She found no relationship between heart disease and levels of testosterone, estrone, and androstenedione in postmenopausal women or in men, nor did she find any relationship with levels of estrogen, cholesterol, LDL, and triglycerides. Other studies have confirmed her findings.

MORE ON RESEARCH BIAS

In Chapter 1, we discussed David Moher's recently published study on the poor reliability and exaggerated results of medical drug trials and the careful selection of control groups in these studies when a particular outcome is the goal.

At one point in our investigations of estrogen and cardiovascular health, the flimsy nature of the evidence for estrogen as a cardiovascular disease treatment, and the clear dangers the drug poses to the cardiovascular system, sparked a thought: *Does a plus b = c?*

My hypothetical equation works like this:

(a) More women today are dying of heart attacks than ever before.
(b) More women today are taking estrogen than ever before.

Do (a) and (b) add up to (c)?

(c) The increasing incidence of heart attacks in women is in part due to the increased use of HRT.

All the evidence needed to decide the question firmly one way or another isn't yet available.

It is interesting to note, however, that the Committee on the Safety of Medicines in the United Kingdom warned in 1996 of a threefold increase in the risk of thrombotic episodes (strokes) in women on HRT. Also interesting is that after three years of the first randomized placebo-controlled study of ET and heart disease, the results reported in the *Journal of the American Medical Association* indicate that *more new cases of heart disease and thromboembolism developed in patients given ET than in those given placebo.* A study published in 1998 reports that the estrogen drug Premarin fails when it comes to prevention of coronary heart disease in postmenopausal women.

Meanwhile, the PEPI trial and the Women's Health Initiative study (WHI) are attempting to show the long-term effects of HRT in relation to cardiovascular disease in women; both will be completed in 2005; the Women's International Study of Long-Duration Estrogen After Menopause is slated for completion in 2017. Recently however the WHI study was halted prematurely due to the increased risks of breast cancer and heart disease.

The National Institute of Health (NIH) announced that the long-term use of estrogen and progestin increased otherwise healthy women's risk of a stroke by 41 percent, a heart attack by 29 percent and breast cancer by 24 percent. The NIH concluded that the hormones' risks outweighed the benefits and stopped the 16,600-woman study three years early. Please remember that this is definitely not the first study to show increased risks of HRT but it is the first one the scientific community seems to be listening to.

Fortunately for those women who haven't decided yet that estrogen replacement is a surefire method of preventing or treating cardiovascular disease, there are other ways to deal with this health concern—ways that are based on solid scientific evidence. For my recommendations on maintaining cardiovascular health, please see the corresponding section in Chapter 9, "Other Common Health Concerns."

Now that we have considered estrogen in some detail, let's move on to the other major hormones involved in the transitional years.

PROGESTERONE

Progesterone is a significant but underappreciated hormone produced by the hormonal symphony orchestra. It is a precursor hormone, meaning the body uses it to make other steroid hormones (see "Hormone Formation" diagram, page 134; estrogen, on the other hand, is an end-point hormone and, other than estrogen byproducts, does not break down into other hormones.) In the corpus luteum of the ovaries, progesterone is the end product of hormone synthesis. In the adrenals the progesterone may be further broken down to form androstenedione. In the testes the process is carried one step further, resulting in testosterone. In the ovary, a series of reactions leads from cholesterol through progesterone, among other substances, to testosterone and finally to estradiol.

Progesterone levels decrease at menopause, although the ovaries and the adrenals continue producing the hormone.

The Physiological Effects of Progesterone

Maintaining adequate progesterone levels is important for overall health. This hormone produces many effects that have an opposing or balancing function with respect to the effects of the estrogens. Its importance becomes obvious when we consider some of its major effects:

- has antistress action—is the precursor of the stress-response hormone cortisone
- facilitates bone formation
- promotes the activity of the endometrium (shedding of the endometrium if conception does not occur)
- protects against fibrocystic breast disease, endometriosis, and breast cancer because it is a natural counterbalance to estrogen
- facilitates the action of thyroid hormone

According to some researchers, such as Dr. John Lee, endogenous progesterone and USP progesterone (a form of bioidentical progesterone discussed in detail below) are needed for normal physiological function in the following areas: blood clotting, blood sugar regulation, cellular oxygenation, and fat metabolism.

Note that these abilities belong to natural and bioidentical progesterone, as made by the body, not to synthetic progestins, most commonly prescribed in HRT.

In addition to the actions of progesterone listed above, it has been reported that progesterone is involved in the repair of myelin. Myelin is a sheath that protects many of the nerve fibres in the body. In multiple sclerosis the myelin sheath degenerates, short-circuiting nerve impulses.

Synthetic Progesterone (Progestins)

The use of synthetic progestins began when doctors started seeing some of the negative effects of their miracle hormone, estrogen. In the early days of its use, in the 1960s, estrogen was widely prescribed as a single hormone (unopposed estrogen). Women taking unopposed estrogen experienced up to a fourteenfold increase in endometrial cancer, cancer of the lining of the uterus. (Remember that one of estrogen's functions is to encourage growth of endometrial and breast tissue.) In the face of this finding, as well as reports of a 30 percent increase in breast cancer amongst users, estrogen therapy lost some its appeal in the 1970s, for a little while anyway. Enter synthetic progestin: this drug is now commonly prescribed along with estrogen for women who have an intact uterus, to reduce the risk of the estrogen overstimulating the uterine lining and causing endometrial cancer. But all is still not well in HRT paradise.

Despite the use of synthetic progestin, the looming risk of cancer contin-ues to haunt HRT. In 1995, a study reported in the *New England Journal of Medicine* showed that combined estrogen and progestin put women at even higher risk for breast cancer than estrogen alone. This study's results came in the wake of an alarming report made in May 1995 suggesting that the long-term use of estrogen heightens the risk of fatal ovarian cancer.

Why has the introduction of synthetic progestin done little to make HRT safer? To begin with, these compounds do not have the same full spec-trum of activity as natural progesterone, and can cause unpleasant side effects. The possible adverse effects of synthetic progestins include:

- breast tenderness; galactorrhea (milk secretion)
- cardiovascular effects: thromboembolic disorders, thrombophlebitis, and pulmonary embolism
- central nervous system symptoms: headaches, nervousness, dizziness, depression, insomnia, fatigue
- gastrointestinal symptoms: bloating, nausea, abdominal discomfort
- miscellaneous difficulties: weight gain, peripheral edema, "moon face"
- reproductive system symptoms: breakthrough bleeding, spotting, change in the menses, amenorrhea, premenstrual syndrome, changes in cervical erosion and secretions
- skin and mucous membrane disorders: acne, alopecia (hair loss), hirsutism (excess hair growth), allergic reactions ranging from skin rashes to anaphylaxis

In addition, progestins actually inhibit natural progesterone production and lower the concentration of the hormone in the blood, thereby worsen-ing any existing hormonal imbalance. Remember, too, that natural proges-terone has anticancer effects. Perhaps the fact that synthetic progestins interfere with natural progesterone production provides some of the expla-nation for why synthetic progestins used in HRT appear to increase the risk of breast cancer. This question has not yet been adequately studied.

Bioidentical Progesterone

Bioidentical hormones may not be as profitable as the synthetics, but by the end of this chapter we hope you will agree with us that they are generally safer than the synthetics, so long as they are used for short periods. Most women experience far fewer side effects from bioidentical progesterone, or USP progesterone, than from synthetic progestins.

Bioidentical progesterone is not without side effects if taken in excess. It may cause the following symptoms: breast swelling and tenderness, decreased libido, depression and fatigue, headaches, hyperinsulinemia (overproduction of insulin by the pancreas), sedation, sinus inflammation and sinus headaches, and water retention.

TESTOSTERONE—LOST YOUR LIBIDO?

Testosterone is considered primarily a male hormone, but it also plays an important part in the overall hormonal health of women—the "Hormone Formation" diagram (see page 134) points out that testosterone is a step on the way to estrogen. Also, contrary to popular belief, men produce estrogen too. The difference is that each hormone is more dominant in one sex. As previously mentioned, in men the precursor to testosterone, androstenedione, is formed in the adrenal gland and then converted to testosterone in the testes. In women, testosterone is produced in the ovaries; most is then converted to estradiol, but some remains as testosterone. Other male hormones (though, again, they are present in both sexes, simply more predominant in males) include:

- the aforementioned androstenedione (ASD);
- dehydroepiandrosterone (DHEA);
- dehydroepiandrosterone-sulphate (DHEAS).

Not all women need testosterone or other male hormones, but there are some situations that may justify its use:
- breast tenderness
- loss of energy
- a complete hysterectomy (uterus and ovaries) or partial hysterectomy (still have the ovaries). In the latter case, the decreased blood supply to the ovaries after a hysterectomy usually results in compromised function. Women who have partial hysterectomies have a 30 percent chance of becoming menopausal within four years of surgery.
- loss of libido
- osteoporosis
- persistent insomnia

UNOPPOSED ESTROGEN IS STILL ALIVE AND WELL

Most medical doctors prescribing for a woman who has had a hysterectomy assume that just because a woman does not have a uterus, progesterone is not necessary—in this case they will generally prescribe
unopposed estrogen. This line of thinking would lead one to believe that
progesterone has only *one* function in the body—the maintenance of the
endometrium. But how could anyone, on reviewing the list of functions of
natural progesterone given above, come to the conclusion that the
absence of a uterus negates the need for progesterone?

It is my opinion that natural progesterone is a requirement for *all* women
taking estrogen in any form. Estrogen and progesterone exist in balance
with one another, each eliciting physiological effects that oppose those
created by the other.

If you feel that you may be a candidate for male hormonal supplementation, please first have your hormone levels checked. (Hormone level tests
are described in more detail later in this chapter.) If levels are low you may
want to consider very low dose transdermal testosterone cream or DHEA for
a short time. As is the case with the other hormones, start with the bioidentical versions, available by prescription from compounding pharmacies.

(Compounding pharmacies belong to a group of pharmacies specializ-
ing in networking on the latest techniques and pharmacokinetics of pharmaceuticals. The Professional Compounding Consultants Association can be
reached at 1-800-331-2498.)

PREGNENOLONE

Pregnenolone, a hormone produced from cholesterol in our adrenal glands,
liver, skin, testicles, ovaries, and brain, has become a subject of interest, along
with DHEA, as a "fountain of youth" hormone. Pregnenolone has been found
to be helpful in reducing stress and fatigue, and enhancing memory, mental
alertness, and joint and tissue function. The body converts pregnenolone into
other hormones, and it is a precursor to both progesterone and DHEA.
Pregnenolone provides another example of both how the whole hormonal

orchestra must work together to perform the hormonal symphony and how important optimal health is. Many organs must be healthy to produce this compound.

DEHYDROEPIANDROSTERONE (DHEA)

DHEA and its breakdown product (sulphate) dehydroepiandrosterone-sulphate (DHEAS) are precursors of both androgenic (male steroid hormones) and estrogenic (female) steroids. When we are younger we have high levels of DHEA and DHEAS. These substances reach their peak level in our late twenties, and from that point on there is a steady decline. The possible benefits of using supplemental DHEA include the following:

- inhibition of breast cancer development
- antidepressant
- diabetes and autoimmune disease prevention
- inhibition of genetic mutations from exposure to cancer-causing substances
- enhanced immune system function
- increased life span
- improved sleep, memory, and mood
- improved stress adaptation
- decreased weight gain

The possible health benefits of DHEA are exciting, and it will be interesting to see what further information comes in over the long term. It should be noted that the safety of long-term DHEA use has not been established.

Given that DHEA is a precursor hormone to both testosterone and estrogen, make sure you establish your baseline level for all the major hormones before taking DHEA, and then monitor the levels while using it. Each body is a unique chemical plant unto itself and is also constantly changing. Hormone supplementation will affect every person differently and will affect the same person differently at different stages of life.

A *word of caution:* *if you have fibroids do not take DHEA. It is likely that the DHEA will choose the estrogen pathway and increase the growth of the fibroids that are already due to excess estrogen.*

PART TWO:
HORMONAL SUPPORT AND
HORMONE REPLACEMENT THERAPY

As is obvious by now, it is our strategy in treating any condition to start with the safest, least toxic, and least invasive remedies possible. Accordingly, this section of the chapter begins by discussing ways to support hormonal balance naturally, without the use of pharmaceutical hormones. For some women, the suggested steps will not have a powerful enough effect, and they will require short-term hormonal support until they are able to rebalance themselves through diet, lifestyle changes, and natural remedies. Remember that natural hormonal support will be more effective if you are already working towards optimal health, using the protocols given in Chapters 2 through 4. This section will conclude with a discussion on how to use HRT as safely as possible.

Earlier in the book, we alluded to plants with phytoestrogenic activity. We're now going to look at some of these plants in detail. Yes, plants have hormones too, and theirs are "Made in Nature." Plant hormones can support a naturally healthy menopausal transition.

PHYTOHORMONES

Phytohormones are plant compounds found in all plants in one form or another; the various types of phytoestrogens are isoflavones, phytosterols, saponins, coumestans, and lignans. The phytoestrogens are not steroidal estrogens such as the estradiol made by the ovaries but belong to a class of estrogens known as phenolic estrogens. They are much weaker than steroidal estrogens—their potency ranges from one-fiftieth to one-twenty-thousandth of that of estradiol. In high doses, however, phytoestrogens can exert estrogenic effects. Many researchers feel this is why women in cultures consuming predominantly plant-based diets rarely experience hot flashes and other menopause-related symptoms.

Phytoestrogens are considered hormone balancers, since they exert both mild estrogenic effects and antiestrogenic (agonist) activity: that is, phytoestrogens compete with more potent steroidal and environmental (remember DDE?) estrogens (xenoestrogens) for "receptor binding sites" on the cells. These binding sites can be thought of as being like parking spots reserved especially for hormones. Once "parked," the hormone can exert its effect on the cell. By taking up more of the limited number of estrogen parking spots, the phytoestrogens reduce the overall activity level of the more potent endogenous (made by the body) and exogenous (from the environment) estrogens. The balancing effects of the phytoestrogens can be seen when we consider their general effects:

- If the steroidal estrogen levels are low (as may occur at menopause), the phytoestrogens gently mimic the role steroidal estrogens would play.
- If the level of steroidal or environmental estrogens is too high, the phytoestrogens block their access to estrogen receptor sites, substituting their own mild estrogenic activity for the excessively strong estrogenic effects created by overabundant steroidal or environmental estrogens.

Let's now look at isoflavones, a class of phytoestrogens.

Isoflavones and Other Plant Constituents

Currently, a class of phytoestrogens called isoflavones is getting a great deal of attention because they appear to have estrogenic activity. Of the isoflavones found in soybeans and other foods—daidzein, genistein, biochanin, and formononetin—genistein and daidzein seem to have the most therapeutic effect. Isoflavones:

- decrease blood cholesterol and triglyceride levels;
- decrease the tendency of blood platelets (which play a critical role in blood clotting) to stick together;
- help to maintain the health of the cardiovascular system;
- inhibit the growth of cancers, especially in the breast and colon;
- ease or prevent menopausal symptoms; and
- are helpful in preventing and treating osteoporosis.

Soy foods, for example, are a source of many other phytoestrogenic constituents (lignans and coumestans, saponins, plant sterols, and phytates) that have considerable health-promoting benefits in addition to their estrogenic and antiestrogenic activity. These substances have been found to have the following properties:

- antibacterial, antiviral, and antifungal activity
- potent antioxidant activity
- protect against the effects of cancer-causing substances; prevent cell mutations
- inhibit growth of cancer cells in breast tissue

- protect the cardiovascular system
- anti-inflammatory activity
- improves the action of the immune system

ISOFLAVONES AND MENOPAUSAL SYMPTOMS

The phytoestrogens in soy and other foods, when consumed in adequate amounts in the diet, can alleviate moderate to severe symptoms of menopause in most women. Soy isoflavones, along with other phytoestrogens, offer a natural alternative to HRT. And given that many of the world's cultures have been eating fermented soybean products for thousands of years without ill effect, we can gather that using soy products to address menopausal symptoms is far safer than taking synthetic hormone replacement.

In pilot studies conducted by Dr. J. Eden and colleagues at the Royal Hospital for Women in New South Wales, Australia, it was found that when women were given 160 mg of isoflavones daily for three months, a significant reduction in several menopausal symptoms, especially hot flashes, occurred. Further studies have shown smaller decreases in menopausal symptoms with a daily consumption of 40 mg of isoflavones. The ideal daily isoflavone intake seems to lie somewhere between 60 and 100 mg.

Phytoestrogens have several advantages over HRT in the treatment of menopausal symptoms. We've already considered some of the exaggerated claims made for synthetic estrogen, and later in this chapter I will detail some of the significant health risks of synthetic HRT—gallbladder disease, cancer, strokes, heart attacks. *Phytoestrogens are not associated with any of these side effects.*

Isoflavones also reduce the risk of several chronic diseases, such as cardiovascular disease and osteoporosis. A word of caution: The jury is still not out on phytoestrogenic plants for women with breast cancer and ovarian cancer. If you have estrogen receptor positive breast cancer, I would recommend using only the food sources of phytoestrogens such as fermented soy, in moderation. Do not use the concentrated formulas of isoflavones in supplement form.

HOW DOES THE BODY METABOLIZE ISOFLAVONES?

In earlier chapters we emphasized that healthy liver and intestine function are central to hormonal health. *The absorption of isoflavones depends on a healthy gut.* In adults, the gut bacteria convert phytoestrogens into compounds simi-lar to steroid hormones. Indeed, they go through extensive metabolism in the intestinal tract prior to absorption. In order for this metabolism to take place, the gut must contain healthy bacteria capable of converting the phytoestrogens to their active forms. Once absorbed, the active isoflavone metabolites are transported to the liver and most are removed from circulation. Some, however, enter the bloodstream and eventually bind to estrogen receptor sites. As you've probably already guessed, dysbiosis interferes with the process. If you haven't addressed your *Candida*/intestine problems or liver congestion yet, start now!

PHYTOPROGESTERONE HERBS

Earlier in this chapter we looked at the many reasons why adequate proges-terone levels are so important for optimal health throughout life and into the transitional years. Wild yam contain various compounds such as diosgenin that appear to support the production of progesterone. Research on the phytoprogesterone herbs is limited, and what has been done does not show a change in blood levels of progesterone after ingestion of wild yam, the most favoured phytoprogestegenic herb. However, reports in herbal jour-nals over hundreds of years and clinical observations support the beneficial hormone balancing effects of these plants, as well as their high degree of safety. As we have seen with isoflavones, the gut bacteria are responsible for converting many of the phytoestrogenic compounds into the bioactive form. Given the number of possible biochemical changes and additional constituents of the phytoprogesterone plants, perhaps there is another mech-anism involved in the conversion of the phytoprogesterone precursors into other bioactive agents that have not yet been determined. Clearly, more research is required. It seems that when it comes to natural substances, nature has provided specific intricate mechanisms that may not always be measurable through our current scientific methods.

USING NATURAL HORMONAL SUPPORT

Whether you are now on HRT and considering switching to a natural hormonal support program, or are still pondering your options, know that there are many ways to add phytoestrogens and phytoprogesterone to the diet.

You can begin your natural hormonal support program by eating more foods rich in phytoestrogens.

Phytoestrogen-Containing Foods

Plant foods that contain phytoestrogens include legumes such as soybeans, lentils, and chickpeas; vegetables such as fennel, celery, and parsley; and the herbs red clover, black cohosh, alfalfa, licorice, dong quai, and hops. These compounds have also been isolated in nuts and seeds and in corn and are found in some quantity in sesame seeds and corn, safflower, flaxseed, and pumpkin oils. Legumes contain 23 to 230 mg of phytoestrogens per 100 g; vegetables, 1 to 200 mg per 100 g. Sprouted seedlings seem to contain the highest amounts. There is so much variation in the phyto-estrogen content of plants because phytoestrogen content depends on their stage of growth, the season, where they are grown, and the nutrient content of the soil in which they grow.

Many of the phytohormone-containing plants are also listed as cancer-preventive foods: licorice, soybeans, flaxseed, barley, and cruciferous vegetables (broccoli, cabbage, kale).

In addition to soy products, many different plants contain phytohormones and can offer support during the transitional years. These plant compounds have phytoestrogenic and/or phytoprogesterone effects and can offer support as the endogenous hormones decrease.

Botanicals and Other Hormonal Support Remedies

The following herbs have been used for hundreds of years in traditional herbal medicine. They are extremely safe, well tolerated, and in comparison to synthetic estrogen replacement, fairly inexpensive.

- **Alfalfa (*Medicago sativa*).** This herb contains the phytoestrogens coumestrol, genistein, and formononetin. Alfalfa also benefits the thyroid and inhibits prolactin levels. Prolactin is, among other things, responsible for stimulating breast tissue. Thus, high levels are thought to play a role in the development of some breast cancers. Alfalfa is a restorative tonic and a blood builder because it is high in vitamins A, C, B2, B3, folic acid, and K and in protein and chlorophyll. Alfalfa works similarly to licorice in that it its beta-sitosterol and saponin content balances estrogen levels and reduces elevated cholesterol.

In menopause, alfalfa is useful for hot flashes, fibrocystic breasts, PMS, breast cancer, and other conditions associated with hyperestrogenism (high levels of estrogen). Due to its ability to inhibit prolactin and balance estrogen levels, it is very effective in the treatment of women with polycystic ovaries. Alfalfa is not recommended in autoimmune diseases.

— *Recommended dosage:* 500 to 1 000 mg powdered leaves and roots daily.

• **Black Cohosh (*Cimicifuga racemosa*).** Black cohosh is the most thoroughly studied herb in the treatment of menopausal symptoms and other female hormonal imbalances. Its effectiveness is thought to be due to the action of key compounds (isoflavones and triterpenes) on a number of the regulatory centres in the body, such as the hypothalamus and pituitary. One of black cohosh's most important effects is that it inhibits the pituitary's release of luteinizing hormone (one of the hormones responsible for hot flashes) without affecting—as estrogen does—the release of prolactin and follicle stimulating hormone (FSH). FSH is responsible for stimulating estrogen, so balancing FSH is a good thing. Further, prolactin is responsible for regulating the development of the mammary gland and milk secretion. In non-lactating women it is critical that this hormone be in balance with FSH and LH. Excess prolactin can also inhibit the maturation of the follicles in the ovary and cause menstrual abnormalities and sterility.

Black cohosh has been found to be very effective in the treatment of the following perimenopausal and menopausal symptoms: hot flashes, profuse perspiration, headaches, heart palpitations, depression, PMS, dysmenorrhea (painful menstruation), sleep disturbances, vaginal atrophy or dryness, nervousness and irritability, and loss of concentration. Positive results usually begin appearing within four to eight weeks of beginning the herb's use.

The German equivalent of the Health Canada lists no contraindications or limitations for use of this herb in cancer patients where estrogen is contraindicated, such as breast cancer. Black cohosh is extremely well tolerated.

— *Recommended dosage:* 250 to 500 mg solid extract two to three times daily. If you use a standardized black cohosh product such as meno or Remefemin, take 2 capsules daily.

• **Dong Quai (*Angelica sinensis*).** Dong quai has been used for centuries in other cultures as a tonifying herb, specifically as a blood builder. In traditional Chinese medicine, blood tonics are used to tonify the yin and promote healthy reproductive function. Because blood tonics build the blood, they indirectly strengthen the heart energy complex, which controls the blood and houses the spirit. In traditional Chinese medicine, insomnia indicates an imbalance in the heart energy complex, and dong quai can be helpful in this case.

In menopausal women this herb is particularly useful for promoting vaginal metabolism and for easing hot flashes. In menstruating women, dong quai has proven its worth in treating infertility and dysmenorrhea. Its efficiency may be due to its phytoestrogenic effects, coupled with the synergism of other components that act to stabilize blood vessels. Scientific investigation has shown that dong quai has both a balancing effect on estrogen activity and a tonic effect on the uterus. Furthermore, one of the active ingredients in dong quai stimulates the corpus luteum in the ovary to secrete progesterone, so this herb shows phytoprogestegenic action as well.

As the Oriental herbal tradition suggests, dong quai has beneficial effects on the cardiovascular system, such as decreasing blood pressure and preventing atherosclerotic plaque formation.

Dong quai has potent antitumour effects. It is also a very effective immune system regulator.

— *Recommended dosage:* 125 to 500 mg solid extract or 0.5 to 2 mL fluid extract or 2.5 mL tincture two to three times daily.

• **Garden Sage (*Salvia officinalis*)**. Garden sage (please note that we are *not* referring to sagebrush, the plant whose Latin name is *Salvia artemesias*) was reported in early research to contain high levels of estrogenic precursors. It is very effective for treating menopausal symptoms, particularly hot flashes. It is tranquilizing and acts as an excellent anxiety remedy. Garden sage also has strong antioxidant properties and improves digestion and assimilation. When digestion is improved, symptoms and illnesses improve.

— *Recommended dosage:* Steep 1 teaspoon leaves in 125 mL boiled water for 30 minutes. Take 1 to 2 tablespoons at a time. If insomnia is a problem, take 1 to 2 tablespoons tea in the evening, or more if required.

- **Hops (*Humulus lupulus*).** This plant has been shown to contain very high levels of phytoestrogens. The active constituents are effective antibacterial, diuretic, and powerful antispasmodic agents. Hops has traditionally been used as a tonic herb and to treat hysteria, restlessness, and insomnia.
  - *Recommended dosage:* 30 to 40 drops tincture (1:5) two to three times in the evening; or tea made with 15 g strobiles (flowers) to 500 mL water and steeped 15 to 20 minutes. Take one or two cups in the evening.

- **Red Clover (*Trifolium pratense*).** This herb contains very high levels of isoflavones , especially formononetin and biochanin. If the gut microflora are intact, they convert these isoflavones into daidzein and genistein, respectively (see the information above on soy isoflavones). Red clover is very beneficial in the treatment of many symptoms during the transitional years. In addition, it has traditionally been used in European, Asian, and native American cultures as food because of its nutritive value. It is commonly used as a diuretic, expectorant, and natural antibiotic, and for skin conditions such as psoriasis, because of its blood-cleansing effects.
  - *Recommended dosage:* 300 to 500 mg dried extract standardized to offer 25 to 40 mg of dietary isoflavones two to three times daily. If you take a standardized red clover supplement called Promensil, use 1 to 2 tablets daily; use 2 capsules daily of meno, in which red clover is combined with other herbs. **Note: Do not take red clover, Promensil, or meno if you know or suspect you are pregnant.**

- **Wild Yam (*Dioscorea spiculifora*).** Traditionally, wild yam has been used as an antispasmodic and a cholagogue (a substance that encourages bile production and secretion by the liver) and for its anti-inflammatory effects in arthritic conditions. Despite its reputation as a progestegenic herb, wild yam in its natural state is phytoestrogenic. We prefer USP progesterone or wild yam cream containing USP progesterone (natural progresterone, see page 161 for further explanation).
  - *Recommended dosage:* 2 to 4 mL fluid extract (1:1) daily; 2 to 10 mL root tincture daily.

- **Hesperidin**, like many other flavanoids, improves vascular integrity, lessening excessive capillary permeability which is a primary factor in hot flashes. When combined with vitamin C it was found that hot flashes were relieved in 53 percent of patients and reduced in 34 percent. Leg cramps, nosebleeds and easy bruising also declined.

— *Recommended dosage:* 900 mg two to four times daily with at least 1,200 mg vitamin C.

• **Gamma-oryzanol (*ferulic acid*)**. A growth-promoting substance found in grains and isolated from rice bran oil, it has been shown to be effective in alleviating menopausal symptoms including hot flashes and also in lowering triglyceride and cholesterol levels.

— *Recommended dosage:* 600 mg twice daily.

• **MenoSense** is an excellent product containing black cohosh, dong quai, gamma-oryzanol and hesperidin to help women deal with hot flashes and other menopausal symptoms. The products meno and Remefemin are also very effective in the treatment of menopausal complaints. Follow the recommended dosage on the label.

Phytoprogesterone Herbs

As with the phytoestrogenic herbs, these plants have long traditions of use; their safety and efficacy have been proven by the experience of many women over many centuries. With the advent of modern research techniques, we have been able to isolate and describe their effects on hormonal balance.

• **Chaste Tree (*Vitex agnus-castus*)**. The berries of this Middle Eastern tree have a long history of use and were first mentioned in the writings of Hippocrates in the fourth century BC. According to Dr. R. Weiss, *Vitex* acts on the pituitary and hypothalamus, regulating LH secretion. The LH increases the level of progesterone (as in the luteal phase of the menstrual cycle), thereby shifting the ratio of estrogen to progesterone in favour of progesterone. The increase in progesterone created by *Vitex* is thus achieved indirectly; the plant does not have direct hormonal action.

Vitex has a strong reputation in the traditional treatment of menstrual abnormalities, PMS, menopausal complaints, and infertility. In 1997 a team of German researchers found in a placebo-controlled double-blind study that *Vitex* was more effective in the treatment of PMS complaints (breast tenderness, edema, tension, headaches, constipation, depression, skin problems) than vitamin B6, which is commonly used for PMS.

— *Recommended dosage:* 30 to 40 mg solid extract standardized to contain 0.5 percent agnusides daily; 175 to 250 mg dried fruit berry twice daily. Note: Do not use *Vitex* if you suspect or know you are pregnant. It is safe to use, however, while breast-feeding. Treating infertility with *Vitex* may take as long as five to seven months before success is achieved.

• **Dong Quai (*Angelica sinensis*).** Dong quai has both estrogenic and progestegenic effects. For a complete description and recommended dosages, see the discussion above in the list of phytoestrogenic herbs.

WILD YAM CREAMS: A CLOSER LOOK

Today wild yam is most commonly associated with the wild yam creams that are advertised as a natural source of progesterone. The creams are becoming extremely popular with women seeking relief from conditions such as PMS and menopausal and osteoporotic symptoms. Please note that in its natural state, wild yam is phytoestrogenic. Although researchers have found that the saponins in wild yam (primarily diosgenin) can be converted into steroid hormones such as corticosteroids, estrogen, androgens, and progesterone, it takes many laboratory steps to achieve such conversions.

It must also be emphasized that natural diosgenin in wild yam and human steroids such as progesterone and DHEA are *not equivalent*, as is so often claimed. Natural wild yam's effects occur not because it contains steroidal hormones but rather because the natural phytohormones have similar effects to the steroidal hormones. The body does not mistake the precursors for its own hormones but instead uses them in a similar manner if needed.

Several brands of wild yam creams are available; all vary in strength and quality and most are advertised as either "wild yam extract" or "derived from" wild yams. The wild yam creams that contain natural progesterone are usually labelled "derived from" and contain USP progesterone, a pharmaceutical product. USP progesterone is bioidentical to natural human progesterone.

Any isolated hormone, even USP progesterone, should be considered a potent therapeutic agent and used only under the supervision of a health care practitioner, if there is a deficiency indicated by lab tests.

Some studies have reported an increase of anywhere from 400 to 20,000 percent in normal progesterone levels from using doses of the cream ranging from one-eighth to one-quarter teaspoon of 5 percent USP progesterone cream twice daily. A lab in the United States that commonly tests salivary hormone levels has found significant elevations in progesterone in 95 percent of women using topical progesterone creams. The most common side effects experienced by these women include water retention, gradual increase in body weight, breast engorgement, and mild to moderate depression that becomes clinically evident after six to nine months of use. Returning to acceptable progesterone levels may take from 30 to 200 days after use is discontinued.

Please remember when taking any hormone that taking amounts greater than is naturally produced by the body will actually inhibit the body's natural production of the hormone. If its use is indicated by low progesterone levels, USP progesterone is a fairly safe alternative to synthetic progestins. In the face of low progesterone levels, our first recommendation, however, is to make diet and lifestyle changes, begin taking extra nutritional support, and use herbs to balance estrogen and progesterone levels, such as dong quai and chaste tree, which naturally stimulate progesterone production. If necessary for immediate relief from symptoms, we recommend short-term use of the USP creams to rebuild natural hormonal balance.

All the above cautions also apply to the estrogen creams now sold in some American health food stores and available from compounding pharmacies in Canada. They are made in much the same way as the USP progesterone creams. They contain bioidentical estrogen molecules, but these are not natural—and at the same time are a powerful biochemical substance. Just because these creams are now freely available in some places does not mean that they should be freely used without being monitored, and without a real need being established first.

We wonder if Mother Nature was counting on laboratory technology to improve on her creations. We hardly think so; therefore, we trust nature's wisdom.

HORMONE REPLACEMENT THERAPY CHOICES

We have now completed our discussion of natural hormonal support. For those who still may require some synthetic hormonal support, the rest of this chapter outlines your choices, discusses how to use HRT safely, and delves in greater depth into the question of the xenoestrogens, the estrogen-like chemicals that currently pollute our water, air, and soil.

Consider Taking Bioidentical Hormones

When we speak of natural hormones or phytohormones, we mean unaltered plant-made hormones; in other words, no laboratory alterations have been made to the original plant molecule. Today we have reached (what we hope) is peak production of synthetic everything, and many people, wanting to return to nature, have become interested in *natural* products. Consequently, the pharmaceutical companies are jumping on the "natural" bandwagon, and some makers of synthetic estrogens are advertising them as "natural plant-based estrogen." While it is true that some pharmaceutical or commercial hormones are made from wild yam or soybeans, the final estrogen or progesterone molecules found in HRT drugs *do not remotely resemble the respective hormones produced by the body*, with the exception of USP progesterone found in Prometrium and USP progesterone creams, and some estrogen products such as Tri-Est, Estrace, and Estraderm. These estrogen products have proven to be patentable because of the unique delivery systems they employ, making them profitable despite the use of bioidentical hormones. In most cases, however, the pharmaceutical advertising carries a hint of truth, as the original substance is natural, but the final product is far from it.

Premarin (made by Wyeth-Ayerst) could be falsely considered natural because horse's urine is natural (to horses). Premarin contains estradiol plus at least two or more horse estrogens, such as equilin and equilenin. *Just say neigh to Premarin.*

In our opinion, whether a hormone is bioidentical or not, if it has been altered in the laboratory or is not as nature made it, *it is not natural.*

As mentioned earlier, there are compounding pharmacies in Canada and the United States that will make prescription hormone drugs from bioidentical molecules. It is further my opinion that these hormones, albeit the results of chemical manipulation, are much safer than alien molecules if prescription hormones are necessary for relief of severe symptoms for short periods. (For more information on compounding pharmacies, see page 150.)

Prescription HRT Choices

Most synthetic estrogens are forms of estradiol or estrone. However, because estradiol is converted to estrone in the small intestine, most HRT supplies mainly estrone. The most common forms in which estrogen is available include the following (we have provided standard dosages so that you know what they are and can therefore question the rationale behind lower, and especially higher, doses than these):

The most common forms in which bioidentical estrogen is supplied include:

Lab Tests and Hormone Levels

To determine your need for hormone replacement and the appropriate dosage, you may require a number of tests.

BLOOD TESTS

The standard blood test for determining menopause is the FSH test. FSH levels go up at menopause (formally defined as occurring when menstrual periods have been absent for one year). However, FSH levels may also be up in perimenopausal women who are still menstruating. The tyranny of the lab test in allopathic medicine (see Chapter 4 on thyroid health for more examples) means that even though these women are still having regular periods, they are told they are in menopause! A woman in her late forties or older who has not menstruated for one year does not need an FSH test to tell her she is in menopause; it isn't that difficult to figure out. What is difficult, however, is determining what hormonal changes are related to any perimenopausal or menopausal symptoms. Blood levels of FSH, progesterone, testosterone, and estradiol can give an overall indication of deficiencies or imbalances but do not measure for estriol. In addition, blood tests measure the hormones "bound" to blood proteins, that is, the inactive ones.

SALIVARY HORMONE TESTS

Salivary hormone tests are very sensitive, much more sensitive than blood hormone tests, and also measure estriol levels. These tests reflect the amount of steroid hormone not bound to carrier proteins in the blood. They can be done without the inconvenience of blood draws done in labs.

There is not one optimal hormonal level that fits every woman, but the saliva tests check for imbalances before initiating a program and to prevent possible excesses once the symptoms improve. Symptom relief should not be the only measurement of success in HRT; we recommend yearly monitoring of hormone levels primarily to prevent excess supplementation and because the body is continuously changing. For example, the amount of replacement hormone required at the onset of menopause will not be the same as for a women who is in her seventies. Monitoring will also help you gauge the pace at which to wean yourself off synthetic hormones as you move towards

Synthetic HRT

- conjugated equine (horse) estrogens, e.g., Premarin (0.3 to 1.25 mg per day)
- esterified estrogens, e.g., Estratab (0.3 to 2.5 mg per day)
- estropipate, e.g., Ogen (0.625 to 1.25 mg per day)

The most common forms in which synthetic progestins are available include:

- medroxyprogesterone acetate, e.g., Provera (2.5 to 10 mg daily or twice daily, on a cyclical basis)
- megestrol acetate, e.g., Megace (20 mg twice daily)

Bioidentical (Natural) HRT

- estradiol transdermal patch, e.g., Estraderm (0.05 to 0.1 mg twice weekly or every three to four days)
- micronized estradiol, e.g., Estrace (0.5 to 1 mg per day)
- estriol, e.g., Tri-Est (available orally or in cream form) (2.5 to 5.0 mg per day)

The most common forms in which bioidentical progesterone is supplied include:

- micronized progesterone, e.g., Prometrium (100 mg twice daily)
- USP progesterone cream (5 to 10 mg twice daily)

optimal health and your adrenal glands become increasingly able to manufacture all the hormones you need.

We urge hormone use for the shortest possible time. Once symptoms are
improved, we suggest weaning oneself from HRT to botanical support.
Remember, we are recommending optimal health as the real goal, so while
you are using HRT, begin making lifestyle changes to address weaknesses in
your organ systems. There is no safe window for synthetic HRT, we prefer as
little time as possible—let's not push our physiological luck.

Health Risks Associated with Estrogen

Most of us have known for a long time that women taking birth control
pills have an increased risk of developing high blood pressure and dangerous blood clots. Abnormal blood clotting can result in stroke if the clot is
in the brain, heart attack if the clot develops in a blood vessel of the
heart, or pulmonary embolus, a lung condition in which a clot in the leg
or pelvis breaks off and travels to the lungs. Any of these conditions can
be fatal.

But how many women are aware of the many *additional* risks of estrogen use, whether for birth control, menopausal symptoms, or other
hormonal symptoms?

Possible adverse reactions to oral contraceptives are listed in the
"Warning" section of the *Physician's Desk Reference* (PDR). This book, which
gives physicians detailed guidance about the uses and side effects of particular drugs, states that there is an increased risk of the following *serious adverse
reactions* associated with the use of oral contraceptives (medical terms are
explained in the glossary):

- arterial thromboembolism, pulmonary embolism, myocar-dial infarction, throm-bophlebitis
- breast cancer
- cerebral hemorrhage, cerebral thrombosis
- endometrial cancer
- gallbladder disease
- hepatic adenomas
- hypercalcemia, severe
- hypertension
- liver cancer
- mesenteric thrombosis, retinal thrombosis

The following adverse reactions have been reported in patients receiving oral contraceptives and are believed to be drug-related:

- acne
- amenorrhea
- appetite changes
- breakthrough bleeding
- breast changes
- Budd-Chiari syndrome
- Candidiasis
- cataracts
- cervical erosion
- cerebrovascular disease with mitral valve prolapse
- cholestatic jaundice
- colitis
- congenital abnormalities

- corneal changes
- cystitis-like syndrome
- dizziness
- depression
- edema
- erythema nodosum/multiforme
- gastrointestinal symptoms
- glucose intolerance
- hair loss
- headaches
- hemorrhage
- hirsutism
- infertility after discontinuation

- kidney function impairment
- libido changes
- lupus symptoms
- melasma, persistent
- menstrual changes
- migraines
- nausea
- nervousness
- optic neuritis
- porphyria
- PMS
- rash
- sickle-cell disease
- T3 uptake decrease
- vomiting
- weight changes (increase/decrease)

TESTS RECOMMENDED FOR WOMEN BEFORE PRESCRIBING HRT

The risks associated with estrogen use increase even more if health status is poor. Before using any synthetic estrogen alone or in combination with synthetic progesterone, the *Canadian Compendium of Pharmaceuticals* (CPS) recommends that all patients should undergo the following medical tests:

- thyroid tests

- blood calcium levels

- blood glucose levels

- endometrial biopsy

- Papanicolaou smear (Pap test)

- lipid panel test (triglycerides, total cholesterol, HDL, LDL)
- liver function tests
- complete physical examination, including blood pressure evaluation and examinations of the breasts and pelvic organs

The first follow-up examination should be done within six months after treatment begins, to assess the response to synthetic hormone use. Thereafter, says CPS, examinations should be made once a year *and should include at least those procedures listed above.* It is also important, emphasizes CPS, that patients be encouraged to examine the breasts frequently. How many women are given these tests before HRT is prescribed? In practice we have yet to meet one!

Have You Been Told ...?

As though all these warning and precautions were not frightening enough, various medical sources have more advisements on the use of synthetic estrogen.

Two studies quoted in *PDR* show that synthetic estrogen results in a persistent risk of cardiovascular disease. One study performed in the United States showed that a higher risk of developing myocardial infarction (a heart attack) after *discontinuing* oral contraceptives persists for at least nine years for women aged 40 to 49 who had used oral contraceptives for more than five years. A British study found that a greater risk of developing cerebrovascular disease (disease of blood vessels in the brain) persisted for at least *six years* after *stopping* oral contraceptive use. The women in both studies had used

Note that the list of adverse effects given in *PDR* is much longer than the one above! Also stated in *PDR* is the fact that the side effects have been reported as occurring in reaction to estrogen use generally, including oral contraceptives, and *they may be encountered in association with any type of estrogen therapy.*

PDR further states that if Premarin is prescribed in conjunction with testosterone or tranquilizing agents, it must be given cyclically and only over a short term because of the risks entailed in this combination, and that the risks of Premarin taken alone can be lowered by administering the drug cyclically and over the short term only.

Last, but certainly not least, *PDR* constantly repeats in reference to estrogen that *it is important to take this drug only when it is really needed.*

oral contraceptives containing 50 mcg of estrogens per pill. In addition, women using this hormone need to know the following facts:

- The development of abnormal blood clots is the most common serious side effect of the use of estrogens, particularly during surgery or bed rest. How many women are advised to stop taking estrogens for at least three to four weeks before surgery, for two weeks after surgery, or when there is a need for bed rest due to prolonged illness?

- Cigarette smoking increases the possibility that estrogen will have serious adverse effects on the heart and blood vessels. This risk increases with age and becomes significant in oral contraceptive users older than 35. We think it would be logical to include in the high-risk category HRT users who smoke. How many young women on the pill or women on HRT are told of the incredibly high increased risk of cardiovascular disease that comes with combining smoking and estrogen use?

- Women who take estrogen for more than one year have a risk of developing endometrial cancer that is on average 14 times higher than normal. The degree of risk depends on both the duration of estrogen use and the dosage taken.

- The risk of developing cancer rises dramatically with the use of HRT. The Nurses' Health Study, organized by the Harvard Medical School, followed 122 000 nurses over 16 years and reported the following regarding its subjects:

  — Women on estrogen alone developed breast cancer at rates 36 percent higher than average.

  — Women taking estrogen and progestin experienced a 50 percent increase in breast cancer rates.

  — Women taking progestins alone experienced a 240 percent increase in breast cancer rates.

  — Women taking estrogen in combination with testosterone experienced a 78 percent increase in breast cancer rates.

  — Women between 60 and 64, taking HRT over five years, experienced a 71 percent increase in breast cancer rates.

  — Women on synthetic HRT were found to be twice as likely to suffer from adult-onset asthma.

- The Collaborative Group on Hormonal Factors in Breast Cancer study, which reported its results in October 1997, found that after five years of estrogen use, women's risk of developing breast cancer increased by 35 percent. The extra risk didn't disappear until *five years* after stopping estrogen use.

- CPS states that women at increased risk of developing breast cancer before menopause are long-term users of oral contraceptives (more than eight years) and those who start using these drugs at an early age.

ANOTHER GOOD REASON TO "FLUSH" THE HORSE'S URINE

It has been found in a 1998 in-depth study of Premarin that the breakdown products of synthetic (non-bioidentical) hormones are different from those of bioidentical hormones. For example, the breakdown products of Premarin are biologically stronger than estradiol itself and have been called the *ultimate carcinogens*. If we are so set on taking estrogen derived from urine, why don't we leave horse's urine for the horses and collect our own? We know how this may sound unappealing, but in India the benefits of urine therapy have been extensively studied; we will leave that one to you!

> "Here we can see in stark outline the vast dangers of 'medicine by advertising' in this country. When the primary driving force behind a drug is expansion of the number of users, untempered by concerns for long-term effects and truth in advertising, the results can be devastating."—Marcus Laux, N.D.

Given the health risks associated with estrogen exposure, it would make sense (at least to us it does) to use it only as needed, as sparingly as possible. But what if we were to add all the estrogen-like chemicals that we get from our environment (xenoestrogens) and in our foods to the HRT doses, then factor in the influence of a congested liver and bowel throwing endogenous estrogen back into circulation? What then?

Please don't take me literally when we say "flush" the horse's urine; treat it as a toxic substance. Remember, what goes around comes around—yes in our environment too!

Estrogen Excess

The fact is that estrogen excess is very common in women, including during the menopausal years, for various reasons we will be covering. The usual allopathic medical assumption, particularly during the menopausal years, is that estrogen is deficient and it is prescribed wholesale, usually, without any verification from blood or saliva testing that it is really needed. The pre-use and follow-up examinations discussed above, needed to determine risks and effectiveness of treatment as well as possible side effects, are rarely done, despite the fact that they are called for by authoritative medical reference books.

Because of the lack of testing, many women whose real problem is low progesterone production (more common at the perimenopause) and a resultant unbalanced estrogen to progesterone ratio (excess estrogen, deficient progesterone) are never properly diagnosed. Add to this the possible sources of estrogens and estrogen-like compounds and you will see that estrogen excess is fairly easy to develop. Sources or causes of high estrogen levels include:

- environmental (exogenous) estrogens
- HRT
- liver congestion and dysbiosis
- oral contraceptives (the birth control pill)
- non-organic animal products (dairy, meat)
- increased estrogen made by the body because of:
  — ovarian function imbalance
  — hysterectomies causing ovarian imbalance
  — adrenal stress

The signs and symptoms of estrogen excess are many, and are also very common. If you frequently experience any of the symptoms listed below, make sure your investigation of the possible causes includes a check of your estrogen levels.

- Acceleration of the aging process
- Increased blood pressure; increased blood clotting
- Impaired blood sugar control; hypoglycemia
- Depression
- Increased body fat, especially around hips; general weight gain
- Fluid retention; sore breasts, fibrocystic breasts

- Headaches; migraines
- Decreased libido
- Memory loss and foggy thinking
- Heavy and long menstrual flow; possible short cycle (21 days), painful periods, PMS acne
- Decreased thyroid function
- Increased triglycerides
- Uterine fibroids, endometriosis

All these symptoms can be made worse by supplemental synthetic estrogen. Estrogen excess also leads to an increased risk of gallbladder disease and an increased risk of breast and endometrial cancer.

XENOESTROGENS AND THEIR INFLUENCE ON THE HORMONAL SYSTEM

One of the biggest culprits in estrogen excess, environmental chemicals with estrogen-like properties, have been mentioned several times throughout this chapter. We sincerely hope the story below and the many others like it are tales that we will not be having to tell our grandchildren—if we are fortunate enough to have any, given the rising rate of sterility in males and infertility in women. The global problem of environmental toxins and xeno-estrogens causing chronic disease and genetic mutations can change; *but we all need to do our part!*

The Tale of Lake Apopka: Are We Listening?

Come with me to the sea, the sea of ... *gender bending chemicals.*

In the early 1970s, scientists began counting alligators in Lake Apopka, Florida, an ideal place to hatch baby alligators. In the early 1980s they would often see up to 2,000 alligators a night on the lake. Then something began to happen. By the late 1980s they were finding at most only 150 per night. What could be going on? It was also found that the poor alligators had some big (or small) worries. The males' penises were only one-quarter the normal size; their testosterone levels were so low they were sterile and unable to do their part in making baby alligators. The researchers eventually found that some poisonous substances (DDT metabolites) had similar effects on mice, and lo and behold, it turned out that thousands of gallons of these same poisons (DDT-

containing pesticides) had spilled into Lake Apopka in the
were living in a sea of gender-bending chemicals—*but* t
The chemicals the alligators had to deal with were si
ture to the estrogen hormones that they were able to tri
into using the imposters as they would estrogen molecules. And yes, human ....
have receptor sites for estrogen too, not just male alligators. Surrounded by
these chemicals, the male alligators started becoming more and more female-
like; they were becoming hermaphrodites, creatures who could not be classified as male or female because they had sex characteristics of both.

The estrogen impostors not only created serious problems in the sexual
development of the male alligators, they interfered with the healthy development of the female alligators too. The result? No more baby alligators.

And if the estrogen impostors are good enough to trick the alligators,
they can sure fool us too.

Beyond Alligators

Florida panthers who eat high on a food chain now contaminated with
estrogen-like pesticides (xenoestrogens) have their own reproductive problems: more infertile females and sterile males, lower sperm counts, and high
estrogen levels. In March 1994, toxicologist C. Facemire of the United
States Fish and Wildlife Service said that the male panthers had estrogen
levels higher than most females.

Literally hundreds of chemicals found in the environment—PCBs, pesticides, polycarbons used in many plastics, chlorine-containing compounds, *and
synthetic estrogens and estrogen metabolites that enter the water supply via the
urine of women taking synthetic estrogens*—all resemble the human hormone
estrogen. These compounds are now called xenoestrogens. Their molecules
are similar enough to human estrogens to fit into the same cell receptor
sites—the estrogen parking spots—that the body's naturally produced
hormones would use. And yes, chlorine is added to our drinking water.

There is plenty of evidence that these environmental estrogen-like chemicals affect the human hormonal system.

- In 1994, the research of Danish endocrinologist Dr. N. Skakkebaek
  indicated that since 1938, sperm counts in men in the United States
  and 20 other countries have decreased by an average of 50 percent and
  testicular cancer rates have tripled since 1938.

Women who eat meat high in PBBs (estrogen mimics) have sons with testicular and penis malformations.

- A German study published in 1994 reported that women with endometriosis were more likely to have high levels of PCBs in their blood.
- A study published in 1993 by New York's Mount Sinai School of Medicine found that women with the greatest number of DDE markers (a DDT metabolite) are four times more likely to get breast cancer.

HOW XENOESTROGENS AFFECT US

Chemicals enter the body when we eat, drink, or breathe and are distributed throughout the body by the blood. Chemicals that are not removed efficiently by detoxification pathways accumulate in the body; those that are fat soluble, notably PCBs and DDT, accumulate in fat stores. Fat stores are mobilized during stress, malnutrition, pregnancy, or perspiration, at which times these chemicals are re-released into the blood circulation.

Hormones made by the body are modified by sex hormone binding substances that bind the majority of the hormones in the blood, thereby reducing their availability for initiating responses. It has been found that numerous xenoestrogens, however, bind far less to the hormone binding substances than do internally produced hormones, leaving more free chemicals available to bind with estrogen receptor sites on the cells and catalyze the responses those cells make to estrogen hormones. It has been found that if several of these chemicals are added together, their effects are additive, so exposure to even small quantities of a range of xenoestrogens can add up to a large impact. Many chemicals, particularly fat-soluble ones, can also travel into a fetus from the mother's blood.

In addition to their estrogenic activity, xenoestrogens have a number of other toxic effects.

- **Blocking non-estrogen hormone receptor sites.** Many receptors, in addition to estrogen receptors, are involved in the hormonal system, for example receptors for male hormones. The xenoestrogens, like DDT metabolites, can bind and inactivate these receptors, decreasing the natural activity levels of male hormones in both women and men and thereby causing problems similar to those experienced by hermaphroditic alligators and sterile and infertile panthers.

- **Modifying natural hormone metabolism.** Some of the environmental chemicals can alter the pathways of estradiol, resulting in the conversion of our healthy estrogens into cancer-causing estrogens. Other of these chemicals increase the metabolism of hormones, disrupting their natural balance. In the testes there are specific enzymes that metabolize estrogens, breaking them down rapidly into a form in which they can no longer bind to receptors. Xenoestrogens reduce the levels of these enzymes, and the exposure of the testes to estrogen is therefore increased. Increased testicular estrogen exposure due to chemical disruption is of particular concern during fetal development, as the fetus is regularly exposed to high estrogen levels from the mother's hormonal production.

- **Modifying the number of hormone receptors in a cell.** A chemical can reduce or increase the number of hormone receptors in a cell, thereby affecting the extent of the cell's response to natural or artificial hormones.

- **Modifying the production of natural hormones.** Xenoestrogenous chemicals interfere with the smooth functioning of the thyroid, immune system, and other organs and systems, resulting in increases or decreases in hormones made by these organs and systems.

In November 1995, an international conference was held in the United States to study the xenoestrogens, or as they are otherwise known, the hormone-disrupting chemicals. The conclusion was that hormone-disrupting chemicals can undermine neurological and behavioural development in children and thereby cut short the potential of the individual. The conference report went on to say that many hormone-disrupting contaminants, even if less potent than natural hormones, are nowadays present in living tissue in most creatures at concentrations millions of times higher than the natural hormones would normally be found in.

However, even after this report, the general medical response is that the situation is definitely worth further study, but *it is not certain* that these hormone-like molecules have any negative effect on humans.

Why do we think that as humans we are immune to the effects our environment has on wildlife? We continue to be blind to the warning signs, and if we don't wake up and change the way we are headed quickly, the chances of being able to reproduce will soon be slim to none—and you can figure out the ending to the story. The present-day plight of alligators and panthers and the human health effects documented so far are more than enough to convince us that rapid change is necessary.

We sincerely hope and trust that the attitude of the general population changes and begins to focus on *health care as health promotion and disease prevention*. Rather than continually waiting for "new and improved" drugs to offer better health through chemistry, let's get back to basics and start taking more responsibility for our own health and our environment: *we need to learn to appreciate and respect the interconnectedness of each and every aspect of our physical, mental, emotional, and spiritual selves, and we need to learn to have reverence for each person and for all other living things—we are all part of, and influenced by, the whole.*

Can Phytoestrogens Contribute to Estrogen Excess?

By this point in the discussion, estrogen must appear to be a scary substance indeed. But remember, the health risks associated with estrogen are all present in relation to estrogen replacement and xenoestrogens, toxic chemicals present in the environment. Phytoestrogens are not associated with increased cancer risks or "gender-bending" effects.

As discussed above, phytoestrogens are natural substances whose estrogenic effects are much weaker than both human estrogens and xenoestrogens. As such, they have an important protective effect: by taking up estrogen receptor sites, they prevent toxic chemicals or strong internal estrogens from using those same sites and causing much stronger estrogenic effects. Phytoestrogens thus do not generally contribute to estrogen excess, but help combat it. At the same time, their mild estrogenic effects ease menopausal symptoms. In certain cases of extreme estrogen excess, however, such as when endometriosis, estrogen-dominant breast cancer, or other serious indications of estrogen excess are present, even phytoestrogenic herbs may need to be used with caution. In such cases, it is first very important to detoxify the body to clear chemicals and to strengthen the liver and bowel so that estrogens can be efficiently excreted.

Estriol in the Spotlight

Now that we have considered the dangers of synthetic HRT, let's take a look at one possibly safer pharmaceutical alternative.

Estrone, estradiol, and estriol are the main three estrogens made naturally by human beings. As explained previously, most commercial estrogens are patented—and therefore slightly altered—forms of estradiol, or combinations of estrone and estradiol. But estriol, in bioidentical form, has recently come into the spotlight in North America. Some family doctors and many complementary practitioners see it as a relatively safer estrogen prescription for the symptoms of menopause. Estriol is said to be a weak estrogen. However, compared to estradiol, it is more biologically active. Estradiol is bound to sex hormone binding globulin (SHBG), making only a portion of circulating estradiol available for entry into the cells. Estriol, on the other hand, has a much lower affinity for SHBG, and therefore a greater percentage is available for biological activity. Dr. C. Northrup, in reviewing the data from Aaron and Madison Pharmacy, has found that Tri-Est, a combination product containing estrone, estriol and estradiol, actually gave users higher levels of estrogen activity than the other commonly prescribed estrogens.

Research done in Europe indicates that estriol appears to be the safest estrogen. However, when the global research record is studied, estriol has somewhat of a mixed record.

One of the leading researchers on estriol, Dr. H. Lemon, reports that estriol is probably a safer form of estrogen than others with regard to breast cancer risks. He bases his theory on the following facts: when estriol is given to animals in conjunction with estradiol, it accelerates the removal of estradiol bound to protein receptors (that is, it exerts an antiestrogenic effect); in addition, larger doses do not cause cancer. Estriol supplementation does not result in the formation of potentially carcinogenic substances as estrone and estradiol supplementation do. Another researcher, A. H. Follingstad, reports further on the research done by Lemon. He states that 37 percent of women supplemented with estriol at 2.5 to 5.0 mg per day demonstrate remission or arrest of metastatic breast cancer lesions. However, other studies indicate that estriol, as well as estrone and estradiol, has a stimulatory effect on human breast cancer cells.

It is well established that unopposed estrogen contributes significantly to the risk of uterine cancer. It has been believed that estriol does not cause endometrial proliferation to the same extent as estradiol and estrone. However, studies indicate that estriol does contribute to endometrial stimulation. More recently, a meta-analysis of 12 studies concluded that the daily use of intravaginal estriol is safe. Other studies on estriol were done on oral estriol, which could explain why some studies indicate a certain amount of risk but the meta-analysis does not.

Estriol is capable of exerting estrogenic or antiestrogenic action depending on dosage, administration schedule, and length of use. Estriol has more stimulatory effects when given in divided doses causing sustained levels rather than when given once daily. Although estriol appears to be much safer than estrone or estradiol, its continuous use seems to have a stimulatory effect on both breast and endometrial tissue.

Given the conflicting results regarding the effect of estriol on the endometrium, we suggest that if your symptoms require HRT, you use USP progesterone with estriol to protect yourself from endometrial proliferation, and use it for a short time only. At this point estriol appears to provide certain benefits associated with HRT without creating as high health risks as those associated with estradiol and estrone—but inside, my *yellow caution lights* are still flashing.

AVAILABILITY OF ESTRIOL

Estriol is available by prescription in the United States and Canada from many compounding pharmacies, either alone or in a combination formula called Tri-Est.

Remember the goal … *let's get healthy!* Then prescription HRT will be unnecessary in most cases, and, if required, will be needed only for a short time.

HORMONE BALANCE PROTOCOLS

These are general protocols that will support your hormonal balance during the transitional years. Remember, we are all individual, and one size does not fit all, ever. Adjust these programs, in consultation with your health care practitioner if need be, to suit your needs.

Asymptomatic Women

Women with few or no symptoms of hormonal changes who want to maintain hormonal balance can use the following protocol:

- Follow the general guidelines for creating optimal health (Chapters 1 to 4).
- Add essential fatty acids to your diet if you aren't taking them already
- Support your liver at least 10 days/month with EstroSense or liv-tone
- Support the adrenal glands with nutrients from Chapter 3.
- Take a good multiple vitamin such as FemmEssentials which also contains 1,000 mg evening primrose oil and 1,600 mg of organic flax.
- Take a calcium supplement, such as OsteoBalance+ or Bone-Up.

Mildly Symptomatic Women

Perimenopausal, menopausal, or postmenopausal women with mild to moderate symptoms will benefit from the following protocol:

- Take all steps outlined above, and add MenoSense, meno or Remefemin (standardized botanical products discussed earlier in this chapter).

- If you have difficulty with insomnia, take valerian, hops, passion flower, and/or chamomile one hour before bed.

Severely Symptomatic Women

Perimenopausal, menopausal, or postmenopausal women with severe symptoms such as debilitating hot flashes or chronic insomnia will benefit from the following treatment:

- Take all steps outlined above and add Tri-Est and USP progesterone for three to six months until symptoms are stable. Then begin with the "weaning process" outlined below, starting with Step Two.

Women on Oral HRT

For women who have been on hormones such as Premarin and Provera for more than five years, following is a two-step weaning process. Note: If you have been taking hormones for less than five years, do not wean to Tri-Est; switch directly to botanical support (e.g., MenoSense, meno, Remefemin) as outlined below and change from Provera to USP progesterone. Your daily amount of HRT will not change, only the frequency of intake.

STEP ONE

Change from standard HRT to Tri-Est and USP progesterone, in oral or cream form. If you have not been taking progesterone of any kind but are taking a synthetic estrogen, add the USP progesterone at the same time that you change to a bioidentical estrogen such as Tri-Est.

After adjusting to Tri-Est and USP progesterone for three to six months, you may want to move to Step Two.

STEP TWO

Follow the charts on the next page to wean yourself from estrogen. Directions for USP progesterone use are given directly below, or use as directed by your health care practitioner.

BASIC PROTOCOL FOR USP PROGESTERONE

The dosages given are for creams containing 3 percent progesterone by volume, or 1.6 percent by weight.

Menstruating Women

- Days 1 to 7 of the menstrual cycle (or until the end of menstruation): no progesterone.
- Approximately Days 8 to 21: one-quarter teaspoon morning and night.
- For approximately one week before the onset of menstruation, one-half teaspoon morning and night. (Note: Stop using progesterone one or two days before the menses would normally start.)
- Or take progesterone for 12 days of every cycle, beginning at the mid-point.

Menopausal Women

- Use a low dose throughout the month. Take one-quarter teaspoon cream morning and night.
- If your symptoms are more severe, take one-half teaspoon cream morning and night. Once symptoms have stabilized, decrease the dose.

WEANING OFF USP PROGESTERONE

To begin decreasing progesterone use, remember that the least amount possible of any hormone is ideal. Try decreasing your progesterone use by one-half. Then try using this halved dosage every other day. Let your sense of well-being, your symptom frequency, and salivary tests guide the process.

Most women will find that once they have made the necessary lifestyle and dietary changes and begin giving support to the adrenal glands, intestines, and liver, they will require only botanical support to maintain hormonal balance. Both for its effects on yourself and your environment, it is a worthy goal for which to work—and getting there can be a whole new adventure.

WOMEN ON ORAL HRT

WEEKS	ESTROGEN	BOTANICAL MENOSENSE	PROGES-TERONE
	(Tri-Est or other)	MenoSense	(USP cream or oral)
1 and 2	4 days per week	3 days per week	as directed
3 and 4	3 days per week	4 days per week	as directed
5 and 6	2 days per week	5 days per week	as directed
7 and 8	0 to 1 day per week	7 days per week	as directed

Take one to two capsules of EstroSense everyday to aid hormone balance

WOMEN ON TRANSDERMAL HRT

WEEKS	APPLY PATCH	BOTANICAL MenoSense	USP PROGES-TERONE
1 and 2	every 5 days then apply new patch, wear for 5 days	evey other day	as directed
3 and 4	wear patch for 7 days	evey other day	as directed
5	do not wear patch for 7 days	daily	as directed
6	wear patch for 7 days	daily	as directed
7	do not wear patch for 7 days	daily	as directed
8	wear patch for 7 days	daily	as directed

Take one to two capsules of EstroSense everyday to aid hormone balance

---

UNDERSTANDING
OSTEOPOROSIS

*"The forces of winter create cold in Heaven and water on Earth.
They create the kidney organ and the bones within the body ...
the emotion fear, and the ability to make the groaning
sound."—Inner Classic*

It is estimated that a 50-year-old woman has a 50 percent chance of suffering an osteoporosis-related fracture during the remainder of her life.

Osteoporosis, a disease in which the bones become porous and easily broken, is one of the most debilitating and costly illnesses that may confront us as we age. It affects one in four women and one in eight men (35 percent of osteoporotic fractures occur in men) and is reaching epidemic proportions in the United States and Canada. Currently, one in four Canadian women and about 400,000 men are affected by osteoporosis annually; as a result, more than 25,000 hip fractures, with costs of $400 million annually, occur in Canada every year. In the United States, more than three million people are diagnosed with osteoporosis each year, and one and a half million osteoporosis-related fractures, most often of the hip, spine, or wrist, occur every year.

Complications of osteoporosis, particularly hip fractures, result in death in 20 percent of cases; of those who survive, 50 percent require long-term care.

Fifty million women of the baby boom generation are entering menopause today. Although osteoporosis can occur at any time, postmenopausal osteoporosis is the most common form of this crippling disease. In 1988, the estimated annual health care costs in the United States for osteoporosis and its consequences were between $7 billion and $10 billion; costs are expected to increase to between $30 billion and $40 billion annually by the turn of the century as the percentage of the population over age 65 increases. More important is the increase in pain and suffering that accompanies osteoporosis.

Osteoporosis needs our full attention, *now*. There are no magic bullets!

Personally, we never thought about osteoporosis as a possibility for ourselves. We have been athletically active all our lives, became vegetarian in our twenties, have never consumed cow's milk (you'll find out later why we feel that has decreased, rather than increased, our risks), and for many years have taken our supplements regularly. But when Karen observed her mother, now in her eighties, become the "incredible shrinking woman" and experience spinal and wrist fractures, osteoporosis got her full attention. In our search to understand more about osteoporosis risk factors and treatments, we realized that the conventional medical approach is very superficial, giving little, if any, attention to the underlying causes of the disease.

Osteoporosis is influenced by genetics, endocrine function, diet and lifestyle, and environmental factors. Osteoporosis prevention and treatment therefore requires a fully integrated approach that addresses all possible contributing factors.

Unfortunately, the widespread incidence of this disease is not met by widespread knowledge about it. Popular ideas about osteoporosis generally run along the line that taking more calcium, especially through consumption of milk and dairy products, will prevent bone problems. If milk fails, assume many women, estrogen or the new antiosteoporosis drugs will save them. This chapter and the next will clarify why these ideas are inadequate.

Doctors do not seem to be knowledgeable about osteoporosis either. Studies have found that 80 percent of patients treated with fractures typical of osteoporosis are not diagnosed as having this bone-wasting disease. The researchers studied the treatment of 108 patients who fractured a hip, wrist, spine, or shoulder in a minor fall—these fractures are usually treated by an orthopedic surgeon. When patients were contacted later, it was found that only one in five had been given the diagnosis of osteoporosis. Thus, at least four out of five patients with fractures due to osteoporosis were not given information that might help them set up a realistic program for treatment and prevention of further bone deterioration.

Granted, the statistics surrounding osteoporosis are grim. But they don't seal our fate. We don't have to become statistics. We always have the choice between being reactive or proactive. And as we become more informed, we can assume more responsibility for our health.

"He is the best physician who is the most ingenious inspirer of hope."— Samuel Taylor Coleridge

The fact is that osteoporosis, like so many other common diseases, is created through the accumulated effects of diet and lifestyle choices we make over the years. Our diets and lifestyles, along with our mental, emotional, and spiritual health, contribute to our overall health—and bone health is no exception.

Prevention has been shown to be the most effective method of dealing with osteoporosis *and we don't mean* drinking lots of milk and taking calcium, vitamin D, and estrogen. If one has already been diagnosed with osteo-porosis, there are safe and effective natural treatments that can be employed as an alternative to more toxic drugs. *We can prevent and treat osteoporosis safely with naturopathic treatments.*

Now, we realize that we are again flying in the face of conventional wisdom. In 1998 a research director of an osteoporosis research program at Women's College Hospital in Toronto, Dr. G. Hawker, stated that diet and exercise are not adequate for addressing osteoporosis and that drugs must be taken to prevent and treat the disease. Her statements could lead one to believe that osteoporosis is simply a deficiency of Didronel and Fosamax (common drugs used to treat osteoporosis). We also believe that this researcher's understanding of preventive diet and other lifestyle choices is probably limited—the allopathic approach to nutritional prevention of osteoporosis is to push dairy products, and, as we shall see, this approach doesn't have a sound scientific basis.

After reading this chapter, you will have a better understanding of the possible causes of osteoporosis and the varied choices you have for prevent-ing and treating this disease. Let's begin by considering the bones.

BONES: WHAT ARE THEY?

When we look at the skeleton in the chiropractor's office we might be led to think that bones are dead matter and don't count for much. Bones, however, are a living substance and one of the most active tissues in the body. They offer support for all the other body structures, as well as protect delicate structures such as the brain, spinal cord, lungs, heart, and major blood vessels. They are also the levers to which the muscles of the body are attached—with-out them the muscles would not be able to move us around. Finally, they are critical in blood cell production.

Despite their importance, it is often forgotten that the bones are more than just a collection of calcium crystals that simply require more calcium to remain healthy. In reality, bone is a composite. Thirty percent of bone mass consists of osteoid, living tissue made up of connective tissue and proteins. Seventy percent of bone is made of minerals; of this, 95 percent is mineral salts, primarily calcium phosphate and calcium carbonate called hydroxyapatite, and small amounts of magnesium, sodium, potassium, chloride, and fluoride.

Structurally speaking, there are two types of bone. Cortical bone, which forms the outer casing of all bones and is concentrated in the shafts of the long bones of the legs and arms, makes up 80 percent of all bone. Trabecular bone, which forms the inner meshwork of the vertebrae, pelvis, and other flat bones and the ends of the long bones, makes up the other 20 percent. As complex structures, bones need complex nutritional support to stay strong and healthy. Bones also becomes stronger as a result of mechanical stress and other stresses involving the effects of gravity.

Bone mass reaches its maximum level, known as peak bone mass, around the age of 30. To reach the highest possible peak bone mass, an individual must have taken in and absorbed optimal levels of the nutrients known to enhance bone density and have avoided the factors that deplete bone mass. Once peak bone mass is reached, about 25 percent of trabecular bone and 3 percent of cortical bone will be broken down and rebuilt every year.

We have already alluded to the fact that because bones are living tissue they are continuously in a process of breaking themselves down (this process is called resorption) and rebuilding themselves. Osteoclasts are the bone cells responsible for breaking down old bone. They detect slightly damaged and older bone and slowly dissolve it, leaving behind an empty space. Enter the osteoblasts, which build new bone to fill the space. When the osteo-clast and osteoblast activity is balanced, bone mass remains stable.

Bones lose mass when there is increased osteoclast activity or decreased osteoblast activity. The result of bone loss is osteoporosis.

WHAT IS OSTEOPOROSIS?

The word "osteoporosis" simply means porous bone. People with osteoporosis experience progressive loss of bone mass involving both the organic and mineral structures of bone, and as a result, increased susceptibility to fractures.

Although the entire skeleton can be involved, bone loss in osteoporosis is usually greatest in the trabecular bone, especially in the spine, hips, and ribs. Other commonly affected areas are the wrists, upper arms, and shoulders. One-third of all North American women and one-sixth of all North American men will fracture their hips in their lifetime.

Bone loss begins between the ages of 35 and 40. During this time, there is an annual rate of loss of 0.3 to 1.0 percent of peak bone mass in both men and women. The loss accelerates to 3 to 5 percent annually in postmenopausal women. However, in many women half of the total vertebral bone loss occurs *before* estrogen levels decline. Therefore, menopause cannot be the only cause of osteoporosis. In most cases, however, bone loss occurs at the most rapid rate for the first four to six years after menopause, and the excess bone loss attributable to menopause is approximately 10 to 15 percent in the limbs and 15 to 20 percent in the spine. Because of age-related decreases in bone density, current statistics indicate that the risk of hip fracture doubles every six to seven years after menopause.

The denser her bone as a woman enters menopause, the less significant the accelerated postmenopausal bone loss.

The most frequently occurring forms of osteoporosis are Type I, post-menopausal osteoporosis, and Type II, age-related osteoporosis. Type I involves greater trabecular bone loss and has a tremendous impact on the vertebrae, especially when one considers that even before menopause many women will have lost close to 50 percent of their vertebral bone. We will be considering the causes of Type I osteoporosis later in this chapter. In Type II osteoporosis the bone loss is equal in both cortical and trabecular bone and the greatest effect is on the femur (hip) and the long bones of the legs and arms. This type of osteoporosis seems to be closely linked to the age-related decline of intestinal absorption of nutrients and the impaired conversion of vitamin D into its active form. A deficiency of vitamin D causes the bones to give up excessive amounts of calcium and phosphorus, causing bone loss (demineralization); this loss tends to be particularly heavy in the bones of the pelvis, legs, and spine.

A study published in the *New England Journal of Medicine* in 1998 reported that vitamin D deficiency is common among older adults and that even daily intake of a multivitamin supplement does not provide enough of this vitamin. The study, done with patients at a Boston hospital, reported that 57 percent of the 290 people tested had too little vitamin D; 22 per cent had a severe deficiency. (Vitamin D will be discussed in more detail in Chapter 8.)

You may have also heard the term "osteopenia." The word refers to decreased bone mass from any cause. Technically, osteopenia is the diagnosis when there is detectable bone mass loss as determined by a bone scan, but the loss is not yet causing symptoms.

Osteoporosis and the Immune System

Scientists have shown that there is an intimate connection between the immune system and osteoporosis. Who would have ever thought that osteoporosis could be caused by our immune system? Research showing that our immune system may cause osteoporosis is so new that even your doctor may not be aware of this important interplay. Calcium and vitamin D supplements alone won't halt osteoporosis if your immune system is not in balance. As we mentioned earlier in the book the immune system is made up of many different types of cells that release certain factors called cytokines. These cells and their cytokines destroy invaders, fight cancer cells and regulate other systems in the body including the body's bone maintenance system. Certain cytokines have a direct effect on bone strength by causing bone loss.

THE STRESS CONNECTION

Stress and its effect on two types of immune cells are the basis of osteoporosis. We have two types of T-helper cells called T-helper-1 and T-helper-2 cells. T-helper-2 cells release three main cytokines that have been shown to cause bone loss of these are interleukin-6, interleukin-8 and interleukin-1. T-helper-1 cells, we can call them the good guys, control T-helper-2 cells making sure that these bad guys don't release too many of the cytokines that cause bone loss. T-helper-1 cells also release cytokines that protect or help build bone so we really want to have more good T-helper-1 cells to enhance bone development. But when we are under stress, especially unrelenting stress, the bad T-helper-2 cells release plenty of interleukin-6, interleukin-8 and interleukin-1 which cause calcium to be pulled from our bones causing bone loss.

Stressful events cause an increase in our stress hormone cortisol and cortisol's job is to get calcium from bone to make it available to the body during the stressful event. What this means is that the odd stressful situation is not a problem but for many individuals today under constant stress from financial pressures, too many activities to complete in a day, inadequate nutrient consumption from our food and more, bone loss can be the result. Each of us handle stress differently and stress does not just mean having a fight with your spouse or disliking your job, you can release cortisol from feeling cold. Cortisol then causes interleukin-6 to pull calcium from bone. Stressors are different for each of us. Yet one thing is clear stress does cause bone loss. For more information on stress, cortisol and health, see Chapter 3.

Our bones are not static they are constantly being broken down and restored. We can take all the calcium citrate, vitamin D, boron and estrogen in the world but if we do not deal with our stress we are missing the key to osteoporosis prevention. Those who are taking Fosamax, hormone replacement therapy and thousands of milligrams of calcium still have bone loss—now we know why. It is our immune system releasing too many of the bad interleukins that cause bone loss.

NUTRIENTS THAT CONTROL CALCIUM LOSS

Researchers found in studies published in the *International Journal of Immunopharmacology* and the *International Journal of Sports Medicine* that plant sterols and sterolins (both studies were using Moducare) controlled the release of cortisol and the subsequent secretion of Interleukin-6 thereby protecting our bones. Plant sterols and sterolins are the missing key—they stop bone loss! Make plant sterols and sterolins the basis of your bone-building program. Then add vitamin D, calcium citrate and other bone building nutrients along with weight-bearing exercise and watch your bone density improve.

Who Is at Risk?

In addition to diet and lifestyle influences on optimal bone mass (see Chapter 8), there are several additional factors that can predispose a person to developing osteoporosis. Risk factors for osteoporosis include the following:

- age—risk of developing osteoporosis increases after age 35
- amenorrhea
- small bones and/or low peak bone mass
- Caucasian or Asian heritage
- genetic and hereditary factors
- hormonal deficiencies and endocrine imbalances, including hyperthyroidism (overactive thyroid) and hyperparathyroidism (overactive parathyroid; this gland is discussed below)
- hydrochloric acid (stomach acid) deficiency
- complete hysterectomy
- early menopause

- obesity
- frequent or regular use of over-the-counter/prescription drugs
- premature grey hair
- sex—women are at greater risk

- stress = increases cortisol = increases bone loss

Genetic and ethnic factors significantly influence bone health. Mothers with low bone mineral content tend to have daughters with low bone mineral content. It also appears that Caucasian women are at greater risk for osteoporotic fractures than women of other races. Studies show that bone mass is greater in black women and men and in white men compared to Caucasian women, and consequently the latter have twice the risk of hip fractures as do black women.

Women generally carry a greater risk for hip fracture than men, particularly women who have a small bone frame. Women's greater risk is due partly to the fact that their bone mass is generally smaller than that of men and that their bone loss accelerates after menopause because of hormonal changes. Age is also considered a risk factor for osteoporosis (see above); an accelerated postmenopausal bone loss of 3 to 5 percent annually occurs in women. With age-related decline in bone mass the risk of fracture increases; an exponential increase in incidence of hip fracture among both men and women begins between the ages of 35 and 44, with the risk doubling every six to seven years.

Another major factor in one's risk of developing osteoporosis is the level of peak bone mass achieved at skeletal maturity (between the ages of 25 and 30 years), which is influenced by activity and nutritional status as a child and young adult. The more bone mass available before age-related bone loss starts, the less risk of fracture.

Early menopause or surgically induced menopause is felt by some to increase risk because of the longer period of estrogen and progesterone deficiency these events cause in a woman's life. In one study, women who had had both ovaries removed had two to three times the risk of hip fracture of other postmenopausal women. Women who have hysterectomies but do not have their ovaries removed are also at increased risk because the blood and nerve supply to the ovaries is altered during such surgery. The ovaries thus become less efficient, resulting in decreased hormone production earlier than in women experiencing natural menopause.

Women who have suffered from anorexia nervosa and competitive female athletes both commonly experience amenorrhea, or loss of menses, and as a result have lower bone density. When body fat falls to very low levels, a woman quits ovulating and bones lose mass as a result of decreased progesterone, since progesterone levels rise after ovulation. The bone loss occurs despite normal estrogen levels. (We will discuss the role of progesterone in bone health later in this chapter.)

Weight is another factor in osteoporosis risk but it represents a double-edged sword. The protective effect of increased weight has been shown consistently in case control studies. There is a 30 to 40 percent reduction in risk of osteoporosis for every 3.4 kg of body weight, according to various studies. Women who have more fat than the recommended 22 percent do not suffer estrogen decline as much as women with low body fat. Fat is the site of much of the conversion of estrogen and other steroid hormones from precursor hormones.

Our society's obsession with thinness in women thus perpetuates potential compromised health in those who buy the image that thin means beautiful. On the other hand, with excessive weight, as in the case of obese people, there is added stress on the bones and surrounding tissues that potentially can cause back problems and pain in the legs and hips. Healthy eating and regular exercise help establish a natural body weight that is right for the person. It is this natural balance in body weight that should be sought.

HORMONES: THEIR INFLUENCE ON BONE HEALTH

Hormones play a very important role in bone health. However, the current almost exclusive focus on estrogens as a critical factor in bone health is seriously misplaced. Many more hormones are involved, and the estrogens alone do not necessarily have the beneficial effects many people think they do.

A healthy hormonal system maintains a delicate balance, with contributions coming from all of the endocrine (hormone secreting) organs. The principal regulators of bone remodelling are parathyroid hormone (PTH); 1,25-hydroxycholecalciferol (1,25-DOHCC, or vitamin D); calcitonin, secreted by the thyroid; and to a lesser extent, estrogens, androgens, progesterone, and thyroid hormone.

SUPPLEMENTAL ESTROGEN AND BONE HEALTH

The effect of estrogen therapy on the bones can be simply summarized, in another, obvious, a + b = c equation that is based on the known actions of the cells involved in remodelling bone:

(a) Estrogens inhibit osteoclasts +

(b) Osteoclasts destroy old, damaged bone =

(c) Increase in old, damaged brittle bone

Calcitonin, PTH, and Cholecalciferol

Calcitonin stimulates the deposition of new bone, and in so doing, decreases blood calcium levels. PTH increases when blood calcium levels are low. PTH also causes breakdown of bone; increases kidney absorption and excretion of calcium; and decreases kidney absorption of phosphates. This last function has importance because phosphates that remain in the blood bind to calcium, making it inactive.

DOHCC is a derivative of vitamin D3, found in meat and fish, and of vitamin D2, found in plants. D3 in the body is synthesized from cholesterol with the help of ultraviolet sunlight. Vitamins D2 and D3 are collectively referred to as cholecalciferol. When PTH increases, causing calcium loss from the bone, 1,25-DOHCC formation is stimulated. This substance, in turn, stimulates increased calcium and phosphate absorption from the intestines.

Thus, the hormones calcitonin, PTH, and 1,25-DOHCC all work together to maintain bone health.

Estrogen

Estrogen stimulates the formation of calcitonin, thus increasing calcium uptake by the bones and inhibiting the action of osteoclasts, the cells that break down bone. For this reason, supplemental estrogen on its own or with supplemental calcium is often touted as a preventive measure and treatment for osteoporosis. Many studies indicate that estrogen therapy decreases bone resorption and seemingly stabilizes bone mass, and may even be involved with a minimal increase in bone density. The promotion of estrogen's benefits for osteoporosis started with the whole "Premarin push," and the theme was well established by the 1970s and 1980s. The actual benefits of estrogen for osteoporosis were greatly exaggerated in the advertising hype.

A more recent eight-year study that involved more than 9 500 American women confirmed other studies that mentioned that the only benefit estrogen has on possibly preventing bone loss is in the first few years around the time of menopause. This study also showed that by seven years after menopause the decline in bone mineral density (BMD) was the same in women who were taking estrogen and women who were not. It is interesting to note that women treated with estrogen who showed less BMD loss during the earlier years of menopause had a higher BMD in the years before menopause, putting to question the so-called positive effects of estrogen on bone loss during the first few years of menopause.

In my opinion, this view of estrogen understates the harm it can do. Think about it ... Osteoclasts seek out and destroy old, damaged bone. Estrogen slows down the action of osteoclasts. If osteoclasts are not breaking down old bone, then the osteoblasts, which would normally fill the space with new healthy bone, become unable to build new bone because there is no space in which to put it. It seems logical that the result would be greater amounts of older damaged and brittle bone. More is not always better, especially when it comes to more old, brittle bone.

> "In the final analysis, the survival of health of the individual and species may depend not so much on further developments in technology as on the collective application of common sense."—S. Bryan Furnass

Studies show that women who have been on estrogen for a long time and suddenly stop have increased rates of bone loss. Given that estrogen inhibits the breakdown of old bone, rapid breakdown will occur once estrogen is stopped because now the osteoclasts, put on hold by the hormone, can finally do their work. In the meantime, so much old, damaged bone has accumulated that when it starts to be resorbed, the bone-building cells probably already at a disadvantage due to the other causes that contribute to poor bone health, cannot fill the spaces fast enough.

Clearly, supplemental estrogen merely temporarily masks the symptoms of osteoporosis while doing nothing to address its causes and putting women's health at risk.

When there are safe, natural, effective remedies and treatments available to support women through menopause, treatments that not only prevent bone breakdown but stimulate new bone growth (see Chapter 8), why is synthetic estrogen replacement so popular?

For more information on synthetic estrogen's side effects and dangers, as well as on natural hormonal support choices, please refer to Chapter 6.

Thyroxin

Thyroxin (T4), one of the thyroid hormones, activates osteoclast activity and bone resorption. Long-term high thyroxin activity, whether it is due to hyperthyroidism or medication for hypothyroidism, results in bone loss.

Thyroxin-treated women with low thyroid stimulating hormone (TSH) levels lose more bone mineral from the spine than those without known thyroid disease. Even a relatively modest degree of overtreatment results in decreased bone mass.

If you take thyroid medication, please have your thyroid hormone levels monitored regularly and have bone density status assessed before menopause.

Progesterone

Progesterone is active in bone metabolism and appears to promote bone formation, a critical function, since the most important contributor to bone health is new bone growth.

Progesterone levels can start decreasing approximately 10 to 15 years before menopause in some women, and therefore the bone thinning that leads to osteoporosis can start as early as the mid-thirties. Given that in many women trabecular bone loss (spine and hip bone loss) appears before the decline in estrogen levels that accompanies menopause, the decline in progesterone that precedes the estrogen decline is of greater significance.

Some of the most significant research done to date on progesterone as a treatment for bone loss has been conducted by Dr. J. Prior at the University of British Columbia. Her research confirms that not only can progesterone stop bone loss, it can also stimulate bone formation.

What is somewhat puzzling is that the medical establishment has not paid any attention to all this new information. Sales of Premarin alone currently exceed $940 million annually; eight million women in the United States alone take the drug—and the rush of baby boomers is close behind, potentially increasing the drug's mass sales. Yet the excessive use of Premarin is simply a result of successful advertising and is not based on its effectiveness or its high safety.

Androgens (Testosterone and DHEA)

It is common for androgen levels to be lower in postmenopausal women with osteoporosis. Androgens have also been found to stimulate osteoblasts, and treatment with testosterone has been reported to increase bone density and elevate total body calcium.

Various studies have compared women taking estrogen only with women taking both estrogen and testosterone. Women who take both hormones show a significant increase in bone density—5.7 percent in the spine and 5.2 percent in the hip. The bone density of women who took estrogen alone remained unchanged. As with any continued use of a hormone, testosterone does not come without risk, but if hormone replacement is necessary, studies show that combining estrogen with testosterone or USP progesterone confers more benefits and fewer risks than using estrogen alone.

Levels of DHEA (dehydroepiandrosterone) decline with age, and several studies have reported that lower DHEA levels positively correlate with lower bone density and could be used as a possible indicator of lowered bone density. Other researchers have not found any clinically significant relationship between DHEA levels and bone density.

However, the body converts DHEA to either estradiol or testosterone, and this could be one of the mechanisms whereby DHEA could be helpful in maintaining bone mass. More research is needed.

We think that by now you may be realizing that the current medical recommendations regarding estrogen for osteoporosis are just too simplistic. The hormonal interactions that influence bone health generally are very intricate and complex, and at menopause this is even more the case. So please let's not blame all our menopausal woes on the ovaries!

Furthermore, overall hormonal imbalances are only part of the big picture when it comes to osteoporosis risks.

FURTHER RISK FACTORS FOR OSTEOPOROSIS

In addition to the risk factors (age, race, sex, body weight and frame) and hormonal influences discussed above, there are other osteoporosis risk factors that you need to know about.

• **Diuretics**. Many people take diuretics without knowing of the risk of calcium loss. All diuretics increase the urge to void, thereby increasing loss of calcium and other minerals. The drug called furosemide (Lasix) causes the greatest loss of calcium. Substitute other diuretics wherever possible, and, in keeping with the search for optimal health, look for the cause of the water retention, rather than relying on diuretics that only mask the symptoms of the underlying problem.

• **Corticosteroid drugs.** Glucocorticoids such as prednisone, as well as other forms of cortisone, decrease the absorption of calcium and inhibit osteoblasts. Indeed, treatment with corticosteroids directly causes osteoporosis. If you are taking a form of cortisone, bioidentical progesterone and calcium and mineral supplementation can protect against some of the negative effects. In ongoing stressful situations the adrenal glands secrete cortisol, one of the glucocorticoids, excessively, which can also increase the risk of developing osteoporosis. (For information on how to reduce your stress load, see Chapter 2.)

• **Antidepressants.** A study reported in 1998 showed that Prozac and other similar antidepressant drugs cause increased risk of hip fractures. The researchers found that seniors prescribed antidepressants were 2.4 times more likely to suffer from hip fractures than seniors who were not taking antidepressants.

• **Other medications.** A number of other drugs can contribute to weakening of the bones: aluminum antacids, anticonvulsants, cyclosporine, lithium, medroxyprogesterone (synthetic progesterone), methotrexate, tetracycline, thyroid hormone (when taken in excess), warfarin (Coumadin), and cortisone (prednisone).

ASSESSING YOUR BONE HEALTH

Now that you have had an introduction to some of the risk factors for osteoporosis you may be wondering what you can do to determine your bone health. It is our recommendation that every women in her mid- to late forties start monitoring bone health. Karen sends patients for bone assessment tests routinely, and it is common to find that women in their forties already have significant bone loss.

Osteoporosis: Possible Early Symptoms

Bone loss that precedes osteoporosis is usually asymptomatic and may go undetected for years, until the slightest trauma causes a fracture. Taking preventive or treatment action as early as possible is extremely important.

Some people do experience early signs and symptoms. If you experience any of the following, have your bone density tested immediately:

- chronic back pain; deep bone aches
- oral bone loss. A recent study shows a relationship between oral bone loss, tooth loss, and increased risk for osteoporosis.
- poor digestion. This symptom could mean that assimilation of calcium and other minerals is poor.
- extreme fatigue
- premature grey hair (before the age of 40). A recent study done at the Maine Center for Osteoporosis Research found that premature greying correlates with low bone mass.
- loss of height. Height normally decreases by 4 cm every 10 years after menopause. If your height appears to be dropping more quickly than this, you have cause for concern.
- kyphosis (dowager's hump)
- night cramps in the legs and feet

Osteoporosis is often asymptomatic. When you reach your mid- to late forties, it is time to assess your risk factors and to use the screening tests described below to ensure that your bone mass is not being lost too quickly.

LOOKING AT OSTEOPOROSIS RISK FACTORS

No risk factor alone or in combination with others will accurately predict which patients will or will not experience osteoporotic fracture. As a general rule, the more risk factors present, the greater the potential for osteoporosis. Assessing risk factors provides important guidance in making further assessment and treatment decisions. The questionnaire on pages 198 and 199 will help you assess your risk of developing osteoporosis. In addition, imaging and biochemical markers can help you and your health care practitioner determine when and how to support bone health.

DUAL ENERGY X-RAY ABSORPTIOMETRY (DEXA)

Simple x-rays do not detect a bone mass loss of less than 30 percent, so they are not reliable for determining early losses of bone mineral density. DEXA, however, measures the bone density of the lumbar spine, hip, and distal forearm with some accuracy. It is a non-invasive technology that exposes

OSTEOPOROSIS QUESTIONNAIRE

Choose the descriptor in each category that best describes you, and fill in the point value for that descriptor in the space to the right. You may choose more than one descriptor in categories marked with an asterisk.

If your total score is greater than 50, you are at significant risk for osteoporosis.

Frame Size	Points	Score
Small-boned or petite	10	_____
Medium frame, very lean	5	_____
Medium frame, average or heavy build	0	_____
Large frame, very lean	5	_____

Ethnic Background

Caucasian	10	_____
Asian	10	_____
Other	0	_____

Activity Level

How often do you walk briskly, jog, do aerobics or weight lifting, or perform hard physical labour for at least 30 minutes?

Seldom	30	_____
1 to 2 times per week	20	_____
3 to 4 times per week	5	_____
5 or more times per week	0	_____

Smoking

Smoke 10 or more cigarettes a day	20	_____

Smoke fewer than 10 cigarettes a day	10	____
Quit smoking	5	____
Never smoked	0	____

Personal Health Factors*

Family history of osteoporosis	20	____
Long-term corticosteroid use	20	____
Long-term anticonvulsant use	20	____
Drink more than 3 glasses of alcohol per week	20	____
Drink more than 1 cup of coffee per day	10	____
Seldom get outside in the sun	10	____
Have had ovaries removed	10	____
Premature menopause	10	____
Have had no children	10	____

Dietary Factors*

Consume more than 120 g meat per day	20	____
Drink soft drinks regularly	20	____
Consume 3 to 5 servings of vegetables per day	-10	____
Take a calcium supplement	-10	____
Consume a vegetarian diet	-10	____
Total Score:		____

Adapted from *The American Journal of Natural Medicine* by Michael T. Murray, N.D., 1995 you to extremely low levels of radiation. In addition to its diagnostic role, it can be used to monitor the efficacy of therapy.

DEXA measures the number of standard deviations (level changes) between a given bone density and the normal bone density of a 35-year-old. (The definition of normal is set by the National Osteoporosis Foundation in the United States.) One standard deviation (SD) below normal is referred to as osteopenia. Osteoporosis is diagnosed when bone density is 2.5 SDs below normal. Severe osteoporosis is present when bone density is greater than 2.5 SDs below normal. Should your results show that you are osteoporotic, we recommend a follow-up DEXA within one year to monitor progress.

OSTEOPOROSIS RISK ASSAY

A urine test, the Bone Restoration Assessment, can assess bone resorption rates; the test distinguishes between people who lose bone rapidly and those who lose it slowly. Approximately 90 percent of bone is collagen, a key component of connective tissue; collagen is the main protein substance of the body and is essential in the formation of bone and connective tissue. All proteins are made of amino acids, and some of these are specifically used in the cross-linking of bone collagen. (Connective tissue is filled with collagen "cross-links" that give it its strength and flexibility. When collagen cross-links deteriorate, connective tissue begins to sag. Wrinkles, for instance, result when collagen cross-links in the skin connective tissue begin to deteriorate.) When bone breaks down, the special amino acids that create the bone collagen cross-links end up in the urine; their levels can determine how rapidly bone loss is occurring. Although urine tests for osteoporosis do not explain why a person is losing bone, they can be useful in determining how fast bone is being lost before actual changes in bone density, and are an easy way to monitor treatment. This test is available through naturopathic and medical doctors. If you would like more information on this urine test for osteoporosis please see www.GSDL.com (Great Smokies Diagnostic Laboratories).

HEIGHT MEASUREMENT

A very simple way to monitor your bone health is to measure your height every three to six months. When osteoporosis is present, the spinal vertebrae shrink, causing a loss of height. One indication that treatment for osteoporosis has been successful is that height becomes stable.

In the next chapter we will consider in detail how to maintain strong and healthy bones throughout life.

8

TAKING CARE OF
"DEM BONES"

"The human body is not really your own. It belongs to life, and it is your responsibility to take care of it. You cannot afford to do anything that injures your body, because the body is the instrument you need for selfless action."—Eknath Easwaran

This chapter will consider the options available for the prevention and treatment of osteoporosis. We will begin by considering allopathic treatment models—and let us be honest here, we are not impressed with conventional medical treatment. But we can always make the choice to be proactive about our health, including bone health. In that spirit we will discuss, from a naturopathic perspective, diet and lifestyle changes that build strong and healthy bone.

You will learn that there are many changes you can make to your diet and lifestyle, as well as botanical and vitamin supplements you can take, to increase bone density and maintain bone health, safely. *It is possible to maintain and/or restore bone health.* You do not need to suffer the pain of osteoporosis.

"Half of what we have taught you is wrong; unfortunately we don't know what half."—Dean Borwell

THE ALLOPATHIC APPROACH TO OSTEOPOROSIS

The most common allopathic treatments for osteoporosis are discussed below, along with the reasons they are ineffective or excessively risky.

Calcium and/or Antacid and/or Synthetic Vitamin D Supplementation

In suggesting supplemental calcium and vitamin D, the allopathic profession is on the right track. Using calcium and vitamin D effectively is covered in detail later in this chapter. Some people, including some doctors, are under the impression that antacids are suitable calcium supplements. This is erroneous. The damaging effects of antacids are discussed in detail in the section on calcium supplementation, where we consider what works and what doesn't.

Supplemental Estrogen

Unfortunately, many women today are under the impression that supplemental estrogen or hormone replacement therapy (HRT) can address osteoporosis. As we saw in the last chapter, however, while estrogen does slow down bone resorption through its effect on the osteoclasts, the cells that break down old bone, it does nothing to help rebuild bone. In fact, when bone is not being broken down, new bone cannot be built. In addition, the osteoclasts break down damaged and brittle bone. When they are less active, we can expect to see a build-up of inferior-quality bone in the skeleton. The last chapter also mentions other hormones involved in bone health, such as progesterone, testosterone, vitamin D, and parathyroid hormone. HRT is not the solution to the problem of osteoporosis that it is often claimed to be.

Slow-Release Sodium Fluoride

Fluoride was once thought to be useful in the treatment of osteoporosis because of its ability to bind to calcium, and it is still thought by some to be of potential help in increasing bone mass. Although a modest increase in bone mass does occur with the use of sodium fluoride, the acquired bone is of poor quality.

The effect of low levels of fluoride on bones, levels such as are found in fluoridated water, has been tested in recent years. The studies show that fluoridation of the water supply increases the incidence of hip fractures due to increased bone fragility. A study reported in the *Journal of the American Medical Association* in 1992 found that fluoridation of the water supply increases the hip fracture rate by 30 percent in women and 40 percent in men. Sodium fluoride is certified rat poison and is toxic at any level.

Calcitonin Nasal Spray

This spray delivers a peptide hormone, calcitonin, that interferes with osteo-clasts and inhibits bone resorption. The *Principles of Medical Pharmacology* states that bone diseases such as osteoporosis, which involve decreased bone density, are unlikely to benefit significantly from a further decrease in bone rebuilding rate induced by calcitonin.

Biophosphonates: Alendronate (Fosamax) and Etidronate Disodium (Didronel and Didrocal)

The mechanism of these drugs is the same: they inhibit the formation, growth, and breakdown of hydroxyapatite (a mineral salt used in the model-ling of new bone; see Chapter 7). Didronel is commonly used to treat Paget's disease, in which there is decreased bone resorption and thickening of the bone. Didronel or Didrocal (etidronate with calcium carbonate) is also commonly used for the treatment of osteoporosis. Only 3 percent of the drug is metabolized; 97 percent must be excreted via the kidneys.

Didronel is contraindicated in osteomalacia (vitamin D deficiency caus-ing bone demineralization), a common causative factor in osteoporosis. It is interesting to read in CPS that the risk of fracture is increased in patients with Paget's disease who receive Didronel doses of 20 mg per kilogram of body weight for more than three months and that this risk may also be greater in patients with a history of multiple fractures or bone lesions. Didronel or Didrocal is taken in 90-day cycles. For the first 14 days of the cycle, 400 mg of etidronate disodium is taken once daily; for the next 76 days, calcium carbonate is taken. Safety and tolerance has been established for 20 cycles (five years). However, Karen commonly see patients who have been taking these drugs in excess of the time periods established as safe.

CPS states that the excretion rate of Fosamax is estimated to exceed 10 years and that alendronate decreases the rate of bone resorption directly, which leads to an indirect decrease in bone formation. Although the medical opinion is that alendronate is well tolerated, the adverse effects can include abdominal pain, diarrhea, esophageal ulcers, abdominal bloating, muscu-loskeletal pain, and headaches, to name the most common.

"Even as the wise physician takes full advantage of the armamentarium available to him, he never misses the opportunity to educate the patient to the truth that drugs aren't always necessary and that the human body is its own best drugstore for most symptoms."—Norman Cousins

Evista (Raloxifene Hydrochloride)

Evista, made by Eli Lilly Canada, is a new drug approved for the treatment of osteoporosis. It is a selective estrogen binder, meaning that the molecules land on estrogen receptor sites, but selectively: Evista molecules are programmed not to land on breast or uterine tissue. Approximately 60 percent of raloxifine is absorbed upon ingestion but only 2 percent is bioavailable, meaning that the rest of the drug must be packaged by the liver and excreted—more stress for the liver.

The increase in bone mass over one year with use of this drug ranges, on average, from 1.3 to 2.3 percent, according to the research done to date.

A promoted benefit of this drug is its effects on lipid metabolism. It increases HDL cholesterol (so-called good) without negatively affecting LDL levels (so-called bad cholesterol), therefore decreasing the risk of atherosclerotic cardiovascular disease. Yet at the same time, the main warning given for this drug is that it may cause deep vein thrombosis, pulmonary embolism, and retinal thrombosis—in other words, blood clots in various parts of the body.

The warnings given for this drug also state that Evista should be discontinued at least 72 hours before prolonged immobilization, to reduce further risk of blood clots.

Clearly, there are no magic bullets that work over the long term in the treatment of disease. At best the so called miracle drugs are only able to mask symptoms temporarily.

THE NATUROPATHIC APPROACH TO OSTEOPOROSIS

In contrast to the allopathic approach to osteoporosis, the naturopathic approach offers no "quick fixes" or powerful pills that "take care of the problem." Instead, the naturopathic perspective is that a serious degenerative disease such as osteoporosis, with a multitude of possible contributing causes, requires methodical, in-depth treatment that takes all the possible causative factors into account. A comprehensive naturopathic program for osteoporosis would take the following objectives into account:

- Arrest vertebral bone loss during the perimenopausal period, and rebuild the lost bone.
- Address the harmful lifestyle factors ("bone busters") contributing to bone loss.
- Ensure adequate intake and absorption of nutrients that support bone health.
- Support the function of the adrenal glands and reduce stress. (Read about osteoporosis and the immune system, page 53.)
- Implement hormonal support (using phytohormones or safe HRT) for those at greatest risk for fracture. (See Chapter 6.)

Let's now consider those points that have not been covered in previous chapters.

Arresting Perimenopausal Vertebral Bone Loss; Restoring Vertebral Bone

In the last chapter we urged all women in their mid- to late forties to begin monitoring bone health. We will repeat that recommendation here. If you are younger but are exhibiting perimenopausal symptoms, you should also start the testing, including having bone density scans.

If your tests come back indicating that you are experiencing significant bone loss, then you need to create an action plan with your health care practitioner. Make sure your plan includes the following steps:

- Assess your risk factors (described in Chapter 7). Which ones can you address?
- Assess your overall stress levels and the functioning of your adrenal glands. What can you do to lower your stress levels? (See Chapters 2 and 3 for guidance.)
- Take botanical phytohormone support such as meno or MenoSense to help you re-establish hormonal balance.

- You may require short-term hormonal therapy with progesterone, DHEA, estriol, or testosterone, hormones that have documented bone-building effects (see Chapter 7). Use these hormones under the supervision of your health care practitioner, making sure to have hormone levels monitored regularly. We strongly recommend that you take the bioidentical forms of the hormones available through compounding pharmacies.

- Read the remainder of this chapter to determine which dietary and lifestyle factors are contributing to bone loss and what you can do about them.

Bone Busters: Diet and Lifestyle Choices That Contribute to Bone Loss

If we believe and accept the current opinions surrounding osteoporosis and women, we'll come to think that women are fated to turn into decrepit sacks of crumbling bones after menopause. Fortunately, this does not have to happen—but to prevent bone loss and fracture, we have to know what to do. Bones are constantly remodelled throughout life under the influence of diet, lifestyle factors, hormones, and stresses placed on them by weight-bearing exercise (exercise done in a standing position). Cutting the "bone busters" out of our life and adding bone-building activities, foods, and supplements will go a long way towards ensuring that we don't become another osteo-porosis statistic.

> "The person who fails to alter his living habits, and especially his eating and drinking habits, because he is afraid that other persons may regard him as queer, eccentric, or fanatic, forgets that the ownership of his body, the responsibility for its well-being, belongs to him, not them."
> —Paul Brunton

The most important bone busters are the following dietary and lifestyle choices:

- lack of exercise; overly vigorous exercise
- high-protein diet or very low protein diet

- stress—prolonged stress raises cortisol levels
- excess phosphorus intake
- excess intake of coffee, sugar, salt, and/or alcohol
- cigarette smoking
- consumption of fluoridated water
- lack of vitamins and minerals; calcium deficiency; vitamin D deficiency
- excessively low fat diet

Let's now look at each of these bone busters—and some antidotes.

EXERCISE IS NOT AN OPTION

Popular knowledge about the general benefits of exercise and, specifically, knowledge of the beneficial effects of weight-bearing exercise on bone health is growing. Many people do not realize, however, that when it comes to preventing fractures, maintaining muscle strength is just as important as maintaining bone strength. Most osteoporotic fractures, including roughly 90 percent of hip fractures, result from falls, and one-third of people over age 65 fall each year. (Other falls, however, are due to spontaneous fracture of a bone.) With the added strength and balance obtained through regular exercise, some falls can be prevented.

Peak bone mass is achieved by a combination of adequate bone-building nutrients and adequate exercise. For exercise to be effective, it must be maintained throughout life; inactivity leads to bone loss. Weight-bearing exercise stimulates the fibres of the bone matrix and initiates the complex interactions of minerals and hormones required to maintain healthy bone. A lack of gravitational stress, such as that experienced by astronauts, causes severe osteoporosis. In addition to its ability to increase bone density, thickness, and strength, regular exercise lengthens life, adding an average six to seven years to life expectancy, and offers a number of other benefits as well:

- better bowel movements and elimination of toxins in general
- decreased risk of breast cancer—regular exercise decreases the risk by 50 percent

- protection against heart disease and better cardiovascular health. Exercise lowers blood pressure, increases blood circulation, and improves blood lipid profiles, increasing high-density lipoproteins (HDL) and decreasing low-density lipoproteins (LDL).
- in menopausal women, decreased or eliminated hot flashes
- if not excessive, increased immunity, thus lower rates of chronic disease
- increased metabolism, therefore less weight gain
- increased muscle mass and strength
- relaxing and stress-relieving effects; more restful sleep
- improved self-esteem

When we review the list of benefits exercise confers, it is surprising to us that everyone does not make the time to exercise for at least 20 to 30 minutes, three to four times a week. We emphatically assert to people that exercise is absolutely essential for good health. One of the most common excuses we hear for not exercising is, "But I don't have time." Sound familiar? Well, what is going to happen to your time when you get sick and can't accomplish any of your goals and meet your commitments?

We assume that if you have scheduled an appointment with a client or a friend, you will keep it. Why not schedule *and keep* an appointment with yourself, at least one-half hour long, four days a week, for physical exercise? If someone calls and wants to see you at the time you have scheduled for your exercise, set a different meeting time with them. Your exercise appointment is *your time*. It gives you one very important way to stay healthy and build stamina so that you are able to withstand the demands of your life. We are complex beings, with mental, emotional, spiritual, and physical aspects. We all certainly seem to get enough mental and emotional exercise, but physical exercise is lacking for many, as well as spiritual exercise (prayer, meditation, contemplation). We will return to this topic in Chapter 10.

When it comes to exercise, beginning is not enough. The key that unlocks the benefits of exercise is *regularity*. Regular exercise is done consistently three or four days weekly over a long time. One of the most important influences on bone density in women is the amount of lifetime weight-bearing, low-intensity exercise done. (We will discuss weight-bearing exercise in detail below.)

But wait a minute! If you haven't done regular exercise throughout your life that's no excuse to not start now. Regular weight-bearing exercise started at any time has benefits! *However, a weekly minimum of 90 minutes is neces-*

sary to preserve or build bone density, and the benefits of increased bone density are seen after approximately one year. Bone mass is lost quickly when exercise decreases to two sessions per week or when exercise is inconsistent. Sorry, the occasional golf game or round of tennis just doesn't do it.

We encourage most forms of exercise, but just as aerobic exercise is the most beneficial for cardiovascular health, *weight-bearing exercise is the best for your bones*.

Weight-Bearing Exercise

Weight-bearing exercise happens when you are standing and have to hold yourself up against the pull of gravity. Bearing weight puts stress on the skeleton, thereby encouraging bone building and preserving bone density. If you are exercising for bone health, it is more important to incur weight stress than to undertake intense activity such as vigorous swimming or cycling.

Studies show that postmenopausal women who engage in weight-bearing exercise will see an average 6.1 percent increase in bone density of the lower spine over one year. One study found that women who participated in vigorous exercise two or more times per week, or whose total physical activity amounted to four hours per week, had significantly higher bone density than women who did less. In general, women who regularly engage in some form of exercise have a 50 to 70 percent lower risk of hip fracture than those who don't. Many other studies confirm that increased bone density results from vigorous weight-bearing exercise and strength training. Walking, however, appears to offer little benefit to the bones, at least when its effects on the wrist bones are measured. We would say that this is probably because walking does not stimulate the wrist bones; try carrying some light weights when you walk.

Non-weight-bearing exercise consists of exercises done in a weightless or semi-weightless position. Cycling, aerobic water exercises, swimming, leg lifts, yoga, and stretching are examples of non-weight-bearing exercise.

Although most research seems to agree that weight-bearing exercise is the most effective for preventing and treating osteoporosis, there is a new small study from Ohio State University that claims that cycling is the most effective form of exercise for maintaining healthy bones. The study followed seven elderly women who were asked to ride a stationary bicycle three times per week. After eight months, the researcher, Dr. Rebecca Jackson, found that the women's bone density had increased.

The consensus, however, remains that weight-bearing exercise is the most beneficial for protecting bones.

It is not necessary to rush out and join a gym to get weight-bearing exercise. This can be expensive for some and generally inconvenient. Instead, incorporate simple exercises into your daily routine.

As mentioned in the previous chapter, the most common areas in which bone density decreases are the wrists, upper arms, shoulders, spine, and hips. Modified push-ups, lunges, and light upper body weight training (see diagrams on the following pages) will strengthen the wrists, upper arms, and shoulders. For the spine and lower body, try adding some weight to a backpack while you are out walking; you can also carry hand-held weights while walking or riding your stationary bike. In addition, leg lifts (see diagram), walking or running stairs, and hiking or walking while using weights will strengthen the hips and spine.

A balanced exercise program includes regular stretching for muscle flexibility, aerobic exercise for the cardiovascular system, strength training (weight training) for muscle strength, and other weight-bearing exercises, such as those described above, for the bones. Very important for general strength training and largely avoided are the often dreaded abdominal exercises.

Exert yourself a bit, balancing the different forms of exercise, and little by little you will develop increased cardiovascular health, greater overall strength and stamina, and healthier bones.

Aerobic exercise, which promotes cardiovascular and respiratory health, needs to be done three to four days a week for 20 to 60 minutes. Aerobic exercises include jogging, walking hills, cross country skiing, dancing, swimming, and cycling.

If you are able to exercise only three days weekly, then combine stretching with aerobic exercise and strength-training exercises each time. Take every alternate day off.

If you can fit four or five exercise sessions per week into your schedule, do the same program with one exception: eliminate the strength training on the additional two days.

Some people feel that aerobic exercise is not beneficial to the heart unless they reach quite high heart rates. In such cases, however, they may be pushing themselves into anaerobic states and really not accomplishing very much except exhausting themselves. The body is composed mainly of aerobic muscle mass, meaning these muscles function best when oxygen is used in the energy-generating process. Anaerobic exercise, in which oxygen is

MODIFIED PUSH-UP   LUNGE

LEG LIFTS

not used to generate energy, taxes the muscles and is generally stress-inducing. An ideal exercise program includes 80 percent aerobic exercises. Note that aerobic exercise burns fat more efficiently than anaerobic exercise, thereby helping to maintain ideal body weight.

A simple formula can help you determine your ideal heart rate. Unlike many exercise guidelines that offer general targets for heart rate, this one,

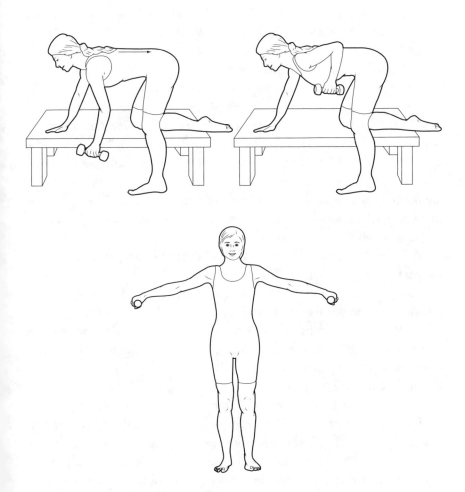

formulated by Dr. Phillip Maffetone, takes into account the individual's level of fitness.

The 180 Formula

- Start by subtracting your age from 180.
- Subtract 10 from the result if you are on medication or recovering from a major illness (operation, heart disease, etc.).
- Subtract a further 5 if you have not been exercising, have recently been injured, or have a weakened immune system.

- Add 5 if you have been exercising for more than two years without any problems.

For an example of how the 180 Formula works, let's calculate the target heart rate for a 52-year-old who has exercised regularly for years:

180 – 52 + 5 =133 beats per minute

If the 52-year-old in question reached a heart rate greater than 133 per minute, she would most likely be in an anaerobic state.

To help yourself design an effective exercise program, I recommend a new health and fitness book, *The Complete Athlete: Integrating Fitness, Nutrition, and Natural Health.* (See the "Further Reading" section at the back of this book.) *The Complete Athlete* offers specific guidelines for everyone from beginner to seasoned athletes. The "how-tos" of lifting weights are outlined as well as how to initiate an exercise program. The book gives more detailed formulas for determining target heart rates for weight-bearing and non-weight-bearing exercises.

A person is never too old or too frail to start weight-bearing and strengthening exercises.

Some of you reading this chapter may protest, "I am hardly able to get around, how can you expect me to exercise?" Good question.

For those of you confined to bed, please make the effort to stand, even on crutches, as much as you can. In addition, start the supplements discussed for osteoporosis later in this chapter. It is never too late—you will be amazed at the healing that can take place.

Overly vigorous exercise can have a negative effect on bone health.

Women who are involved in high levels of physical activity, such as long-distance running, may develop amenorrhea (lack of menses) because of a disturbance in the hormonal system from lack of body fat. Several studies of endurance athletes experiencing prolonged amenorrhea show that these women develop a significant reduction in bone mineral density, particularly in the trabecular bone. If you are exercising intensely enough to disrupt your normal menstrual cycle, we recommend rethinking your exercise regime.

Now that we are all going to start putting out the effort to exercise regularly and sensibly for optimal health, let's look at some of the dietary choices that could be counterproductive.

"As to disease, make a habit of two things … to help or at least to do no harm."—Hippocrates

DIETARY BONE BUSTERS

Like any other living tissue, bone has specific and diverse nutritional needs; failure to meet those needs compromises the strength and integrity of the bones.

Our Standard (North) American Diet (SAD) is less than adequate for optimal health. We need only to listen to the daily news, giving its litany of disease-related statistics and deaths, to recognize how SAD things really are. Since the early 1900s, per capita consumption of fruits and vegetables has declined by 60 percent and soft drinks have replaced water and fruit juices. Diets high in empty-calorie foods (non-foods), low in vitamins and minerals, and too high in animal proteins can contribute to the development of osteoporosis. Also, as some people age, their lifestyle becomes more sedentary, digestive enzyme output decreases, prescription drug use increases, outside activity and sunshine exposure lessens creating vitamin D deficiency, and hormones decrease. These and other possible risk factors relating to osteoporosis will be discussed throughout this chapter.

High Animal Protein and Dairy Intake

Many dietary factors are associated with the development of osteoporosis, and excess animal protein is one of the front runners. Although we am not advocating vegetarianism for everyone, we do recommend that people cut back on the amount of animal protein in their diet. In North America it is generally recommended that we consume two to three servings of dairy foods and at least 90 g of meat per day. Some sources, however, suggest that this is too much and that the proper intake is in the range of 40 g per day for a person weighing 70 kg. In his book *Enter the Zone*, B. Sears offers a formula for calculating your individual protein requirements (see the "Further Reading" section).

What's more, the body uses proteins for building and repair and does not store them. When intake exceeds the body's demands, the excess must be excreted via the kidneys as waste product. Protein waste products, in addition to increasing the urinary calcium, increase urinary oxalate and uric acid, which in turn could cause gout, kidney stones, or kidney damage.

All protein is composed of amino acids; dairy protein is high in sulphur amino acids, which produce sulphates in the body. Sulphates prevent calcium from being absorbed.

Several researchers have studied the effects of high levels of animal protein on calcium loss. One study showed that increasing daily intake of protein from 48 g to 95 g resulted in a 50 percent increase in the amount of calcium excreted in the urine. When diets are extremely high in animal protein, a calcium deficit results because it becomes impossible to maintain the calcium balance no matter how much calcium is taken; this same study showed that when approximately 140 g of protein was consumed daily, calcium balance could not be maintained with an intake of calcium as high as 1 400 mg daily.

Researchers have looked at the correlation between animal protein intake and the risk of hip fracture. The results are summarized in the table on the next page.

You can see from this chart the correlation between a high intake of animal foods and increased hip fracture. Note also that the highest inci-

ANIMAL PROTEIN INTAKE AND HIP FRACTURE RATE IN VARIOUS COUNTRIES

COUNTRY	ANIMAL PROTEIN INTAKE (G/DAY)	HIP FRACTURE RATE PER 100 000 PEOPLE
South Africa	10.4	6.8
New Guinea	16.4	3.1
Singapore	24.7	21.6
Hong Kong	34.6	45.6
Israel	42.5	93.2
Spain	47.6	42.4
The Netherlands	54.3	87.7
United Kingdom	56.6	118.2
Denmark*	58.0	165.3
Sweden*	59.4	187.8
Norway*	66.6	190.4
United States	72.0	144.9
New Zealand	77.8	119.0

Adapted from M. Messina and V. Messina, *The Simple Soybean and Your Health*. Avery Publishing Group, 1994.

PLANT AND ANIMAL SOURCES OF PROTEIN

Protein amounts refer to grams per 100 g of the food in question.

PLANTS

all fruits	0.2 to 2	all vegetables	1 to 5
Grains		**Legumes**	
rice	7	lentils	25
corn	9	adzuki beans	22
millet	10	dried peas	24
hard red wheat	14	soybeans	35
spelt	15	**Yeast**	
quinoa	18	nutritional yeast	15
Nuts and Seeds		**Algae**	
almonds	19	blue-green	60
hazelnuts	13	chlorella	55
sesame seeds	19	spirulina	68
sunflower seeds	24	**Ferments**	
Sea Vegetables		amasake	3
dulse	22	miso	15
hijiki	6	tempeh	20
kelp	16	tofu	8
kombu	7	soy powder	16
nori	35	(fermented)	

ANIMAL PRODUCTS

Dairy		**Fish/Seafood**	
cheese	25 to 31	bass	18
cottage cheese	14	clams	14
milk (whole)	9	cod	18
yoghurt	9 to 15	herring	17
Meat and Eggs		mackerel	19
Eggs	3	oysters	6
Fowl	16 to 24	sardines	24
Organ meats	20 to 22	tuna	29
Red meat	17 to 21		

J. Winterdyk and K. Jensen, *The Complete Athlete: Integrating Fitness, Nutrition and Natural Health.* Alive Books, 1998.

dence of fracture is in countries known to consume the highest amount of dairy products (those countries marked with an asterisk).

On average, North Americans eat approximately 85 to 95 g of protein daily. Sound like a lot? Let's look at the protein content of various vegetable and animal foods. As you can see, you do not have to consume a great deal of animal food to reach an average intake of more than 100 g of animal protein a day.

Note, however, that not all protein causes excess calcium excretion—only too much *animal* protein. To achieve and maintain general health, including bone health, a diet high in fruits, vegetables, whole grains, legumes such as soy, and nuts and seeds is optimal. Vegetarians have a much lower incidence of osteoporosis than people who eat meat. At the same time, 20 percent of the bone matrix is made from protein, so adequate protein intake is also very important. Most North Americans probably consume excess protein, but there are those who are not getting enough. The possibility of inadequate protein intake may be of particular concern in teenagers consuming a diet high in junk foods, and vegetarians who do not consume enough legumes and other plant foods high in protein.

Acidifying and Alkalizing Foods: A Recipe for Life

The chart on the following pages provides information that shows the contribution of various food substances to the acidifying or alkalizing of body fluids and, ultimately, to the urine, saliva, and venous blood.

In general, it is important to eat a diet that contains foods from both sides of the chart. Allergic reactions and other forms of stress tend to produce acids in the body. The presence of high acidity indicates that more of your foods should be selected from the alkalizing group.

The kidneys help to maintain the neutrality of body fluids by excreting the excess acid or alkali in the urine. You may find it useful to check your urine pH using pHydrion paper in order to find out if your food selection is providing the desired balance. Check urine pH three times a day.

A urine pH of between 6.8 in the morning and 7.4 in the afternoon is ideal, but it will vary over the day depending upon the foods you eat as well as allergic reactions and other stress factors. Your urine pH should average 7.0.

ALKALIZING FOODS

Vegetables
Cucumber
Rutabaga
Garlic
*Eggplant
Sea Veggies
Asparagus
Kale
Spirulina (algae)
Fermented Veggies
Kohlrabi
Sprouts (all types)
Watercress
Lettuces (all types)

Squashes
Beets
Mushrooms
Alfalfa Grass
Broccoli
Mustard Greens
Barley Grass
Brussels Sprouts
Nova Scotia Duke
Wheat Grass
Cabbage
Dandelions
Wild Greens
Carrot

Edible Flowers
Cauliflower
Onions
Celery
Parsnips
(high-glycemic)
Chard
Peas
Chlorella (algae)
*Peppers
Collard Greens
Pumpkin

Fruits
Apple
Apricot
Avocado
Banana (high-glycemic)
Blackberry
Blueberry
Cantaloupe

Cherries, Currants
Dates, Figs
Grapes
Grapefruit, Lime
Honeydew
Nectarine
Orange, Lemon
Peach, Pear
Pineapple

Raspberry
(all berries)
Strawberry
Tangerine
*Tomato
Tropical Fruits
Watermelon

Protein
Free-range Eggs
Whey Protein Powder
Fat-Free Cottage Cheese
Lean Chicken Breast

Organic Yogurt
Almonds
Chestnuts
Tofu (fermented)
Flax Seeds
Pumpkin Seeds
Tempeh (fermented)

Squash Seeds
Sunflower Seeds
Millet
Sprouted Seeds
Nuts

Other
Apple cider vinegar
Bee Pollen

Lecithin Granules
Dairy-free Probiotic Cultures

Beverages
GREENS+
Veggie Juices
Fresh Fruit Juice (unsweetened)
Organic Milk (unpasteurized)

Mineral Water (non-carbonated)
Quality Water

Sweeteners
Stevia

Teas
Green Tea
Herbal Tea
Dandelion Tea
Ginseng
Bancha Tea
Kombucha

Spice & Seasonings
Cinnamon
Curry
Ginger
Mustard
Chili Peppers
Salt (Sea, Celtic)
Miso

Tamari
All Herbs

Oriental Vegetables
Maitake
Daikon
Dandelion Root
Shiitake

Kombu
Reishi
Nori
Umeboshi
Wakame
Sea Veggies

ACIDIFYING FOODS

Fats & Oils
  Avocado Oil
  Canola Oil
  Corn Oil

Hemp Seed Oil
Flax Oil
Grape Seed Oil
Lard

Olive Oil
Safflower Oil
Sesame Oil
Sunflower Oil

Grains
  Rice Cakes
  Wheat Cakes
  Amaranth
  Barley
  Buckwheat
  Corn
  Oats (Rolled)
  Quinoa

Rice
(Brown, Basmati)
Rye
Spelt
Kamut
Wheat
Hemp See Flour

Fruits
  Cranberries

Dairy, Milk, Hard Cheeses
  Cheese, Cow
  Cheese, Goat
  Cheese, Processed
  Cheese, Sheep
  Milk
  Butter

Nuts & Butters
  Cashews
  Filberts
  Brazil Nuts
  Peanuts
  Peanut Butter
  Pecans
  Tahini
  Walnuts

Animal Protein
  Beef
  Carp
  Clams
  Duck
  Fish, White Meat
  Lamb
  Lobster
  Mussels

Oysters
Pork
Rabbit
Salmon
Shrimp
Scallops
Tuna
Turkey
Venison

Pasta (White)
  Noodles
  Macaroni
  Spaghetti

Other
  Distilled Vinegar
  Brewers Yeast
  Wheat Germ
  *Potatoes

Sweets & Sweeteners
  Molasses
  Candy
  Honey
  Maple Syrup
  Saccharin
  Soft Drinks
  Sugar
  Aspartame
  Fruit-Flavoured
  Drinks

Alcoholic Beverages
  Beer
  Spirits
  Hard Liquor
  Wine

Drugs & Chemicals
  Drugs, Medicinal
  Drugs, Psychedelics
  Pesticides
  Herbicides

Beans & Legumes
  Black Beans
  Chick Peas
  Green Peas
  Kidney Beans

Lentils
Lima Beans
Pinto Beans
Red Beans
Soybeans

Soy Milk
White Beans
Rice Milk
Almond Milk

* Nightshade family foods

Note: Use organically grown whenever possible.

ISOFLAVONES AND OSTEOPOROSIS

One of the vegetarian staples, the soybean, actually demonstrates a calcium sparing effect in the body, delaying age-related bone loss. Soy products also contain phytoestrogens, called isoflavones, as discussed in Chapter 6.

Studies done on osteoporosis and soy products show unequivocally that soy isoflavones, in particular genistein and daidzein, are effective in preventing bone loss and reversing the low bone densities associated with hormonal changes during the menopausal years.

Amazing results were obtained in a six-month study of postmenopausal women. One group of women was asked to ingest a daily intake of 40 mg of soy protein, containing 2.25 mg of total isoflavones. Significant increases in bone mineral content and bone mineral density in the lumbar spine were found in this group, compared to women in the control group, who were given lower levels of isoflavones or casein (a milk protein) and non-fat milk.

People with kidney problems should know that diets high in animal protein can be very hard on the kidneys because of the extra work the kidneys must do to filter ammonia, one of the byproducts of animal protein metabolism. Plant proteins do not place this stress on the kidneys.

Note, however, that as a general rule animal proteins are complete—that is, they contain all the essential amino acids that our bodies use to make their own proteins, whereas vegetables, grains, and nuts and seeds provide fewer complete proteins. This does not in any way imply that vegetables and grains are less desirable sources of protein. They simply are less complete, not incomplete. As long as you regularly vary the mix of grains, legumes, and nuts you eat, you will consume all the essential amino acids you need.

In reading the information above on diet and acid/alkaline balance, you see that an acid pH can deplete calcium from the muscles and bones. Prolonged stress can also cause the body to become more acidic with the same results. In addition, research has shown that high cortisol levels resulting from stress, exert an inhibitory effect on bone resorption.

Other Dietary Factors Associated with Bone Loss

When it comes to bone health, knowledge is your best ally. Let's now examine other dietary choices that could seriously affect your bone health.

• **Excess phosphorus intake.** Phosphorus is an essential nutrient and is necessary for proper calcium absorption. However, it must be taken in at the proper ratio to calcium, one to one (1:1). The SAD, meanwhile, supplies approximately four times more phosphorus than calcium because of the high levels of phosphorus in soda pop, junk foods, meats, and dairy foods. When more phosphorus than calcium is taken in, the body starts pulling calcium from the bones to regain the proper one-to-one balance of the two minerals in the blood and tissues. The result is decreased calcium in the bones, resulting in lower bone density.

• **Caffeine.** Various studies show that calcium and other important minerals associated with bone health, specifically cortical bone mass, are lost in the urine as a result of caffeine consumption. Coffee is a diuretic (it increases urination) and thereby doubles the rate of calcium excretion. Coffee also tends to be highly acid creating, so the body will draw on its own calcium to buffer the acids its metabolism leaves in the system. In general, caffeine increases the risk of osteoporosis by reducing blood calcium levels. A moderate caffeine intake (two to three cups per day) can cause enough calcium loss in the urine to significantly increase the risk of bone fracture. We may think only of coffee as containing caffeine, but tea, caffeinated soft drinks, and chocolate all do as well.

• **Sugar**. Beware of sugar's disguises! There are many forms of sugar and you may not realize just how much you eating. Read labels and you will probably find dextrose, sucrose, maltose, fructose, corn syrup, beet sugar, cane sugar, honey, and molasses all listed as ingredients of various processed foods. All these substances are refined sugars. The list of sugar's harmful effects is extensive, but for now we are focusing on bone health.

Sugar interferes with vitamin and mineral storage in the body, can create hormonal fluctuations that in turn affect the bones, inhibits calcium absorption, contributes to digestive problems, and it suppresses the immune system. Sugar encourages the growth of yeast and harmful microflora in the intestines, a problem discussed in detail in Chapters 2 and 3. This microflora imbalance can cause a deficiency of vitamin K, which is essential for bone building and repair. My message to menopausal women and anyone else at risk for osteoporosis? *Curb your sweet tooth.*

CALCIUM CONTENT OF COMMON FOODS

FOOD	CALCIUM CONTENT IN MG
PLANT FOODS	
100 g hijiki (sea vegetable)	1 400
100 g wakame (sea vegetable)	1 300
100 g kelp (sea vegetable)	1 100
250 g sesame seeds	900
250 g almonds	660
250 g filberts	450
250 g turnip greens	450
250 g chickpeas	450
250 g tofu	400
250 g quinoa	340
250 g bok choy	330
250 g black beans	315
250 g kale	315
25 mL blackstrap molasses	300
7 corn tortillas	300
250 g broccoli	160
ANIMAL FOODS	
250 g goat's milk	330
250 g cow's milk	300
65 g Parmesan cheese	300
125 g plain yogurt	300
125 g ricotta cheese	300
30 g Cheddar cheese	300
250 g ice cream	240

• **Salt**. Like sugar, salt is overused in the western diet, for, like sugar, it is inexpensive yet enhances the flavour and extends the shelf life of various foods. If you have ever looked at the food labels in the supermarket you know that salt and sugar are listed in most processed foods. Various studies show that diets high in sodium increase the excretion of calcium; the body adapts to the increased excretion of calcium by drawing calcium from the bone, resulting in bone thinning (osteopenia). Osteopenia can lead to osteoporosis. A good place to start if you want to curb salt consumption is to cut back on your intake of processed and preprepared foods and begin incorporating more fresh whole foods into your diet.

• **Alcohol.** It is common knowledge that prolonged use of alcohol can cause a variety of heart, brain, and liver diseases. It is less commonly known that alcohol can cause significant bone loss and osteoporosis. Studies have reported a *40 percent increase in risk of hip fracture with each 7 ounce increase per week in alcohol consumption.*

Alcohol decreases the activity of the bone-building cells (osteoblasts), therefore decreasing bone mineralization and bone formation. It is interesting to note that alcohol increases estrogen levels yet causes calcium excretion and osteoporosis—yet another reason to question the effectiveness of estrogen in osteoporosis treatment. Prolonged use of alcohol also results in numerous nutrient deficiencies, including vitamin D deficiency, which is essential for bone health. (Vitamin D will be discussed in detail later in this chapter.)

• **Smoking.** Smoking is associated with lower cortical bone mass and bone mineral content. Women who smoke and are also thin experience a sixfold increase in their risk of fractures; studies also indicate a 60 percent increase in the risk of hip fracture among such women. The risk of hip fracture seems to increase with the amount smoked.

• **Fluoride.** As previously discussed, fluoride is still claimed by some to be a treatment for osteoporosis. It is, in fact, toxic to bone cells. Fluoride may slightly increase bone mass, but the quality of the bone formed is highly inferior and brittle, thereby significantly increasing the risk of fracture. Fluoride is commonly found in our water, in many juices, and is concentrated in processed foods, many processed beverages, and many toothpaste brands.

RECOMMENDED DAILY CALCIUM INTAKE	
AGE	AMOUNT (MG)
Birth to 6 months	400
1 to 10 years	800 to 1 200
11 to 24 years	1 200 to 1 500
Women	
20 to 50 years	1 000
Over 50, on HRT	1 000
Over 50, not on HRT	1 500
Over 65	1 500
Lactating/pregnant	1 200 to 1 500

Adapted from the NIH Consensus Statement, vol. 12(4), June 6–8, 1994.

VITAMINS AND MINERALS: THEIR INFLUENCE ON BONE HEALTH

One of the greatest influences on bone mineral density and bone health is an adequate intake of vitamins and minerals. Bone matrix is made from calcium and other minerals, with calcium deficiency being a major player in osteoporosis. A deficiency of calcium in childhood and adolescence is strongly associated with an increased risk of osteoporosis in adulthood. We will therefore discuss calcium now in some detail. However, it will become clear below that calcium does not stand alone as the hero in the healthy bone battle.

Calcium

Calcium is a mineral that constitutes approximately 50 percent of all the mineral content in the body; almost 100 percent of the body's calcium is found in the bones and teeth. Calcium does much more, however, than contribute to bone structure. It is involved in transporting nutrients across cell membranes, regulating the contractions of the heart and other muscles, maintaining balanced blood acid-alkaline levels, assisting iron absorption, and contributing to the process of cell division.

It will be surprising to some of you that many epidemiological studies (studies that look at the prevalence of a particular illness) show that there is not a direct relationship between calcium intake and the incidence of osteoporosis. The incidence of osteoporosis is low in Southeast Asian countries and in several Third World countries where calcium intake is low. The intake of animal protein in these countries is also quite low. In the richer countries, where the intake of animal proteins such as meats and dairy products is high, there is a greater incidence of osteoporosis even though dietary calcium levels are also higher than in the poorer countries.

Such information (combined with the knowledge of the effects of animal protein on bone health we gained above) would indicate that dairy products should not be viewed as a primary source of calcium; many of us have forgotten that the real primary source of calcium is green leafy vegetables.

If we believe what the Canadian Dairy Association pumps out in their aggressive advertising campaigns, we would think that cow's milk is the only source of dietary calcium. But do cows drink milk in order to provide the calcium in milk? No, they eat grass! In fact, humans are the only species on the planet that continues to drink milk after weaning. Yet vegetable sources of calcium are more readily absorbed and easily utilized by the body than dairy sources, and occur in abundance. Furthermore, three out of four North American adults have some degree of lactose intolerance (sensitivity to milk sugars), while others are allergic or sensitive to casein, the protein in milk. Pasteurizing milk kills the enzymes that assist in the breakdown of these products, often causing digestive difficulties that result in poor assimilation of the calcium and other nutrients in milk. Dr. D. Cramer, along with other researchers, has shown that "wholesome" milk is toxic to the ovaries and increases the risk of ovarian cancer in lactose-intolerant women, inhibits fertility, and, used during pregnancy, may cause birth defects. Leave the milk to baby "moos"!

The table on the previous page demonstrates how much calcium abounds in the vegetable kingdom. Foods are listed in order from highest calcium content to lowest. As you compare the amount of calcium in vegetable and plant foods, remember that the vegetable calcium is more easily absorbed and assimilated, and that unlike dairy products, vegetables do not cause leaching of calcium from bone in order to buffer acidic metabolites. Note that cooking does not destroy calcium.

CALCIUM AND OSTEOPOROSIS

Calcium intake varies throughout life; calcium levels are determined by the balance between what is absorbed from the gastrointestinal tract and what is lost via the skin, urine, and feces.

Research shows that although dietary calcium is essential throughout a woman's lifetime, it is not effective as a single agent in the prevention and treatment of osteoporosis. The positive effects of calcium are greatest in women whose baseline calcium intake is low, in older women, and in women with osteoporosis, and several studies have reported very favourable results on bone loss reduction in postmenopausal women who have used multiple nutrient therapy with calcium as the focus.

These studies are yet another reminder that osteoporosis is a multi-factorial disease. We will be discussing other nutrients important in bone health below.

Adult bone building requires that approximately 600 mg of calcium per day be absorbed. If your diet and lifestyle choices do not contribute to high calcium excretion, your calcium needs could be met by your diet, so long as you are conscientious about your food choices.

According to national health surveys conducted in the United States, calcium intake in adult women is 40 to 50 percent lower than in men, with 75 to 80 percent of women consuming less than 800 mg of calcium per day; one-quarter of American women consume less than 300 mg daily.

In general the recommended daily allowance for calcium intake in menopausal women is 1 500 mg a day. Recommended intakes throughout life are summarized in the above table.

These recommendations were created by scientists working for the United States government. What the scientists do not mention or consider is how the calcium source itself influences the total amount the body is able to readily absorb and metabolize—as we have seen, this amount will also vary considerably depending on a person's lifestyle and diet.

If, given your health history, current diet, and digestive strength, you determine that you need supplemental calcium (your health care practitioner can help establish whether supplementation is necessary), know that throwing calcium at your bones and expecting it to stick won't work. Your health, the type of calcium consumed, and the overall balance of minerals and vitamins taken in are critical factors in optimal absorption and assimilation.

Many people have difficulty digesting and assimilating the form of calcium most commonly recommended by medical doctors, calcium carbonate. Research has shown that whereas about 45 percent of calcium in the citrate form is absorbed, only 4 percent of calcium in the carbonate form is absorbed in people with low stomach hydrochloric acid (HCl) levels. It has also been demonstrated that calcium citrate is more readily absorbed than carbonate in normal subjects. One study demonstrated that subjects absorbed more calcium from 500 mg of calcium citrate than from 2,000 mg of calcium carbonate.

It is not uncommon for people to become deficient in stomach acid as they age; in studies of menopausal women it has been shown that approximately 40 percent are severely deficient in HCl. Large amounts of HCl are required to absorb calcium carbonate. Due to the high prevalence of hypochlorhydria (low stomach acid) in postmenopausal and geriatric women, use of calcium carbonate increases the risk of calcium deficiency and osteoporosis. HCl is also important for the absorption of other nutrients needed for optimal health. If you show signs of developing osteoporosis or other chronic illness, or your digestion is poor, get your HCl levels tested. The best test for doing so is called the Heidelberg gastric analysis test. The results may indicate that you need supplemental HCl to help you digest your food. As nutrient absorption increases with the supplemental HCl, your own ability to produce HCl will improve.

The Most Absorbable Calciums

A relatively new calcium complex, calcium citrate-malate, has been shown to have superior absorption into both cortical and trabecular bone; it is better absorbed gram for gram than any other complex calcium. Trabecular bone density increases by 25 percent after four weeks of supplementation with 1,000 mg of calcium citrate-malate daily, and by 44 to 47 percent after twelve weeks. Other studies confirm citrate-malate's ability to retard bone loss in premenopausal and postmenopausal women.

To build bone, calcium works in concert with other minerals such as phosphorus, magnesium, manganese, boron, strontium, silica, zinc, and copper. All minerals in the body are in delicate balance with one another, and if a deficiency in calcium exists, other minerals will also be compromised. Vitamins that join in to complete the orchestration of bone building are folic acid, vitamin B6, vitamin D, and vitamin K.

Another excellent form of calcium is microcrystalline hydroxyapatite concentrate (MCHC), a whole bone preparation made from raw calf long bones. MCHC contains minerals in their natural ratio as well as the proteins that help build bone. MCHC has been shown both to help shorten the amount of time it takes fractured bone to reunite and to facilitate reunion in slow-healing fractures. It is easily absorbed and has been shown to halt bone loss in postmenopausal osteoporosis.[31]

Antacids

The power of advertising never ceases to amaze us. The antacid industry certainly has done a good job of convincing people that antacids that buffer stomach acid are a good source of calcium. Many medical doctors accept these claims and commonly recommend antacids as a "good" source of calcium. Following are some facts you need to know.

The type of calcium in antacids is calcium carbonate, the least absorbable form of calcium. Calcium carbonate requires large amounts of HCl for its absorption, but antacids decrease stomach acid levels, thereby interfering with digestion. Antacids also deplete the body of phosphorus, and disrupt the calcium-phosphorus interactions necessary to maintain bone. Some antacids contain aluminum, which is a possible causative factor in osteoporosis because it can inhibit the osteoblast cells; aluminum also contributes to Alzheimer's disease.

Please do not rely on antacids for your calcium intake. Even better, don't rely on antacids for gastric disturbances; treat the underlying cause.

Contrary to popular ideas, heartburn is often a result of deficiency, not excess, of stomach acid. A meal high in protein requires high amounts of HCl to break down the protein. When there is a deficiency, the stomach starts to overproduce HCl to compensate, and may produce so much that the stomach lining becomes irritated. If you suffer from heartburn, get your HCl levels tested.

We now know the important relationship between maintaining adequate calcium levels throughout life and bone health. Deficiencies of other nutrients over a prolonged period, however, may play an even greater role in the onset of osteoporosis than calcium deficiency.

As we will refer to them often when discussing nutrient levels, let us explain the terms minimal daily intake (MDI), used in Canada, and recommended daily intake (RDI), used in the United States (formerly the recommended daily allowance, or RDA). The MDI and RDI values for a particular nutrient show how much of that nutrient needs to be ingested daily to prevent a deficiency disease, such as the vitamin C deficiency disease, scurvy. The guidelines were developed by government-sponsored scientists to help researchers estimate the adequacy of the general food supply—if daily intake of the general food supply yields the nutrient levels listed in the MDI and RDI, then the food supply is deemed sufficiently nutritious. Only healthy subjects were tested to set the guidelines; these subjects were deprived of one nutrient at a time, a situation that rarely, if ever, occurs in real life. The MDI and RDI guidelines do not take into account the following facts:

- Nutrients work together, not independently of one another.
- Nutrient requirements vary from person to person, depending on genetic heritage, health status and history, environmental context, stress levels, and others; indeed, some people have quite particular nutrient needs that cannot possibly be addressed simply by following MDI or RDI guidelines.
- There is a significant difference between the minimum amount of a nutrient needed to prevent disease in a formerly healthy subject and the minimum needed to support optimal health.

Because of the inadequacies of the MDI and RDI guidelines, the recommended intake levels for nutrients given below will be higher that the guidelines suggest.

Minerals

First let us consider the minerals besides calcium that play a role in bone health, in order of importance.

- **Magnesium** helps maintain bone health because of its effects on hormones and other substances that regulate the bones and mineral metabolism.

Magnesium is also required for the conversion of vitamin D to the biologically active metabolite, vitamin D3.

Sixty percent of the body's magnesium is contained within the bones, primarily the trabecular bones. The North American diet is commonly low in magnesium. Dietary surveys have shown that 80 to 85 percent of women between the ages of 15 and 50 ingest less than 70 per cent of the RDI of magnesium. Magnesium deficiency adversely affects all stages of skeletal development, stopping bone growth, decreasing osteoblastic and osteoclastic activity, and causing bone fragility.

— **Suggested Daily Intake:** 300 to 800 mg. Note: Some people taking higher levels of magnesium get loose stools and will need to decrease their intake.

— **Food Sources:** Beans (especially black, mung, lima, and adzuki); whole grains (especially buckwheat, millet, corn, barley, rye, and rice); nuts and seeds (especially almonds, cashews, sesame seeds, and filberts), and sea vegetables.

   Magnesium sits at the centre of the chlorophyll molecule; therefore, foods high in chlorophyll, such as wheat or barley grass products, and micro-algae such as spirulina, provide easily assimilated magnesium. One of the best products I know of for adding more of the green chlorophyll-containing foods to one's diet is greens+ or GreenAlive, which can be found in most health food stores.

• **Boron** is a trace mineral thought previously to be essential only for plants. Consequently there is no MDI for boron. Now it appears that it has a very significant role to play in the absorption of calcium and magnesium and in the conversion of vitamin D to its active form, vitamin D3. In a recent study, it was found that the urinary excretion of calcium and magnesium is reduced by 44 percent in postmenopausal women when they are given 3 mg of boron per day. The women also developed increased blood levels of an estrogen, 17 beta-estradiol, and its precursor, testosterone. The exact mechanisms by which boron acts are not known; however, it seems to be required in the formation of steroid hormones.

   This fact does not in any way suggest that boron poses the same risks as estrogen replacement therapy. Boron seems capable of producing a mild estrogenic effect without the risks associated with the higher does prescribed in HRT.

   Boron has been used in Germany for years, where it is considered very effective in the treatment of arthritic conditions such as osteoarthritis, rheumatoid arthritis, and juvenile arthritis.

— **Suggested Daily Intake:** 3 to 9 mg of boron chelate for osteoporosis prevention and treatment. Boron in the form of sodium tetraborate decahydrate is considered the best type to take for arthritic conditions. In this case the suggested daily intake is also 3 to 9 mg.

— **Food Sources:** Fruits and vegetables are the best dietary sources but the level of nutrient available in foods depends on the level of that nutrient in the soil. As mentioned in Chapter 2, soils are commonly deficient in minerals and trace minerals.

• **Manganese.** Research indicates that inadequate dietary manganese may play a significant role in the development of osteoporosis. Manganese is required for bone mineralization and for the creation of connective tissue in both joint cartilage and bone. This makes manganese very important for preventing and treating osteoarthritis, a degenerative condition of the cartilage in the joints. Today the dietary consumption of refined foods is extremely high; when whole grains are replaced with refined flour, manganese is lost.

— **Suggested Daily Intake:** 15 to 30 mg.

— **Food Sources:** Whole grains, especially brown rice, meat, nuts and seeds, and leafy vegetables.

• **Zinc.** Zinc deficiency is common in North America; in one survey it was found that 68 percent of American adults consume less than two-thirds of the RDI for zinc. Zinc is an important contributor in the formation of bone cells and also enhances the actions of vitamin D. In the elderly, zinc deficiency is common because of decreased absorption, low intake, and the effects of certain medications. It has also been shown that high calcium supplementation in older women can increase zinc requirements.

— **Suggested Daily Intake:** 15 to 50 mg. Note: Zinc should be taken with copper in an approximate 8:1 (Zn:Cu) ratio.

— **Food Sources:** Legumes, oysters, meats, seafood, poultry, egg yolks, brewer's yeast, pumpkin seeds, soybeans, and whole grains.

• **Silicon** The theory of biological transmutation advanced by Louis Kervran, a French chemist, proposes that all living organisms have the ability to transmute, or change, minerals from other living organisms into other minerals through the action of enzymes. In mammals, the mineral silicon, found in all plants as silica, is transmuted to calcium, according to Kervran's theory. Standard scientific research asserts that silicon is found in high concentrations at the calcification sites in growing bones and that it strengthens the body's connective tissues. Silica is available in liquid and capsule forms in health food stores.

— **Suggested Daily Intake:** 1 to 20 mg.
— **Food Sources:** Alfalfa, beets, brown rice and whole grains, soybeans, and leafy green vegetables.

Nutrients for Bone Health

As is now obvious, calcium is not the only mineral affecting bone health. I hope that you will use the information presented above to introduce more mineral-rich foods into your diet, and to supplement as necessary. Your bones will thank you! Let's now consider the vitamins that have a strong influence on bone health.

• **Vitamin D.** Chapter 7 mentioned the importance of vitamin D for intestinal calcium absorption. It is common for people to become deficient in this vitamin as they age. One reason is that many older people become less able to convert vitamin D to its biologically active form, 1,25-hydroxycholecalciferol (vitamin D3); the conversion can be facilitated by treatment with magnesium and boron, as discussed above. Other causes of vitamin D deficiency include decreased dietary intake, drug interactions, and reduced sun exposure—vitamin D is synthesized from cholesterol on skin exposure to ultraviolet light from the sun.

A recent study strongly suggests that widespread deficiencies of vitamin D play a big role in causing osteoporosis among older Americans. Published in the *New England Journal of Medicine*, the study suggests that the current RDI for vitamin D, 400 IU for people 51 to 70 years of age and 600 IU for people over 70 years, may be inadequate.

There are two major forms of vitamin D: vitamin D2, the form often added to milk and other foods, and used in nutritional supplements, and vitamin D3, the most natural and biologically active form, found in cod and halibut liver oils. Not only may the RDI be low, it does not distinguish between these two forms of vitamin D; however, many people, even if they have adequate D2 intake, will not be able to convert enough of it into D3, the form so important for bone health.

— **Suggested Daily Intake:** 600 to 800 IU for adults; 1,000 IU for adults over 50 years of age. Note: The upper limit determined by the National Research Council is 2 000 IU.

— **Food Sources:** Butter, egg yolks, and cold-water fish.

• **Pyridoxine (Vitamin B6).** Vitamin B6, along with vitamin C, is an important factor in the formation of collagen. Collagen increases the strength of the connective tissue, an important structural element of bone and, indeed, the whole body. The body also requires vitamin B6 in the many enzymatic pathways involved in maintaining hormonal balance and proper immune function. As is the case with other nutrients, vitamin B6 is depleted by exposure to or ingestion of herbicides, food colourings, and cadmium (present in cigarettes). Diets high in animal protein increase the intake requirements for B6. Dietary surveys done in the United States suggest that B6 deficiency is common in more than half of American women.

— **Suggested Daily Intake:** 25 to 50 mg. Most B-complex supplements provide this amount. We prefer vitamin B6 in the form of pyridoxyl-5-phosphate (P5P) whenever possible.

— **Food Sources:** Avocados, bananas, whole grains, kale, legumes, peppers, prunes, raisins, sunflower seeds, soybeans, spinach, and nutritional yeast (brewer's and torula).

• **Vitamin K.** The protein matrix that provides the foundation for calcium crystallization in bone requires vitamin K to form and maintain itself. Therefore, vitamin K is necessary for bone formation, remodelling, and repair. Vitamin K deficiency is more common than previously thought and occurs in people who don't eat enough vegetables or have intestinal microbial imbalances—vitamin K is formed by healthy intestinal microflora.

In one study of osteoporotic patients, treatment with vitamin K decreased urinary calcium loss by 18 to 50 percent. Generally, people with osteoporosis are found to have lower concentrations of vitamin K than people of the same age without osteoporosis. It has also been found that the severity of an osteoporotic fracture strongly correlates with the level of circulating vitamin K—the less vitamin K present, the worse the fracture is likely to be.

Vitamin K is available in three forms: vitamin K1 from plants; vitamin K2 from the bacteria in the gastrointestinal tract; and vitamin K3, a synthetic form. Perhaps one of the reasons that vegetarians have less incidence of osteoporosis is their higher dietary intake of vitamin K–rich green leafy vegetables.

— **Suggested Daily Intake:** 200 to 500 mcg. Note: There are no known side effects or toxicity levels for vitamin K. However, vitamin K may interfere with the actions of anticoagulant drugs like warfarin and Coumadin, which work by blocking vitamin K's action in the bloodstream.

— **Food Sources:** Asparagus, broccoli, cabbage, kale, lettuce, spinach, green peas, and green tea (raw vegetables and fresh juices provide the richest vitamin K content).

• **Vitamin B12 and Folic Acid** function in tandem in many body processes. Folic acid helps prevent and treat osteoporosis through its ability to lower homocysteine levels—homocysteine interferes with the collagen cross-linking process in the formation of connective tissue.

Menopause is a time of increased requirements for folic acid. Folic acid deficiency is fairly common, with the average North American diet supplying less than one-half of the RDI/MDI. Folic acid deficiency is exacerbated by oral contraceptives, smoking, and drinking alcohol.

Vitamin B12 promotes the metabolism of osteoblasts and is therefore important in bone remodelling. Folic acid and B12 should be taken together because folic acid taken alone can mask an underlying deficiency of B12.

— **Suggested Daily Intake, Folic Acid:** 400 mcg to 1 mg.

— **Food Sources:** Beans (especially black-eyed peas, soy, kidney, lima, mung, navy beans and chickpeas), whole grains, nuts (especially filberts, peanuts, and almonds), green vegetables, and nutritional yeast (brewer's).

— **Suggested Daily Intake, Vitamin B12:** The most common recommendation for oral B12 is 1 000 mcg per day, which results in approximately 2 to 3 mcg per day absorption. If stores are low I would suggest 2 000 mcg per day for a few months, then decrease the dose to 1 000 mcg per day.

— **Food Sources:** Liver (beef, chicken, and lamb), oysters and sardines; lower levels are found in cheese, eggs, trout, salmon, and tuna. As you can see, all of the food sources for vitamin B12 are animal foods, so I strongly recommend that vegetarians supplement their diet with vitamin B12 and folic acid.

• **Vitamin C** is commonly known as an antioxidant and has many beneficial effects on the immune system as well. The primary function of vitamin C, however, is to participate in the manufacture of collagen, which makes it essential in the formation of bone and connective tissue. Vitamin C deficiency has been found in more than 20 percent of elderly women, even those consuming more than the RDI of the vitamin—60 mg per day). In our opinion, the RDI for vitamin C is extremely low.

Almost all other animals manufacture vitamin C internally, but the human body does not, so adequate daily intake is necessary and essential for optimal health. Most people consider citrus fruits a good source of vitamin C and think that drinking their orange juice daily gives them enough. Unfortunately, exposure to air destroys vitamin C, as does transport, storage, and display under fluorescent lighting. Most of us do not have the luxury of going out and picking fresh oranges, grapefruits, lemons, and limes, or any other fruits and vegetables for that matter, and end up with fruits and vegetables that have lost most of their vitamin C. The result is that outright scurvy, the classic vitamin C deficiency disease, is now rare in our country, but subclinical vitamin C deficiency is common, especially in the elderly. This is especially worrisome given that age is a risk factor for osteoporosis.

Other common conditions and situations in which vitamin C has been shown to be of benefit include asthma, cancer prevention, cardiovascular disease, cataracts, eczema, fatigue, glaucoma, hepatitis, and osteoarthritis.

— **Suggested Daily Intake:** 500 mg. Note: For treatment of any of the conditions mentioned above, increased doses could start at 1 000 mg per day and go up from there to the bowel tolerance level. When your intake of vitamin C is in excess of what you are assimilating, you will experience gas or loose stools. Your dosage has reached your bowel tolerance level. If you experience these symptoms, decrease your daily intake.

I take between 3 000 and 5 000 mg of vitamin C daily and can tolerate even higher doses over the winter when my exposure to people with colds and flus is high.

— **Food Sources:** Vitamin C is quickly destroyed by today's food transport, storage, and processing methods. Don't depend on food to supply the vitamin C you need.

Now that we've covered the major vitamins and minerals, let's look at a few other diet and lifestyle factors that have a contribution to make to bone health.

- **Essential fatty acids.** High dietary fat intake, especially of saturated fats, can cause problems for bone health because saturated fats combine with calcium to form unabsorbable calcium soaps. However, the essential fatty acids (EFAs) introduced in Chapter 2 are important for the health of the bones and the surrounding tissues. Omega-3 and omega-6 fatty acids must be obtained from the diet, as they cannot be manufactured by the body. They are needed to make hormones. They are also the primary constituent of cell membranes and direct hormones to their target cells.

If dietary amounts of the EFAs are inadequate, insufficient hormonal levels result, and this in turn has a harmful effect on the health of the skeletal system.

  — **Suggested Daily Intake:** 1 to 3 g omega-3 fatty acids daily; 500 to 1,000 mg omega-6 fatty acids daily.

  — **Food Sources:** Fish (salmon, sardines); oils (black currant seed oil, borage oil, fish oils, flaxseed oil).

- **Ipriflavone** is a synthetic molecule that is classified as a flavonoid. I previously discussed the bone health benefits conferred by the naturally occurring soy isoflavonoids, particularly genistein and daidzein. The chemical structure of Ipriflavone is very close to that of these natural isoflavones. Although a more recent arrival in North America, Ipriflavone has been used in Europe and Japan for years to treat osteoporosis. I prefer to prevent and treat osteoporosis with soy and red clover isoflavones, since they are found in nature. However, if one of my patients is diagnosed with moderate to severe osteoporosis, I recommend Ipriflavone; many studies show its ability to prevent bone loss and promote bone formation. Ipriflavone does not have the unwanted side effects that so often accompany pharmaceutical treatment of osteoporosis.

— **Suggested Daily Intake:** 200 to 300 mg two to three times daily.

OSTEOARTHRITIS

Osteoarthritis is a common condition in both women and men, particularly after the age of 65, and is often, but not always, associated with osteoporosis. The osteoarthritis remedies discussed here are also useful for preventing and treating osteoporosis.

Osteoarthritis primarily affects the joint cartilage and adjacent tissues. Joint cartilage is a cushioning tissue that softens the impact between two bones at a joint. In osteoarthritis, the mechanical wear and tear of the years, along with slowing cartilage repair rate that occurs with age, combine to weaken and tear cartilage, resulting in higher stress on the bones where they meet at the joint. Tissues in and around the affected bones become inflamed, and fissuring and linear fractures appear in the bone.

The most common drugs used in the management of pain associated with osteoarthritis and osteoporosis are non-steroidal anti-inflammatory drugs (NSAIDs), including Aspirin. Chronic use of these agents can cause potentially serious side effects such as peptic ulcers, upper and lower gastrointestinal bleeding, liver damage, and kidney impairment; the use of NSAIDs is a major public health concern.

In Canada, the United States, and the United Kingdom, respectively, 10, 70, and 20 million prescriptions or dispensations of NSAIDs are handed out annually. Studies indicate that up to 3 percent of NSAID users will bleed from their guts and more than one-quarter of the users will require medications to treat peptic ulcerations. These statistics are probably low, given the common over-the-counter use of these drugs.

We have covered the importance of nutritional treatment of bone difficulties in the osteoporosis chapters, and osteoarthritis is no exception. Several studies demonstrate the effectiveness of natural, safe remedies in the treatment of osteoarthritis. We will cover briefly here some of the most important supplements used in the natural treatment of osteoarthritis, chondroitin sulphate and glucosamine sulphate. In addition, the nutritional information given above applies in osteoarthritis.

Common Osteoarthritis Remedies: Glucosamine Sulphate and Chondroitin Sulphate

Glucosamine sulphate is a substance that occurs naturally in the body; it is composed of glucose and the amino acid glutamine. It is an important component of healthy joints, and when taken in supplemental form, the body uses it to rebuild joint cartilage and thereby begin repair of the osteoarthritic joint. Studies of glucosamine show that it is as effective in reducing pain as are NSAIDs, without the risk of side effects. Of course, NSAIDs do not help the osteoarthritic joints repair themselves; they simply mask pain. Glucosamine reduces pain because it helps correct the problem that causes the pain. In fact, NSAIDs inhibit cartilage repair and accelerate cartilage destruction. Their use is actually associated with acceleration of osteoarthritis and increased joint destruction.

- **Suggested Daily Intake:** 500 mg three to four times daily.

Many of the glucosamine supplements include a substance called chondroitin sulphate because the two materials together have synergistic potential. Chondroitins are complex sugars that form part of the cartilage. They facilitate the absorption of nutrients into the cartilage and inhibit the action of enzymes that may damage the matrix of cartilage.

- **Suggested Daily Intake:** 125 mg two to three times daily.

There is also growing evidence that the benefits of these two substances for osteoarthritis and osteoporosis are further enhanced if they are combined with trace minerals and added antioxidants—which, you'll recall, prevent accelerated cellular damage—such as vitamin C and proanthocyanidins (grape seed extract, pine bark extract).

IN CONCLUSION: PROTOCOLS FOR OSTEOPOROSIS PREVENTION AND TREATMENT

Evaluating the risk of osteoporosis or diagnosing osteoporosis involves looking at your health history, lifestyle (how prevalent are the bone busters?), getting a thorough physical examination, and making use of the appropriate medical tests outlined earlier in this chapter.

RECOMMENDED DAILY NUTRIENT INTAKE FOR THE PREVENTION AND TREATMENT OF OSTEOPOROSIS

MINERALS	PREVENTION	TREATMENT
Boron	1 to 3 mg	3 to 6 mg
Calcium hydroxyappetite	600 to 800 mg	800 to 1,000 mg
Calcium citrate	400 to 600 mg	600 to 1,200 mg
Copper	1 to 2 mg	1 to 2 mg
Magnesium	300 to 600 mg	400 to 800 mg
Manganese	15 to 20 mg	20 to 30 mg
Silicon	1 to 10 mg	5 to 20 mg
Zinc	15 to 20 mg	20 to 30 mg

VITAMINS	PREVENTION	TREATMENT
B-complex vitamins	10 to 25 mg	25 to 50 mg
B12	500 to 1,000 mcg	1,000 to 2,000 mcg
Folic Acid	400 to 500 mcg	500 mcg to 1 mg
Vitamin C	300 to 500 mg	500 to 2,000 mg
Vitamin D	400 to 600 IU	800 to 1,000 IU
Vitamin K	100 to 300 mcg	300 to 500 mcg

ADDITIONAL NUTRIENTS

- Soy isoflavones (e.g. Women's Whey) are extremely beneficial for osteoporosis.
- Omega-3 essential fatty acids are essential for calcium metabolism.
- Glucosamine sulphate and chondroitin sulphate regenerate joints.
- Hydrochloric acid and digestive enzymes aid in the assimilation and utilization of calcium.
- Calcium formulas (e.g. OsteoBalance+)
- Support for the adrenals to decrease cortisol levels (see Chapter 3).

While you're waiting for the test results to come in, there's no reason not to be proactive. Below is a summary of the prevention and treatment strategies discussed in this chapter that apply to everyone, regardless of present health status. If you do not have osteoporosis, give thanks—and begin to implement the general strategies given below. If you do have osteoporosis, know that the situation is reversible—and begin to implement the strategies given below! More specific directions for your situation follow.

Exercise, use it or lose it; **Eat a bone-supportive diet,** keep your animal protein and emphasize whole grains, legumes, leafy greens and green foods; **Supplement your food intake,** add a good multinutrient formula such as FemmEssentials; **Establish good bowel health,** eliminate Candida (see Chapters 2 and 3); **Take care of your liver,** without strong liver function, you cannot have proper detoxification of the body, hormone balance, vitamin and mineral assimilation, or protein creation. Liver support remedies such as EstroSense especially for women with estrogen dominant conditions, and liv-tone for general liver drainage and support can simplify things; **Take care of you adrenal glands,** when the body is stressed, cortisol levels increase causing a decrease in bone resorption. Consider adding an adrenal support product to keep cortisol levels in check (see Chapter 3).

A proactive approach to bone health may include supplemental nutrients to ensure that the bones are getting the nutrients they need to remain strong and healthy. The following table gives general guidelines for bone-supportive nutritional supplementation for women and men.

Suggested Treatment Protocols

When your test results come in, you may discover that you have osteoporosis. What a relief that you already have a full treatment program in swing! In addition, you can take the following measures, depending on whether your bone loss is mild, medium, or severe.

• **Mild.** Take a multinutrient formula such as FemmEssentials and a calcium supplement such as OsteoBalance+ or Bone-Up or in the forms listed earlier. Help keep your stress in check by using an adrenal supplement such as adrena+.

- **Moderate.** As above. In addition, you should add meno, Remefemin or MenoSense for phytohormone support. Women with moderate osteoporosis also need to test for progesterone levels and consider short-term use of USP progesterone cream, under medical supervision.

- **Severe.** Take all the steps above. Women will need to consider short-term "friendly" HRT use (for example, Tri-Est and progesterone cream 6%), to temporarily slow bone loss while beginning to tip the balance towards rebuilding bone. We would also recommend taking additional Ipriflavone, 600 to 800 mg once or twice daily.

In addition, consider the use of biophosphonates (alendronate or etidronate) for a *short* time, again, to temporarily slow bone loss. These drugs may be more beneficial in the elderly. Stop use if you experience side effects.

Now that we have considered the major health concerns associated with menopause—hormone replacement therapy and osteoporosis—let's look at other common health concerns of women.

OTHER COMMON
HEALTH CONCERNS

"Health is the normal and harmonious vibration of the elements
and forces composing the entity on the mental and moral
(emotional) planes of being, in conformity with the constructive
principle (great law of life) in nature."—Henry Lindlahr

In keeping with the overall themes of this book, this chapter touches mainly
on the hormone-related problems most likely to be encountered by women.
In addition we look at two common conditions, anemia and dysglycemia
(blood sugar imbalance), and at cardiovascular disease. Many of the hormonal
and reproductive-related disorders covered in this chapter, such as premenstrual syndrome (PMS), painful periods, and endometriosis, are, of course,
illnesses that often occur well before the transitional years. It is important to
address these and other hormone imbalances as early as possible to lower
the risk for more serious endocrine health problems down the road. Here, as
elsewhere, natural interventions can provide effective help.

More and more women seem to be experiencing conditions related to
hormonal imbalance. Diet, lifestyle, and the environment can be contributing causes at the physical level. Remember, however, that no disease of the
body is strictly physical; it always has its mental/emotional and spiritual
aspects. Most women today are so busy with life, juggling family responsibilities and careers, that they have little time left to nurture themselves.
When our natural innermost needs are not being met, our mental, emotional,
and physical energy suffers and can become severely compromised. Chronic
disease such as cancer may result.

Energetically speaking, anyone who experiences chronic problems in a
particular area of the body has blocked energy flow (blocked chi). Such

blockages can be due to underlying spiritual or mental/emotional conflicts, and complete healing may be impossible to achieve until the blockages (conflicts) are removed at the spiritual or mental/emotional levels. Disease specifically involving female functions and processes can often indicate that we are at some level trying to reject or disown our femininity. In a society that for many centuries has tended to denigrate women for their cyclical changes, rather than celebrating the natural power, creativity, and fertility inherent in women's cycles, many women go to war with their own female nature. Developing a loving and accepting attitude towards our hormonal cycles and transitions will often help create major shifts in our symptoms, away from pain and towards an enriching and deepening experience of being female.

There are many ways to aid the restoration of full and free energetic flow; in this section we will be covering dietary, botanical, and nutritional remedies that strengthen energy flow primarily at the physical level. For more information and healing techniques related to working with the mental/emotional and spiritual aspects of life, please refer to Chapter 10.

Anemia

Anemia is one of the most common deficiency diseases in people of all ages. In this condition, the blood contains too few red blood cells, or the red blood cells are low in hemoglobin, the portion of the cell that contains iron. Blood that is deficient in this way cannot transport oxygen and nutrients at adequate levels to properly nourish the cells. Chronic anemia may be present at a subclinical level even though it has not been confirmed by standard laboratory tests. As a result it is often overlooked. Most medical practitioners do only routine hemoglobin tests to determine whether anemia is present, but hemoglobin measurements do not provide a good baseline for determining iron deficiency anemia. The more accurate indicator for this condition is the blood's iron storage level, called serum ferritin. Hemoglobin levels can be normal while serum ferritin is very low.

The symptoms of anemia in the initial stages can include fatigue, headaches, irritability, or depression. Shortness of breath, rapid heart beat, tinnitus, angina pain, disturbances in equilibrium, and fainting may develop later, even though hemoglobin levels may still be within the normal range.

Any level of anemia impairs the normal functioning of the blood. The endocrine organs, such as ovaries and the adrenal glands depend on the directives of the hormonal messengers that are transported in the blood to the target tissue in the organs. Therefore, when anemic conditions compromise hormonal messages, hormonal imbalance results, with a variety of different complaints. In women, therefore, anemia may contribute to menstrual irregularities. Anemia can not only be the result of excessive menstrual bleeding (menorrhagia), it can also be the cause.

Uterine fibroids, which can cause excessive menstrual bleeding and are discussed in detail below, can contribute to anemia. Anemia can also be caused by deficiencies of dietary iron, vitamin B12, folic acid, vitamin C, vitamin B6, and vitamin E. All of these contribute to the uptake of iron and the formation of healthy red blood cells. Supplemental forms of iron such as aqueous liver extracts and liquid iron/herbal formulas (Floradix) can be extremely beneficial. To determine your exact nutritional needs respecting anemia, consult with a qualified health care practitioner.

Dysglycemia (Blood Sugar Imbalance) and Adrenal Function

One of the most common conditions that we see in people of all ages is functional dysglycemia (blood sugar dysregulation). Glucose (blood sugar) is the main fuel for the brain and is required by all the cells of the body. Thus, it is important to maintain balanced blood glucose levels, adequate for meeting demand. Many people, women in particular, have difficulty with the metabolism of carbohydrates. The result is dysglycemia.

Blood sugar illnesses such as diabetes and hypoglycemia are well recognized and easily diagnosed by looking at fluctuations in blood glucose levels and the associated symptoms. Subclinical blood sugar dysregulation, however, referred to in this book as dysglycemia, can often not be confirmed by blood tests. Symptoms are very similar to those produced by the more serious blood sugar imbalances, though not as dramatic. The main symptoms include, but are not limited to, anxiety, fatigue, irritability, and poor concentration. Symptoms generally occur two to three hours after carbohydrate ingestion.

There are laboratory tests that may be helpful in assessing dysglycemia: the two-hour postprandial (post-meal) blood glucose test, the four- or six-hour glucose tolerance test, or the more sensitive four- or six-hour glucose and insulin tolerance test. The fasting blood glucose test (the most routinely done) is a single, isolated measurement and cannot provide information on overall blood glucose regulation.

We feel that a combined cataloguing of symptoms and assessment of the risk factors for dysglycemia is probably the most accurate and cost-effective way to determine whether dysglycemia is present.

The questionnaire is extremely helpful in assessing your level of dysglycemia. A total score of less than 50 indicates occasional or extremely mild dys-glycemia; 50 to 110 indicates mild dysglycemia; 110 to 150 means moderate dysglycemia; and greater than 150 means severe dysglycemia.

Insulin and glucagon are the main hormones regulating blood glucose metabolism. Insulin is produced by the pancreas. Diets high in simple refined carbohydrates overwork the pancreas, so it is no wonder so many people have symptoms of dysglycemia to varying degrees. Adrenal hormones are very important in blood sugar regulation as well, so if the adrenals are overtaxed, blood sugar balance will be impaired. We know how stress affects the function of the adrenal glands. Chronic stress has also been known to cause chromium depletion; chromium is crucial for normal blood sugar regulation.

Progesterone appears to be able to affect insulin's ability to suppress glucose production by the liver. Several studies have found impaired glucose metabolism in women taking oral contraceptives containing synthetic estrogen and progestins or progestins alone.

DYSGLYCEMIA: NATUROPATHIC TREATMENT OPTIONS

The critical role the adrenal glands play in the maintenance of blood sugar is obvious in the dysglycemia questionnaire; many of the symptoms listed were also listed in the adrenal stress symptom list (Chapter 3) and as symptoms of menopause (Chapter 5). Restoring balanced adrenal function is important for blood sugar health; please see Chapter 3 for recommendations.

Adequate intake of minerals such as magnesium, zinc, and especially chromium are also necessary to prevent dysglycemia. Those exhibiting symptoms need 200 to 400 mcg per day of chromium, 400 to 800 mg per day of magnesium, and 30 to 60 mg per day of zinc. We also recommend a multivitamin and mineral tablet that contains high levels of vitamins such as FemmEssentials and adrenal support (see Chapter 3).

A diet high in refined carbohydrates (sugar and white flour) is a major contributor to the high incidence of non-insulin-dependent diabetes

DYSGLYCEMIA SYMPTOM LIST

To arrive at your final score, write:
- 0 beside symptoms you never or almost never experience;
- 1 beside symptoms you occasionally have, but which do not affect you severely;
- 2 beside symptoms you occasionally have and that affect you severely;
- 3 beside symptoms you experience frequently, but which do not affect you severely; and
- 4 beside symptoms you experience frequently and that affect you severely.

1. Afternoon headaches ___
2. Awaken after a few hours sleep
    —hard to get back to sleep ___
3. Aware of breathing heavily ___
4. "Butterfly stomach," cramps ___
5. Can't decide easily ___
6. Can't start in the morning without coffee ___
7. Can't work under pressure ___
8. Crave candy or coffee in the afternoons ___
9. Cry easily for no apparent reason ___
10. Eat when nervous ___
11. Fatigue, relieved by eating ___
12. Get "shaky" if hungry ___
13. Irritable before meals ___
14. Lack of energy ___
15. Reduced initiative ___
16. Sleepy after meals ___
17. Sleepy during day ___
18. Weakness ___
19. Symptoms come before breakfast ___
20. Afternoon exhaustion ___
21. Depression ___
22. Insomnia ___
23. Anxiety ___
24. Irritability (general) ___

25. Headaches   ___
26. Dizziness   ___
27. Sweating   ___
28. Internal trembling   ___
29. Palpitation of heart   ___
30. Muscle pain and backache   ___
31. Difficulty in concentration   ___
32. Chronic indigestion   ___
33. Cold hands or feet   ___
34. Blurred vision   ___
35. Muscular twitching or cramps   ___
36. Joint pain   ___
37. Restlessness   ___
38. Obesity   ___
39. Forgetfulness   ___
40. Nervousness   ___
41. Indecisiveness   ___
42. Craving for sweets   ___
43. Moodiness   ___
44. Allergies   ___
45. Sighing and yawning   ___
46. Peculiar breath or perspiration odor   ___
47. Noise or light sensitivity   ___
48. Mood swings   ___
49. Crave chocolate   ___
50. Crave bread   ___
51. Feeling "spacey" or "unreal"   ___
52. Crave alcohol   ___
53. Poor exercise tolerance   ___
54. Night urination   ___
55. Frequent urination   ___
56. Premenstrual symptoms (PMS)   ___
57. Constantly hungry   ___

Total: ___

(NIDDM) in North America and definitely contributes to dysglycemia as well. A diet consisting of 40 percent unrefined carbohydrates, 30 percent protein (as we have seen in the chapter on osteoporosis, the emphasis should be on plant proteins), and 30 percent fat (nuts, seeds, nut butters, extra virgin olive oil, and high-quality expeller-pressed oils are the best sources) has been shown to be preventive against blood sugar abnormalities. This diet encourages a more moderate release of insulin than does one high in refined carbohydrates. When insulin is not being released as often or in such high levels after meals, there is less stress on the pancreas and less fluctuation in blood sugar levels.

Studies have shown that other health problems that can be helped by treating dysglycemia include carbohydrate cravings, accelerated aging, PMS, depression, muscle cramps, and fibromyalgia. Diseases that can be prevented by addressing dysglycemia include hypertension, NIDDM, obesity, and atherosclerosis.

Premenstrual Syndrome (PMS)

PMS is very common, with roughly 50 percent of women—some reports claim 70 percent—experiencing some form of PMS during the premenstrual time. It is so common, in fact, that many women think that PMS is normal.

Women experience the various symptoms of PMS at different times during the cycle and to varying degrees. Some suffer to such an extent that they may experience only a few days during the month when they feel normal. Recurrent signs and symptoms that many women develop during the seven to fourteen days before menstruation include the following:

• **Female organs:** tender and enlarged breasts; uterine cramping; altered libido.

• **Gastrointestinal:** abdominal bloating; constipation or diarrhea; change in appetite with increased cravings, usually for carbohydrates, chocolate, and sugar.

• **General:** fatigue; migraines and headaches; backaches; skin problems; water retention with edema of fingers, face, and ankles; heart palpitations; dizziness with or without fainting; insomnia; herpes and decreased immunity.

- **Mental/emotional:** Nervousness, anxiety, irritability, mood swings, depression.

THE CAUSES OF PMS

Premenstrual tension was known as a type of hysteria by the herbalists of earlier days and was treated as a nervous condition associated with loss of emotional control and functional disturbances. The term "hysteria" was taken from a Greek word for uterus, *hystera,* because this condition was more commonly recognized in women.

As recently as 1987, the American Psychiatric Association concluded that severe PMS was a *psychiatric illness,* characterized by a pattern of significant emotional and behavioural symptoms occurring during the luteal phase of the menstrual cycle.

From a naturopathic perspective, the main causes of PMS are poor diet, lack of exercise, liver and bowel congestion, and general toxicity. Once these factors are addressed, along with short-term botanical, nutritional, or homeopathic support, most women that I treat for PMS symptoms no longer experience them.

The naturopathic perspective has points in common with traditional Chinese medicine, which sees PMS as being caused by congested liver chi and a deficiency of yin energy, which is treated with herbs such as dong quai and licorice.

The difficulties that generally cause PMS can result in the following imbalances, all of which have been identified in women with PMS:

- **Dysglycemia (blood sugar imbalances).** Poor blood sugar control, which can lead to further emotional and physical symptoms.
- **Hormonal imbalances:** estrogen excess; progesterone deficiency or excess; thyroid hormone imbalances; prolactin excess; high aldosterone levels (aldosterone is an adrenal hormone that in excess can cause muscle spasms).
- **Nutritional deficiencies:** magnesium, B-complex vitamins, especially vitamin B6, vitamin A, and vitamin E.
- **Prostaglandin imbalances.** Prostaglandins (PGs) are hormone-like compounds made in every cell of the body that function as regulators of a variety of physiological responses including inflammation, muscle contraction, blood vessel dilation, blood platelet stickiness (platelets are

blood cells involved in blood clotting), and some reproductive functions. Symptoms can result with prostaglandin excesses or deficiencies. In PMS, there is often a decrease of compounds in the prostaglandin-1 series (PG1), and an increase in prostaglandin-2 series (PG2) compounds.

- **Psychological difficulties.** In researching PMS and its causes, Dr. Guy Abraham, a leading researcher in the field, has identified four distinct types of PMS, each with specific symptoms, hormonal patterns, and metabolic mechanisms. Some women will find that their symptoms fit almost perfectly into one of the PMS types described below; others will have symptoms that fit into one or more PMS types. If you are unsure which PMS types best describe your symptom pattern, you may find it useful to fill in the Menstrual Symptom Questionnaire (see page 253).

PMS TREATMENT

Following are the general recommendations that will benefit all women with PMS, and conclude with treatment recommendations specific to the various PMS types. To treat your PMS, implement the general protocols in combination with the specific remedies and diet and lifestyle changes given for the PMS types.

Diet

Diet plays a very important role in PMS. Generally it has been found that PMS sufferers consume more refined sugars and carbohydrates, salt, dairy products, and meats than women who do not have PMS. Vegetarian women do not have the same incidence of PMS as non-vegetarian women, because they consume more fibre and less low-quality or harmful fat. Studies show that vegetarian women also have lower estrogen levels than women who eat meat.

Chapter 2 discusses in detail how to eat to support health and lower nutritional and digestive stress. I recommend that all PMS sufferers review the information given there and begin moving towards a healthier diet. See also the "Further Reading" section for more information on this topic.

In addition to a good diet, the following basic program of nutritional supplementation has been found very helpful for PMS.

- B-complex vitamins, 25 mg per day; vitamin B6, 50 mg per day
- Vitamin C, 500 mg twice per day

- Vitamin E, 400 to 800 IU per day (use natural-source vitamin E for best results)
- Evening primrose oil capsules, 1 to 2 g per day. Evening primrose oil, taken monthly at least three to five days before the usual onset of symptoms, has been shown to be extremely effective in the treatment of PMS

PMS-C (CRAVINGS)

SYMPTOMS	MECHANISMS	PREVALENCE
• Increased appetite • Craving for sugar, carbohydrates, salt • Fatigue, dizziness, fainting • Heart palpitations • Headaches	• Increased carbohydrate tolerance • Low levels of prostaglandin PGE1	• 24 to 35 percent

Deficiency of PGE1 in the pancreas and central nervous system leads to increased insulin secretion and lowered blood glucose levels (hypoglycemia).

PMS-D (DEPRESSION)

SYMPTOMS	MECHANISMS	PREVALENCE
• Depression and insomnia • Crying • Forgetfulness and confusion	• Low estrogen • High progesterone • Elevated adrenal androgens • Possible heavy metal toxicity (lead)	• 23 to 37 percent

The increase in estrogen results from a stress-induced increase in adrenal androgens or progesterone. It has been found that PMS-D patients often have higher heavy metal levels and lower magnesium levels as determined by hair mineral analysis. The heavy metal lead binds estrogen to receptor sites and has no effect on progesterone.

- Flaxseed oil (expeller- or cold-pressed and stored in the refrigerator or freezer in an opaque bottle), 2 to 4 tablespoons per day
- Magnesium, 400 to 800 mg per day
- Zinc, 30 mg per day, or
- Keep it simple: take FemmEssentials containing all the nutrients above

PMS-H (HYPERHYDRATION)

SYMPTOMS	MECHANISM	PREVALENCE
• Weight gain • Abdominal bloating • Breast tenderness and congestion • Fluid retention, with swelling face, fingers, hands, or ankles	• Increase in adrenal aldosterone production • Estrogen excess • Deficient dopamine (a central nervous system compound)	• 60 to 66 percent

Increased levels of aldosterone (adrenal hormone) due to stress, estrogen excess, and dopamine deficiency cause sodium and water retention.

PMS-A (ANXIETY)

SYMPTOMS	MECHANISMS	PREVALENCE (% OF PMS SUFFERERS)
• Anxiety • Irritability • Mood swings • Nervous tension	• Estrogen excess • Progesterone deficiency	• 68 to 80 percent

The estrogen excess in PMS-A is due to decreased breakdown of estrogen by the liver. It creates a relative progesterone deficiency, that is, not enough progesterone is normally produced to balance the excess estrogen. Again we see the importance of a healthy liver for hormonal balance.

Support the Liver and Treat the Gut

As can be seen when we look at the hormone imbalances charted by Dr. Abraham, many symptoms of PMS are related to gut problems, which contributes directly to hormone imbalance and to liver congestion, which further affects hormone levels. We recommend that all women with PMS follow the program outlined in Chapter 3 to restore healthy microflora to the bowel for four to six weeks, and institute a program of liver support. You can do this in conjunction with the appropriate nutritional supplementation and botanical remedies (outlined below). Once symptoms have improved, a simple maintenance program consisting of a healthy whole food diet, exercise, and a good multivitamin and mineral may be all that is required.

Treatments for PMS

Botanical remedies have been used for centuries to regulate abnormal hormonal symptoms. Since good adrenal functioning is so important for hormone balance, you could start with Adrena+, and if you need further support, consider the "specialty" herbs below.

Start the botanical remedy that seems to suit your symptoms 10 days before your PMS symptoms usually start, and take it until you begin menstruating, unless your symptoms continue during menstruation, in which case you can continue with the remedy. If you experience PMS symptoms for most of the month, as some women do, take the remedy throughout the month. After you have made the necessary lifestyle and dietary changes and corrected the underlying cause, whether liver congestion, adrenal fatigue, or thyroid problems, you will most likely be able to decrease or even stop taking the specific PMS remedy altogether.

• **Alfalfa (*Medicago sativa*)** is a source of phytoestrogens, and therefore acts as an estrogen balancing herb. For more details, please see Chapter 6.

— *Recommended dosage:* 500 to 1 000 mg powdered extract (4:1) daily.

• **Black cohosh (*Cimicifuga racemosa*)** can address an estrogen excess and inhibit prostaglandin production. Traditionally, it has also been used to treat "hysterical" PMS symptoms such as restlessness and nervous excitement. It is also beneficial in the treatment of breast tenderness and headaches associated with menstruation.

MENSTRUAL SYMPTOM QUESTIONNAIRE

Date: ___ / ___ / ___
Present Contraception: None ___ Pill ___ I.D. ___ Other ___
History of Taking Contraceptive Pills: Yes ___ No ___
If YES, months ago: ___ For how long ___ months
Your last period started (Date) ___ / ___ / ___
Your last period lasted ___ days.
Your last menstrual cycle was ___ days long.
Your last period was: Light ___ Moderate ___ Heavy ___
Number of Pregnancies: ___ Children: ___
Occupation: _____

Grading of Symptoms

1 none
2 mild—present but does not interfere with activities
3 moderate—present and interferes with activities but not
   disabling
4 severe—disabling (unable to function)

Grade Your Symptoms for Last Menstrual Cycle Only

Symptoms	Week After Period	Week Before Period
PMS-A		
Nervous tension	___	___
Mood swings	___	___
Irritability	___	___
Anxiety	___	___
	Total ___	Total ___
PMS-H		
Swelling of extremities	___	___
Breast tenderness	___	___
Abdominal bloating	___	___
	Total ___	Total ___

PMS-C

Headache	—	—
Craving for sweets	—	—
Increased appetite	—	—
Heart pounding	—	—
Fatigue	—	—
Dizziness or fainting	—	—
	Total ___	Total ___

PMS-D

Depression	—	—
Forgetfulness	—	—
Crying	—	—
Confusion	—	—
	Total ___	Total ___

Other symptoms

Oily skin	—	—
Acne	—	—

During First Two Days of Periods

Menstrual cramps	—
Menstrual backache	—

From: Abraham, G.E., "Nutritional Factors in the Etiology of the Premenstrual Tension Syndromes," J. Reprod. Med., 1983, 28:446-464.

— *Recommended dosage:* 250 to 500 mg solid extract (4:1) twice daily; 40 mg solid extract standardized to contain 2.5 percent triterpene glycosides once or twice daily.

• **Black haw (*Viburnum prunifolium*)** is an excellent tonic for the female organs and gastrointestinal system. It also helps calm the nervous or overly excitable tendencies sometimes associated with PMS. Herbalists of European origin learned of its use from Native Americans.

— *Recommended dosage:* 2 to 8 mL bark tincture (1:5) daily.

• **Blue cohosh (*Caulophyllum thalictroides*)** has been used traditionally in the treatment of PMS where there are "hysterical" or emotional symptoms and ovarian or breast pain. It is very effective for uterine spasm in dysmenorrhea.

— *Recommended dosage:* 20 to 30 drops root tincture three to four times daily.

• **Chaste tree (*Vitex agnus-castus*).** Chaste tree is the number-one botanical remedy used in Europe to treat PMS symptoms. Its action in the body increases progesterone levels relative to estrogen levels. It is described in more detail in Chapter 6.

— *Recommended dosage:* 250 mg solid extract standardized to contain 0.5 percent agnusides twice daily.

• **Ginkgo (*Ginkgo biloba*)** has been shown to be effective for congestive effects experienced in PMS, particularly breast tenderness.

— *Recommended dosage:* 120 to 140 mg solid extract (4:1) one to two times daily; 80 mg solid extract standardized to contain 24 percent ginkgoflavonglycosides two to three times daily.

Specific Treatment Recommendations for PMS

• **PMS-A.** It has been found through diet surveys that women who experience the PMS-A symptom pattern consume five times more dairy products and three times more refined sugars than women who experience the other PMS symptom patterns. If you have PMS-A and are making dietary changes, explore whether your idea of what constitutes moderate or minimal sugar and dairy intake is still too generous. Try replacing more of these foods with healthier choices and see how you feel.

You will also benefit from supplementing your diet with quercetin and other bioflavonoids (500 mg two times per day). You may require short-term, supervised use of USP progesterone (see Chapters 6, 7 and 8).

• **PMS-C.** Use evening primrose oil (500 to 1 000 mg two times per day). Throughout the day have four to six smaller meals or snack on foods high in protein and complex carbohydrates (whole grains, vegetables, nuts and seeds, fruits) to encourage more evenly sustained blood sugar levels. Adequate B-complex, magnesium, and zinc intake is important if you suffer PMS-C symptoms.

- **PMS-D.** Implementing full adrenal and liver support (Chapter 3) is very important for PMS-D treatment. Also use the general nutritional support recommendations outlined and have yourself checked for heavy metal toxicity through hair analysis.

- **PMS-H.** Implement an adrenal support program such as Adrena+ (Chapter 3) and *eliminate all coffee, tea, chocolate, and caffeine* from your diet. These substances stress the nervous system; further, caffeine is hard on the liver. Studies show that women who consume it are more likely to suffer from PMS. EstroSense can be of help for PMS in general, but particularly PMS-H due to estrogen excess.

Dysmenorrhea (Painful Menstruation)

Dysmenorrhea is one of the most common gynecological conditions, affecting almost half of all women sometime during their life. Symptoms include abdominal cramping that may radiate to the thighs or lower back, headaches, nausea, gastrointestinal problems, and sometimes increased urinary frequency. Typically these symptoms occur just before the onset of menstruation or on the first or second day of the menses and subside as the flow progresses. Primary dysmenorrhea, the most common form of this condition, is characterized by the absence of any organic problem. It is thought to be due either to estrogen excess or deficiency or to psychological factors. Secondary dysmenorrhea is caused by specific diseases such as endometriosis, ovarian cysts, pelvic inflammatory disease, or uterine displacement.

Prostaglandins have already been mentioned with respect to PMS. Some influence the contraction of the smooth muscle of the uterus, and the PG2 prostaglandin series is commonly found in higher concentrations in women with primary dysmenorrhea and menorrhagia.

Many women with primary dysmenorrhea therefore use prostaglandin inhibitors (non-steroidal anti-inflammatory drugs, or NSAIDs) such as ibuprofen or naproxen. However, 22 percent of women do not benefit from these medications. In these cases the cause of the dysmenorrhea may be an organic disease, such as endometriosis. NSAIDs do not come without side effects, which can include dizziness, heartburn, nausea, vomiting, headaches, and, with continued use, possible gastrointestinal damage. Oral contraceptives are also used to alleviate the pain and, in rare cases, surgery may be done. By now we are sure you know that there are usually natural alternatives to drug treatment; dysmenorrhea is no exception.

TREATMENTS FOR DYSMENORRHEA

Let's begin with the nutritional supplements that have proven very helpful to many women with dysmenorrhea.

• **Essential Fatty Acids (EFAs)**. The body converts the essential fatty acid linoleic acid (LA; omega-6) first into the gamma-linolenic acid (GLA), and then into the anti-inflammatory PG1 prostaglandin series. This process is promoted by vitamin B6, zinc, niacin, vitamin C, and magnesium. Diets high in saturated fats and heated oils inhibit the production of the PG1 series as well as increase the release of stress hormones (catecholamines) by the adrenal glands. The PG2 series, thought to be at least partially responsible for the pain during the period, is derived from arachidonic acid (AA), which is found in animal fats. A deficiency of the essential fatty acid LA, a poor ability to convert LA into GLA and PG1 prostaglandins, and a diet high in saturated animal fats can result in an overproduction of AA and, consequently, of PG2 prostaglandins. The result is increased inflammation.

Supplementation with borage oil, black currant seed oil, or evening primrose oil, all high in GLA, can reduce the production of the PG2 series in favour of the anti-inflammatory PG1 series.

Many women choose to take GLA supplements daily because of their many positive effects. Studies show that taking evening primrose oil standardized to contain 9 percent GLA only three days before the onset of menstruation has positive effects on PMS.

— *Recommended dosage:* 250 to 500 mg GLA one to two times daily.

• **Vitamin B6 (Pyridoxine Hydrochloride)**. This essential nutrient is used in many biochemical pathways and is needed for the conversion of LA into the PG1 series and for the breakdown of estrogen in the liver. Vitamin B6 also helps intracellular magnesium levels to stay higher.

— *Recommended dosage:* 100 to 200 mg daily.

• **Magnesium**. We have already seen the importance of this mineral for bone health and blood sugar regulation. Magnesium also regulates the entry of calcium into smooth muscle, such as the uterine muscle, thereby influencing the ability of the uterine muscle to contract and relax. Magnesium plays an important role in the conversion to LA to GLA in the synthesis of the PG1 series and may inhibit the synthesis of PG2 series prostaglandins. It also is involved in the liver's estrogen-eliminating activity, in activating the B vitamins, in energy production and dopamine synthesis (dopamine is an important central nervous system chemical), and general hormone balance. The population at large is generally deficient in magnesium, with teenage girls and adult women having among the lowest intakes; this could be one of the reasons for the high levels of estrogen found nowadays in both men and women. Magnesium deficiency can be worsened by alcohol, high dietary fat intake, high use of dairy products, stress, diuretics, and malabsorption.

— *Recommended dosage:* 400 to 800 mg per day. Note: Magnesium can cause loose bowel movements or diarrhea; decrease your intake if you experience these symptoms.

• Or once again, keep it simple with FemmEssentials.

The commonly recommended herbal remedies for dysmenorrhea include blue cohosh, helonias, black cohosh, wild yam, cramp bark, and black haw. For most women taking these botanicals, starting three to four days before the onset of the menses and continuing during the days on which discomfort is usually felt is all that is required. These remedies will be much more effective when combined with diet and lifestyle changes and extra nutritional support: essential fatty acids and vitamins and minerals. Herbs already discussed in the PMS section can be used at the same dosages as given there.

• **Black cohosh (*Cimicifuga racemosa*).** Use this herb when there is congestive headache and uterine congestion with bearing-down pain, throbbing muscular pains that are due to uterine contractions, and backaches.

• **Black haw (*Viburnum prunifolium*)** is especially useful when the uterus is engorged and there is severe intermittent cramping.

• **Blue cohosh (*Caulophyllum thalictroides*)** is a menstrual flow stimulant, antispasmodic, and uterine tonic. Use it for severe pain.

- **Cramp bark (*Viburnum opulus*).** This herb is useful for spasmodic dysmenorrhea, when it feels as if something is being expelled.

  — *Recommended dosage:* 2 to 8 mL root tincture (1:5) daily.

- **Helonias (*Chamaelirium luteum*)** is an excellent remedy for dysmenorrhea and is used specifically for feelings of fullness and bearing-down sensations in the pelvis, which are often associated with menorrhagia. The woman with these symptoms often has mental irritability as well.

  — *Recommended dosage:* 1 to 2 g powdered rhizomes and roots two to three times daily.

- **Wild yam (*Dioscorea* spp).** Use wild yam when the pains are colicky in nature. It is antispasmodic and tonifying.

  — *Recommended dosage:* 2 to 4 mL fluid extract (1:1) daily; 4 to 10 mL tincture (1:5) daily.

ESTROGEN DOMINANT CONDITIONS

Endometriosis Epidemic

The Endometriosis Association states it is extremely rare that a woman in this day and age should ever need a hysterectomy for endometriosis, no matter how severe. Yet, three out of four gynecologists Lorna saw said, "You have already had your children, so if we find that you have extensive endometriosis, the best option is to perform a hysterectomy." This was in response to yet undiagnosed severe pelvic pain.

The thought of a hysterectomy in Lorna's mid-thirties sent her searching for the cause for the intense pain she was experiencing. All her symptoms seemed to point to endometriosis. Finally, the fourth gynecologist she visited discussed diagnosis and treatment options without mentioning hysterectomy as a "cure." That was a decade ago and now she is still free of endometriosis.

SYMPTOMS OF ENDOMETRIOSIS

Endometriosis is one of the most misunderstood female diseases. Approximately 15 percent of women between 20 and 45 years of age are affected with this painful and debilitating disorder. Symptoms can begin with the onset of menstruation and progressively increase with pending menopause. Painful periods, pain with intercourse and infertility may also be present. The pain some women experience can be devastating. Pain worse than childbirth was Lorna's only symptom and the pain radiated from the left hip into her back. Many women also experience pain when they have a full bladder or bowel. Some women experience no pain but may have infertility, ovarian or menstrual problems. The symptoms are many and varied from woman to woman.

CAREFUL DIAGNOSIS

Pelvic examinations by a highly skilled gynecologist may disclose nodules or lesions on the ovaries but ultrasound tests rarely confirm endometriosis. The only way to know for certain is through a procedure called laparoscopy. This surgery, performed under general anesthetic, involves inserting a light-containing telescope through a small incision in your navel and another one or two small incisions along the bikini line for the instruments.

Remember, a laparoscopy is only as good as the surgeon who performs the exam. To remove all the endometriosis tissue requires a physician who is committed to biopsy and getting rid of all suspicious abnormalities. Endometrial tissue can look like tiny blueberries or black spots, white, yellow or red-like cysts varying from tiny bluish or dark brown blisters to large chocolate cysts up to 20 centimeters in diameter. Only biopsy can confirm which tissue is truly endometriosis.

It is not uncommon for endometrial cells to grow on the ovaries, the fallopian tubes, the pelvic ligaments, the outer surface of the uterus, bladder, the large intestine and the covering of the abdominal cavity. Women are often misdiagnosed with irritable bowel syndrome, bladder infections, appendix attack, "just" PMS or painful cramps. But you know your body better than anyone. If you feel bad, something is wrong!

WHAT CAUSES ENDOMETRIOSIS?

Until recently, the most widely accepted theory to explain the cause of endometriosis was that of retrograde menstruation. Supposedly, tiny fragments of normal endometrial tissue (from the lining of the uterus) travel up the fallopian tubes and take residence in the abdominal or pelvic cavity.

Here this tissue acts as it would in the uterus in accordance with the monthly menstrual cycle. The blood often cannot escape, however, and causes the formation of deposits.

OUR IMMUNE SYSTEM IS THE KEY

New research points to a glitch in the immune system. Dr David Redwine, world renowned expert and director of the Endometriosis Institute of Bend, Oregon, believes that some women are born with abnormally located endometrial cells and that something goes astray with the immune system, causing the cells to become active. This theory gained acceptance because endometrial implants have been found in the nose, lungs and organs far from the uterus.

ENVIRONMENTAL ESTROGENS LINKED TO ENDOMETRIOSIS

Convincing evidence has linked dioxin exposure, a group of 75 chemicals which mimic estrogen in the body that are used to make PVC plastics (our drinking water runs through pipes made from PVC in our homes), solvents, pesticides, refrigerants and in the pulp and paper industry, to the development of endometriosis. These same chemicals also persist in the fats of meat and dairy products. Women should refuse to use bleached paper products including toilet paper, sanitary napkins and especially tampons. See page 48 for more information on environmental estrogens.

STRESS AND ENDO

Constant stress as we learned earlier causes an imbalance in the adrenal glands and the immune system. When we are under stress our adrenal glands secrete the hormone cortisol, which in turn, causes certain immune cytokines to be released worsening the endometriosis. In one study baboons who developed endometriosis in captivity were found to have higher stress and a decreased ability to react to stress compared to those in the wild, suggesting a stress connection to this condition. Reducing stress in your life, especially the self-inflicted type, is essential. Working women are the most vulnerable to endometriosis. If you have a laparoscopy to remove endometriosis but do nothing to change your lifestyle, the endometriosis will be back. Rest, relaxation and knowing when to say 'no' are important to your health.

THE HORMONE CONNECTION

Because of the hormone connection, medical therapy for endometriosis has concentrated on altering a woman's hormonal chemistry with drugs. These drugs include Danazol and gonadotropin-releasing hormones (GnRH) such as Nafarelin and birth control pills. Sometimes these drugs are successful in controlling the symptoms of endometriosis but not without side effects. Oily skin, acne, decreased breast size, growth of facial hair, weight gain and depression are symptoms. Some cause menopausal symptoms like hot flashes, decreased bone density, vaginal dryness and decreased libido. None of the drugs cures the disease. After the drug is stopped, the endometriosis symptoms return. The following holistic approach to treatment wherein the body heals itself is more effective and safer.

The mainstay of any endometriosis treatment is a diet that decreases the amount of circulating estrogens in the bloodstream to the point where the endometriosis symptoms subside but not so far as to cause pseudo-menopause. A vegetarian diet containing no more than 20 to 25 grams of saturated fat a day and eliminating all dairy products works well. The fat you do eat should come from organically grown nuts and seeds and their oils. Look in the refrigerator at your health food store. Many women get relief by simply removing dairy products. Lorna was one of those people. She eliminated all dairy products to obtain maximum relief.

Supplementing the diet with a multivitamin with minerals is essential. A high potency B-complex supplement will help ease symptoms of endo and balance hormonal states, elevate mood and control fluid retention. Cold-pressed oils containing gamma-linoleic acid or GLA are important both as a possible pain inhibitor and immune strengthener. GLA may offset the symptoms of prostaglandin production. Prostaglandins are involved with uterine contractions producing menstrual cramps. Or keep it simple by taking FemmEssentials multinutrient formula.

Nutrients that help the liver detoxify environmental estrogens and keep our healthy estrogen from converting to toxic form are essential. Curcumin, Indole-3-carbinol, calcium D-glucarate, Milk thistle, green tea extract, lycopene and rosemary found in EstroSense will help balance your hormones naturally.

BE GOOD TO YOURSELF

Castor oil packs are excellent at controlling pain. For instructions on how to make them, see Chapter 3. Endometriosis is an insidious disorder but it can be cured forever if you examine your stress level, the types of environmental toxins you are exposed to and improve your nutrition. Lorna cured her endometriosis and you can too.

Fibroids and Fibrocystic Breast Disease

Fibroids are common in women of all ages. The fibroid is a hard mass of fibrous tissue rich in blood vessels, growing on the inside wall of the uterus, on the outside of the uterus, or within the uterine muscle itself. Fibroids vary in size; some grow very large and come to weigh several kilograms. Although fibroids themselves are not fatal or detrimental to health, they can give rise to complications that can be annoying, painful, and in some cases fatal.

One of the most common symptoms of fibroids, particularly large ones, is profuse menstruation. Blood may flow to such an extent that the affected woman becomes anemic and extremely fatigued. Fibroids can also cause pressure on the organs surrounding the uterus, such as the bladder and bowels, causing serious problems with urination and bowel movements; digestion is compromised, and pain with or without intercourse is often

Seven Early Warning Symptoms of Endometriosis

- Menstrual cramps that increase in severity
- Intermenstrual pain, usually at mid-month
- Painful intercourse or dyspareunia
- Infertility of unknown origin
- You feel like you have bladder infections but the test results are always negative
- Pelvic pain that is all-encompassing
- History of ovarian cysts.

present. Today many physicians recommend removing fibroids, even small ones, but thousands of women go through life with fibroids without suffering any major symptoms, even when large fibroid tumours are present.

Fibroids are caused by an estrogen excess that, from a naturopathic perspective, is due to bowel toxicity, liver congestion, and exposure to environmental xenoestrogens. Another common finding in naturopathic assessments of women with fibroids is undiagnosed clinical or subclinical hypothyroidism.

Going through menopause can have one of two effects on fibroids: some begin to shrink, or atrophy, because of decreased estrogen levels, others grow larger and in rare cases become malignant.

If you do have fibroids and your symptoms are so severe that surgery is required to remove them, find a gynecologist who will remove the fibroids only (this operation is called a myomectomy), keeping the uterus and ovaries intact. If this is impossible because of the large size of the fibroids, then insist that the cervix is kept intact. Most women who have the cervix removed are no longer capable of experiencing orgasm and their sexual desire is generally considerably diminished or eliminated completely with the surgeon's knife. Finally, of course, keep your ovaries! It is common for women to be talked into having their ovaries removed along with the uterus (complete hysterectomy) as a preventive measure against ovarian cancer. Removing a healthy, needed organ because of possible disease strikes me as a poor health care strategy. Work towards optimal health instead to significantly lower your risk of cancer.

TREATING ESTROGEN DOMINANT CONDITIONS

Once you understand that fibroids, fibrocystic breasts and endometriosis are directly related to estrogen excess, you are in an excellent position to treat them naturally and watch them shrink or even disappear.

- Begin by adopting the general dietary and nutritional recommendations given for PMS. These help your body balance itself.

- Pay particular attention to restoring the full health of the liver and bowel. (See Chapters 2 and 3 yet again!)

- Reduce your exposure to environmental chemicals (Chapter 2) and use the detoxification protocols in Chapter 3 to rid yourself of excess estrogenic chemicals picked up from the environment.

- Use EstroSense fermented soy to help reduce the number of stronger endogenous and environmental estrogens taking up your cell receptor sites and to maintain hormonal balance.

- Use castor oil packs over the fibroid three times per week (see Chapter 3 for directions).

Hysterectomy

More than 60,000 hysterectomies are performed each year in Canada—our hysterectomy rate is one of the highest in the world, second only to that of the United States, and almost double that found in most European countries. Thirty-seven percent of all Canadian women will have had a hysterectomy by the age of 60. In the United States, approximately 772,000 hysterectomies are performed annually; the only major surgery that takes place more often in that country is the cesarean section. Between 1988 and 1990, more than 1,700,000 hysterectomies were performed in the United States, each costing about $5,500 US, or between $7,000 and $10,000 Canadian, depending on length of hospital stay.

According to the reports of the United States National Health Center for Health Statistics, one in every three American women will have a hysterectomy. In Britain the statistics are one in five, while in Norway only one in nine women will have the procedure. In California, one of every two women are likely to have a hysterectomy.

"Virtue is never as respectable as money."—Mark Twain

In 1945, an eminent surgeon, Dr. N. Miller, delivered a paper, now a classic, to his peers: "Hysterectomy: Therapeutic Necessity or Surgical Racket." It was published in the *American Journal of Obstetrics and Gynecology* in 1946. Dr. Miller states that the "uterus in the non-pregnant state is one of the more important revelations of our age," meaning that the organ's importance above and beyond the gestation of children has been highly underestimated. He asserts that hysterectomy in the absence of disease cannot be justified any more than can the removal of a normal breast or gallbladder. He also states that in his research he found that one-third of all hysterectomies performed were done despite a complete absence of disease or else disease that would not benefit from hysterectomy.

Dr. Miller warned us in 1945 that if these unnecessary hysterectomies continue, we will witness a tragedy, painful and far-reaching in its implications.

Today, almost half of all hysterectomies are done to remove healthy uteri and ovaries, in which no disease whatsoever is present.

Dr. Joseph Pratt, gynecologist, is quoted as saying, "Let the woman have her family, then at her 35th or 36th birthday have a vaginal hysterectomy." He justifies his position by saying that the woman will be free of menstruation and what he terms the accompanying embarrassing accidents, will experience relief of menstrual discomfort and the fear of pregnancy, and will save on the cost of tampons.

Is his argument enough to convince you? It all sounds harmless, doesn't it? And if you are not yet convinced, how about this? A leading gynecologist, Dr. Neils Lauersen, recommends routine removal of the ovaries for all women over 55 who are having hysterectomies, to eliminate the risk of ovarian cancer, which increases with age. This line of thinking is very foreign to us—removing a critical part of the anatomy just in case, one day, one just might get some disease. Such a strategy represents a rather warped form of preventive medicine. Think of the reaction if the same were recommended for men: the routine removal of the testicles at age 55 because the risk of testicular cancer rises with age.

The fact is that ovarian cancer is rare. Only 4 percent of women get ovarian cancer. One out of every eight women, however, will get breast cancer—this disease is the leading cause of death in North American women between 40 and 45 years of age. But no one in their right mind would suggest routine removal of the breasts to prevent breast cancer ... Or would they?

After speaking with thousands of women over the years it was easy for us to think that we have heard every possible story they may have experienced regarding women's health conditions. But we were wrong. One woman told of how both of her breasts were removed, on her doctor's recommendation, because her grandmother had had breast cancer (after having lived into her eighties) and he felt that this radical surgery was necessary to protect her from the same plight. We know that this story is not as uncommon as we are sure you would want to think, and hope.

EFFECTS OF HYSTERECTOMY

As comments such as those by Dr. Pratt indicate, the allopathic profession typically views the uterus as useless once a woman is past childbearing age—

hence the exceedingly high numbers of so called harmless, if unnecessary, hysterectomies.

The allopathic viewpoint misses a great deal, including a growing body of research that totally refutes the idea of a "useless" uterus. For starters, despite the popular belief to the contrary amongst physicians who haven't experienced hysterectomy, this operation seriously interferes with sexual fulfillment—which may be a surprise to those who think that the sensations of intercourse are limited to the clitoris and vagina! Sexual desire is usually completely lost or severely diminished after hysterectomy. In fact, for most women, libido and sex life after a hysterectomy, even if the ovaries have been left intact, are worse than after menopause. During menopause the libido gradually slows down and the change is usually manageable, but after the trauma of a hysterectomy the sexual desire can stop abruptly. Hysterectomy results in shortening, narrowing, and drying of the vagina, loss of sensitivity, decreased blood flow to the ovaries, as well as damage to the nerves that enter the ovaries, and frequent pain caused by pressure from any source on the scar tissue that develops after the operation.

Studies show that in 50 percent of patients, hysterectomy, especially when done for prolapsed uterus (see below), *ends sexual intercourse for life.*

The uterus is also vital for immunity. Evidence indicates that it produces a variety of prostaglandins that regulate the female immune system, even after menopause. Prostaglandins, as previously mentioned, are hormone-like compounds that function as regulators of a variety of physiological responses, including inflammation, muscle contraction, vascular dilation, and platelet aggregation. They are made in every cell of the body and in the female influence the shedding of the endometrium. They may also affect luteinizing hormone levels and ovulation. The uterus also produces prostacyclin, a compound that prevents blood from clumping and forming clots, thereby helping prevent cardiovascular disease.

Many women lose most of their ovarian function when the uterus is removed, even when the ovaries are conserved. Current studies indicate that the uterus may regulate ovarian hormone production via prostaglandins. Studies also indicate that hysterectomized women, even those who retain their ovaries, have a much higher risk of cardiovascular disease and depression than women who have never had a hysterectomy. They also are more prone to osteoporosis at an earlier age and develop osteoarthritis more frequently than women who go through menopause with all their parts intact. One study of 986 hysterectomized women who retained one or both healthy ovaries showed that they experienced more severe menopausal symptoms than women who had not undergone hysterectomy.

Nature never makes an organ that loses its usefulness at a particular stage of life.

The heart goes out of life for many women who have hysterectomies, even partial ones. Many women lose their passion and zest for love and life after hysterectomy and up to 50 percent lapse into repressed anger or severe depression.

We are finding writing this extremely difficult as we realize that so many women have undergone hysterectomies without ever being told the other side of the story.

"Hysterectomy is unnecessary for almost everything except cancer of the genital tract."—Dr. G. Vilos

To prevent hysterectomy, we need to know how to deal with the underlying difficulties that all too often result in a recommendation to proceed with the operation.

In an analysis done by the Mayo Clinic, the number-one reason for the operation was prolapse of the uterus. Certain ligaments and muscles hold the uterus in its normal position. The muscles involved can become weak for various reasons. On losing its muscular support, the uterus will drop between the bladder and the large intestine—it is then said to be prolapsed. Symptoms include dull pains in the low back, a heavy dragging sensation in the groin, pressure on the bladder, and bowel difficulties such as constipation.

We suppose one way to correct a situation is to get rid of it. Another way to correct the problem is to give oneself nutritional and hormonal support. Botanical remedies that have been found to help with uterine prolapse include the female reproductive tonics already discussed: blue cohosh, helonias, wild yam, and black haw. As well, specific abdominal exercises, as shown below, help the womb fall back into place.

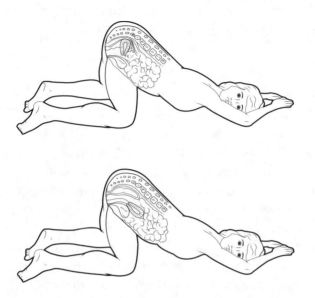

In many cases prolapse of the uterus can be remedied by daily taking the position in the first illustration above until symptoms improve (the second illustration shows the normal position of the uterus). You'll need to get on your knees, raise the posterior high, and allow your chest to touch the floor. Allow as much air to pass into the vagina as possible. Breathe deeply. Continue this exercise two to three times weekly to maintain the change.

If the exercise is done properly the entire contents of the abdominal cavity will drop forward. The first few times getting the uterus to move may require gentle self-massage over the uterus while doing the exercise.

Those women who do not find relief from the exercises and hormonal and nutritional support can opt for various *simple* surgeries that repair a displaced uterus. It is my opinion that a hysterectomy should be the last option when it comes to the repair of uterine prolapse.

The second most frequent reason for hysterectomies listed in the Mayo Clinic study was sterilization. Hysterectomy, especially when the ovaries are removed as well, is the exact equivalent of male castration, carrying with it the concomitant problems of instant menopause, loss of sexuality, loss of well-being, and increased risk for a host of diseases. How about something a little less catastrophic, like a tubal ligation?

The third most common reason for performing a hysterectomy, the Mayo researchers found, was excessive menstrual bleeding—menorrhagia and metrorrhagia.

MENORRHAGIA

Menorrhagia is heavy, prolonged menstrual bleeding that may occur occasionally or on a chronic basis. The normal menstrual blood flow lasts about five days and involves a loss of 60 to 250 mL of blood. In menorrhagia the blood flow can last up to 10 and sometimes 15 days, with a total blood loss ranging from 80 mL to overt hemorrhage. Metrorrhagia is uterine bleeding that occurs between menstrual periods. It usually involves only spotting, but can be as excessive as hemorrhage.

Menorrhagia and metrorrhagia are common experiences for perimenopausal women. Several botanical remedies, homeopathic remedies, and nutritional supplements are very effective in the treatment of menorrhagia and metrorrhagia in most women; see the section above on treatment for dysmenorrhea for natural remedies that are also effective in the treatment of menorrhagia. In addition, herbs such as shepherd's purse, cotton root, and agrimony leaf have proven very beneficial for excessive blood flow.

Given the simple, effective, and often natural alternatives available, we can see that if a prolapsed uterus, sterilization, and menorrhagia account for three-quarters of all hysterectomies performed, then *most are unnecessary*.

Breast Cancer—Prevention is the Key

I (Lorna) was ten years old when I visited my maternal grandmother for the last time. It was Christmas and my grandmother had prepared a fabulous turkey dinner with all the trimmings but she ate baby food from a jar—she was dying of breast cancer and the cancer had spread to her digestive tract. Fear stopped her from seeking an early diagnosis and she waited until the cancer was growing outside of her breast before visiting her doctor. Breast cancer has left an indelible mark on my life, the images of my dying grandmother still strong in my mind. Prevention is a word we speak often in our household with two daughters aged 17 and 24 and a family history of this terrible disease.

Breast cancer is the leading cause of death in women ages 35-54. And our risk is rising in 1960 one in 20 developed breast cancer. Today 1 in 8 women will get breast cancer and of those who have breast cancer 1 in 4 will die. Younger and younger women are also developing breast cancer. Genetics plays a role in less than 10 percent of breast cancer cases. With this fact in mind we should be asking what is causing the other 90 percent of breast cancers. The answer—80 percent of all cancers are thought to be related to environmental factors, while diet plays a role in at least 35 percent of all cancers. We can reduce our risk, we can adopt a prevention strategy but first we have to know what the factors are that are increasing our risk of breast cancer. Take the breast cancer risk test below to evaluate your own personal risk. It is beyond the scope of this book to discuss breast cancer treatment strategies so we will just look at prevention. Lorna has a new book available in 2003 on breast cancer that will explore all aspects of the disease.

There are three factors that the American Cancer Society states are the 'only' known risk factors, these include: hereditary (genetics), starting periods early and going through menopause late (this exposes you to too many years of estrogen), and a high fat diet. Yet there is a tremendous amount of research showing that common environmental factors are potential breast cancer causing agents. We have been trained to believe that the only way to prevent breast cancer is through regular mammograms. This is a diagnostic method, to diagnose breast cancer once you have it—not a prevention method. Early diagnosis is key to acquiring fast and appropriate treatment but it does not prevent breast cancer.

What are the most common but unpublicized risks for breast cancer? Estrogen replacement therapy in high doses with prolonged use; oral contraceptive use in young women with prolonged use; pre-menopausal mammography with early and repeated exposure; non hormonal prescription drugs such as some anti-hypertensive medications; silicone gel breast implants, especially those wrapped in polyurethane foam; diets high in fat contaminated with undisclosed carcinogens and estrogenic chemicals; exposure in the workplace or home to household chemicals or pollution from chemical plants and waste sites; alcohol and tobacco use with early or excessive use; lack of exercise; use of dark hair dyes with early or prolonged use.

ESTROGEN: FRIEND OR FOE?

Excess or cancer causing estrogens have also been linked to the development of breast cancer. Scientists have discovered that certain foods, stress, a lack of exercise and environmental toxins call all wreak havoc with our estrogens. These factors have also been shown to cause good estrogens to

be converted to cancer-causing estrogens. And now a new and more serious alarm bell has been raised—estrogen mimickers in our environment
called xenoestrogens (pronounced 'zeno' estrogens) found in plastics, pesti-
cide and herbicide-laden foods, cosmetics, hair dyes, bleached feminine
hygiene products, plastics, some prescription drugs, dry cleaned clothing
and nail polish are further disrupting our estrogen balance increasing our
risk of breast cancer, infertility and birth defects. Xenoestrogens, we believe
are the biggest contributing factor to increased rates of breast cancer. Yet
most women do not know that common substances they use everyday are
increasing their risk—things that they could avoid if they knew what they
were.

HRT AND BREAST CANCER

The single biggest questions that we get are "Should I take Hormone
Replacement Therapy (HRT) or How do I get off of HRT?" The baby
boomers are just starting to enter menopause or peri menopause (over 55
million North American women) and prescriptions for hormone replacement therapy a combination of synthetic estrogen and progestin called HRT
are being written in increasing numbers to prevent everything from hot
flashes to protection from cardiovascular disease. In Canada HRT is the
number three most prescribed drug with 12 million prescriptions written in
2001. In the United States in the year 2000 over 22 million prescriptions were
written.

Did you Know? The following HRT drugs, PremphaseTM (which contains
Premarin), PremproTM and Premarin(r) deplete the body of magnesium,
vitamin B6 and zinc.

Now the study that ends the debate has been published in the *Journal of
the American Medical Association* in July 2002 and women are being warned
of the risks of stroke, heart attack, blood clots and breast cancer. This study
of 16,608 women found that the reduction of hot flashes, night sweats and
vaginal dryness offered by HRT may come with disastrous health consequences. The Women's Health Initiative randomized controlled trial scheduled to run 8.5 years was abruptly halted at 5.2 years because women in the
treatment group had a 26% increased risk of invasive breast cancer. This
increased risk was seen around the third year of the study. This is not the first
study to show increased risk of breast cancer but this is the one that the
scientific community is listening too. We have heard advocates trying to
rescue HRT saying it is 'only' 8 women in 10,000 that will get breast cancer

as a result of HRT. We would like those making this statement to make it personal —those 8 women could be their mother, sisters, daughters, wife, grandmother and aunts.

The study also concluded that women who took HRT were 41 percent more likely to have a stroke and they also had a 29% increased risk of heart attack and this was in a group of healthy women not at high risk for heart disease. The increased risk of coronary heart disease caused by HRT was seen within the first 1 to 2 years of the study. No longer will women be prescribed HRT for to reduce the incidence of coronary heart disease. The study did show a reduction in the risk of fracture and colorectal cancer but the risks of stroke, heart attack and breast cancer outweigh any benefit for these conditions. Women taking HRT are also at risk of gallbladder and liver disease and blood clots.

We know that women who still have a uterus can't take estrogen alone because it increases her risk of uterine or endometrial cancer dramatically. Estrogen dominance or too much estrogen as mentioned earlier is also cause for concern for everything from endometriosis, heavy periods, weight gain to uterine fibroids. A study in the *Journal of the American Chemical Society* has also reported a by-product of Premarin(r) (horse urine derived estrogen) damaged DNA in a way that could cause cancer.

BREAST CANCER RISK ASSESSMENT

Take the following breast health test and discover your true risk for breast cancer. Less than 10 percent of breast cancers are genetic. Knowing genetics is a minor factor in the development of breast cancer we need to understand the other rarely mentioned factors that increase our risk of breast cancer.

Have not had children and are under 25	1
Have not had children and are 25 to 35	2
Have had no children and don't intend to	3
Did not breastfeed	2
Had an abortion of a first pregnancy	1

Took birth control pills during teens or early 20s.
A few months use may increase risk of breast
cancer by 30%. Ten years use may double it.   3

Have taken or are taking HRT
(Premarin, Provera, Prempro)   3

Have had regular mammograms before menopause   2

Don't exercise three times per week   2

Have had depression where tricyclic anti-depressants
were prescribed (studies showed increase in
mammory tumors in rats)   2

Have breast implants (cause breast trauma)   1

Had chest x-rays as a teenager or during 20s   2

Are exposed to EMFs due to excessive computer
usage, hair dryer usage or live close to power lines   1

Dye your hair with dark-coloured dyes (a source of
xenoestrogens)   2

Wear dry-cleaned clothing (a source of xenoestrogens)   1

Use bleached sanitary products, eg tampons, pads
(a source of xenoestrogens)   2

Eat pesticide- and herbicide-laden foods   3

Use nail polish remover that is not tolulene-
or phthalate-free   1

Periods started before the age of 12   2

Late onset menopause starting after the age of 50   2

Eat a diet high in animal fat, dairy and meat
(a source of xenoestrogens)   3

Smoke, with early or excessive use   3

Alcohol, with early or excessive use   3

Don't eat cruciferous vegetables (these vegetables
    detoxify carcinogenic estrogens   3

Take cholesterol-lowering drugs which depletes the
    body of Q10 (Q10 is used to treat breast cancer)   3

Using anti-hypertensives for lowering high blood
    pressure which deplete Q10   3

Using tranquilizers (studies show an increase
    in breast tumors)   2

Using ulcer medications which disrupts estrogen
    metabolism which decreases good estrogen   2

You are overweight or obese (fat stores estrogens)   3

Use or have used Flagyl for yeast infections
    (studies show an increase in mammory tumors)   2

Family history in a first degree relative
    (mother, sister, or daughter)   1

                                    Total Score:_____

0-18   lower risk
19-35   moderate to high risk
35-65   high risk

We can choose alternatives to many of the risk factors above and we can make dietary and lifestyle changes that will protect us from developing breast cancer or at least reduce our risk.

DIET AND BREAST CANCER

Knowing that poor diet plays a role in 35 percent of breast cancer cases we will want to improve this area first. Insist on organic fruits and vegetables to reduce your exposure to xenoestrogens. Eat plenty of organic vegetables, especially those from the cruciferous family: broccoli, cauliflower, kale and Brussels sprouts they contain indole-3-carbinol and sulphoraphane known breast cancer inhibitors. Reduce your intake of sugar as it suppresses the immune system. Eat organic dairy products and meats that don't contain xenoestrogens. Reduce the amount of animal products you eat and choose more fruits, vegetables, whole grains and eat curry three times a week. Never microwave foods in plastic or cover with plastic wrap (especially baby formula). This releases the xenoestrogens in the plastics. Store foods in glass or pyrex containers. Ensure that the fats you eat are those that are rich in essential fatty acids including flax seed oil. Eat high lignan flax seeds (ground and sprinkled on your cereal everyday) which have been shown to reduce the risk of breast cancer.

ISOFLAVONES AND BREAST CANCER

Many studies have shown the protective benefits of soy foods in the prevention and treatment of breast cancer. Soy foods, as we have seen, are high in phytoestrogens called isoflavones. Isoflavones have positive effects in breast cancer prevention and treatment; they bind to estrogen receptors, where they exhibit weak estrogenic activity while at the same time reducing the effects of the much more potent estrogens and xenoestrogens. Many case-controlled, epidemiological, *in vitro*, and animal studies confirm the effectiveness of soy isoflavones in the prevention of breast cancer. A study published in the *Lancet* in 1997 demonstrated that the soy isoflavone equol and the soy lignan enterolactone had the most significant impacts on breast health in pre- and postmenopausal women.

More evidence comes from cross-cultural studies. North American women have three times the rate of breast cancer of Asian women eating a traditional diet high in soy foods. Other data also indicate that rates of other cancers, including prostate, lung, stomach, and colon, are also lower in Asian cultures.

For more information on soy isoflavones and hormonal health, please refer to Chapter 6.

NUTRIENTS FOR BREAST CANCER PREVENTION/TREATMENT

• **Indole-3-carbinol (I3C)** is an anti-cancer phytonutrient found in cruciferous vegetables. Research has shown that I3C helps to breakdown cancer-causing estrogens to non-toxic forms. It has also been shown to inhibit breast cancer tumors.

— *Recommended dosage:* 150 to 300 mg daily.

• **Calcium D-glucarate** is a powerful detoxifier of excess estrogens from the liver and important for both the prevention and treatment of breast cancer.

— *Recommended dosage:* 150 to 300 mg daily.

• **Curcumin** is the yellow pigment of turmeric, the chief ingredient in curry. It is a powerful anti-inflammatory agent and it works to inhibit all steps of cancer formation: initiation, promotion, and progression. Curcumin also protects against inflammatory calcium loss from our bones.

— *Recommended dosage:* 50 to 100 mg daily.

• **Green tea extract** contains polyphenols, catechins and flavonoids shown to be protective against estrogen-dominant breast cancers.

— *Recommended dosage:* 100 to 200 mg daily.

• **Milk thistle** enhances detoxification from the liver, inhibits breast cancer cells from replicating and reduces the toxic effects of chemotherapy.

— *Recommended dosage:* 50 to 100 mg daily.

• **Rosemary extract,** a potent antioxidant, inhibits breast cancer development and it helps to detoxify carcinogenic estrogens.

— *Recommended dosage:* 25 to 50 mg daily.

• **Lycopene** found in tomatoes, pink grapefruit, papaya, guava and watermelon, was recently shown to reduce a women's risk of breast cancer by 36 percent when those women took 6.5 mg per day.

— *Recommended dosage:* 5 to 10 mg daily.

• **Sulfurophane,** from broccoli sprout extract, has been shown to stimulate the body's production of detoxification enzymes that eliminate xenoestrogens. Recent research points to this nutrient as a powerful anti-breast cancer agent. Sulfurophane is also a powerful antioxidant. All of the eight nutrients above are found in EstroSense.

— *Recommended dosage:* 200 to 400 mg daily.

- **Coenzyme Q10,** which occurs naturally in the body, has been shown in recent studies to cause regression of breast tumors and prevent metastasis (spread of cancer) in some women.

  — *Recommended dosage:* The daily dose administered in the studies was between 90 and 340 mg.

- Keep it simple and take FemmEssentials multinutrient formula with FemmOmega essential fatty acids.

  — *Recommended dosage:* as directed on the label.

WHAT ELSE CAN WE DO?

We can avoid pesticides, use nail polish that is tolulene and phthalate-free (pronounced thalate) and choose hair dyes that are safe. Safe hair dye and nail polish are available at the health food store. We can choose unbleached sanitary products again these can be found at your health food store. We can avoid certain prescription drugs that caused mammory tumors in rats and mice. We can limit the amount of dry cleaned clothing we wear. We can choose to exercise 30 minutes three times a week and eat healthy foods that don't disrupt our estrogens and take nutritional supplements that protect against environmental estrogens and support the liver and body to fight cancer before it begins.

We can support new mothers to breast feed for as long as possible. Breast feeding has been shown to be a powerful protector from breast cancer. We can clean up our environment to reduce our exposure to xenoestrogens. We can reduce the number of yearly x-rays we have from dental x-rays, chest x-rays and have a baseline mammogram and then only if required thereafter. These are things that can reduce our risk of breast cancer and prevent this rapidly rising disease.

MENTAL, EMOTIONAL AND SPIRITUAL ISSUES
IN BREAST CANCER

Visualization and spiritual exercises such as contemplation and prayer are powerful tools for healing. Please refer to Chapter 10 for techniques that I have found very effective.

It is not uncommon for women to put themselves last, taking care of everyone else's needs while sacrificing their own. What is more symbolic of the ability to nurture life than a woman's breast? Approximately 30 to 40 percent of the female patients in Karen's practice have, or have had, breast cancer. Almost 100 percent of these women do not feel that their feminine nature has been or is being nurtured. It is up to each one of us to ensure that our own needs are met, to learn to communicate these needs to others, and to make time in our lives to nurture ourselves.

Cancer of any kind is an insidious disease, permeating every level of our being. At the same time it is an *impeccable teacher*, should we choose to embrace the opportunity it offers.

We have now covered some of the main hormone-related conditions that occur in perimenopausal and menopausal women. For more information on women's health and specific conditions, both those discussed here and those not, such as endometrial and ovarian cancer, polycystic ovaries, infertility, and pregnancy and childbirth, please refer to the "Further Reading" section at the back of this book.

We will now look at the basics of treatment for cardiovascular disease in women, a common health condition not as closely linked with the endocrine system as the other illnesses we have discussed.

Cardiovascular Disease

We noted in Chapter 6 that heart disease is the main cause of death in women 50 or older and that two out of three women in this age group are at risk for developing cardiovascular disease. We also noted that synthetic HRT, which has been touted as protective for the heart and circulatory system, based on the results of a handful of contradictory and poorly designed studies, has bitten the dust. Finally, we looked at the fact that synthetic drug estrogen is recognized by the medical community to increase blood clotting, increase triglyceride levels, and to cause other side effects that all increase the likelihood of heart attack, stroke, or other serious cardiovascular problems. To review the results of the WHI study recently published in the Journal of the American Medical Association (JAMA): there was a 29 percent increase in coronary heart disease, a 41 percent increase in stroke and a 26 percent increase in invasive breast cancer.

Do we need to take a dangerous drug like estrogen to reduce the risk of heart disease? The answer is an emphatic no! So, what's a woman (or man supposed to do?

DECREASE YOUR RISK FACTORS
FOR CARDIOVASCULAR DISEASE

There are lifestyle and dietary choices that can help you decrease the like-lihood of heart disease.

• **Alcohol use/abuse** increases blood estradiol levels by 300 percent in postmenopausal women using estrogen replacement therapy. Alcohol use also increases incidence of breast cancer, osteoporosis, and depression. If you must drink, save alcohol for very special occasions only.

• **Birth control pills and HRT.** Find safer alternative methods of birth control and hormone replacement.

• **High blood pressure.** Monitoring blood pressure as we age is impor-tant since high blood pressure increases the heart's workload, causing the heart to enlarge and weaken over time. Exercise, diet and take care of yourself. Find your own way to relax. Relaxation may look different for each person —for some it is a walk in the park, for others yoga or medita-tion, or perhaps finding a creative outlet, etc. Whatever it might be for you, "Just Do It!"

• **Low consumption of fibre and soy products.** Oat bran and psyllium fibre bind bile and cholesterol in the intestines and remove it, thereby decreasing low-density lipoprotein (LDL) levels and increasing high-density lipoprotein (HDL) levels. (LDLs are excreted via the intestines.) Foods high in isoflavones also decrease LDL levels, as well as total blood cholesterol and triglycerides.

• **Water, Water, Water.** Dehydration causes the blood to become sludge-like (platelet aggregation). As the blood pump (heart) attempts to push the sludgy blood through the pipes (arteries and veins), pressure builds up in the pipes. If the pressure becomes too great, a valve bursts (stroke). Something as simple as drinking 2.5 liters of water daily will help to prevent dehydration and may prevent heart disease.

• **Obesity.** People who have excess body fat are more likely to develop heart disease and stroke even if they have no other risk factors.

• **"Non-food" consumption.** Sugars, fast foods, and refined foods stress the whole body, including the heart. Eat whole foods instead: fresh fruits and vegetables, whole grains, raw nuts and seeds, and hormone-free animal products.

- **Sedentary lifestyle.** A lack of exercise is a primary factor in the risk of developing heart disease. Exercise can help control cholesterol, Type II diabetes, and obesity, and can help decrease blood pressure.

- **Eliminate refined carbohydrates.** High sugar levels in the blood, as a result of eating "non-foods", stimulate the release of insulin that causes many harmful effects in the body. The higher and faster the rise in blood sugar increases, the more insulin is secreted. Through a series of steps in the body the high insulin levels promote the removal of triglycerides from the bloodstream and deposition in fat cells thereby promoting fat storage. Insulin also directly increases blood pressure, shuts off fat-burning pathways and turns on pathways that produce fat and triglycerides. Arterial damage and plaque formation (atherosclerosis) are also increased. (See Further Reading for two good books we highly recommend: *The Schwatrbein Principle* and *Heart Sense.*)

- **Smoking** is the greatest single cause of death over which we have control. Women who smoke have a higher risk of death from heart disease and stroke; combining oral contraceptive use with smoking increases the risk many times more.

- **High stress levels.** Taking time out for rest and recreation, family, fun, and quiet time (focused relaxation, contemplation, prayer) is a must for heart health. A recent study reported in the *Journal of the American Medical Association* found that leisure time and physical activity decreased heart disease incidence by 50 percent in postmenopausal women. The activities these women engaged in were not strenuous and consisted of walking, gardening, swimming, biking, golf, and bowling.

  Catecholamines such as adrenaline and dopamine are released by the adrenal glands, along with cortisol, during stressful situations and it has been suspected that high-circulating levels of catecholamines contribute to heart disease. Newer research indicates that it is the oxidized products of catecholamines, the free radicals and other toxic substances, that cause cell damage in the heart. During oxidative stress a number of mechanisms which regulate calcium become unbalanced. Calcium regulation is vital for the proper contraction and relaxation of the heart's muscle cells.

- **Emotional state.** Don't worry, be happy. Researchers have found that depression is an independent risk factor for heart failure among women. In a large sampling of older adults, depression was associated with a greater than 50 percent risk of developing heart failure. The depressed mood influences the neuroendocrine (hormonal) system. Depressive moods can cause an increase in cathecholamine levels causing increased oxidative damage to the cells of the heart. The free radicals and other toxic oxidized products contribute to congestive heart failure. (For more information on stress and the adrenal glands, and stress reduction tips see Chapter 3.)

• **Consumption of unhealthy fats and oils.** Don't get caught up in "Fat Phobia". Good fats do not promote heart disease or high cholesterol problems. Instead of hydrogenated and heated oils, such as margarines, deep-fried foods and processed oils, use essential fatty acids (omega-3 and omega-6 fatty acids) from flax oil, olive oil, pumpkin seed oil, and fish oils, or an oil blend. Essential fatty acids lower blood cholesterol and triglyceride levels and decrease platelet "stickiness," reducing the risk of blood clots. Animal fats are not the bad guys; heated, refined oils and refined carbohydrates are. (See Chapter 2 for more information on fats and oils.)

THE BIG FAT LIES ABOUT LOW-FAT DIETS

Before 1920 coronary heart disease was rare in North America but today heart disease causes at least 40 percent of all deaths. What changed? It isn't the increased consumption of animal products. In fact, since the 1950s and the popularization of the theory that increased fat consumption caused an increased risk for heart disease, the consumption of animal products such as red meat and butter, has decreased. The proportion of animal fat declined from 83 percent to 62 percent and butter consumption fell from eighteen pounds to four pounds per person, per year while the consumption of sugar and processed foods increased about 60 percent. The obesity epidemic started to increase in the 1980s when the 'medical experts' started advocating low-fat diets to prevent heart disease and obesity. Type II diabetes also increased significantly during this period. Low-fat weight loss and heart protective diets fail in clinical trials and in real life. (see Chapter 2 for more information on fats and oils)

New Heart Tests That Could Save Your Life

• **Homocysteine:** Dozens of studies suggest that even slightly elevated levels of this amino acid might double, triple, or even quadruple your risk of heart attack or stroke, even when cholesterol levels are normal. Tests are available from naturopathic or medical doctors.

• **C-Reactive Protein:** A substance produced in the liver when arteries are inflamed, C-reactive protein will tell us whether or not the plaque in the artery is likely to rupture. Ask for the high-sensitivity CRP test (hs-CRP).

• **Lipoprotein (a):** Researchers at Oxford University in England found that in studies involving 5,200 people with heart disease or were heart attack survivors, those with the highest levels of LP(a) had a 70 percent greater risk of having a heart attack over 10 years than those with the lowest. Specialized test: ask your N.D. or M.D.

• **ApolipoproteinA-1 (apoA-1) and ApolipoproteinB (apoB):** ApoA-1 and apoB move through the bloodstream delivering chunks of cholesterol to places where they don't belong, such as the arterial walls. The cholesterol itself is innocent, it is the proteins that determine whether cholesterol ends up as plaque or safely leaves the body. Specialized test: ask your N.D. or M.D.

• **Live Blood Cell Analysis (Darkfield Microscopy):** A good diagnostic for fibrinogen levels. Research indicates that too much fibrinogen, an inflammatory product of blood coagulation, can make the blood clot too fast. Narrowing of the arteries (arteriosclerosis) is the most common cause of heart disease but in younger women heart attacks are most often triggered by blood clots caused from high fibrinogen levels. Specialized test: Ask your N.D.

Also, have your insulin levels checked along with your triglyceride levels. These tests are over and above the basic lipid panel that simply measures HDL (high density lipoprotein), LDL (low density lipoprotein) and total cholesterol.

CARDIOVASCULAR DISEASE PREVENTION: SUPPLEMENTS AND HERBS

A number of natural substances support the good health of the heart and entire cardiovascular system, but remember: no supplement or magic pill can take the place of exercise, good quality unrefined foods, water, rest and relaxation, and giving and receiving love in your life.

- **Cayenne pepper (*Capsicum annum*).** Cayenne benefits the cardio-vascular system in a number of ways. It reduces the risk of atherosclerosis (a degenerative condition of the arteries in which lipids, or fats, accumulate in them) by lowering cholesterol and triglyceride levels and reducing platelet aggregation, or stickiness.

    — *Recommended dosage*: 1/4 to 1 teaspoon pepper powder daily.

- **Coenzyme Q10.** The key to our body's electron transport system and cellular energy production, it also participates in the normal metabolism of fat and energy. CoQ10 is manufactured by the body and stored in the organs: liver, kidneys and heart. Heart tissue biopsies in patients with various heart conditions show a CoQ10 deficiency in 50 to 75 percent of the cases. Many studies show this natural compound's usefulness in the treatment of high blood pressure, atherosclerosis, angina, mitral valve prolapse, congestive heart failure, and cardiomyopathy. It works even better when taken in combination with vitamin E. According to Dr. Julian Whitaker, M.D., CoQ10 is the most powerful treatment of cardiomyopathy available. He states that it increases the survival rate of patients tenfold, compared to the combined therapy of ACE inhibitors, diuretics and digitalis drugs.

    — *Recommended dosage*: 50 to 150 mg per day or 2 mg daily for each kilogram of body weight. When heart failure is severe up to 360 mg (doses of 120 mg at a time) may be needed. Experts say "the sicker the cardiac patient, the weaker the heart, the higher the CoQ10 dose needs to be.

- **Essential fatty acids.** These help blood to stay unclotted, and also help keep every cell in the body nourished and oxygenated. They can be added to the diet in the form of flax oil, pumpkin seed oil, or mixed oil blends containing omega-3 and omega-6 fatty acids. (See Chapter 2 for more information.) Some people prefer taking essential fatty acids in capsule form—especially the fish oils!

    — *Recommended dosage*: 1,000 mg fish oil one to three times daily; 3 to 6 1,000 mg flax oil capsules daily; 2 to 4 teaspoons pumpkin seed oil and oil blends daily.

- **Garlic (*Allium sativa*)** lowers cholesterol and triglycerides, inhibits platelet aggregation, and increases HDL levels.

— *Recommended dosage:* Use fresh garlic liberally in foods; we also recommend the supplement Garlinase. Take enough to gain 8 mg allicin daily.

- **Hawthorne (*Crataegus oxyacantha*).** Preparations of this herb have been used clinically to prevent oxidation of LDL, reduce blood pressure, lower cholesterol, and prevent and treat atherosclerosis. Studies show that it is the proanthrocyanidin (bioflavonoid) component of the herb that is largely responsible for its effects. Hawthorne is a well-known restorative and nutritive tonic for the coronary system. Circulation to the heart muscles is improved due to mild vasodilation, thus reducing heart spasms and angina. It is also an effective treatment for hypertension, palpitations, irregular heartbeat and tachycardia.

  — *Recommended dosage:* 100 to 250 mg solid extract (4:1) up to three times daily; 4 to 5 mL tincture (1:5) up to three times daily.

- **Jiaogulan (*Gynostemma pentaphyllum*)** is an adaptogenic herb that helps the body adapt to physiological and psychological stress. The favorable actions of Gynostemma on the cardiovascular system are many: prevention of free radical damage and platelet aggregation (sticky blood), blood pressure regulation, cholesterol levels moderation, improvement of fat metabolism and strengthening the immune system.

  — *Recommended dosage:* 80 to 100 mg capsule standardized to 20% gypenosides, two to three times daily.

- **Soy isoflavones.** There have been several case-controlled studies of the effects of soy products on cardiovascular disease; control groups were fed diets containing animal protein. Overall, blood lipid levels decreased significantly in the soy groups. The changes were most significant in those people who had increased cholesterol levels to begin with. Studies also indicate that humans and animals on high-soy diets have increased clearance of cholesterol from the bloodstream as well as inhibition of platelet aggregation. Furthermore, studies indicate that the isoflavone content of soy lowers LDL, very low density lipoprotein (VLDL), and total cholesterol to HDL ratios, while at the same time increasing HDL levels.

  — *Recommended dosage:* 40 to 100 mg daily, or two servings of Women's Whey.

- **Calcium** regulation is vital to the proper contraction and relaxation of the heart's muscle. As we have mentioned oxidative stress (free radical damage) is a common cause of heart disease in many people. Oxidative stress causes a number of mechanisms important to the regulation of calcium to become unbalanced.
  - — *Recommended dosage:* 400 to 600 mg daily (daily doses of calcium and magnesium can be found in OsteoBalance or Bone-Up).

- **Magnesium.** This little-appreciated mineral seems to pop up everywhere, doesn't it? Magnesium is very important for the health of the heart. It strengthens the contraction of the heart muscles, lowers blood pressure, increases HDL levels, and inhibits platelet aggregation.
  - — *Recommended dosage:* 400 to 600 mg daily.

- **Vitamin C.** Well known as an antioxidant that prevents oxidation of LDL (a process that damages blood vessels), raises HDL levels, and lowers total cholesterol and triglycerides, vitamin C is an essential of any health program. Its many actions help prevent atherosclerosis and reduce the death rate in people who have suffered heart attacks and strokes.
  - — *Recommended dosage:* 1,500 to 2,000 mg daily.

- **Vitamin E** is probably the most studied vitamin in relation to cardiovascular disease. It helps to prevent atherosclerosis by decreasing the oxidation of LDL. Effective when taken with CoQ10.
  - — *Recommended dosage:* 400 to 800 IU daily.

- **Alpha Lipoic Acid (lipoic acid)** is a powerful antioxidant that prevents free radical formation, thereby protecting the cardiovascular system. Lipoic acid is both fat and water-soluble and it is readily transported in the blood to all the tissues and cells of the body. It plays a role in preventing atherosclerosis, preventing cataracts, improving sugar metabolism, rejuvenating the skin and preventing heavy metal toxicity. If we had to choose only one antioxidant, lipoic acid would be our first choice.
  - — *Recommended dosage:* 50 to 150 mg daily (up to 500 mg daily can be taken without fear of side effects).

- **FemmEssentials** is a good combined multivitamin formula containing important heart protective nutrients including lipotropic factors, folic acid, magnesium, B vitamins and the necessary vitamins and minerals needed for heart health.

A Note of Caution: for those people who are taking blood thinners (e.g. Coumadin), avoid the following: feverfew, gingko biloba and omega-3 (in therapeutic dose). These remedies have anti-clotting effects.

SOMETHING MORE TO THINK ABOUT...

One reason for the current increase in heart disease in women could be the fact that women are having to ignore the responses that come naturally. As more women move into predominantly male-dominated careers, they must learn to adapt (or adjust) and become more analytical. This is not within the more intuitive and emotional (heart-felt) nature of the woman and has a profound effect on the heart chakra, which governs the health of the physical heart. (Chakras will be described in more detail in Chapter 10.) All emotional triggers initially register in the solar plexus chakra, the seat of the emotions, and are then transferred to the heart centre, where the emotion is felt more intensely, integrated, and then channelled through the throat chakra to be expressed. Currently, North American men's emotional process typically starts at the solar plexus, stops very briefly at the heart centre, then proceeds directly to the intellectual centre, largely bypassing the heart centre, and then returns to the throat chakra for expression—that is, men tend to intellectualize their feelings, so their heart centre tends to become congested or blocked.

Women, in the past, typically went through the heart centre, felt the emotion, but then got stuck in the verbal expression of the emotion (put up and shut up), and the throat chakra energy got blocked, affecting the thyroid. Today, however, many women are taking on more and more of the stereotypic male role in business and to survive must assume more of the typically male patterns. In doing so, many women stop honouring the feminine ways of being, such as finding emotional integration through the heart centre. Therefore, the heart centre energy is becoming blocked in many women. The result is an increase in heart-related problems.

We must take care of our hearts on all levels. There are many factors outside of our hormones and basic biochemistry that influence our overall health.

We will discuss in detail the more subtle influences on health in the next chapter.

THE INTRICATE WEB OF LIFE

"Life is the expression of love in sound waves and energy
current, through the creation and in man. Love is light, which
crystallizes as beauty in the spectrum, becomes colour and
gases as it is reduced in its speed of vibration."
—Dr. Randolf Stone, 1890–1981

At this point in this book, we have covered in detail many of the physical
aspects of optimal health and touched on many of its mental/emotional
aspects as well, with a specific focus on the transitional years. From the
holistic viewpoint, there is a third aspect of health that has been largely
ignored or overlooked—the spiritual, which is the most important. Yet,
historically speaking, be it in the traditional practices of Buddhism,
Christianity, Islam, or other religions, the power of prayer, contemplation, or
meditation has always been seen as an integral part of health and healing.

More than eight in ten Americans think prayer or meditation can
augment medical treatment, according to a survey of 1 007 people released
by the sponsor of Harvard Medical School's Spirituality and Healing in
Medicine seminars. As many as 74 percent feel a doctor should discuss a
patients' spiritual needs with them, suggest prayer, or refer them to a spiritual
counsellor, and 41 percent said their medical conditions have been cured
or improved through personal prayer or meditation.

Just as we need physical exercise and good whole foods to keep our physical body healthy, we need daily spiritual exercises (contemplation, prayer,
or meditation) to keep our spiritual bodies balanced. Life is moving so quickly
today that spiritual practice is more necessary than ever before—it is easy to
lose balance if spiritual exercises are not done every day. We see the pace of
life today as being like that of a treadmill with the speed turned up to ten and
the fitness level (physical, mental/emotional, and spiritual) at around five.
And the treadmill shows no signs of slowing its movement towards greater

and greater speed. There are going to be more and more casualties as the speed increases unless people start to take responsibility for strengthening themselves on all levels.

Spiritual health is the foundation of optimal health on all other levels of life.

During a time of transition, whether it be the hormonal and physical changes that occur during menopause, or a change in our work or relationship life, every part of our being is affected. It is up to us to support the physical body with the right fuel and regular exercise. Many people turn to friends and loved ones for mental/emotional support. However, we will repeat again, the greatest influence on our whole state of health is the work we undertake in the spiritual realm. We need daily spiritual exercises to maintain the highest degree of health for our incredible journey in this life. However you perceive the spiritual side of your life, we urge you to choose to regularly access this part of yourself ... Just do it!

WHAT IS THE SPIRITUAL LIFE?

My basic answer to this question is very simple. The various forms of spiritual exercises are ways of communicating with the Divine Power. Each religion has its own terms that refer to the divine being (Jesus, Buddha, Ala, Mahanta, etc.). For the purpose of this chapter, I will be referring to this nameless one or being of many names, depending on how you look at it, as God, Holy Spirit, or Divine Power. Please associate with my names the name or names that fit with your own beliefs. For me, communicating with the Divine Power is the same thing as opening my heart to love, as becoming acquainted with the love, the God-like qualities within. Life has taught me that as we are more able to give and receive love, this all-powerful yet unseen vibration will begin to heal us.

This chapter will present various ways of communicating with Spirit that you may want to integrate into your own daily prayer or other spiritual practices, as well as a view of what it is to be a human that we hope will expand the possibilities you see for communion with Spirit. All of what we present here is based on ancient traditions and new thoughts founded on old concepts. Feel free to let your intuition guide you in this area of life. After all, we are regularly creative in other aspects of our lives, making changes in our clothing and hairstyle, rearranging the furniture in our homes, undertaking new work projects or relationships. Becoming more creative in our spiritual lives will have an exponentially larger impact on our feelings of enthusiasm, excitement, and vitality.

Now let's examine the spiritual aspect of life and how to work with it in more detail.

OUR MULTI-DIMENSIONAL BEING

I said above that as we expand our ability to give and receive love through communion with the Divine Power, we will begin to heal. The healing begins in our subtle bodies.

> "A doctor is not merely a dispenser and synthesizer of scientific knowledge, nor is a patient an inert receptacle. As Norman Cousins said, 'Ultimately it is the physician's respect for the human soul that determines the worth of his science.' "—Paul Roud

It is commonly held as truth that our body, including its various biochemical processes, is a purely physical phenomenon. In fact, we all actually possess two bodies. Beyond the ordinary reach of the senses, beyond the chemical bonding of molecules and atoms, are the fields of pure energy from which the atoms and matter of our physical bodies arise—these energy fields are the subtle body, composed of vibrational sheaths. It is the state of health of the subtle bodies that determines the health of the physical body—all physical disease begins in these energetic fields. Shifts towards less harmonious energetic vibrations in the subtle bodies will, if not addressed at the energetic level, lead to pathological physical changes.

The energetic bodies were described by Paracelsus in the sixteenth century: "The vital force is not enclosed in man, but radiates round him like a luminous sphere, and it may be made to act at a distance. In these semi-natural rays the imagination of man may produce healthy or morbid effects. It may poison the essence of life and cause diseases, or it may purify it after it has been made impure, and restore the health." Paracelsus also stated that the ultimate cause of illness is a weakness of the spirit and he advised his fellow physicians to search within themselves for spiritual insight to assist in the healing of their patients. The Father of Medicine, Hippocrates, also asserted the importance of healing the spiritual, or subtle, energy bodies as well as the physical body of the patient.

At this point you may be feeling uneasy about reading further, wondering whether we are crazy, and trying to figure out how we could assert that such a thing as the subtle bodies exist. A helpful place for you to start pondering the question may be in considering the limits of the senses.

Start by assuming that everything is energy; there is fundamentally nothing else. In his famous equation, $E = mc^2$, Albert Einstein, possibly this century's greatest scientist, proved that matter and energy are equivalent. Energy, as we can experience by going to the seaside, standing in the sun's rays, or allowing the breeze to play in our hair, *vibrates*. It emits waves of light and sound. (Using Einstein's equation, the world's nuclear scientists were able to force atoms to release the energy within themselves, which, in the detonation of an atomic bomb, vibrates in the form of extremely forceful light, sound, and heat.)

"A new scientific truth is not usually presented in a way to convince its opponents. Rather, they die off, and a rising generation is familiarized with the truth from the start."—Max Planck

All phenomena vibrate at their own rate. Different colours, for instance, are produced by light waves vibrating at different rates. An object feels hot or cold to us depending on the rate at which the atoms and molecules within it vibrate. Whether a phenomenon is physically visible or invisible, audible or inaudible, perceptible or imperceptible depends upon the rate at which the phenomenon vibrates—our senses generally have upper and lower limits to the vibratory rates they can perceive (some people, however, have a more expanded range of perception). We cannot see the motion of electrons that creates electricity, nor can we see the wind; we cannot feel the rotation of the earth or hear the sounds emitted by many of our fellow creatures on the planet; we cannot see, or hear, or touch, or taste, or smell love—but we know these phenomena exist, and we know love exists. Why? Because our physical senses and technologies feel and see the effects of invisible and inaudible energies, feel and see the effects of love. Who is to say that at this point in time we have mapped out in their totality all the ordinarily imperceptible energies in the universe, including our own? And what a dull world we would be living in if that were the truth!

Have you ever found yourself saying, "That person has such strong presence," or "I feel his or her energy"? Your senses have registered something, even though the other person may not have said or done anything specific to create your impression. You are using your own subtle bodies to sense the vibrations of the other person's subtle bodies; you can't see them but they affect you, and the information filters down to your physical senses. If a person in your vicinity is angry, this negative emotion indicates a discordant frequency in the subtle bodies, and you may feel uncomfortable or even sick around that person. A person may not understand why she is disliked and avoided even when she has not said or done anything "improper."

This person does not understand that it is not what one says but the totality of one's being that speaks louder than anything one says or does.

Now we hope that the idea of subtle bodies no longer seems so strange— as we have tried to show, the subtle bodies are like the physical body, but their form and functioning is different because they vibrate at different speeds than the physical body. The world's rhythms not only are outside and within us but they *are* us; from the oscillating particles that make up the atoms of our bones to the rhythms that flow in our minds. You may also be familiar with how many people who have had near death experiences talk about a spiritual body that has little form and can move through doors and walls and move rapidly. They too are referring to the subtle bodies.

As we touched on above, before physical symptoms develop, energetic vibrations in the subtle body change, becoming discordant. Such a discordance first affects the body's electromagnetic field. If the discordant vibration is constant enough or strong enough, it will eventually result in changes at the cellular level. Many things can influence the subtle bodies, including harmful thought forms (your own and other people's), poor nutrition, the standard electromagnetic frequencies in our electrical grid, and environmental toxins. Note that environmental toxins, processed foods, and the like, especially in this day and age of greater information about the effects of these substances, must inevitably be created by people who are involved with limiting and harmful thought forms.

Energy Diagnostic:
Polycontrast Interference Photography (PIP)

In Karen's practice she uses the PIP to help assess disruptions in the energetic body closest to the physical. The intention is to "catch" disease patterns before they have had a chance to affect cellular functioning (at which point the problem will have become more difficult to deal with) and to gain a better understanding of the energetic disruptions associated with any physical symptoms.

The PIP system, developed by scientist Harry Oldfield, analyzes the different light intensities emanating from the body. Harry says, "We believe that we are showing up an energy interaction with light, which is giving us insight into the energetic counterpart on which our physical molecules are strung."

On average, every atom in the body is replaced every seven to nine years. If we think of the body not as just a physical structure, but as a constant moving fountain of molecules that are constantly being replaced, we start to realize the importance of subtle energy diagnosis. The PIP is actually able to photograph the acupuncture points and meridians used in traditional Chinese medicine and the chakra centers, two systems of medicine known for thousands of years. For more information on this topic, see the Further Reading section at the back of this book.

Who We Really Are

Any scientific knowledge based on the analysis of separate body parts is working only with the bubbles on the surface while remaining unaware of the massive creative ocean surrounding and within us. A view of life accepted by many is that our life begins with birth and ends with death and that's it—there is no greater meaning to our existence. People also talk about my body, this body, my soul. But who is represented by the word "my"? Where is the part of us called "I"?

> "All know that the drop merges into the ocean but few know that the ocean merges into the drop."—Kabir

The body is a shimmering ocean of energetic movement, an energy dance, a web of interconnections, and within this web lies soul, who we really are. You are soul. Just as the cell in the human body contains all the genetic material of the whole, soul is a living vibration with the qualities and characteristics of God.

Each soul is a drop of the endless ocean of creativity called God; it is surrounded by a multi-layered web of energy patterns, the subtle anatomy that houses soul on its journey home. We all have the inner desire to return to our true home, to develop towards the highest good, towards the divine love. Each one of us chooses the extent to which we resist this journey. Conflict between our soul and our mind results in disease on one or more levels of our being.

Subtle Anatomy

Let's now look in more detail at the various energy fields, or subtle bodies, surrounding and interpenetrating the energy field known as the physical body. The wisdom teachings spanning many cultures and thousands of years explain the structure and function of the various fields or subtle bodies that make up the totality of human consciousness. There may be differences in the details from one culture or teaching to the next, but the foundation of these teachings remains the same.

- The *human being is a multi-dimensional entity;* the physical or gross body is but one of our dimensions.
- The other levels of the human entity are composed of more subtle frequencies than the physical body.
- All of the levels of consciousness coexist with and interpenetrate each other, even though we may be completely unaware of our multi-dimensional self.
- Communication between the various fields of consciousness exists and is continuous.
- Matter is not the prerequisite for life in the physical dimension; life in the physical dimension is the prerequisite for matter.

Modern science is slowly catching up to the teachings of the wisdom traditions.

THE INTERCONNECTED UNIVERSE: WE ARE ALL PART OF THE WHOLE

Quantum mechanics has found that all life is interconnected. A physicist at Princeton University, J. Wheeler, stated that the spin of one subatomic particle forces a twin particle, miles away, to have the opposite spin. Einstein converted consciousness (his perception of a recurring truth present in the natural universe) into mathematical symbols: $E = mc^2$. *Energy and matter, this equation states, are the same universal substance.* Let's now look at the matter/energy forms that make up the totality of the human body: our subtle anatomy.

- **The Physical Body.** In the view of the wisdom teachings, the physical body could be compared to a rental vehicle that gets us through this lifetime and others. It is structured in accordance with the vibratory rate of this physical plane of existence. It is a temple for soul in this lifetime. The physical body is surrounded by the subtle bodies composed of varying frequencies, each with its own function, purpose, colour/light, and sound.

- **The Aura.** The aura is a kind of subtle extension of the character, capable of giving and receiving impressions. For example, a person may feel an instant attraction or repulsion to another person; this is because of the harmony or disharmony of the vibratory rates between the two auras. The auric field is also the receptive vehicle for the life forces that flow into the body from the atmosphere, the sun, Earth and the other planets, and light and sound (the cosmic energies).

- **The Supraphysical Body.** This is the subtle body closest to the physical body in vibrational frequency. It is the point of intake and distribution of the vibrational influences from the more subtle bodies and functions as a mold or energy field for the body's cellular structures. This is the transitional zone through which souls travel before entering the first level of heaven, the astral plane.

- **The Astral Body.** Also called the emotional body, the astral body is lighter and finer than the physical body. It takes shape in accordance with the character of the individual. The astral body is involved with the emotions, desires, and passions. Because the astral body deals with emotions and the expression of emotions, its actions can have a powerful effect on our physical bodies. It is also very closely linked to the causal body, the first of the mental bodies.

- **The Causal Body.** Consisting of even finer vibrations than the astral body, the causal body is referred to as the beginning of the mental body. It is here that all the information is stored from the individual's experiences of this life and past lives that are affecting the present lifetime. It is here that the "seeds" are planted for things to take place in our lives. The function of the causal body is to transmit impressions between the mind and soul. The seeds of disease start here; *disease is a conflict between the mind and our true self, soul.*

• **The Mental Bodies.** The causal body is the lower mental body, while the etheric body is a higher mental body. The highest mental body (intuition) is part of the universal mind and has great creative power taken from soul. It is through the mental bodies that soul controls all the lower bodies. The vibrations of the mental bodies are the finest except for the soul body, and these bodies are so closely interwoven and reinforcing of each other that it is difficult to separate them from one another as distinct bodies of consciousness. These bodies create the rational mind, which makes intellectual comparisons and abstractions, as well as judgments, feelings, desires, and attachments that follow from the mental concepts. The various levels of the mental plane are heaven for most religions.

• **The Soul Body.** The soul is the last of the subtle bodies; it is the divine spark of God, sent to this world to learn and experience and then to return to its true home. The soul body has the finest of all the vibrations, so fine, in fact, that it cannot be in this world without the protective sheaths provided by the other bodies. Soul knows all by direct perception or knowingness. All power and consciousness reside in soul. We are soul residing within the multi-dimensional body with a specific purpose for this lifetime. Living on the soul plane represents spiritual freedom and self-realization. *If you are looking for your purpose, what you are here to do, simply look at what it is you love to do.*

THE CHAKRA CENTRES

Within the subtle energy bodies there are centres, called chakra centres. The chakras transform the life force energy from the Divine Spirit into forms our system can use; for instance, the chakras transform life force energy into electrochemical impulses within the cells. The chakras also distribute the life force given by God throughout our subtle anatomy, and they transmit and receive various subtle energy frequencies within our being and our environment.

For simplicity's sake, we will cover only the seven major centres that are located along the major nerve plexus of the body; these are the principal power stations in a vast network of life force energy distribution. However, to give you an idea of the complexity of the subtle anatomy, some of the subtle bodies have fewer or more than seven chakra centres. There are, in addition, approximately 22 minor chakra centres, 49 subminor locations, and more than 200 points of distribution that are linked to the acupuncture points.

The word "chakra" is derived from the Sanskrit word meaning wheel.

Those who can visually perceive aspects of the subtle bodies have described the chakras as vortices of beautiful pulsating, spinning, and shifting colours and sounds spinning in our subtle anatomy. Let's look briefly at the properties of the seven major chakras.

- **First chakra (sacral/root chakra).** Located at the very base of the spine, this chakra is associated with our will to live. It supplies energy to the spinal column, the adrenal glands, and the kidneys. It governs the endocrine extension of the autonomic nervous system. On the mental/emotional level it is associated with unresolved issues and how safe we feel in the world. The colour of this chakra is red, and its sound is *LUM* (LUUU … M).

- **Second chakra (splenic chakra).** Located just above the pubic bone, the second chakra is related to the sacral nerve plexus and supplies energy to our sexual organs and to the immune system. This chakra is associated with our relationships: control, guilt, or blame towards ourselves, our friends, or our family all indicate dysfunctions in this chakra. The functioning of this chakra is also related to our financial sense of security. Its colour is orange, and its sound is *VOM* (VOOO … M).

- **Third chakra (solar plexus).** Known as the seat of the emotions, this chakra is represented as the counterpart of the pancreas, the heart of the intestinal tract. Just as the digestive system discriminates amongst the chemical substances we ingest, the solar plexus makes emotional discriminations. It is located between the thoracic vertebra number twelve and the lumbar vertebra one and supplies the stomach, gallbladder, liver, pancreas, spleen, and nervous system with energy. The solar plexus chakra is also related to who we are in the universe, to our self-esteem. And it marks the point of fusion between our upward and downward moving energies.

The solar plexus is the centre where we receive our instinctive impressions (intuition); it is not uncommon for people to experience problems in the organs related to this chakra because of conflicts between the instinctive and the analytical mind. If you experience an emotional shock, you may feel a tightness just under the diaphragm, or you may feel like someone has just hit you in that area. The colour of the solar plexus chakra is yellow, and its sound is *RAM* (RAAA … M).

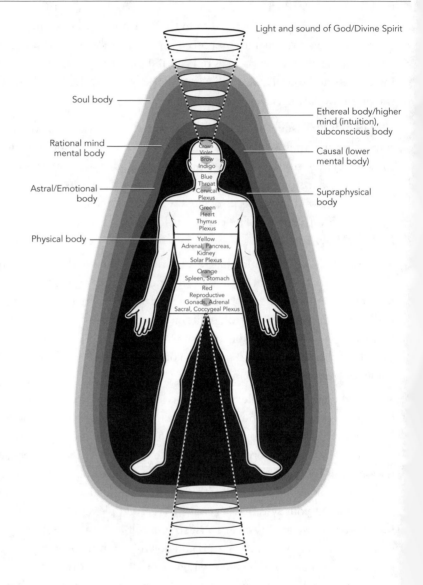

Light and sound of God/Divine Spirit

Soul body

Ethereal body/higher mind (intuition), subconscious body

Rational mind mental body

Causal (lower mental body)

Astral/Emotional body

Supraphysical body

Physical body

Crown
Violet
Brow
Indigo
Blue
Throat
Cervical
Plexus
Green
Heart
Thymus
Plexus
Yellow
Adrenal, Pancreas,
Kidney
Solar Plexus
Orange
Spleen, Stomach
Red
Reproductive
Gonads, Adrenal
Sacral, Coccygeal Plexus

Fourth chakra (heart chakra). The energy of this chakra is physically manifested by the heart and the thymus gland. It is located at the level of thoracic vertebra five. It supplies energy to the circulatory system, the heart, breasts, lungs, thymus gland, upper back, and vagus nerve. This is the centre of unselfish, unconditional love, and the will. When health problems arise in the organs this chakra regulates, they are the result of an inability to give love to or receive love from God, self, or others, unresolved grief, lack of forgiveness, or criticism and blame of self or others. In Chinese medicine, the emotion associated with the lungs is grief. The heart chakra and its associated organs are activated by positive thoughts and when we become a vehicle for love. This chakra's colour is green, and its sounds are *HUM* or *EYAM* (HUUU ... M).

• **Fifth chakra (throat chakra).** The throat centre is located at the level of cervical vertebra three. Its physical manifestation is the thyroid gland; in addition, the quality of a person's voice can be as penetrating as that of the eyes and is an indication of the degree to which this chakra is developed. The throat centre is related to the higher forms of expression—speaking our truth. Women typically have problems in the throat chakra area because socially we have been told to "put up and shut up." Thus, expression of our true thoughts and feelings becomes blocked. The colour of this chakra is blue, and its sounds are *AH* or *HUM* (AH ...; HUUU ... M).

• **Sixth chakra (brow chakra).** Located behind the eyes and between the eyebrows in the centre of the brain cavity, the sixth chakra supplies energy to our pituitary gland, lower brain, left eye, ears, nose, and nervous system. Its colour is indigo, and its sound is *AUM* (AUUU ... M).

The sixth chakra is associated with the pineal gland. Today little attention is given to the pineal gland, other than that we are told it starts to degenerate when we are six or seven. This is just around the age when we usually begin to forget who we are, as soul. At the age of six or seven, the pineal is said to join the three-fifths of the brain that lies dormant in most of us; according to science, these areas of the brain have no apparent function; however, science does recognize the importance of melatonin, a hormone secreted by the pineal gland.

The pineal is known to contain retinal tissue and could be likened to a third eye, atrophied but still containing photoreceptors. The third eye is thought by some cultures to be in the brow chakra and by others in the crown chakra.

• **Seventh chakra (crown chakra).** Located on top of the head, this chakra, like the sixth chakra, dips into the central part of the brain. Physically, this chakra is connected to the right eye and governs the upper half of the brain. Traditions such as those held in the Greek mystery schools and among the Egyptians see the crown chakra as the "seat of the soul." Descartes, who theorized at length about the pineal gland, saw it as the link between the body and, in his terminology, the "rational mind." In Hinduism the state of this chakra is believed to be a microcosmic reflection of the states of all the other chakras in the body; it is also believed that with its development the adept—a person thoroughly skilled in the knowledge of a particular spiritual path—moves into a whole new level of awareness. Hindus also believe that through this area alone a person can project her awareness beyond the confines of the physical senses. For this chakra represents the blending of the human nature with the deepest wisdom of God and represents direct knowingness. Its colour is violet, and its sound is silence.

For more information on the psychological and physical aspects of the chakra centres, please refer to two works by Norman Shealy and Carolyn Myss, *The Creation of Health: Merging Traditional Medicine with Intuitive Diagnosis* and *The Anatomy of the Spirit* (see the "Further Reading" section).

Putting It All Together

Picture the subtle bodies with their spinning chakras as an onion with its many layers. To perceive our true self requires navigating our way through the various layers of the onion, seeing through the illusions of self created by dysfunctions in the subtle bodies or chakras, or by our attachment to the activity of one or more of the subtle bodies or chakras. As with peeling away the layers of an onion, stripping away illusory self-concepts can be painful and may even cause us to weep.

Such a healing of the subtle bodies, however, is necessary for our optimal health on all levels. Each experience we go through in life's adventure can teach us more about leaving behind attachments to thought patterns, feelings, and desires and developing more love and compassion for ourselves, others, and all of life. As we make changes on one level, all of the other bodies are affected also.

During the transitional years, many changes occurring at the physical level may require us to turn to nutritional, botanical, and other remedies in order to stay in balance. These remedies will affect the subtle bodies. There will also be changes happening on the mental and emotional and spiritual levels. For many men and women during these years, their children may be leaving home, and they may be entering retirement or semi-retirement, allowing them more time to really look at themselves and review their lives. Some people may become more introspective, searching inside for a deeper meaning to their life, searching for themselves, as soul.

The one constant in our lives is change; the process of life is a process of growth. During these times of transformation, one level of being and self-organization is changing to a different, new, more advanced level. However, changes of any kind can result in a period of upheaval and chaos that in some cases manifests as emotional or physical crisis, before the new level of being is established.

Although we may not have a choice around the naturally occurring hormonal or physiological changes accompanying our transitional times, we do have a choice regarding our attitude towards the events. Transitions, especially hormone-related ones, are times of increasing creative energy. The extent to which we do or do not suppress our creative expression of our true self is one of the greatest influences on how we experience the transitional years.

Undertaking spiritual exercise supports our creative flowering, and, as already explained, helps maintain the health of the subtle bodies, and therefore health on all levels.

Let us now consider the practical aspects of spiritual practice.

We have already explained that discordant energetic vibrations stress the subtle bodies and can lead to disease. Harmonious energetic frequencies can heal us. Love is the ultimate healer.

LOVE AND THE LIGHT AND SOUND OF GOD

"Let there be light," said God, and light there was, and this was the beginning of life on earth, according to the biblical scriptures (Genesis 1:3).

Also mentioned in the Bible is the Word, the sound of God that existed before the light came into being: "In the beginning was the Word, and the Word was with God, *and the word was God*" (John 1:1).

Take a moment and visualize the love that comes from the Divine Spirit as a brilliant light and audible sound—for light and sound are manifestations of Spirit. As it enters into human experience, the magnificent energy beam travelling from the Divine Spirit filters itself through a giant prism and unfolds itself into the millions of frequencies of light/colour, sound, scent, and other sensations that make up our being. The divine frequencies descend and ascend in vibratory currents producing life in all forms. In this chapter we will focus on the light and sound frequencies emanating from the one Divine Spirit, as these provide an accessible starting point for opening to love, to communion with Spirit.

Sound

Orpheus is not only known as one of the greatest musicians and poets the world has ever known, but he is also regarded as the first theologian and founder of the Greek mystery schools. Orpheus was the patron saint of Pythagoras, who believed that the principles underlying the harmony of the musical scales underlay harmony in the universe as well. In Greek, the word "harmonia" means the fitting together of opposites: spirit and matter, unity and multiplicity, order and chaos.

Socrates also spoke of the importance of sound, telling us that more than anything else rhythm and harmony find their way to the innermost soul, bringing harmony and grace. He emphasized that this occurs not because music is "supreme" but rather because it is "form itself," an earthly echo of the Divine Form. Plato, in his dialogue entitled "Timaeus," explains that the fabric of the world and individual soul reflects the ratios of musical harmony, seen as the underlying foundation of all healthy systems. Plato maintained that sickness results when the harmony of the whole system is upset, that is, when the greater systems (our world) are out of harmony, the individual is affected. If one was to embrace this concept, a disease such as cancer would be viewed as a state of malfunctioning rhythm, resonance, and vibration that starts first in the world and eventually causes disharmony within our own being.

The effects of vibrations on solid and liquid bodies have been extensively studied by a Swiss scientist, Hans Jenny. He has stated that the more he studies sound vibrations, the more he realizes that sound is the most fundamental embodiment of the creative principle; it must be regarded as primordial.[2]

> "Every self-respecting medical practitioner would not only know music theory but feel it in pulse."—Peter of Abano, medieval physician/philosopher

Sound waves are rhythmic oscillations of energy that pass through a medium, most commonly air or water. We call these oscillations of energy sound because they occur within a frequency (rate of vibration) range that the ear can detect. (A broad range of rhythmic oscillations can be detected by the eye—these are called light.) It was the German physicist Heinrich Hertz (1857–1894) who first discovered that every sound and musical note has its own frequency. In other words, each specific sound is created by a specific number of rhythmic oscillations occurring within a specified unit of time; the number of rhythmic oscillations occurring within the specified unit of time are called the sound's frequency. Sound frequencies are now measured with a unit called the hertz (Hz), which stands for number of cycles, or rhythmic oscillations, per second. The lower a sound, the lower its frequency; the higher a sound, the higher its frequency. Due to the properties of our world, every sound sets in motion a number of other simultaneously sounding sounds, called overtones, which are vibrations oscillating at ever higher rates, theoretically to infinity. Overtones always oscillate at rates that are multiples of the original tone to which they are related. Within a certain range, these oscillations will occur at a rate quick enough to produce light. Thus, each sound frequency has a mathematically definable relationship to a specific range of colours, or light frequencies.

The law of resonance holds that anything that vibrates reacts to vibrations, even the most minute vibrations, so our bodies will respond to all sound, especially the primordial sounds (discussed below).

The law of resonance also means that sound is a universal language, a language that all our bodies respond to. Sound is effortlessly absorbed through the skin. Every physical organ and gland, the meridians, even the bones, respond to the frequencies of sound, colour, and other vibrational therapies, such as homeopathy. An expanding body of clinical research lends support to the healing ability of sound.[3] This research is rediscovering, in modern terms, the reasons music and medicine have been linked from the beginning of recorded history.

Healing of the subtle bodies that in turn effects the healing of the physical body can also be done with the sounds of music, nature, or animals, sounds used in prayer or meditation, or simply the sound of silence.

THE DIFFERENT SOUNDS OF "THE SOUND"

The sound of God manifests in different ways in the various subtle bodies and may sound like thunder, the roaring of the sea, the jingling of bells, running water, buzzing of bees, or twittering of birds, until it finally becomes the *hu*, the universal name of God (pronounced "hugh"), the most sacred of all sound frequencies. The hu is the beginning and end of all sounds, the origin of all words, the spirit of all sounds; it does not belong to any language or religion.

The English word "human" explains two aspects characteristic of all humanity. "Hu" means God and "man" means mind—the Sanskrit word "*mana*," mind, referred to the ordinary person. The two words taken together represent the God-conscious person.

The many sounds that emanate from the various levels of the subtle bodies, or planes of consciousness, can be powerful healing tools. The sounds corresponding to the various bodies are described below. In addition, you have the ability, over time, to know intuitively which patterns in your life or which attitudes towards life are associated with each of the subtle bodies and chakras, and you may want to use the word associated with each body or the sound associated with each chakra to access knowledge or insights stored within it.

A Spiritual Exercise

Nowhere is the power of sound more apparent than when we use such sounds as Amen, Hallelujah, Hosanna, Om, and Hu in our prayers or mantras.

Choose the sound that resonates with you, either from those in the paragraph above, or those associated with the various bodies or chakras, and with it do the exercise given below. It is extremely beneficial to do this exercise for 10 to 20 minutes each day. This exercise can also be done even for only a few minutes at any time in the day if you find that you are losing your centre of balance, are feeling stressed, or find yourself dealing with an uncomfortable situation. You needn't use the same sound each day. Before beginning your spiritual exercise, ask God or your spiritual guide to let you experience whatever knowledge or insights are best and necessary for your highest good.

Then, sit and listen to the voice of God, the Holy Spirit, and contemplate the light of God. God knows what we truly need; God does not need to be directed by us.

- Find a quiet, comfortable place.
- Close your eyes and take three deep breaths. Let the current thoughts and worries of the day leave with each exhale.
- Focus your attention between your eyebrows, where the spiritual eye is.

- Fill your heart with love by thinking of someone who opens your heart, such as a loved one or your spiritual guide (Jesus, Buddha, the Mahanta, or other spiritual guides).

- If you have a specific question or concern that you would like answered, gently place the question in your mind.

- Sing silently or outwardly the word you chose to help bring more insight and awareness into your life. For example, if you chose the Hu, you would gently sing either out loud, or silently, "Huuu, Huuu." You may also just want to sit in silence, filling your heart with love and waiting to see what sounds and colours may come to you.

- You may then see a particular colour in your mind's eye, hear a sound, or see a particular scene. Just continue to sit quietly, filled with love and your sound for 10 to 20 minutes.

- You may want to write down any insights or experiences when you are finished.

- Thank Spirit for the blessings and guidance you have received and are about to receive.

You have asked for help; now pay attention throughout the day for the answers to your questions. The process by which Spirit gives answers is different for everyone. For example, you may have a waking dream, like a very vivid and involuntary daydream, that gives you answers. Or right after your spiritual exercise, a friend who does not call you regularly may call, suggesting that you read a particular book. Your answers could come in any form. *Listen with your heart.* It is so important to hear Spirit's call.

In our lives we have often experienced what we call the "sledgehammer technique." This has happened when we didn't hear, or perhaps heard but didn't respond to, the inner guidance and more subtly stated directions from the Divine Spirit. When God wanted our attention and just couldn't get it with softer communication, something happened that we couldn't ignore, such as a major illness or a broken pelvis. Now we do our best to listen to the gentle messages that direct and guide our life.

It is through awareness and understanding of why something is happening that we can heal it and make changes so as to prevent it from occurring again. When we do our form of spiritual exercise, this helps us understand our lives, and to receive more of the divine love of Spirit. Then we are able to give more back to all of life. Life itself is a spiritual exercise when we live it with our hearts open to the love of Spirit.

Life will teach us if we let it. Take time daily to listen to the Holy Spirit.

IF YOU CAN THINK IT, YOU CAN BE IT

As we begin to listen to the promptings of Spirit, it is important that we have a clear understanding that negative emotions or attitudes can manifest in physical or mental disturbances. Evidence supporting this view is found in the traditional wisdom teachings as well as in the observations accumulated by psychiatry and medicine—all these fields substantiate the fact that thought and behaviours, attitudes and emotions have a profound impact on our state of health.

Dr. Hans Selye established the relationship between emotional states and blood chemistry; certain emotions cause the release of the hormones adrenalin or norepinephrine from the adrenal glands into the bloodstream. Furthermore, the mind (conscious and unconscious thoughts and emotions) and the body are linked up by nerve pathways and hormones. A neurohormonal relationship exists between the hypothalamus, pituitary, and adrenal glands (hypothalamic-pituitary-adrenal axis) that actually links thought and emotion with the physiological responses created by the endocrine system's hormonal releases. The field of psychoneuroimmunology has found a distinct connection between the mind and the immune system (thymus gland).[5-7] Knowing this gives us more of an appreciation of the complexity of hormonal changes.

Dr. Candace Pert and other researchers have found that brain and nervous system chemicals released in response to thoughts and feelings land on and activate receptor sites in the body's endocrine and immune system cells, as well as in nerve cells. Pert's research has revealed that organs such as the kidney and bowel also have receptor sites for these so-called brain chemicals, and the organs and immune system manufacture these same chemicals. In other words, chemicals associated with thought and feeling are produced by, and affect, all aspects of our bodies.

"Our entire concept of the mind needs to be expanded considerably. One of my colleagues says, 'The mind is the space between the cells.' "—Dr. Christiane Northrup

Whether we assess the matter by means of scientific exploration of biochemistry or via observation of the subtle energy fields, the message is the same: persistent harmful or unbalanced patterns in thoughts, actions, and attitudes cause physical, emotional, and mental illness. The effects of our actions, thoughts, words, deeds, desires, and emotions all condition the quality of the whole energy field and our life experiences. At the root of all damaging thoughts, feelings, and actions is fear.

Fear, the Primary Toxin; Love, the Ultimate Healer

Fear is the toxin from which all other mental and emotional toxins evolve. When there is fear, there is absence of love; the two can't live together in the same space. Fear is at the root of all problems and disease because it is involved at the roots with self-identity and can invade all aspects of the self. It has multiple tentacles: fear of death, fear of disease, fear of injury, fear of poverty, fear of being alone. If we do not take action to transform fear, it becomes like an old movie that plays itself out over and over with the projector stuck on rerun and its operator asleep.

> "Experience of man as a force-field connected to others and in turn to the force fields of the earth, where the power of attraction and symbiosis and unstinting exchange of energy are operating, leads easily to a more rational concept of love. When the psyche, therefore the body, constricts itself with fear, it also severs the life force of love from itself."—Buckminster Fuller

Love is at the root of all health and healthy self-identity. It is the life energy from which all aspects of the self are nurtured and regenerated, and there is always a never-ending supply from Spirit. We need only accept it. The more love we give out the more we can receive. When we recognize the reality of the never-ending supply of the love of God, what is there to fear, really? *Seize the day—do not be afraid to plunge into life. Learn to live by the dictates of soul, to fear no man and to follow the fulfillment of our purpose in life, the rendering of help to our fellow man. Remember, the more we give to life, the more life gives to us.*

Creating Your Health, Creating Your Life

As we release fear, we come into creativity.

By reconnecting ourselves with the light and sound from the Divine Spirit that permeates all existence and changing our thoughts, we become connected to *who we really are, and why we are here in this life.*

"Experiences with the same rate of vibration will fuse."
—Susan Hiller, artist

We discussed in Chapter 2 how our thoughts create our world. Thought forms are no less than different modes of energetic frequency. They exhibit patterns that if held for long enough will crystallize into physical manifestation. In relation to disease or imbalance in our body, *disease is a thought* that has been held long enough and constantly enough to manifest physically. That which I think, that I am. Our thoughts affect our subtle bodies, and changes in the subtle bodies precede pathological changes and disease at the physical levels. In the same way, what we create with our thoughts and actions each lifetime follows with us. If a baby is born deformed or with a disease, at some other time the deeds or thought forms were enough to create the present situation; that soul needed experience for growth in this life.

We can change our lives by changing our thoughts and attitudes towards life. We may not necessarily be able to *cure* ourselves of disease, but in many cases our attitude can change the course of a disease. A positive attitude held towards the condition will make it an incredible opportunity for growth; a negative attitude holds a person where they are and does not allow them to break the pattern of thought or deed that may have been the root of the condition—who knows when.

A *miracle is simply a change in consciousness, nothing more.*

Many people may say, "Well, attitude is all well and good, but my thoughts alone can't solve everything." This is very true. When thoughts have been held long enough to crystallize into physical patterns, then diet, nutritional supplements, and natural or prescription medications may be necessary for the healing—in other words, the physicalized manifestations of helpful, rather than harmful, thoughts. Even when you are using physical remedies, your attitude towards the experience will influence how you heal.

IMAGINE!

If harmful thoughts and feelings create difficulties, it is only logical that constructive and loving thoughts and feelings will allow us to flourish. It is through our imaginative faculty that we individually and collectively create our lives; once we fully understand that what we imagine for ourselves is what we get, we come to realize that the majority of our limitations are created by our own limited imaginings about what is and is not possible. The conditioned consciousness that generally shapes our lives is the creation of individual and society-wide habits—but we can rise above habit to create the life we choose. Further below, you will find an exercise that helps you begin to refocus the power of your imagination.

We can challenge our limiting beliefs about the possibility of change by looking at the metaphor provided by a computer. Most of us recognize the capability of computers to store information that, with the right command, can be accessed at any time. We can also revise the files, adding and subtracting material, anytime we choose, and save the new versions for later use. Our personal memory banks are like this. We can change them at any time: we can refile material from "awful experience" to "learning opportunity," from "I hate So-and-so" to "I have compassion for So-and-so's pain." Undertaking this task will force us to review events in the past that influence our present.

Even after going through the memory banks, however, many people are not able to see a direct cause for a particular condition; this often occurs because past lives influence this life, and they are often difficult to remember. Past life events may have caused us pain, or aroused anger, excess greed, vanity, or any of the other passions. Qualified therapists can help us recover past life memories and clear away any destructive thoughts and emotions stored in those lives that interfere with our ability to create the life we imagine for ourselves. We can also ask during prayer or meditation for insights into the reasons for those things in our lives that limit us.

All revisions to our memory banks need to be done in the spirit of forgiveness for oneself and others, and with a willingness to surrender oneself to the final outcome of the process.

Since we have introduced several important ideas here, we are going to make some quick digressions to expand our understanding of them before moving on with this discussion of how to create the life we want. Many people feel discouraged about making certain changes because they feel that even if they undertake a new and fulfilling direction, others won't, which will undercut their own efforts. For instance, if we decide to quit smoking because we want to breathe clean air and stay healthy, but our friends and neighbours insist on smoking and using their cars even when they could walk, bike, or use public transit, we will feel frustrated in our inability to create the life we want. For those going through this experience, we offer the story of the hundredth monkey; it proves that individual actions eventually make a big difference. I also introduced the idea of past lives above. You may or may not believe in reincarnation; below we offer evidence that reincarnation is a reality.

The Hundredth Monkey

In his book *The Hundredth Monkey*, Ken Keyes Jr. tells the following story. In the 1950s, scientists working off the coast of Japan were observing populations of monkeys. They supplied them with sweet potatoes, dropped into the sand. The monkeys liked the sweet potatoes, but not the dirt that clung to them. One day a young female monkey went to the sea and washed her potato before eating it. Her playmates, mother, and relatives started doing the same thing, and between 1952 and 1958, the idea of washing the potatoes spread gradually. A certain number of monkeys were practising the new idea—let's say 99 of them, Keyes suggests. (No one knows the exact number.) Then one day, in the autumn of 1958, right after the hundredth monkey joined in, the new idea was suddenly observed being put into practice by almost all the monkeys *and* on two completely separate islands by monkeys who, until that moment, had shown no inclination to wash their potatoes.

The idea of washing the potato suddenly became a part of the whole group's consciousness when there were enough monkeys thinking the same way. The new idea was able to affect even groups of monkeys living at a distance, separated from those who initiated the idea by impenetrable ocean.

We can see from this example that when enough members of a species hold something to be true, then it becomes true for everyone. When a myth is shared by large numbers of people, it becomes reality. It is through the introduction and gradual acceptance of new truths that greater wisdom and insights are born.

Another aspect of our lives that forms an important part of many religions is the belief in reincarnation. Have you ever considered this concept? It is a valuable one. Through greater understanding of our soul's journey throughout many different lifetimes of experiences, we can obtain a greater awareness of the influences on our current situation.

Have I Really Lived Before?

Gallup Canada has reported that 33 percent of Canadians polled believe in rebirth, and a Gallup/USA *Today*/CNN TV poll found that 27 percent of adult Americans believe in reincarnation. A *Newsweek* report published in

1994 showed that 33 percent of North Americans have had a religious or mystical experience. Hundreds of millions of people throughout the world also believe in reincarnation, including Australian Aborigines, Native North Americans, Hindus, and Buddhists. In Ghana, West Africa, the newborn is called *ababio* —"He is come again." Believers in past lives possibly outnumber the disbelievers.

One of the most renowned researchers of past lives in our time is Ian Stevenson, M.D., who works at the University of Virginia. He has studied more than 1,250 people who claim they remember their own reincarnation and has found similar patterns in these accounts all around the world, regardless of the person's religious beliefs or culture. His findings have been published in books, the *Journal of the American Medical Association*, and the *American Journal of Psychiatry*. Children, says Stevenson, usually remember their past lives up until the age of five or six; most will have forgotten by the age of eight. Ask a child between two and five "Who were you when you were big?" You will probably be surprised by the detail of their answer.

Back to the main thread we return—our ability to shape our lives, including our well-being, with our thoughts and feelings.

EXAMINE YOUR ATTITUDE

Attitude plays an important part in imagination because of the feeling it generates—feeling gives the fuel for the creation of what one imagines. Creative imagination is a combination of thought and attitude (feeling). We shape each experience according to our own individual attitude and state of awareness or consciousness. If you don't like what you see, undertake to change it.

It is not our environment that determines our lives, but we ourselves. Our thoughts and our actions are responsible for our surroundings and our lives. Granted, things do happen in our lives that seem outside of our control; however, we *always* have a choice about how we respond to these events.

When you are doing the spiritual exercise outlined earlier in this chapter, you may want to start by asking yourself what attitude or viewpoint you hold towards a problem: do you view it as an inconvenience, perhaps as overpowering and all-encompassing, or do you see it as a valuable lesson that will teach you something? Your attitude to your problem is the key that will determine whether you are able to hear Spirit's response and grow in love and compassion, or whether your experience leads to the growth of fearfulness, embitteredness, defensiveness, and possibly poor physical health as well.

Creating the Life You Imagine: A Practical Exercise

The seat of the imagination in the body is the third eye, the sixth chakra centre, deep in the brain, between the brows. Allow yourself to focus on this area for a moment. Then form a mental image, a picture, of what it is you want, and hold it there; take a picture with your inner camera. Concentrate on the feeling that the completed picture brings into your world, then fill the picture with love and let it go.

We always leave the creation of the final "print" up to the Divine Spirit or God by completing our creative imagining of what it is we desire by saying or writing, "If it be for the good of the whole." Then we surrender ourselves to whatever the outcome may be by saying or writing, "Thy will be done." Thus we create within according to our awareness of what is best, surrender the creation up to inputs and adjustments from the Spirit, and then trust in the outcome. Whatever happens then becomes the product not of our will but of the will of the Divine Power.

ACCEPTANCE

There is another process without which our creative abilities may be limited: *acceptance*. Everything is already here, just waiting for us to accept it. We do not have to be worthy of any experience in life—*we need only to accept it and live accordingly*. In other words, live assuming that you have already received your heart's desire.

Use your imagination to decide how it feels, sounds, looks to live within your creation. Collapse time and remove the barriers between you and your desire. In the deepest part of your mind tell yourself that you are willing to accept what you desire into your life. For example, say or write to yourself, "I accept God's love"; "I accept my love"; "I accept excellent health"; "I accept the love of my family and loving relationships in my life"; "I accept wealth and prosperity"; "I accept a heightened spiritual consciousness (self-realization, God-realization)"; "I accept abundance on all levels." You will be amazed at the results. Be careful what you ask for, you may just get it!

Other exercises that help with acceptance include the following.

• **Collage.** Make a collage of the picture you imagine and put it somewhere where you will see it regularly. You can add and remove pictures as
the picture changes in your mind's eye. This will help you hold the vision.

• **Writing.** Write out what it is you wish to bring into your life *15 times*
daily for a few weeks, always starting with the words "I am." For example, "I
am healthy on all levels of my being." Watch what happens in your life.[11]

The Attitude of Gratitude: Remember to Say Thank You!

Take time, in your meditations or writings, to say thank you for the divine
gifts of spirit that are and will be forthcoming. Know that you will receive your
answers or solutions to your questions and problems. Gratitude for the gifts
of Spirit opens our heart to more divine love and guidance.

As you begin to work with these exercises your life will begin to change.
Any outward change is preceded by inward change. For example, as you
begin to experience better health you may not know how to use your new-
found energy, and the transition from the original state of being or consciousness to the new one may be initially challenging or confusing.

A Patient's Story: "Years ago I had a patient who had been seeking help
for her problem for years from a variety of practitioners. After a few months
of seeing me she started getting better, so we arranged to start spacing out her
appointments over a longer time. The next time I saw her she had regressed
to where she had been initially and admitted to me that she hadn't known
what to do with her new life—that she had identified with her illness for so
long she was afraid to embrace what was ahead. Without the illness giving
her the attention she needed and an identity she was familiar with, she
didn't know any longer who she was or what she wanted to do with her life.
Do you want to change?"

THE ABILITY TO ADAPT TO CHANGE

Health depends on our ability to adapt to change. This ability in turn depends
on our ability to know that everything that happens in our life provides the
perfect opportunity needed at that moment to spur us on to more love,
learning, and growth. We can thus surrender with confidence to the Divine
Power and have faith that if we are willing to love, we will receive the
resources necessary to meet any challenge. On a personal level, flowing with

life is made easier when we determine to cultivate the ongoing presence of the following qualities:

- Hope—a vision for tomorrow
- Faith—both in one's self (self-esteem) and in God
- Purpose—a sense of personal meaning about what we are here to do
- Control—a sense of having choice in our lives, created when we choose to have a choice!
- Enthusiasm—a vital passion for life

In order to change, we must evaluate all we have learned and accumulated. We must also learn to recognize the feeling that something is not right, or no longer fits. Doing so could result in a decision to find a new path that resonates more strongly with who we really are. The next step is finding the courage and faith to act on this knowingness, to give up the old experience for the new.

We often receive inner nudges or impulses telling us that things must change, but it is all too easy to get caught up in our illusions of comfort and security and reject the opportunity for change. That's okay, life will just push a little harder next time. Whether we choose to accept the challenge is up to us. Each of us has our own journey, filled with individual experiences fuelled by actions of this and past lives. Each of us has to pass our own examinations, and has to travel through our own territory, with all its happiness and pain.

What is right for one person may not be right for another. There is no such thing as one truth that fits all; this is dogma. *The only absolute truth remains within us—in our own connection with Spirit.*

The exercises suggested above as well as the following techniques can help us balance ourselves and heal all levels of our being (all the bodies) and assist us as we embrace change in our life.

VIBRATIONAL HEALING

When any one of our bodies is shifted from equilibrium it begins oscillating at a less harmonious frequency than previously. In the physical body, such a shift leads to a general state of cellular energetic imbalance, and the immune system becomes unable to defend us. If provided with a model of its healthy, harmonious frequency in the form of light and sound, an unbalanced body will again begin to oscillate at the proper vibration.

Many of the healing tools used by complementary practitioners, such as homeopathy, flower essences, and acupuncture, help to adjust the finer frequencies of the body. Yoga, tai chi, massage techniques, gem therapy, Shen therapy, reiki therapy, and of course the practice of daily spiritual exercises are examples of therapies that work at the energetic level.

When women are experiencing one of the greatest transitions in their lives during the menopausal years, changes occur on all levels. The spiritual exercises previously mentioned can be very beneficial during this time. There are also specific acupuncture and reflexology points on the body that can help balance the endocrine system. When one aspect of our multidimensional being changes, all the other aspects change.

Acupuncture-based Therapies

Treatment of the acupuncture points is based on the idea that the human body contains a dense network of invisible channels, called meridians, through which the chi, the fundamental life force, flows. Over the course of a very long history, the Chinese acupuncturists gradually discovered that by applying needles to particular points they could affect the symptoms of disease and evoke a healing. The procedure can be traced back to about 2000 BC. The acupuncture points have a different electrical resistance and skin tension than all other areas of the skin, making it possible to determine exactly where they are.

Many people are puzzled by the fact that the points used to treat a symptom are often far away from the area under treatment. For instance, to treat symptoms in the large intestine, a point on the hand is used. This is possible because energetic information from the acupuncture point is transported via the meridians to the actual area affected by the sickness or imbalance.

It is also possible to stimulate the acupuncture points with pressure, electrical stimulus, and colour.

Acupressure

In this technique, the therapist applies pressure with the hands to various acupuncture points to loosen stagnated chi or stimulate a rebuilding of deficient chi in a particular meridian. The technique is capable of overcoming energetic blockages and establishing a new, more vital and harmonious flow of energetic information through the meridians. The points chosen for treatment depend on the patient's symptoms and underlying imbalance. Acupressure acts more slowly than the Acu-stim mechanism described below.

Electrical Acupuncture Point Stimulation

In electrical acupuncture point stimulation, a device called an Acu-stim is used to give a small electrical charge to various points. The Acu-stim provides a fast-acting energy-directing treatment. For information on sources for the Acu-stim device, please contact Karen at her website given in the back of this book.

Colour Puncture

In colour puncture, light is applied to the skin, usually at the acupuncture points, via projection through a quartz or glass rod. The skin absorbs colour easily; when it is applied at an acupuncture point, the vibrational energy of the colour is distributed via the meridian system. Various frequencies of light—that is, colours—are very powerful and work at a deep level at the acupuncture points, not only to stimulate chi but also to offer the healing effects of each colour frequency to the organ systems being treated and to their associated chakras. For information on sources for colour puncture equipment, please contact my office at the address given in the back of this book. (Some therapists working with colour use colour therapy instead of, or in addition to, colour puncture. In colour therapy, colour is applied via colour gels attached to lamps. The patient lies under the lamp with the colour radiating onto the area of the body needing treatment.)

THE INFLUENCE OF LIGHT AND COLOUR ON LIFE FUNCTIONS

Light, like sound, exists in the form of waves, and colour simply depends on the frequency of a wave of light (the rate at which it vibrates or oscillates). For a long time there was no explanation of why the leaves are green, the clouds white, the sky blue. What was colour? Sir Isaac Newton provided an explanation in the seventeenth century when he discovered that a prism would split white light into the various colours that combine to create it. The colour of an object is determined by the extent to which its molecular structure will allow the various colours in light to pass through. Those colours that cannot pass through and are reflected are the ones we perceive as the object's colour.

SELF-MASSAGE ZONES FOR HEALING ORGAN SYSTEMS

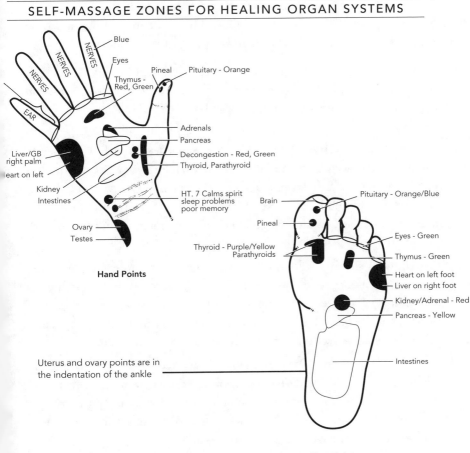

Hand Points

Uterus and ovary points are in
the indentation of the ankle

Foot Points

Colour has been used for healing since ancient times, and in 1903 a Danish physician, Niels Finsen, was awarded the Nobel Prize for medicine for his research on light and colour in the treatment of disease. Modern medicine also makes use of colour therapy to treat complaints, as in the case of ultraviolet and infrared therapy. It is therefore surprising that the majority of doctors still tend to reject colour therapy. Red and violet are electromagnetic vibrations that lie at opposite ends of the colour spectrum and have specific effects on the body. It seems logical that the colours between them are also capable of having healing and therapeutic effects. The experience of colour therapists is that coloured light contains information that is understood by the cells because each cell emits light and sound frequencies of its own.

Each colour of the spectrum has its own healing properties. The following list begins with the primary colours, blue, red, and yellow, and then considers the colours created by blends of the primary colours.

- **Blue.** The colour of the endocrine system and the pituitary gland, blue is a cold colour and has relaxing effects. It is an excellent colour to use for menopausal complaints, impotence, sleeplessness, and relaxation of muscles.

- **Red.** A hot positive colour, red has a stimulating effect. It will strongly stimulate the flow of blood and is therefore useful for poor circulation. It has a cheering effect, helps to release blocked mental energy, and helps combat lethargy and laziness. Red is effective in the treatment of the lungs, bones, heart, and muscles and is good for strengthening the kidney and adrenal chi.

- **Yellow.** Also a hot colour, yellow promotes digestion, strengthens the nerves, and has a general cheering effect. It also fortifies the endocrine system. It is very effective for treatment of imbalances of the liver, gall-bladder, and stomach and it activates the lymphatic and immune systems. Yellow is associated with left brain activity and an alert intellect.

- **Green.** A combination of blue and yellow, green is the most common colour in nature and is sedative and cooling. It has a balancing effect and promotes feelings of contentment and relaxation. Green is a pituitary stimulant and promotes healthy bones. It is also an excellent detoxifier—all chronic conditions respond well to green.

- **Orange.** A combination of red and yellow, orange is the colour of joy and happiness. It encourages warmth of the heart and is beneficial in cases of depression, pessimism, fear, and discontentment. Exposure to orange light for a brief period in the morning will help people who are chronically tired. It is very effective in sclerotic processes such as arteriosclerosis and cerebral congestion. Blue and orange work in close coordination to balance the endocrine system.

- **Turquoise.** A combination of blue and green, turquoise is the colour of mental relaxation. It helps people make enhanced contact with themselves in that it bridges various aspects of the psyche. It is relaxing, tones the skin, and is very effective in inflammatory conditions. Turquoise also helps to regulate the lung and large intestine organ system.

- **Violet.** A combination of red and blue, violet is often associated with spirituality. Accordingly, violet acts on the unconscious and promotes awareness and individual spiritual strength. It is regarded as the colour of inspiration. Violet has positive effects on the spleen and is especially beneficial for women during menopause. It promotes the function of the lymphatic system and relaxes the heart. It is physically sedative and emotionally stimulating.

The points and areas indicated in the diagrams can be stimulated with pressure, the Acu-stim device, or colour puncture. In addition, you can use colour breathing or colour-charged water to provide yourself with the vibrational energies you need at a given time.

Colour Breathing Meditation

Choose the colour that resonates with you, either with reference to the qualities listed above or because your intuition indicates you need to work with a particular chakra and its associated colour.

- Find a quiet, comfortable place.

- Close your eyes and take three deep breaths. Let the current thoughts and worries of the day leave with each exhale.

- With each breath, see yourself breathing in the colour of your choice to a count of six, then mentally direct the colour to the area of your body or the chakra you want to heal. Hold the breath to the count of six and feel the energy of the colour saturating the area you are working with.

- Exhale to the count of six. As you do so, continue to hold the colour in the area you have chosen, while feeling any discordant frequencies leaving with the exhale. Know that they too will find their way back to love.

- Adjust the count if needed; use what works for you.

- Continue for at least 10 to 20 minutes.

- Thank Spirit for the blessings and guidance you have received and are about to receive.

Colour Charge Your Water

Using colour-charged water is a simple technique that is very effective. And since you've now started regularly drinking water anyway, you'll find this technique easy to integrate into your daily life.

Start by choosing the colour you want. Get a glass or pitcher (depending on the amount of colour water you want) of that colour. Fill it with pure water, and leave it in the sun for at least an hour. The energy of the sun's rays will transmit the energy of the colour to the water. After preparing the colour-charged water, keep it in a cool place and sip as needed. Only a few tablespoons will be required whenever you want the healing properties of the colour-charged water.

Colours at the blue end of the spectrum (violet, blue, indigo, green) have more antiseptic qualities; colour-charged water made with these colours can usually be kept for up to 10 days. Waters made with the hotter colours at the red end of the spectrum (red, orange, yellow) need to be changed every two days or so.

IN CONCLUSION

Any of the remedies mentioned throughout this book, whether lifestyle changes, nutritional supplements, or colour puncture and gemstones, are simply tools available to help us maintain health. Just as we need tools to help us build a house, we need tools such as these to help sustain our multidimensional being, our house for soul.

We believe that each person's inner communication with Divine Power/God is the true spiritual healer. When it comes to really looking for the *cause point* of a problem or disease, tuning in to your highest self through your prayer or other spiritual exercises and quietly listening to the Holy Spirit, the voice of God, will offer you spiritual insights that are right for you.

Excellent counsellors are available who may help you glean greater insights; many of them work with powerful tools and techniques that can assist you with your healing. *However, do not surrender your own knowingness and power to anyone or anything else; work with someone who can help to awaken your inherent abilities and facilitate the discovery of your personal truth.*

Our only purpose here, in this body, is to learn to give and receive love, to become more God-like. A friend of Karen's told her a wonderful, simple story of an expression of love. Her friend's young daughter said to him, "Daddy, I *love* you!" He asked his daughter in return, "What is love?" The little girl looked him in the eye and said, "Daddy, it's when a heart grows another heart." We encourage you to embrace the gift of love and life on soul's incredible journey home to God and to continue to grow new hearts.

Our individual health and universal wellness depends on humanity learning to honour the laws of nature and Spirit, by adapting ourselves with humility and love to these laws. The role of the physician is to inspire the patient to gain knowledge and truth; to administer remedies only as needed; and to gently and safely harmonize and strengthen the physical body for this exciting journey of life.

We wish you healthy, happy transitioning, now and always, on all levels.

REFERENCES

Chapter One

Eisenberg, D.M., *et al.*, "Unconventional medicine in the United States: Prevalence, costs and patterns of use," *New Engl. J. Med.*, 1993, 328: 246–52.

Moher, D., *et. al.*, "Does quality of reports of randomised trials affect estimates of intervention efficacy reported in meta-analyses?" *Lancet*, 1998, 352: 609–13.

U.S. Congress, Office of Technology Assessment, "The Implications of Cost-Effective Analysis of Medical Technology," Washington, DC, 1980.

Chapter Two

___"Glacial Toxins Melting into Rivers, Scientist Says," *Calgary Herald*, Oct. 4, 1998.

___"Canadian Rates for Cancer Amongst Highest in the World," *Calgary Herald*, April 8, 1998.

Anderson, L.E., "ELF: Exposure levels, bioeffects and epidemiology," *Health Physics*, 1991, 61(1): 41–6.

Beasley, J.D., and Swift, J., "The Kellogg Report: The Impact of Environment and Lifestyle on the Health of Americans," Institute of Health Policy and Practice, Bard College Center, Annadale-on-Hudson, NY, 1989, pp. 214–5.

Brodeur, P., *Currents of Death: Power Lines, Computer Terminals and the Attempt to Cover Up Their Threat to Your Health*, Simon and Schuster, Uppersaddle River, NJ, 1989.

Kujala, V.M., *et al.*, "Relationship of leisure time physical activity and mortality, the Finnish Twin Cohort," *JAMA*, 1998, 279: 440–4.

Sheppard, A.R., and Eisenbud, M., *Biological Effects of Electric and Magnetic Fields of Extremely Low Frequency*, New York University Press, NY, 1977.

Statistics Canada, *Environment and Natural Resources Program Report*, 1994.

Vojdani, A., *et al.*, "Immunological cross reactivity between Candida albicans and human tissue," *J. Clin. Lab. Immuno.*, 1996, 48: 1–15.

Chapter Three

Beasley, J.D., and Swift, J., "The Kellogg Report: The Impact of Environment and Lifestyle on the Health of Americans," Institute of Health Policy and Practice, Bard College Center, Annadale-on-Hudson, NY, 1989, p. 213.

Edelson, R.L., and Fink, J.M., "The Immunologic Function of Skin," *Scientific American*, 1985, 252(6): 46–53.

Gaginella, T.S., and Phillips, S.F., "Ricinoleic acid: Current view on an ancient oil," *Digestive Diseases*, 1975, 20(12): 1171–7.

Gard, Z.R., and Brown, E.J., "Literature Review and Comparison Studies of the Sauna and Illness: Part II," *Townsend Letter for Doctors and Patients*, July 1992: 650–60.

Hahn, G., *et al.*, "On the pharmacology and toxicology of silymarin, the antihepatotoxic active principle of Silybum marianum," *Arzneimittelforschung*, 1968, 18(6): 698–704.

Kulkarni, R.R., *et al.*, "Treatment of osteoarthritis with a herbomineral formulation: A double-blind, placebo-controlled, cross-over study," *J. Ethnopharmacol.*, 1991, 33(1–2): 91–5.

Morita, K., Kada, T., and Namiki, M., "A dismutagenic factor isolated from burdock (Arctium lappa Linne)," *Mutat. Res.*, 1984, 129(1): 25–31.

Punnonen, R., and Lukola, A., "Estrogen-like effect of ginseng," *Br. Med. J.*, 1980, 281: 1110.

Schroeder, H.A., *The Poisons Around Us*,. Indiana University Press, Bloomington, 1974; Keats Publishing, New Canaan, CT, 1978.

Wagner, H., "Plant Constituents with Antihepatotoxic Activity," in *Natural Products as Medicinal Agents*, ed. Beal, J.L., and Reinhard, E, Hippokrates-Verlag, Stuttgart, 1981.

Chapter Four

Barnes, B.O., and Galton, L., *Hypothyroidism: The Unsuspected Illness*, Harper and Row, New York, 1976.

Kagawa, Y., "Impact of westernization of the Japanese: Changes in physique, cancer, longevity and centenarians," *Preventative Medicine*, 1978, 32: 205–17.

Wescott, Patsy, *Thyroid Problems*, HarperCollins, San Francisco, 1995, p. 3.

Xiao, S., *et al.*, "Hyperthyroidism treated with yiqiyangyin decoction," *Journal of Traditional Chinese Medicine*, 1986, 6(2): 79–82.

Chapter Five

Hammer, M., *et al.*, "Does physical exercise influence the frequency of post-menopausal hot flushes?" *Acta. Obstet. Gynecol. Scan.*, 1990, 69: 409–12.

Kubo, M., *et al.*, "Studies on Scutellariae radix. Part II: The antibacterial substance," *Planta Medica*, 1981, 43: 194–201.

Rhoades, F.P., "Minimizing the menopause," *Journal of the American Geriatric Society*, 1967, 15(4): 346–54.

Volz, H.P., and Kieser, M., "Kava-kava extract WS 1490 versus placebo in anxiety disorders: A randomized placebo-controlled 25-week outpatient trial," *Pharmacopsychiat.*, 1997, 30: 1–5.

Wise, P.W., "Influence of estrogen on aging of the central nervous system: Its role in declining female reproductive function," *Menopause Evaluation, Treatment and Health Concerns*, 1989: 53–70.

Wohlfart, R., Haensel, R., and Schmidt, H., "An investigation of sedative hypnotic principles in hops, Part 3," *Planta Medica*, 1982, 45: 224.

Chapter Six

Adlercreutz, H., "Lignans and phyto-estrogens: Possible preventive role in cancer," *Frontiers of Gastrointestinal Research*, 1988, 14: 165–76.

Barrett-Connor, E., "Postmenopausal estrogen and prevention bias," *Ann. of Int. Med.*, 1991, 115: 455–6.

Barrett-Connor, E., and Goodman-Gruen, D., "Prospective study of endogenous sex hormones and fatal cardiovascular disease in postmenopausal women," *British Med. J.*, 1995, 311: 1193–6.

Begley, Sharon, with Glick, Daniel, "The Estrogen Complex," *Newsweek*, March 21, 1994, pp. 76–7.

Begley with Glick, "The Estrogen Complex," *Newsweek*.

Bolton, J.L., and Shen, L., "Quinone methides are the major decomposition products of catechol estrogen o-quinones," *Carcinogenesis*, 1996, 17(5): 925–9.

Caragay,AB, "Cancer-preventing foods and ingredients," *Food Technology*, 1992, 46: 65–8.

Cassidy, A, "Hormonal effects of isoflavones in humans" (abstract), p. 38. See note 26.

Colditz, G.A., *et al.*, "The use of estrogens and progestins and the risk of breast cancer in postmenopausal women," *New Engl. J. Med.*, 1995, 332(24): 1589–993.

Coronary Drug Project Research Group, "The Coronary Drug Project: Findings leading to discontinuation of the 2.5 mg/d estrogen arm," *JAMA*, 1973, 226: 652–7.

Cummings, S.R., *et al.*, "Risk factors for hip fracture in white women," *New Engl. J. Med.*, 1995, 332: 767–73.

Cutler, W., *Hysterectomy: Before and After*, Harper and Row, New York, 1990.

Duker, E.M., *et al.*, "Effects of extracts from *Cimifuga racemosa* on gonadotropin release in menopausal women and ovariectomized rats," *Planta Medica*, 1991, 57: 420–4.

Eden, J., *et al.*, "Hormonal effects of isoflavones" (abstract), p. 41, Second International Symposium on the Role of Soy in Preventing and Treating Chronic Disease, Brussels, Sept. 15–18, 1996.

Follingstad, A.H., "Estriol, the forgotten estrogen," *JAMA*, 1978, 239: 29–30.

Grady, D., *et al.*, "Hormone replacement therapy and endometrial cancer risk: A meta-analysis," *Obs. and Gyn.*, 1995, 85(2): 304–13.

Grodstein, F., and Stampfer, M.J., "The epidemiology of coronary heart disease and estrogen replacement in postmenopausal women," *Prog. Cardiovasc. Dis.*, 1995, 18: 199.

Hirano, T., *et al.*, "Antiproliferative activity of mammalian lignan derivatives against the human breast carcinoma cell line ZR-75-l," *Cancer Invest.*, 1990, 8: 595–602.

Hulley, S., *et al.*, "Randomized trial of estrogen plus progestin for secondary prevention of coronary heart disease in postmenopausal women," *JAMA*, 1998, 280: 605–13.

Ilyia, E., McLure, D., and Farhat, M., "Topical progesterone cream application and overdosing," *J. Altern. Compl. Med.*, 1998, 4: 1.

Inman, WHW, *et al.*, "Thromboembolic disease and the steroidal content of oral contraceptives. A report to the committee on Safety of Drugs," *British Med. J.*, 1970, 203.

Jeppesen, J., *et al.*, "Triglyceride concentration and ischemic heart disease: An eight-year follow-up in the Copenhagen male study," *Circulation*, 1998, 97(11):1029–36.

Knight, D.C., and Eden, J.A., "A review of the clinical effects of phytoestrogens," *Obstet. Gynecol.*, 1996, 87: 897–904.

Koenig, B., *et al.*, "Progesterone synthesis and myelin formation by schwann cells," *Science*, June 9, 1995, p. 268.

Kumazawa, Y., Mizunoe, K., and Otsuka, Y., "Immunostimulating polysaccharide separated from hot water extract of Angelica acutiloba Kitagawa (Yamatotohki)," *Immunology*, 1982, 47(1): 75–83.

Laurizen, C.H.D., *et al.*, "Treatment of premenstrual tension syndrome with *Vitex agnus-castus*. Controlled double-blind study versus pyridoxine," *Phytomedicine*, 1997, 4(3): 181–9.

Lemon, H.M., "Estriol prevention of mammary carcinoma induced by 7,12-dimethyl-benzanthracene and procarbazine," *Cancer Res.*, 1975, 35: 1341–52.

Lippman, M., Monaco, M.E., and Bolan, G., "Effects of estrone, estradiol, and estriol on hormone-responsive human breast cancer in long-term tissue culture," *Cancer Research*, 1977, 37: 1901–7.

MacRae, W.D., Hudson, J.B., and Towers, G.H., "The antiviral action of lignans," *Planta. Med.*, 1989, 55: 531–55.

Marderoslan, A.D., and Liberti, L., *Natural Product Medicine*, George F. Stickley, Philadelphia, 1988, p. 60.

Montoneri, C., *et al.*, "Effects of estriol administration on human postmenopausal endometrium," *Clin. Exp. Obst. Gyn.*, 1987, 14: 178–81.

Physician's Desk Reference, 49th edition, Medical Economics Data Production Company, Montvale, NJ, 1995, p. 2724.

Physician's Desk Reference, p. 2744.

Shapiro, S, "Oral contraceptives: A time to take stock," *N. Engl. J. Med.*, 1986, 315: 450.

Shen, L., *et al.*, "Alkylation of 2'-deoxynucleosides and DNA by the Premarin metabolite 4-hydroxyequilenin simiquinone radical," *Chem. Res. Toxicol.*, 1998, 11(2): 94–101.

Soto, A.M., *et al.*, "The E-SCREEN assay as a tool to identify estrogens: An update on estrogenic environmental pollutants," *Environ. Health Persp.*, 1995, 103: 113–22.

Vooijs, G.P., and Geurts, T.B.P., "Review of the endometrial safety during intravaginal treatment with estriol," *Eur. J. Obstet. Gynecol. Reprod. Biol.*, 1995, 62: 101–6.

Wallis, Claudia, "The Estrogen Dilemma," *Time*, June 26, 1995, pp. 32–39.

Wei, H., *et al.*, "Inhibition of tumour promoter-induced hydrogen peroxide formation *in vitro* and *in vivo* by genistein," *Nutr. Cancer*, 1993, 20: 1–12.

Wilson, P.W., *et al.*, "Prevalence of coronary heart disease in the Framingham offspring study: Role of lipoprotein cholesterols," *Am. J. Cardiol.*, 1980, 46: 649.

Writing Group for the PEPI Trial, "Effects of estrogen or estrogen/progestin regimens on heart disease risk factors in postmenopausal women: The postmenopausal estrogen/progestin interventions (PEPI) trial," *JAMA*, 1995, 273(3): 199–208.

Writing Group for the Women's Health Initiative Investigators, "Risks and benefits of estrogen plus progestin in healthy postmenopausal women," *JAMA*, 2002, 288:321-333.

Yamada, H., *et al.*, "Structural characterization and antitumour activity of a pectic polysaccharide from the roots of Angelica acutiloba," *Planta Med.*, 1990, 56(2): 182–6.

Yoshihiro, K., "The physiological actions of Tang kuei and Cnidium," *Bulletin of the Oriental Healing Arts Institute of U.S.A.*, 1985, 10(7): 269–78.

Zhiping, H., *et al.*, "Treating amenorrhea in vital energy-deficient patients with Angelica sinensis–Astragalus membranaceus menstruation-regulating decoction," *J. Trad. Chin. Med.*, 1986, 6(3): 187–190.

Chapter Seven

Barbel, U.S., "Estrogen in the prevention and treatment of postmenopausal osteoporosis: A review," *Am. J. Med.*, 1988, 85: 847–50.

Brown, S., *Better Bones, Better Body*, Keats Publishing, New Canaan, CT, 1996.

Christeinsen, C., Christiansen, M.S., and Transbol, I., "Bone mass in postmenopausal women after withdrawal of oestrogen/gestragen replacement therapy," *Lancet*, 1981, 28: 459–61.

Cummings, S. R., *et al.*, "Risk factors for hip fracture in white women," *New Engl. J. Med.*, 1995, 332: 767–73.

Dempster,DW, & Lindsay,R, "Pathogenesis of osteoporosis," *Lancet,* 1993,341: 797–801

Farmer, M.E., *et al.*, "Race and sex differences in hip fracture incidence," *Am. J. Public Health*, 1984, 74(12): 1374–80.

Hemenway, D., *et al.*, "Fractures and lifestyle: Effect of cigarette smoking, alcohol intake and relative weight on the risk of hip and forearm fractures in middle-aged women," *Am. J. Public Health*, 1988, 78(12): 1554–8.

Holbrook, T.L., Barrett-Connor, E., and Wingard, D.L., "Dietary calcium and risk of hip fracture: 14-year prospective population study," *Lancet*, 1988, ii: 1046–9.

Jeffcoat, M.K., "Osteoporosis: A possible modifying factor in oral bone loss," *Ann. Peridontol.*, 1998, 3: 312–21.

Kreiger, N., *et al.*, "An epidemiologic study of hip fracture in postmenopausal women," *Am. J. Epidemiol.*, 1982, 116: 141–8.

Lung, A.W., Lorentz, T., and Tam, S.C., "Thyroxine suppressive therapy decreases bone mineral density in postmenopausal women," *Clin. Endocrinol.*, 1993, 39: 535–40.

Lee, J., "Osteoporosis reversal: The role of progesterone," *Int. Clin. Nutr. Rev.*, 1990, 0: 384–91.

Papp, Leslie, "Bone Disease Undetected," *Toronto Star*, Jan. 24, 1998.

Prior, J.C., and Vigna, V.M., "Spinal bone loss and ovulatory disturbances," *New Engl. J. Med.*, 1990, 323: 1221–7.

Prior, J.C., Vigna, Y.M., and Alojado, N., "Progesterone and prevention of osteoporosis," *Canadian Journal of Obstetrics/Gynecology & Women's Health Care*, 1991, 3: 178–84.

Riggs, B.L., and Melton, L.J., "Clinical Review 8: Clinical heterogeneity of involutional osteoporosis: implications for preventive therapy," *J. Clin. Endocrinol. Metab.*, 1990, 70(5): 1229–32.

Riggs, B., *et al.*, "Rates of bone loss in appendicular and axial skeletons of women," *J. Clin. Invest.*, 1986, 77: 1487–91.

Rosen, C.J., *et al.*, "Premature graying of hair is a risk marker for osteopenia," *J. Clin. Endocrinol. Metabol.*, 1994, 79: 854–7.

Savvas, M., *et al.*, "Increase in bone mass after one year of percutaneous oestradiol and testosterone implants in postmenopausal women who have previously received long-term oral estrogens," *Br. J. Obstet. Gynecol.*, 1992, 99(9): 757–60.

Taylor, Paul, "Medication Linked to Hip Fractures: New Antidepressants No Better: Study," *Globe and Mail*, May 1, 1998.

Townsend Letter for Doctors and Patients, June 1998, p. 27. "Vitamin D deficiency is common," *New Engl. J. Med.*, 1998, 338: 777–83, 828–9.

Trotter, M., Broman, G.E., and Peterson, R.R., "Densities of bones of white and Negro skeleton," *J. Bone Joint Surg.*, 1960, 42A: 50–8.

Wood, Rebecca, "Diet and Exercise Not Always Enough to Prevent Bone Loss," *Calgary Herald*, May 16, 1998.

Chapter Eight

_____"Vitamin D deficiency is common," *New Engl. J.Med.*, 1998, 338: 777–83, 828–9; cited in *Townsend Letter for Doctors and Patients*, June 1998, p. 27.

Agnusdei, D., *et al.*, "Effects of ipriflavone on bone mass and calcium metabolism in postmenopausal osteoporosis," *Bone Miner.*, 1992, 19: S43–S48.

Arjmandi, B.H., *et al.*, "Dietary soybean protein prevents bone loss in an ovariectomized rat model of osteoporosis," *J. Nutr.*, 1996, 126: 161–7.

Bales, C.W., Drezner, M.K., and Hoben, K.P., *Eating Well, Living Well with Osteoporosis*, Duke University Medical Center/Viking Penguin Books, New York, 1996.

Blair, H.C., "Action of genistein and other tyrosine kinase inhibitors in preventing osteoporosis" (abstract), p. 19. See note 12.

Civitelli, R., "In vitro and in vivo effects of ipriflavone on bone formation and bone biomechanics," *Calcif. Tissue Int.*, 1997, 61: S12–S14.

Civitelli, R., *et al.*, "Dietary L-lysine and calcium metabolism in humans," *Nutrition*, 1992, 8: 400–5.

Coats, C., "Negative effects of a high-protein diet," *Family Practice Recertification*, 1990, 12: 80–8.

Cramer, D.W., *et al.*, *Amer. J. Epidemiol.*, 1994, 139: 282–89, cited in Colgan, M.,*The New Nutrition: Medicine for the Millennium*, Apple Publishing, Vancouver, 1994, p. 60.

Cumming, R.G., "Calcium intake and bone mass: A quantitative review of the evidence," *Calcif. Tissue Int.*, 1990, 47: 194–201.

Daksky, G.P., *et al.*, "Weight-bearing exercise training and lumbar bone mineral content in postmenopausal women," *Ann. Intern. Med.*, 1988, 108: 824–8.

Danielson, C. Lyon, *et al.*, "Hip fractures and fluoridation in Utah's elderly population," *JAMA*, 1992, 268: 746–8.

Dawson-Hughes, B., *et al.*, "A controlled trial of the effect of calcium supplementation on bone density in postmenopausal women," *New Engl. J. Med.*, 1990, 232: 878–83.

Dovanti, A., Bignamini, A.A., and Rovati, A.L., "Therapeutic activity of oral glucosamine sulphate in osteoarthrosis: A placebo-controlled double-blind investigation," *Clin. Ther.*, 1980, 3(4): 266–72.

Drinkwater, B.L., *et al.*, "Bone mineral content of amenorrheic and eumenorrheic athletes," *New Engl. J. Med.*, 1984, 311: 277–81.

Fanti, O., *et al.*, "Systematic administration of genistein partially prevents bone loss in ovariectomized rats in non-estrogen-like mechanism" (abstract), p. 20, Second International Symposium on the Role of Soy in Preventing and Treating Chronic Disease, Brussels, Sept. 15–18, 1996.

Felson, D.T., *et al.*, "Alcohol consumption and hip fractures: The Framingham study," *Am. J. Epidemiol.*, 1988, 128(5): 1102–10.

Gaby, A., *Preventing and Reversing Osteoporosis: Everywoman's Essential Guide*, Prima Publishing, Rockland, CA, 1994, pp. 29–36.

Gennari, C., *et al.*, "Effect of chronic treatment with ipriflavone in postmenopausal women with low bone mass," *Calcif. Tissue Int.*, 1997, 61: S19–S22.

Goulding, A., "Osteoporosis: Why consuming less sodium chloride helps to conserve bone," *N.Z. Med. J.*, 1990, 103: 120–2.

Hart, J.P., *et al.*, "Electrochemical detection of depressed circulating levels of vitamin K in osteoporosis," *J. Clin. Endocrinol. Metab.*, 1985, 60: 1268–9.

Harvey, J.A., Zobitz, M.M., and Pak, C.Y.C., "Dose dependency of calcium absorption: A comparison of calcium carbonate and calcium citrate," *J. Bone Min. Res.*, 1988, 3(3): 253–8.

Heaney, R.P., and Recker, R.R., "Effects of nitrogen, phosphorus and caffeine on calcium balance in women," *J. Lab. Clin. Med.*, 1982, 99: 46–55.

Heany, R.P., "The calcium controversy: Finding a middle ground between the extremes," *Public Health Rep.*, 1988, 1986 (suppl.): 36–46.

Hernandez-Avila, M., *et al.*, "Caffeine, moderate alcohol intake and risk of fractures of the hip and forearm in middle-aged women," *Am. J. Clin. Nutr.*, 1991, 54: 157–63.

Holt, S., *Soya for Health*, Mary Ann Liebert, Larchmont, NY, 1996.

Kirksey, A., *et al.*, "Vitamin B6 nutritional status of a group of female adolescents," *Am. J. Clin. Nutr.*, 1978, 31: 946–54.

Kochanowski, B.A., "Effect of calcium citrate malate on skeletal development in young growing rats," *Journal of Nutrition*, 1990, 120: 876–81.

Linkswiler, H.M., *et al.*, "Protein-induced hypercalciuria," *Fed. Proc.*, 1981, 40: 2429–33.

McClellan, W.S., Rupp, V.R., and Toscani, V., "Prolonged meat diets with a study of the metabolism of nitrogen, calcium, and phosphorus," *J. Biol. Chem.*, 1986, 87: 669–80.

Melis, B.G., *et al.*, "Ipriflavone prevents bone loss in postmenopausal women," *Menopause*, 1996, 3: 27–32.

Morgan, A.F., Gillum, H.L., and Williams, R.I., "Nutritional status of aging. III: Serum ascorbic acid and intake," *J. Nutr.*, 1955, 55: 431–8.

Morgan, K.J., *et al.*, "Magnesium and calcium dietary intakes of the U.S. population," *J. Am. Coll. Nutr.*, 1985, 4: 195–206.

Nevitt, M.C., "Epidemiology of osteoporosis," *Rheum. Dis. Clin. North Am.*, 1994, 20(3): 535–59.

Nicar, M.J., and Pak, C.Y.C., "Calcium bioavailability from calcium carbonate and calcium citrate," *J. Clin. Endocrinol. Metabol.*, 1985, 61: 391–3.

Paganini-Hill, A., *et al.*, "Exercise and other factors in the prevention of hip fracture: The leisure world study," *Epidemiology*, 1991, 2: 16–25.

Principles of Medical Pharmacology, 4th edition, Department of Pharmacology, University of Toronto, 1985, p. 566.

Ruegsegger, P., *et al.*, "Comparison of the treatment effects of ossein-hydroxyapatite compound and calcium carbonate in osteoporotic females," *Osteo. Int.*, 1995, 5: 3034.

Sandler, R., *et al.*, "The effects of walking on the cross-sectional dimensions of the radius in postmenopausal women," *Calcif. Tissue Int.*, 1987, 41(2): 65–9.

Smith, K.T., *et al.*, "Calcium absorption from a new calcium delivery system (CCM)," *Calcif. Tissue Int.*, 1987, 51: 351–2.

Sowers, M.F.R., *et al.*, "A prospective study of bone mineral content and fracture in communities with differential fluoride exposure," *Am. J. Epid.*, 1991, 133: 649–60.

Tomita, A., "Post menopausal osteoporosis Ca study in vitamin K2," *Clin. Endocrinol.* (Jpn), 1971, 19: 731–6.

Vaz, A.L., "Double-blind clinical evaluation of the relative efficacy of ibuprofen and glucosamine sulphate in the management of osteoarthritis of the knee in out-patients," *Curr. Med. Res. Opin.*, 1982, 8(3): 145–9.

Chapter Nine

Amias, A.G., "Life after gynecological operations," *Brit. Med. J.*, 1975, 2: 680–1.

Amirika, H., and Evans, T.N., "Ten-year review of hysterectomies, trends, indication and risks," *Am. J. Obstet. Gynecol.*, 1979, 134: 431–7.

Anderson, J.W., Johnstone, B.M., and Cook-Newell, M.E., "Meta-analysis of the effects of soy protein intake on serum lipids," *New Engl. J. Med.*, 1995, 333: 276–82.

Brush, M.G., "Evening primrose oil in the treatment of the premenstrual syndrome," in Horrobin, D.F., ed., *Clinical Uses of Essential Fatty Acids*, Eden Press, Montreal, 1982, pp. 155–62.

Bunker, J.P., and Brown, B.W., "The physician-patient as an informed consumer of surgical services," *New Engl. J. Med.*, 1974, 290: 1051–5.

Centerwall, B.S., "Premenopausal hysterectomy and cardiovascular disease," *Am. J. Obstet. Gynecol.*, 1981, 139: 58–61.

Cerami, A., Viassara, H., and Brownless, M., "Glucose and aging," *Scientific American*, May 1987, pp. 90–6.

Clark, L.C., *et al.*, "Effects of selenium supplementation for cancer prevention in patients with carcinoma of the skin," *JAMA*, 1996, 276: 1957–63.

Cutler, W.B., *et al.*, "The psychoneuroendocrinology of the ovulatory cycle of women," *Psychoneuroendocrinology*, 1980, 5: 89–95.

Denverstein, L., *et al.*, "Sexual response following hysterectomy, oophorectomy and estrogen therapy on libido," *Int. J. Gynecol. Obstet.*, 1975, 13: 97–100.

Epstein, S. *The Breast Cancer Prevention Program*, Macmillan, USA, 1998

Erickson, K. *Drop Dead Gorgeous*, Contemporary Books, 2002

Ginsburg, E., *et al.*, "Effects of alcohol ingestion on estrogens in postmenopausal women," *JAMA*, 1996, 4(276): 1747–51.

Goldin, B.R., *et al.*, "Estrogen excretion patterns and plasma levels in vegetarian and omnivorous women," *New Engl. J. Med.*, 1982, 307: 1542–7.

Grant, J.M., *et al.*, "An audit of abdominal hysterectomy of a decade in a district hospital," *Brit. J. Obstet. Gynecol.*, 1984, 91: 73–7.

Guthrie, N., *et al.*, "Palm oil tocotrienols and plant flavonoids act synergistically with each other and with Tamoxifen in inhibiting proliferation of and growth of estrogen receptor-negative MDA-MB-435 and -positive MCF-7 human breast cancer cells in culture," *Asia Pacific J. Clin. Nutr.*, 1997, 6(1): 41–5.

Guthrie, N., and Carroll, K., "Inhibition of Human Breast Cancer Cell Growth and Metastasis in Nude Mice by Citrus Juices and Their Constituent Flavonoids," in *Biological Oxidants and Antioxidants: Molecular Mechanisms and Health Effects*, Packer, L., and Ong, A.S.H., eds., AOCS Press, Champaign, IL, 1998, pp. 310–6.

Ingram, D., *et al.*, "Case-control study of phyto-oestrogens and breast cancer," *Lancet*, 1997, 350: 990–4.

Keuneke, R. *Total Breast Health*, Kensington Books, 1998

Konhie, J.C., Otolorin, E.O., and Ladipo, O.A., "Changes in carbohydrate metabolism during 30 months on Norplant," *Contraception*, 1991, 44(2): 163–70.

Kujala, U.M., *et al.*, "Relationship of leisure-time physical activity and mortality: The Finnish twin cohort," *JAMA*, 1998, 279: 440–4.

Lauersen, N., *Listen to Your Body*, Berkeley Books, Los Angeles, 1983.

Lee, J. *What Your Doctor May Not Tell You About Breast Cancer*, Warner Books, 2001

Linder, M.C., *Nutritional Biochemistry and Metabolism with Clinical Applications*, 2nd edition, Appleton and Lange, Norwalk, CT, 1991.

Lockwood, K., *et al.*, "Apparent partial remission of breast cancer in 'high risk' patients supplemented with nutritional antioxidants, essential fatty acids and coenzyme Q10," *Molec. Aspects Med.*, 1994, 15(suppl.): S231–40.

Lockwood, K., *et al.*, "Progress on therapy of breast cancer with vitamin Q10 and regression of metastases," *Biochem. Biophys. Res. Comm.*, 1995, 212: 172–7.

In Heinerman, John, *The Treatment of Cancer with Herbs*, Biworld Publishers, Orem, UT, 1980, pp. 124–7.

Hunter, D.J., *et al.*, "A prospective study of the intake of vitamins C, E, and A and the risk of breast cancer," *New Engl. J. Med.*, 1993, 329: 234–40.

Morell, V., "Zeroing in on how hormones affect the immune system," *Science*, 1995, 269: 773–5.

National Health Center for Health Statistics, "Hysterectomies in the United States," DHSS Publication no. (PHS) 88–1753, Public Health Service, Hyattsville, MD, 1988.

Nelson, T, *et al.*, "Progesterone administration induced impairment of insulin suppression of hepatic glucose production," *Fertility Sterility*, 1994, 62(3): 491–6.

Oldenhave, A., *et al.*, "Hysterectomized women with ovarian conservation report more severe climacteric complaints than do normal climacteric women of similar age," *Am. J. Obstet. Gynecol.*, 1993, 168: 765–71.

Owen, P.R., "Prostaglandin synthetase inhibitors in the treatment of primary dysmenorrhea," *Am. J. Obstet. Gynecol.*, 1984, 148: 96–103.

Peterson, G., and Barnes, S., "Genistein inhibition of the growth of human breast cancer cells: Independence from estrogen receptors and the multi-drug resistance gene," *Biochem. Biophys. Res. Commun.*, 1991, 179: 661–7.

Peterson, G., and Barnes, S., "Genistein inhibits both estrogen and growth factor-stimulated proliferation of human breast cancer cells," *Cell Growth Differ.*, 1996, 7: 1345–51.

Peterson, T.G., *et al.*, "The role of metabolism in mammary epithelial cells growth inhibition by the isoflavones genistein and biochanin A," *Carcinogenesis*, 1996, 17: 1861–9.

Potter, S.M., "Overview of proposed mechanism for the hypocholesterolemic effect of soy," *J. Nutr.*, 1995, 125: 606–11.

Pratt, J.H., "The unnecessary hysterectomy," *Southern Med. J.*, 1980, 79: 1360–5.

Riales, R, and Albrink, M, "Effect of chromium chloride supplementation on glucose tolerance and serum lipids, including HDL, of adult men," *Am. J. Clin. Nutr.*, 1981,34: 2670–8.

Richard, D.H., "A post-hysterectomy syndrome," *Lancet*, 1974, 2: 983–5.

Rose, D.P., "Effect of a low-fat diet on hormone levels in women with cystic breast disease. Serum steroids and gonadotropins," *JNCL*, 1987, 78: 623–6.

Rossignol, A.M., "Caffeine-containing beverages and premenstrual syndrome in young women," *Am. J. Public Health*, 1985, 75(11): 1335–7.

Shabert, J., "Nutrition and women's health," *Curr. Prob. Obstet. Gynecol. Fertil.*, 1996, 19: 115–66.

Simard, A, Vobecky, J, & Vobecky, JS, "Vitamin D deficiency and cancer of the breast: An unprovocative ecological hypothesis," *Canadian J. Public Health*,1991, 82: 300–3.

Spector, T.D., *et al.*, "Increased rates of previous hysterectomy and gynecological operations in women with osteoarthritis," *Brit. Med. J.*, 1988, 297: 899–900.

Vanderhaeghe, L. *Healthy Immunity, Scientifically Proven Natural Treatments for Conditions from A-Z*, Macmillan Books, 2001

Wilcox, J.N., and Blumenthal, B.F., "Thrombotic mechanisms in atherosclerosis: potential impact of soy proteins," *J. Nutr.*, 1995, 125: 631–8.

Wu, A.H., Ziegler, R.G., and Horn-Ross, P.L., "Tofu and risk of breast cancer in Asian-Americans," *Cancer Epidemiol. Biomarkers Prev.*, 1996, 5: 901–6.

Wurtman, R.J., and Wurtman, J.J., "Carbohydrates and depression," *Scientific American*, Jan. 1989, pp. 68–75.

Zussman, L,, *et al.*, "Sexual response after hysterectomy-oophorectomy," *Am. J. Obstet. Gynecol.*, 1981, 140: 725–9.

Chapter Ten

Anderson, L., *35 Golden Keys to Who Your Are and Why You're Here*, Eckankar, Minneapolis, 1977, pp. 198–9.

Anderson, L., *35 Golden Keys to Who Your Are and Why You're Here*, Eckankar, Minneapolis, 1977, p. 133.

Bowman, L., "Prayer Augments Medical Treatment, Majority Says," Scripps Howard News Service, Dec. 15, 1998.

Darko, D., "A brief tour of psychoneuroimmunology," *Ann. Allergy*, 1986, 57: 233–8.

Eckankar seminar by Harold Klemp, San Francisco, April 10–12, 1998.

Jenny, H., *Cymataics: Wave Phenomena Vibrational Effects Harmonic Oscillations with Their Structure, Kinetics and Dynamics*,vol. 2, Basilius Presse, Basel, Switzerland, 1974, p 100.

Kantrowitz, B., *et al.*, "In Search of the Sacred," *Newsweek*, Nov. 28, 1994, pp. 52–5.

Marwick, C., "Leaving the concert hall for clinic: Therapists now test music's 'charms,'" *JAMA*, 1996, 275(4): 267–8.

Solomon, G., "Psychoneuroimmunology: Interactions between central nervous system and immune system," *J. Neurosci. Res.*, 1987, 18: 1–9.

Stevenson, Ian, *Children Who Remember Previous Lives: A Question of Reincarnation*, University Press of Virginia, 1987, p. 25.

Tecoma, E., and Huey, L., "Psychic distress and the immune response," *Life Sciences*, 1985, 36: 1799–1812.

FURTHER READING

Chapters One and Two *Optimal Health; Minimizing Stress*

Carter, J. P. Racketeering in Medicine: The Suppression of Alternatives. Hamptom Roads Publishing, 1993.

Coulter, H. L. Divided Legacy. North Atlantic Books, 1982.

Lanctot, G. *The Medical Mafia*. Here's The Key, 1995.

Rachlis, M., and Kushner, C. *Second Opinion*. Collins, 1989.

Schmidt, M. A., Smith, L. H., and Schnert, K. W. *Beyond Antibiotics*. North Atlantic Books, 1993.

Batmanghelidj, F. *Your Body's Many Cries for Water*. Global Health Solutions, 1995.

Beasley, J. D. *The Betrayal of Health*. Random House, 1991.

Beasley, J. D., and Swift, J. J. *The Kellogg Report*. The Institute of Health Policy and Practice, Bard College Center, New York, 1989.

Becker, R. O. *Cross Currents*. Jeremy P. Tarcher, 1990.

Carson, R. *Silent Spring*. Houghton Mifflin, 1987.

Crook, W. G. *The Yeast Connection*. 3rd ed. Professional Books, 1986.

Glenn, K. *I'm Sorry, But Your Perfume Makes Me Sick*. Bluebird Books, 1997.

Locke, S., and Colligan, D. *The Healer Within: The New Medicine of Mind and Body*. E. P. Dutton, 1986.

Pelletier, K. *Mind as Healer, Mind as Slayer: A Holistic Approach to Preventing Stress Disorders*. Dell, 1977.

Robbins, J. *Diet for a New America*. Avon Books, 1992.

Selye, H. *The Stress of Life*. McGraw-Hill, 1956.

Winterdyk, J., and Jensen, K. *The Complete Athlete: Integrating Fitness, Nutrition and Natural Health*. Alive Books, 1998.

Chapter Three and Four
Cleansing, Detoxification, and Strengthening; Hormonal Balance and the Endocrine System

Crook, W. G. *The Yeast Connection: A Medical Breakthrough*. Professional Books, 1985.

Gates, D., and Schatz, L. *The Body Ecology Diet*. B.E.D. Publications, 1996.

Krohn, J., Taylor, F. A., and Prosser, J. *Natural Detoxification*. Hartley and Marks, 1996.

Lappe, Marc. *When Antibiotics Fail: Restoring the Ecology of the Body*. North Atlantic Books, 1986.

Matsen, J. *Eating Alive*. Alive Books, 1997.

Papadogianis, P. *Treat the Cause*. Prentice Hall Canada, 1998.

Pitchford, P. *Healing with Whole Foods*. North Atlantic Books, 1993.

Barnes, B., and Barnes, C. *Heart Attack Rareness in Thyroid-Treated Patients*. Charles C. Thomas Publishers, 1972.

Barnes, B., and Galton, L. *Hypothyroidism: The Unsuspected Illness*. Harper and Row, 1976.

D'Adamo, P. *Eat Right for Your Type*. G. P. Putnam's Sons, 1996.

Wilson, E. D. *Wilson's Syndrome: The Miracle of Feeling Well*. Cornerstone Publishing, 1991.

Winterdyk, J., and Jensen, K. *The Complete Athlete: Integrating Fitness, Nutrition and Natural Health*. Alive Books, 1998.

Chapters Five and Six
Women in Transition; Hormone Replacement Therapy

Barbach, L. *The Pause*. Penguin Books USA, 1993.

Huston, J. E., and Lanka, L. D. *Perimenopause: Changes in Women's Health After 35*. New Harbinger Publications, 1997.

Laux, M., and Conrad, C. *Natural Woman, Natural Menopause*. HarperCollins, 1997.

Love, S. M., and Lindsen, K. *Dr. Susan Love's Hormone Book*. Random House, 1997.

Northrup, C. *Women's Bodies, Women's Wisdom*. Bantam Books, 1995.

Sheehy, G. *The Silent Passage*. Random House, 1995.

Chapters Seven and Eight
Understanding Osteoporosis; Taking Care of "Dem Bones"

D'Adamo, P. J. *Eat Right for Your Type*. G. P. Putnam's Sons, 1996.

Gaby, A. R. *Preventing and Reversing Osteoporosis*. Prima Publishing, 1993.

Graci, S. *The Power of Super Foods*. Prentice Hall Canada, 1997.

Kamen, B. *Hormone Replacement Therapy: Yes or No?* Nutrition Encounter, 1993.

Lee, J. R. *What Your Doctor May Not Tell You about Menopause*. Warner Books, 1996.

Messina, M., Messina, V., and Setchell, K. *The Simple Soybean and Your Health*. Avery Publishing Group, 1994.

Oski, F. A. *Don't Drink Your Milk!* Teach Services, 1992.

Sears, B. *Enter the Zone*. Harper and Row, 1995.

Winterdyk, J., and Jensen, K. *The Complete Athlete: Integrating Fitness, Nutrition and Natural Health*. Alive Books, 1998.

Chapter Nine and Ten
Other Common Health Concerns; The Intricate Web of Life

Austin, S., and Hitchcock, C. *Breast Cancer: What You Should Know (But May Not Be Told) about Prevention, Diagnosis and Treatment.* Prima Publishing, 1994.

Brown, D. *Herbal Prescriptions for Better Health.* Prima Publishing, 1996.

DeMarco, C. *Take Charge of Your Body.* The Well Woman Press, 1995.

Erasmus, U. *Fats That Heal, Fats That Kill.* Alive Books, 1993.

Love, S. *The Breast Book.* Addison-Wesley, 1990.

Murray, M., and Pizzorno, J. *Encyclopaedia of Natural Medicine.* Little, Brown (UK), 1990.

Northrup, C. *Women's Bodies, Women's Wisdom.* Bantam Books, 1995.

Rinzler, C. A. *Estrogen and Breast Cancer: A Warning to Women.* Macmillan, 1993.

Schwarzbein, and D., Deville, N. *The Schwarzbein Principle.* Health Communications, Inc.

West, S. *The Hysterectomy Hoax.* Doubleday, 1994.

Anderson, L. C. *35 Golden Keys to Who You Are and Why You're Here.* Eckankar, 1997.

Babbitt, E. *The Principles of Light and Color: The Healing Power of Color.* 1878. Reprint. The Citadel Press, 1976.

Becker. R. O. *The Body Electric.* William Morrow, 1985.

Brennan, B. *Hands of Light: A Guide to Healing Through the Human Energy Field.* Bantam Books, 1987.

Clark, L. *The Ancient Art of Color Therapy.* Pocket Books, 1975.

Dossey, L. *Healing Words: The Power of Prayer and the Practice of Medicine.* HarperCollins, 1993.

Dumitresc, I., and Kenyon, J. *Electronic Imaging in Medicine and Biology.* Neville Spearman, 1983.

Gerber, R. *Vibrational Medicine.* Bear and Company, 1988.

Greaves, H. *Testimony of Light.* C. W. Daniel Company, 1996.

Kahn, H. I. *The Music of Life.* Omega Publications, 1988.

Myss, C., and Shealy, N. *The Anatomy of the Spirit.* Harmony Books 1996.

Newton, M. *Journey of Souls: Case Studies of Life Between Lives.* Llewellyn Publications, 1994.

Serinus, J. *Psychoneuroimmunology and the Healing Process.* Celestial Arts 1986.

Shealy, N., and Myss, C. *The Creation of Health: Merging Traditiona Medicine.* Stillpoint Publications, 1987.

Sinatra, S.T. *Heart Sense for Women.* Penguin Group.

Vanderhaeghe, Lorna. *Move Over Mammogram.*

Zukav, G. *The Dancing Wu Lei Masters: An Overview of the New Physic.* William Morrow, 1979.

Index

Incontinence, urinary, 114
Indigestion, 66, 113
Indoor office environment, 18
Infertility, 95, 97, 138
    treating, 158
Insomnia, 40, 50, 74, 78, 79, 91, 94, 97, 107, 112,
    122, 127, 179, 247
    prescription drugs for, 130
    remedies for, 127-30
    treatments for, 125-27
Insulin, 56, 149, 244, 247, 250, 281, 283
Intercourse, painful, 113, 263
Iodine, 93, 98, 101, 102, 104, 108
Ipriflavone, 235, 238
Iron, 131, 222, 242, 243
Irradiation, 25
Irritability, 63, 97, 113, 157, 242, 243, 248
Isoflavones, 152, 154, 159, 235, 238, 276, 285
    as HRT alternative, 152-53
    and osteoporosis, 219

Jasmine, yellow, 121, 128
Jaundice, 68
Jiaogulan, 79, 285
Joints, aching, 32, 50, 59, 246

Kelp, 102, 104, 105, 215, 221
Kidneys, 50, 133, 216
Kombu, 103
Kyphosis, 196

Lachesis (venom), 119
Lactobacillus, 122
Lactose intolerance, 224
Laparoscopy, 260
Lasix, 194
Lavender, 126
LDL. See Lipoprotein, low-density
Learning disorders, 31
Lecithin, 30
Leucotrienes, 42
Levothyroxine, 106
Libido, 113, 116, 136, 149, 172, 262
Licorice, licorice root, 124, 156, 248
Light and colour, 316
Lighting, fluorescent, 18, 234
Lipoic acid, 60-61
Lipoprotein, low- and high-density, 29, 133
Lithium, 195
Liver, 22, 41, 48, 57, 58, 59-68, 80, 88, 102, 104,
    110, 125, 150, 159, 168, 239
    congested, sluggish, 65, 66, 170, 248
    disease, 49-50

food sources for healthy, 62-63
and menstrual cycle, 110
Liver spots, 40
Love, 34, 37, 115, 288-296, 297
Low-density lipoprotein (LDL) cholesterol, 29,
    133
Lung cancer, 69
Lycopene, 61
Lycopodium (club moss), 122
Lymphatic drainage, massage, 86

Magnesium, 64, 226, 228, 231, 244, 248, 255, 256,
    257, 258, 272, 286
    and bone health, 228-31
    deficiency, 248
Malabsorption, 40
Manganese, 226, 230, 238
    and bone health, 230
Massage, 10, 33
MCHC. See Microcrystalline hydroxyapatite
    concentrate
Medication, pharmaceutical,
See also Drugs; specific medicines
Meditation, contemplation, 80, 127, 207, 280,
    288, 303, 309
Medroxyprogesterone, 165, 195
Megace, 165
Megestrol acetate, 165
Memory, 73, 97, 113, 122, 136, 151, 172, 309
Menarche, 111
Menopausal symptoms, 1, 78, 94, 97, 112, 118,
    122, 136, 138, 157, 158, 160, 164, 166, 176,
    262, 268. See also specific symptoms
    allopathic treatment for, 133
    and isoflavones, 153-154
Menopausal transition, 114
Menopause, 1, 2, 12, 44, 62, 76, 90, 92, 94, 110-
    11, 112, 113
    and acupuncture, 315
    and aging, 112
    blood tests for determining, 164
    and estrogen production, deficiency, 132-33
    and HRT decisions, 140
    and libido slowdown, 116, 262, 267
    and osteoporosis risk, 188
    role of ovaries in, 108
Menorrhagia, 243
    and hysterectomy, 270
MenoSense, 120, 124, 160, 179, 181, 204, 240
Menstrual bleeding, excessive. See Menorrhagia
Menstrual cycle(s), 95, 109-110, 133
Menstrual periods, 164, 270, See also
    Dysmenorrhea
Mental and emotional stress, 46
Metabolism, 23, 38, 41, 62, 92, 96
Metal toxicity, 256

Dr. Karen Jensen, N.D., graduated from the Canadian College of Naturopathic Medicine (CCNM) in 1988 and she currently has offices in Calgary, Alberta and Vancouver, British Columbia. Her clinical focus is on women's health, immune disorders, allergy disorders, chronic fatigue syndrome, disease prevention, cardiovascular health, and energy medicine. She is past president of the Alberta Naturopathic Assocation and is a frequent guest on radio and television and she writes extensively for health magazines across Canada. For more information call 604-742-0800 or go to **www.drkarenjensen.com**

Lorna R. Vanderhaeghe, B.Sc., is a medical journalist who has been researching and writing on nutritional medicine for over 20 years. She is currently completing her Masters in Science in Human Nutrition. Her list of accomplishments include: associate editor for *Total Health* magazine in the United States and *Alive* magazine in Canada; senior editor of the *Encyclopedia of Natural Healing* (winner of the prestigious Benjamin Franklin Award in 1998); past editor-in-chief of *Canada's Healthy Living Guide*; and working at the *Journal of Orthomolecular Medicine*. Lorna is also co-author of the award-winning, best-selling book *The Immune System Cure* now published in six countries and four languages and *Healthy Immunity, Scientifically Proven Natural Treatments*

for Conditions from A-Z a national bestseller. She is an internationally known lecturer who believes in empowering people with health knowledge so they can achieve optimal wellness. Visit **www.healthyimmunity.com** or **www.hormonehelp.com** and sign up for her free newsletter online.